A Course of Classic British and American Short Stories

英美经典短篇小说教程

吴泽庆　杨纪平　编著

中央民族大学出版社
China Minzu University Press

图书在版编目（CIP）数据

英美经典短篇小说教程：英文、汉文 / 吴泽庆、杨纪平编著 . -- 北京：中央民族大学出版社，2025. 4.

ISBN 978-7-5660-2483-1

Ⅰ. H319.4

中国国家版本馆 CIP 数据核字第 2025W9E015 号

英美经典短篇小说教程

编　　著	吴泽庆　杨纪平
责任编辑	买买提江 · 艾山
封面设计	舒刚卫
出版发行	中央民族大学出版社
	北京市海淀区中关村南大街 27 号　　邮编：100081
	电话：（010）68472815（发行部）　传真：（010）68933757（发行部）
	（010）68932218（总编室）　（010）68932447（办公室）
经 销 者	全国各地新华书店
印 刷 厂	北京鑫宇图源印刷科技有限公司
开　　本	787×1092　1/16　　印张：28.25
字　　数	450 千字
版　　次	2025 年 4 月第 1 版　2025 年 4 月第 1 次印刷
书　　号	ISBN 978-7-5660-2483-1
定　　价	98.00 元

内容简介

《英美经典短篇小说教程》选取英国文学和美国文学中具有代表性作家的作品，通过对作者介绍、作品赏析、文本阅读、讨论和拓展阅读等环节，引导读者领会英美文学中的瑰宝，品味文学魅力，启迪人生。

本书共分英国文学和美国文学两个部分，选取20位著名小说家及其代表作。各章以时间为经，以文学流派为纬，贯穿文学发展的基本脉络。每个单元的编写力求明晰、简洁，便于读者阅读。全书配有英文注释、课后设有讨论问题和拓展书目，供读者加深对文本的理解。

《英美经典短篇小说教程》适用于高校英语专业本科生和英美文学方向研究生教学，也可用作非英语专业高年级学生选修英美文学鉴赏课程或通识课教材。

前　言

英美文学是高校英语专业一门必不可少的课程，加强文学阅读不仅能够提高读者的文学鉴赏水平，培养其语言能力，更能增强人文素养，深化对西方文化的理解。作为重要的文学形式，短篇小说以其篇幅短小、形式活泼、主题突出、语言凝练等特色，在文学中占据日益重要的地位。英美短篇小说的阅读对于学生文学鉴赏能力和文学理论运用能力的培养具有重要作用，为其学习英美戏剧、诗歌、散文、长篇小说等课程奠定坚实的基础。作为英语专业本科生和研究生的教材，本书具有以下特点。

一、题材多样，内容丰富

本书主要选取19至20世纪具有代表性的英美作家作品，精选的20部短篇小说，涵盖了从19世纪小说家华盛顿·欧文（Washington Irving）到现代意识流文学代表作家詹姆斯·乔伊斯（James Joyce）的作品。包括重要英国作家有乔治·艾略特（George Eliot）、约瑟夫·康拉德（Joseph Conrad）、弗吉尼亚·伍尔夫（Virginia Woolf）、戴维·赫伯特·劳伦斯（D.H. Lawrence）、凯瑟琳·曼斯菲尔德（Katherine Mansfield）；美国代表作家埃德加·爱伦·坡（Edgar Allan Poe）、纳撒尼尔·霍桑（Nathaniel Hawthorne）、马克·吐温（Mark Twain）、伊迪斯·沃顿（Edith Wharton）、杰克·伦敦（Jack London）、舍伍德·安德森（Sherwood Anderson）等。涵盖了浪漫主义、现实主义和现代主义等文学流派，主题涉及清教主义、西部文学、自然主义、南方文学、女性文学、少数族裔文学等多个领域。

二、重点突出，名篇主导

20部短篇小说均为英美学界公认为经典之作，包括英国作品：康拉德的《秘密的分享者》、伍尔夫的《邱园记事》、乔伊斯的《阿拉比》、劳伦斯的《木马赢家》，吉卜林的《巴赫斯夫人》；美国作品：欧文的《瑞普·凡·温克尔》、爱伦·坡的《红死魔的面具》、霍桑的《教长的黑面纱》、马克·吐温的《跳蛙》、伊迪斯·沃顿的《罗马热病》等都是脍炙人口的佳作，主题覆盖英美生活的方方面面，作者文笔精妙，语言优美流畅。

三、思想性强，艺术性高

所选作品兼具思想深度与艺术高度，实现知识性与审美性的统一。凯特·肖邦（kate Chopin）的《一个小时的故事》通过人物对话、戏剧化场景及心理描写，揭示了女主人公失去话语空间、思维空间直至整个生存空间的悲剧主题。舍伍德·安德森（Sherwood Anderson）的《林中之死》展示了小镇中的普通人在商品经济冲击下的生活，作者通过呈现生活中的“断片”来构造情节，“断片”是人物内心的某种思绪，或是生活中的某处场景，或是不断呈现的某个意象等。其他所选作品呈现出对讽刺、幽默、象征等艺术手法的灵活运用，这增长了读者的知识，培养了其审美鉴赏能力。

本书的特点

①选读配有英文注释，有助于学生更好地理解文本；

②每篇选文后附有讨论题，可以引发学生深入思考，帮助教师开展启发式、讨论式、探究式教学；

③文本后配有拓展阅读书目，能够帮助学生进一步对作品进行深入研究，为提高学生的研究能力提供便利。

本书基于编者多年教学经验编写而成。内容设计和体例兼顾教师备课、学生预习、课堂研讨及课后研读要求。

感谢中央民族大学出版社编辑的辛勤工作。

限于编者水平，本书在选材和注释中难免存在疏漏，恳请读者批评指正。

编者

CONTENTS

PART ONE BRITISH SHORT STORIES

George Eliot (1819 — 1880)

The Lifted Veil

Introduction to the author

George Eliot (November 22, 1819 — December 22, 1880) was an English novelist, journalist and one of the leading Victorian writers. She is best remembered for her novels, including *Adam Bede, The Mill on the Floss, Silas Marner, Middlemarch, Daniel Deronda*, etc. Eliot depicted rural society in her works and explored the lives of real persons. In the meanwhile, her novels were full of political factors and religious elements including alienation from the church. Eliot's important role in twentieth-century literature can never be ignored.

George Eliot's original name is Mary Ann Evans, the third child of Robert and Christiana Evans. She was born in England on November 22, 1819. George Eliot was very intelligent and loved reading. She boarded at various schools in her childhood, which instilled in her a strong sense of Christian. Eliot carried her self-education by the library of Arbury Hall, where the Greek tragedy she read became themes of her works. After her mother died in 1836, Eliot and her father moved to Foleshill near Coventry, whose society introduced Evans to more liberal theologies and to writers such as David Strauss and Ludwig Feuerbach. Her contact with free-thinking intellectuals led her away from her early beliefs. This resulted in her conflicts with her father and she demonstrated the conflicts in her writing. Her father died in 1849. Eliot move to London in 1851, where she met more free-thinking intellectuals of her age, including George Henry Lewes, a leading journalist and drama critic of the day. Despite the fact that Lewes was a married man, they developed a romantic relationship. Although they lived together happily and their union lasted for over 20 years until Lewes's death in 1878, Eliot suffered a loss of social status, including complete disaffection from her favorite brother, Issac. Encouraged by Lewes, George Eliot started to publish under the pseudonym George Eliot in 1858. In 1880, Eliot married John Walter, Cross, who was 20 years her junior. This legal marriage helped to restore her relationship with her brother Issac. On December 22, 1880, Eliot died, aged 61. She was buried next to Lewes in Highgate Cemetery, London.

Major works by George Eliot

Novels

Adam Bede, 1859

The Mill on the Floss, 1860

Silas Marner, 1861

Romola, 1863

Felix Holt, the Radical, 1866

Middlemarch, 1871–72

Daniel Deronda, 1876

Poetry

The Spanish Gypsy (a dramatic poem), 1868

Agatha, 1869

Brother and Sister, 1869

Armgart, 1871

Stradivarius, 1873

The Legend of Jubal, 1874

Arion, 1874

A Minor Prophet, 1874

A College Breakfast Party, 1879

The Death of Moses, 1879

Appreciation

The Lifted Veil is a novella, first published in 1859. The tale of horror starts with the confession of the first-person narrator Latimer, a dying man, exactly one month before his death. The story is told in a flashback structure, beginning with Latimer's childhood, when he first discovers that he has superadded consciousness, an otherworldly ability to see into the future and the thoughts of other people. Latimer becomes fascinated with Bertha, his brother's fiancée. One day, Latime has a vision many years into his own future, during which bertha, now his wife, suggests, with hatred in her voice, that he commit suicide. Latimer can clearly predicts that their marriage is doomed to be unhappy and even a disaster, but he cannot resist his desire for the girl. After his brother's death, Latimer marries Bertha. Bertha's manipulative and untrustworthy nature does result in a terrible relationship. Latimer's friend, scientist Charles Meunier, performs a blood transfusion from himself to Bertha's recently deceased maid. For a few moments the maid comes back to life and accuses Bertha of a plot to poison Latimer. Bertha flees and Latimer soon dies.

The story demonstrates Eliot's interest in contemporary science and pseudoscience, including physiology, phrenology, mesmerism and clairvoyance. It involves the themes of fate, extrasensory perception, the mystery of life, life after death, the relationship between science and the supernatural, and human desire to play God. It fits well into the Victorian tradition of Gothic horror stories.

Selected Reading

The Lifted Veil

Chapter I

The time of my end approaches. I have lately been subject to attacks of angina pectoris[①] ; and in the ordinary course of things, my physician tells me, I may fairly hope that my life will not be protracted[②] many months. Unless, then, I am cursed with an exceptional physical constitution, as I am cursed with an exceptional mental character, I shall not much longer groan under the wearisome burthen of this earthly existence. If it were to be otherwise — if I were to live on to the age most men desire and provide for — I should for once have known whether the miseries of delusive expectation can outweigh the miseries of true provision. For I foresee when I shall die, and everything that will happen in my last moments.

Just a month from this day, on September 20, 1850, I shall be sitting in this chair, in this study, at ten o'clock at night, longing to die, weary of incessant insight and foresight, without delusions and without hope. Just as I am watching a tongue of blue flame rising in the fire, and my lamp is burning low, the horrible contraction will begin at my chest. I shall only have time to reach the bell, and pull it violently, before the sense of suffocation will come. No one will answer my bell. I know why.

My two servants are lovers, and will have quarrelled. My housekeeper will have rushed out of the house in a fury, two hours before, hoping that Perry will believe she has gone to drown herself. Perry is alarmed at last, and is gone out after her. The little scullery-maid is asleep on a bench: she never answers the bell; it does not wake her. The sense of suffocation increases: my lamp goes out with a horrible stench: I make a great effort, and snatch at the bell again. I long for life, and there is no help. I thirsted for the unknown: the thirst is gone. O God, let me stay with the known, and be weary of it: I am content. Agony of pain and suffocation — and all the while the earth, the fields, the pebbly brook at the bottom of the rookery, the fresh scent after the rain, the light of the morning through my chamber-window, the warmth of the hearth after the frosty air — will darkness close over them for ever?

---

① angina pectoris: a disease that repeatedly causes sudden strong pains in the chest because blood containing oxygen is prevented from reaching the heart

② protracted: lasting for a long time or made to last longer

Darkness — darkness — no pain — nothing but darkness: but I am passing on and on through the darkness: my thought stays in the darkness, but always with a sense of moving onward...

Before that time comes, I wish to use my last hours of ease and strength in telling the strange story of my experience. I have never fully unbosomed① myself to any human being; I have never been encouraged to trust much in the sympathy of my fellow-men. But we have all a chance of meeting with some pity, some tenderness, some charity, when we are dead: it is the living only who cannot be forgiven — the living only from whom men's indulgence and reverence② are held off, like the rain by the hard east wind. While the heart beats, bruise it — it is your only opportunity; while the eye can still turn towards you with moist, timid entreaty, freeze it with an icy unanswering gaze; while the ear, that delicate messenger to the inmost sanctuary of the soul, can still take in the tones of kindness, put it off with hard civility, or sneering compliment, or envious affectation of indifference; while the creative brain can still throb with the sense of injustice, with the yearning for brotherly recognition — make haste — oppress it with your ill-considered judgements, your trivial comparisons, your careless misrepresentations. The heart will by and by be still — " ubi saeva indignatio ulterius cor lacerare nequit"; the eye will cease to entreat; the ear will be deaf; the brain will have ceased from all wants as well as from all work. Then your charitable speeches may find vent; then you may remember and pity the toil and the struggle and the failure; then you may give due honour to the work achieved; then you may find extenuation for errors, and may consent to bury them.

That is a trivial schoolboy text; why do I dwell on it? It has little reference to me, for I shall leave no works behind me for men to honour. I have no near relatives who will make up, by weeping over my grave, for the wounds they inflicted on me

① unbosomed: expressed oneself to others

② reverence: to greatly respect and admire someone or something when I was among them. It is only the story of my life that will perhaps win a little more sympathy from strangers when I am dead, than I ever believed it would obtain from my friends while I was living.

My childhood perhaps seems happier to me than it really was, by contrast with all the after-years. For then the curtain of the future was as impenetrable to me as to other children: I had all their delight in the present hour, their sweet indefinite hopes for the morrow; and I had a tender mother: even now, after the dreary lapse of long years, a slight trace of sensation accompanies the remembrance of her caress as she held me on her knee — her arms round my little body, her cheek pressed on mine. I had a complaint of the eyes that made me blind for a little while, and she kept me on her knee from morning till night. That unequalled love soon vanished out of my life, and even to my childish consciousness it was as if that life had become more chill I rode my little white pony with the groom by my side as before, but there were no loving eyes looking at me as I mounted, no glad arms opened to me when I came back. Perhaps I missed my mother's love more than most children of seven or eight would have done, to whom the other pleasures of life remained as before, for I was certainly a very sensitive child. I remember still the mingled trepidation[①] and delicious excitement with which I was affected by the tramping of the horses on the pavement in the echoing stables, by the loud resonance of the groom's voices, by the booming bark of the dogs as my father's carriage thundered under the archway of the courtyard, by the din of the gong as it gave notice of luncheon and dinner. The measured tramp of soldiery which I sometimes heard — for my father's house lay near a county town where there were large barracks — made me sob and tremble; and yet when they were gone past, I longed for them to come back again.

I fancy my father thought me an odd child, and had little fondness for me; though he was very careful in fulfilling what he regarded as a parent's duties. But

① trepidation: fear or worry about what is going to happen

he was already past the middle of life, and I was not his only son. My mother had been his second wife, and he was five-and-forty when he married her. He was a firm, unbending, intensely orderly man, in root and stem a banker, but with a flourishing graft of the active landholder, aspiring to county influence: one of those people who are always like themselves from day to day, who are uninfluenced by the weather, and neither know melancholy nor high spirits. I held him in great awe, and appeared more timid and sensitive in his presence than at other times; a circumstance which, perhaps, helped to confirm him in the intention to educate me on a different plan from the prescriptive one with which he had complied in the case of my elder brother, already a tall youth at Eton. My brother was to be his representative and successor; he must go to Eton and Oxford, for the sake of making connexions, of course: my father was not a man to underrate the bearing of Latin satirists or Greek dramatists on the attainment of an aristocratic position. But, intrinsically, he had slight esteem for " those dead but sceptred① spirits"; having qualified himself for forming an independent opinion by reading Potter's Aeschylus, and dipping into Francis's Horace. To this negative view he added a positive one, derived from a recent connexion with mining speculations; namely, that a scientific education was the really useful training for a younger son.

Moreover, it was clear that a shy, sensitive boy like me was not fit to encounter the rough experience of a public school. Mr. Letherall had said so very decidedly. Mr. Letherall was a large man in spectacles, who one day took my small head between his large hands, and pressed it here and there in an exploratory, auspicious manner — then placed each of his great thumbs on my temples, and pushed me a little way from him, and stared at me with glittering spectacles. The contemplation appeared to displease him, for he frowned sternly, and said to my father, drawing his thumbs across my eyebrows —

---

① sceptre: a decorated stick that is carried by a queen or king during some official ceremonies as a symbol of their authority

" The deficiency is there, sir — there; and here," he added, touching the upper sides of my head, " here is the excess. That must be brought out, sir, and this must be laid to sleep."

I was in a state of tremor, partly at the vague idea that I was the object of reprobation, partly in the agitation of my first hatred — hatred of this big, spectacled man, who pulled my head about as if he wanted to buy and cheapen it.

I am not aware how much Mr. Letherall had to do with the system afterwards adopted towards me, but it was presently clear that private tutors, natural history, science, and the modern languages, were the appliances by which the defects of my organization were to be remedied. I was very stupid about machines, so I was to be greatly occupied with them; I had no memory for classification, so it was particularly necessary that I should study systematic zoology and botany; I was hungry for human deeds and humane motions, so I was to be plentifully crammed with the mechanical powers, the elementary bodies, and the phenomena of electricity and magnetism. A better-constituted boy would certainly have profited under my intelligent tutors, with their scientific apparatus; and would, doubtless, have found the phenomena of electricity and magnetism as fascinating as I was, every Thursday, assured they were. As it was, I could have paired off, for ignorance of whatever was taught me, with the worst Latin scholar that was ever turned out of a classical academy. I read Plutarch, and Shakespeare, and Don Quixote by the sly, and supplied myself in that way with wandering thoughts, while my tutor was assuring me that " an improved man, as distinguished from an ignorant one, was a man who knew the reason why water ran downhill." I had no desire to be this improved man; I was glad of the running water; I could watch it and listen to it gurgling① among the pebbles, and bathing the bright green water-plants, by the hour together. I did not want to know why it ran; I had perfect confidence that there were good reasons for what was so very beautiful.

① gurgling: (of water, especially small streams) to flow quickly while making a low, pleasant sound

There is no need to dwell on this part of my life. I have said enough to indicate that my nature was of the sensitive, unpractical order, and that it grew up in an uncongenial① medium, which could never foster it into happy, healthy development. When I was sixteen I was sent to Geneva to complete my course of education; and the change was a very happy one to me, for the first sight of the Alps, with the setting sun on them, as we descended the Jura, seemed to me like an entrance into heaven; and the three years of my life there were spent in a perpetual sense of exaltation, as if from a draught of delicious wine, at the presence of Nature in all her awful loveliness. You will think, perhaps, that I must have been a poet, from this early sensibility to Nature. But my lot was not so happy as that. A poet pours forth his song and believes in the listening ear and answering soul, to which his song will be floated sooner or later. But the poet's sensibility without his voice — the poet's sensibility that finds no vent but in silent tears on the sunny bank, when the noonday light sparkles on the water, or in an inward shudder at the sound of harsh human tones, the sight of a cold human eye — this dumb passion brings with it a fatal solitude of soul in the society of one's fellow-men. My least solitary moments were those in which I pushed off in my boat, at evening, towards the centre of the lake; it seemed to me that the sky, and the glowing mountain-tops, and the wide blue water, surrounded me with a cherishing love such as no human face had shed on me since my mother's love had vanished out of my life. I used to do as Jean Jacques did — lie down in my boat and let it glide where it would, while I looked up at the departing glow leaving one mountain-top after the other, as if the prophet's chariot of fire were passing over them on its way to the home of light. Then, when the white summits were all sad and corpse-like, I had to push homeward, for I was under careful surveillance,② and was allowed no late wanderings. This disposition of mine was not favourable to the formation of

---

① uncongenial: not friendly and pleasant

② surveillance: the careful watching of a person or place, especially by the police or army, because of a crime that has happened or is expected intimate friendships among the numerous youths of my own age who are always to be found studying at Geneva. Yet I made one such friendship; and, singularly enough, it was with a youth whose intellectual tendencies were the very reverse of my own. I shall call him Charles Meunier; his real surname — an English one, for he was of English extraction — having since become celebrated. He was an orphan, who lived on a miserable pittance while he pursued the medical studies for which he had a special genius. Strange! that with my vague mind, susceptible and unobservant, hating inquiry and given up to contemplation, I should have been drawn towards a youth whose strongest passion was science. But the bond was not an intellectual one; it came from a source that can happily blend the stupid with the brilliant, the dreamy with the practical: it came from community of feeling.

Charles was poor and ugly, derided by Genevese gamins, and not acceptable in drawing-rooms. I saw that he was isolated, as I was, though from a different cause, and, stimulated by a sympathetic resentment, I made timid advances towards him. It is enough to say that there sprang up as much comradeship between us as our different habits would allow; and in Charles's rare holidays we went up the Salcvc together, or took the boat to Vevay, while I listened dreamily to the monologues in which he unfolded his bold conceptions of future experiment and discovery. I mingled them confusedly in my thought with glimpses of blue water and delicate floating cloud, with the notes of birds and the distant glitter of the glacier. He knew quite well that my mind was half absent, yet he liked to talk to me in this way; for don't we talk of our hopes and our projects even to dogs and birds, when they love us? I have mentioned this one friendship because of its connexion with a strange and terrible scene which I shall have to narrate in my subsequent life.

This happier life at Geneva was put an end to by a severe illness, which is partly a blank to me, partly a time of dimly-remembered suffering, with the presence of my father by my bed from time to time. Then came the languid monotony of convalescence[①], the days gradually breaking into variety and distinctness as my strength enabled me to take longer and longer drives. On one of these more vividly remembered days, my father said to me, as he sat beside my sofa.

" When you are quite well enough to travel, Latimer, I shall take you home with me. The journey will amuse you and do you good, for I shall go through the Tyrol and Austria, and you will see many new places. Our neighbours, the Filmores, are come; Alfred will join us at Basle, and we shall all go together to Vienna, and back by Prague" ...

My father was called away before he had finished his sentence, and he left my mind resting on the word Prague, with a strange sense that a new and wondrous scene was breaking upon me: a city under the broad sunshine, that seemed to me as if it were the summer sunshine of a long-past century arrested in its course — unrefreshed for ages by dews of night, or the rushing rain-cloud; scorching the dusty, weary, time-eaten grandeur of a people doomed to live on in the stale repetition of memories, like deposed and superannuated[②] kings in their regal gold-inwoven tatters. The city looked so thirsty that the broad river seemed to me a sheet of metal; and the blackened statues, as I passed under their blank gaze, along the unending bridge, with their ancient garments and their saintly crowns, seemed to me the real inhabitants and owners of this place, while the busy, trivial men and women, hurrying to and fro, were a swarm of ephemeral visitants infesting it for a day. It is such grim, stony beings as these, I thought, who are the fathers of ancient faded children, in those tanned time-fretted dwellings that crowd the steep before me; who pay their court in the worn and crumbling pomp of the palace which stretches its monotonous length on the height; who worship wearily in the stifling air of the churches, urged by no fear or hope, but compelled by their doom to be ever old and undying, to live on in the rigidity of habit, as they live on in perpetual midday, without the repose of night or

① convalescence: recovering from illness

② superannuated: old, and almost no longer suitable for work the new birth of morning.

A stunning clang of metal suddenly thrilled through me, and I became conscious of the objects in my room again: one of the fire-irons had fallen as Pierre opened the door to bring me my draught.

My heart was palpitating violently, and I begged Pierre to leave my draught beside me; I would take it presently.

As soon as I was alone again, I began to ask myself whether I had been sleeping. Was this a dream — this wonderfully distinct vision — minute in its distinctness down to a patch of rainbow light on the pavement, transmitted through a coloured lamp in the shape of a star — of a strange city, quite unfamiliar to my imagination? I had seen no picture of Prague: it lay in my mind as a mere name, with vaguely-remembered historical associations — ill-defined memories of imperial grandeur and religious wars.

Nothing of this sort had ever occurred in my dreaming experience before, for I had often been humiliated because my dreams were only saved from being utterly disjointed and commonplace by the frequent terrors of nightmare. But I could not believe that I had been asleep, for I remembered distinctly the gradual breaking-in of the vision upon me, like the new images in a dissolving view, or the growing distinctness of the landscape as the sun lifts up the veil of the morning mist. And while I was conscious of this incipient[①] vision, I was also conscious that Pierre came to tell my father Mr. Filmore was waiting for him, and that my father hurried out of the room. No, it was not a dream; was it — the thought was full of tremulous exultation — was it the poet's nature in me, hitherto only a troubled yearning sensibility, now manifesting itself suddenly as spontaneous creation? Surely it was in this way that Homer saw the plain of Troy, that Dante saw the abodes of the departed, that Milton saw the earthward flight of the Tempter. Was it that my illness

① incipient: just beginning

had wrought some happy change in my organization — given a firmer tension to my nerves — carried off some dull obstruction? I had often read of such effects — in works of fiction at least. Nay; in genuine biographies I had read of the subtilizing or exalting influence of some diseases on the mental powers. Did not Novalis feel his inspiration intensified under the progress of consumption?

When my mind had dwelt for some time on this blissful idea, it seemed to me that I might perhaps test it by an exertion of my will. The vision had begun when my father was speaking of our going to Prague. I did not for a moment believe it was really a representation of that city; I believed — I hoped it was a picture that my newly liberated genius had painted in fiery haste, with the colours snatched from lazy memory. Suppose I were to fix my mind on some other place — Venice, for example, which was far more familiar to my imagination than Prague: perhaps the same sort of result would follow. I concentrated my thoughts on Venice; I stimulated my imagination with poetic memories, and strove to feel myself present in Venice, as I had felt myself present in Prague.

But in vain. I was only colouring the Canaletto engravings that hung in my old bedroom at home; the picture was a shifting one, my mind wandering uncertainly in search of more vivid images; I could see no accident of form or shadow without conscious labour after the necessary conditions. It was all prosaic effort, not rapt passivity, such as I had experienced half an hour before. I was discouraged; but I remembered that inspiration was fitful①.

For several days I was in a state of excited expectation, watching for a recurrence of my new gift. I sent my thoughts ranging over my world of knowledge, in the hope that they would find some object which would send a reawakening vibration through my slumbering genius. But no; my world remained as dim as ever, and that flash of strange light refused to come again, though I watched for it with palpitating

① fitful: often stopping and starting and not happening in a regular or continuous way eagerness.

My father accompanied me every day in a drive, and a gradually lengthening walk as my powers of walking increased; and one evening he had agreed to come and fetch me at twelve the next day, that we might go together to select a musical box, and other purchases rigorously demanded of a rich Englishman visiting Geneva. He was one of the most punctual of men and bankers, and I was always nervously anxious to be quite ready for him at the appointed time.

But, to my surprise, at a quarter past twelve he had not appeared.

I felt all the impatience of a convalescent who has nothing particular to do, and who has just taken a tonic in the prospect of immediate exercise that would carry off the stimulus.

Unable to sit still and reserve my strength, I walked up and down the room, looking out on the current of the Rhone, just where it leaves the dark-blue lake; but thinking all the while of the possible causes that could detain my father.

Suddenly I was conscious that my father was in the room, but not alone: there were two persons with him. Strange! I had heard no footstep, I had not seen the door open; but I saw my father, and at his right hand our neighbour Mrs. Filmore, whom I remembered very well, though I had not seen her for five years. She was a commonplace middle-aged woman, in silk and cashmere; but the lady on the left of my father was not more than twenty, a tall, slim, willowy figure, with luxuriant blond hair, arranged in cunning braids and folds that looked almost too massive for the slight figure and the small-featured, thin-lipped face they crowned. But the face had not a girlish expression: the features were sharp, the pale grey eyes at once acute, restless, and sarcastic. They were fixed on me in half-smiling curiosity, and I felt a painful sensation as if a sharp wind were cutting me. The pale-green dress, and the green leaves that seemed to form a border about her pale blond hair, made me think of a Water-Nixie — for my mind was full of German lyrics, and this pale, fatal-eyed woman, with the green weeds, looked like a birth from some cold sedgy stream, the daughter of an aged river.

" Well, Latimer, you thought me long," my father said...

But while the last word was in my ears, the whole group vanished, and there was nothing between me and the Chinese printed folding-screen that stood before the door. I was cold and trembling; I could only totter forward and throw myself on the sofa. This strange new power had manifested itself again… But was it a power? Might it not rather be a disease — a sort of intermittent delirium① , concentrating my energy of brain into moments of unhealthy activity, and leaving my saner hours all the more barren?

I felt a dizzy sense of unreality in what my eye rested on; I grasped the bell convulsively,② like one trying to free himself from nightmare, and rang it twice. Pierre came with a look of alarm in his face.

" Monsieur ne se trouve pas bien?" he said anxiously.

" I'm tired of waiting, Pierre," I said, as distinctly and emphatically as I could, like a man determined to be sober in spite of wine; " I'm afraid something has happened to my father — he's usually so punctual. Run to the Hotel des Bergues and see if he is there."

Pierre left the room at once, with a soothing " Bien, Monsieur"; and I felt the better for this scene of simple, waking prose. Seeking to calm myself still further, I went into my bedroom, adjoining the salon, and opened a case of eau-de-Cologne③ ; took out a bottle; went through the process of taking out the cork very neatly, and then rubbed the reviving spirit over my hands and forehead, and under my nostrils, drawing a new delight from the scent because I had procured it by slow details of labour, and by no strange sudden madness. Already I had begun to taste something

---

① delirium: a state of being unable to think or speak clearly because of fever or mental confusion

② convulsively: sudden movements of the muscles in your body that you cannot control

③ eau-de-Cologne: a pleasant-smelling liquid that you put on your body to make yourself smell fresh; perfumes of the horror that belongs to the lot of a human being whose nature is not adjusted to simple human conditions.

Still enjoying the scent, I returned to the salon, but it was not unoccupied, as it had been before I left it. In front of the Chinese folding-screen there was my father, with Mrs. Filmore on his right hand, and on his left — the slim, blond-haired girl, with the keen face and the keen eyes fixed on me in half-smiling curiosity.

" Well, Latimer, you thought me long," my father said...

I heard no more, felt no more, till I became conscious that I was lying with my head low on the sofa, Pierre, and my father by my side. As soon as I was thoroughly revived, my father left the room, and presently returned, saying –

" I've been to tell the ladies how you are, Latimer. They were waiting in the next room. We shall put off our shopping expedition to-day."

Presently he said, " That young lady is Bertha Grant, Mrs. Filmore's orphan niece. Filmore has adopted her, and she lives with them, so you will have her for a neighbour when we go home — perhaps for a near relation; for there is a tenderness between her and Alfred, I suspect, and I should be gratified by the match, since Filmore means to provide for her in every way as if she were his daughter. It had not occurred to me that you knew nothing about her living with the Filmores."

He made no further allusion to the fact of my having fainted at the moment of seeing her, and I would not for the world have told him the reason: I shrank from the idea of disclosing to any one what might be regarded as a pitiable peculiarity, most of all from betraying it to my father, who would have suspected my sanity ever after.

I do not mean to dwell with particularity on the details of my experience. I have described these two cases at length, because they had definite, clearly traceable results in my after-lot.

Shortly after this last occurrence — I think the very next day — I began to be aware of a phase in my abnormal sensibility, to which, from the languid and slight nature of my intercourse with others since my illness, I had not been alive before.

This was the obtrusion on my mind of the mental process going forward in first one person, and then another, with whom I happened to be in contact: the vagrant, frivolous ideas and emotions of some uninteresting acquaintance — Mrs. Filmore, for example — would force themselves on my consciousness like an importunate,① ill-played musical instrument, or the loud activity of an imprisoned insect.

But this unpleasant sensibility was fitful, and left me moments of rest, when the souls of my companions were once more shut out from me, and I felt a relief such as silence brings to wearied nerves.

I might have believed this importunate insight to be merely a diseased activity of the imagination, but that my prevision of incalculable words and actions proved it to have a fixed relation to the mental process in other minds. But this superadded consciousness, wearying and annoying enough when it urged on me the trivial experience of indifferent people, became an intense pain and grief when it seemed to be opening to me the souls of those who were in a close relation to me — when the rational talk, the graceful attentions, the wittily-turned phrases, and the kindly deeds, which used to make the web of their characters, were seen as if thrust asunder by a microscopic vision, that showed all the intermediate frivolities, all the suppressed egoism, all the struggling chaos of puerilities, meanness, vague capricious② memories, and indolent make-shift thoughts, from which human words and deeds emerge like leaflets covering a fermenting heap.

At Basle we were joined by my brother Alfred, now a handsome, self-confident man of six-and-twenty — a thorough contrast to my fragile, nervous, ineffectual self. I believe I was held to have a sort of half-womanish, half-ghostly beauty; for the portrait-painters, who are thick as weeds at Geneva, had often asked me to sit to them, and I had been the model of a dying minstrel in a fancy picture.

But I thoroughly disliked my own physique and nothing but the belief that it

---

① importunate: repeatedly asking for something, in a forceful and annoying way

② capricious: changing frequently

was a condition of poetic genius would have reconciled me to it. That brief hope was quite fled, and I saw in my face now nothing but the stamp of a morbid organization, framed for passive suffering — too feeble for the sublime resistance of poetic production. Alfred, from whom I had been almost constantly separated, and who, in his present stage of character and appearance, came before me as a perfect stranger, was bent on being extremely friendly and brother-like to me. He had the superficial kindness of a good-humoured, self-satisfied nature, that fears no rivalry, and has encountered no contrarieties. I am not sure that my disposition was good enough for me to have been quite free from envy towards him, even if our desires had not clashed, and if I had been in the healthy human condition which admits of generous confidence and charitable construction. There must always have been an antipathy between our natures. As it was, he became in a few weeks an object of intense hatred to me; and when he entered the room, still more when he spoke, it was as if a sensation of grating metal had set my teeth on edge. My diseased consciousness was more intensely and continually occupied with his thoughts and emotions, than with those of any other person who came in my way.

I was perpetually exasperated with the petty promptings of his conceit and his love of patronage, with his self-complacent belief in Bertha Grant's passion for him, with his half-pitying contempt for me — seen not in the ordinary indications of intonation and phrase and slight action, which an acute and suspicious mind is on the watch for, but in all their naked skinless complication.

For we were rivals, and our desires clashed, though he was not aware of it. I have said nothing yet of the effect Bertha Grant produced in me on a nearer acquaintance. That effect was chiefly determined by the fact that she made the only exception, among all the human beings about me, to my unhappy gift of insight. About Bertha I was always in a state of uncertainty: I could watch the expression of her face, and speculate on its meaning; I could ask for her opinion with the real interest of ignorance; I could listen for her words and watch for her smile with hope and fear: she had for me the fascination of an unravelled destiny. I say it was this fact that chiefly determined the strong effect she produced on me: for, in the abstract, no womanly character could seem to have less affinity① for that of a shrinking, romantic, passionate youth than Bertha's. She was keen, sarcastic, unimaginative, prematurely cynical, remaining critical and unmoved in the most impressive scenes, inclined to dissect all my favourite poems, and especially contemptous towards the German lyrics which were my pet literature at that time. To this moment I am unable to define my feeling towards her: it was not ordinary boyish admiration, for she was the very opposite, even to the colour of her hair, of the ideal woman who still remained to me the type of loveliness; and she was without that enthusiasm for the great and good, which, even at the moment of her strongest dominion over me, I should have declared to be the highest element of character. But there is no tyranny more complete than that which a self-centred negative nature exercises over a morbidly② sensitive nature perpetually craving sympathy and support. The most independent people feel the effect of a man's silence in heightening their value for his opinion — feel an additional triumph in conquering the reverence of a critic habitually captious③ and satirical: no wonder, then, that an enthusiastic self-distrusting youth should watch and wait before the closed secret of a sarcastic woman's face, as if it were the shrine of the doubtfully benignant deity who ruled his destiny.

For a young enthusiast is unable to imagine the total negation in another mind of the emotions which are stirring his own: they may be feeble, latent, inactive, he thinks, but they are there — they may be called forth; sometimes, in moments of happy hallucination, he believes they may be there in all the greater strength because he sees no outward sign of them. And this effect, as I have intimated, was heightened to its utmost intensity in me, because Bertha was the only being who remained for me

① affinity: a close similarity between two things

② morbidly: too interested in unpleasant subjects, especially death

③ captious: critical and uncomplimentary

in the mysterious seclusion of soul that renders such youthful delusion possible.

Doubtless there was another sort of fascination at work — that subtle physical attraction which delights in cheating our psychological predictions, and in compelling the men who paint sylphs, to fall in love with some brave femme, heavy- heeled and freckled.

Bertha's behaviour towards me was such as to encourage all my illusions, to heighten my boyish passion, and make me more and more dependent on her smiles. Looking back with my present wretched knowledge, I conclude that her vanity and love of power were intensely gratified by the belief that I had fainted on first seeing her purely from the strong impression her person had produced on me. The most prosaic woman likes to believe herself the object of a violent, a poetic passion; and without a grain of romance in her, Bertha had that spirit of intrigue which gave piquancy① to the idea that the brother of the man she meant to marry was dying with love and jealousy for her sake. That she meant to marry my brother, was what at that time I did not believe; for though he was assiduous in his attentions to her, and I knew well enough that both he and my father had made up their minds to this result, there was not yet an understood engagement — there had been no explicit declaration; and Bertha habitually, while she flirted with my brother, and accepted his homage in a way that implied to him a thorough recognition of its intention, made me believe, by the subtlest looks and phrases — feminine nothings which could never be quoted against her — that he was really the object of her secret ridicule; that she thought him, as I did, a coxcomb, whom she would have pleasure in disappointing. Me she openly petted in my brother's presence, as if I were too young and sickly ever to be thought of as a lover; and that was the view he took of me. But I believe she must inwardly have delighted in the tremors into which she threw me by the coaxing way in which she patted my curls, while she laughed at my quotations. Such

① piquancy: something interesting and exciting, especially because of being mysterious caresses were always given in the presence of our friends; for when we were alone together, she affected a much greater distance towards me, and now and then took the opportunity, by words or slight actions, to stimulate my foolish timid hope that she really preferred me. And why should she not follow her inclination? I was not in so advantageous a position as my brother, but I had fortune, I was not a year younger than she was, and she was an heiress, who would soon be of age to decide for herself.

The fluctuations of hope and fear, confined to this one channel, made each day in her presence a delicious torment. There was one deliberate act of hers which especially helped to intoxicate me.

When we were at Vienna her twentieth birthday occurred, and as she was very fond of ornaments, we all took the opportunity of the splendid jewellers' shops in that Teutonic Paris to purchase her a birthday present of jewellery. Mine, naturally, was the least expensive; it was an opal ring — the opal was my favourite stone, because it seems to blush and turn pale as if it had a soul. I told Bertha so when I gave it her, and said that it was an emblem of the poetic nature, changing with the changing light of heaven and of woman's eyes. In the evening she appeared elegantly dressed, and wearing conspicuously all the birthday presents except mine. I looked eagerly at her fingers, but saw no opal. I had no opportunity of noticing this to her during the evening; but the next day, when I found her seated near the window alone, after breakfast, I said, " You scorn to wear my poor opal. I should have remembered that you despised poetic natures, and should have given you coral, or turquoise, or some other opaque unresponsive stone." " Do I despise it?" she answered, taking hold of a delicate gold chain which she always wore round her neck and drawing out the end from her bosom with my ring hanging to it; " it hurts me a little, I can tell you," she said, with her usual dubious① smile, " to wear it in that secret place; and since your poetical nature is so stupid as to prefer a more public position, I shall not endure the

① dubious: dubious and not scientifically proven

pain any longer."

She took off the ring from the chain and put it on her finger, smiling still, while the blood rushed to my cheeks, and I could not trust myself to say a word of entreaty that she would keep the ring where it was before.

I was completely fooled by this, and for two days shut myself up in my own room whenever Bertha was absent, that I might intoxicate myself afresh with the thought of this scene and all it implied.

I should mention that during these two months — which seemed a long life to me from the novelty and intensity of the pleasures and pains I underwent — my diseased anticipation in other people's consciousness continued to torment me; now it was my father, and now my brother, now Mrs. Filmore or her husband, and now our German courier, whose stream of thought rushed upon me like a ringing in the ears not to be got rid of, though it allowed my own impulses and ideas to continue their uninterrupted course. It was like a preternaturally heightened sense of hearing, making audible to one a roar of sound where others find perfect stillness. The weariness and disgust of this involuntary intrusion into other souls was counteracted only by my ignorance of Bertha, and my growing passion for her; a passion enormously stimulated, if not produced, by that ignorance. She was my oasis of mystery in the dreary desert of knowledge. I had never allowed my diseased condition to betray itself, or to drive me into any unusual speech or action, except once, when, in a moment of peculiar bitterness against my brother, I had forestalled some words which I knew he was going to utter — a clever observation, which he had prepared beforehand. He had occasionally a slightly affected hesitation in his speech, and when he paused an instant after the second word, my impatience and jealousy impelled me to continue the speech for him, as if it were something we had both learned by rote. He coloured and looked astonished, as well as annoyed; and the words had no sooner escaped my lips than I felt a shock of alarm lest such an anticipation of words — very far from being words of course, easy to divine —

should have betrayed me as an exceptional being, a sort of quiet energumen, whom every one, Bertha above all, would shudder at and avoid. But I magnified, as usual, the impression any word or deed of mine could produce on others; for no one gave any sign of having noticed my interruption as more than a rudeness, to be forgiven me on the score of my feeble nervous condition.

While this superadded consciousness of the actual was almost constant with me, I had never had a recurrence of that distinct prevision which I have described in relation to my first interview with Bertha; and I was waiting with eager curiosity to know whether or not my vision of Prague would prove to have been an instance of the same kind. A few days after the incident of the opal ring, we were paying one of our frequent visits to the Lichtenberg Palace.

I could never look at many pictures in succession; for pictures, when they are at all powerful, affect me so strongly that one or two exhaust all my capability of contemplation. This morning I had been looking at Giorgione's picture of the cruel-eyed woman, said to be a likeness of Lucrezia Borgia. I had stood long alone before it, fascinated by the terrible reality of that cunning, relentless face, till I felt a strange poisoned sensation, as if I had long been inhaling a fatal odour, and was just beginning to be conscious of its effects. Perhaps even then I should not have moved away, if the rest of the party had not returned to this room, and announced that they were going to the Belvedere Gallery to settle a bet which had arisen between my brother and Mr. Filmore about a portrait. I followed them dreamily, and was hardly alive to what occurred till they had all gone up to the gallery, leaving me below; for I refused to come within sight of another picture that day. I made my way to the Grand Terrace, since it was agreed that we should saunter① in the gardens when the dispute had been decided. I had been sitting here a short space, vaguely conscious of trim gardens, with a city and green hills in the distance, when, wishing to avoid the

① saunter: to walk in a slow and relaxed way, often in no particular direction proximity[①] of the sentinel, I rose and walked down the broad stone steps, intending to seat myself farther on in the gardens.

Just as I reached the gravel-walk, I felt an arm slipped within mine, and a light hand gently pressing my wrist. In the same instant a strange intoxicating numbness passed over me, like the continuance or climax of the sensation I was still feeling from the gaze of Lucrezia Borgia. The gardens, the summer sky, the consciousness of Bertha's arm being within mine, all vanished, and I seemed to be suddenly in darkness, out of which there gradually broke a dim firelight, and I felt myself sitting in my father's leather chair in the library at home. I knew the fireplace — the dogs for the wood-fire — the black marble chimney-piece with the white marble medallion of the dying Cleopatra in the centre.

Intense and hopeless misery was pressing on my soul; the light became stronger, for Bertha was entering with a candle in her hand — Bertha, my wife — with cruel eyes, with green jewels and green leaves on her white ball-dress; every hateful thought within her present to me... " Madman, idiot! why don't you kill yourself, then?" It was a moment of hell. I saw into her pitiless soul — saw its barren worldliness, its scorching hate — and felt it clothe me round like an air I was obliged to breathe. She came with her candle and stood over me with a bitter smile of contempt; I saw the great emerald brooch on her bosom, a studded serpent with diamond eyes. I shuddered — I despised this woman with the barren soul and mean thoughts; but I felt helpless before her, as if she clutched my bleeding heart, and would clutch it till the last drop of life-blood ebbed away. She was my wife, and we hated each other.

Gradually the hearth, the dim library, the candle-light disappeared — seemed to melt away into a background of light, the green serpent with the diamond eyes remaining a dark image on the retina. Then I had a sense of my eyelids quivering, and

① proximity: the state of being near in space or time

the living daylight broke in upon me; I saw gardens, and heard voices; I was seated on the steps of the Belvedere Terrace, and my friends were round me.

The tumult① of mind into which I was thrown by this hideous vision made me ill for several days, and prolonged our stay at Vienna. I shuddered with horror as the scene recurred to me; and it recurred constantly, with all its minutiae, as if they had been burnt into my memory; and yet, such is the madness of the human heart under the influence of its immediate desires, I felt a wild hell-braving joy that Bertha was to be mine; for the fulfilment of my former prevision concerning her first appearance before me, left me little hope that this last hideous glimpse of the future was the mere diseased play of my own mind, and had no relation to external realities. One thing alone I looked towards as a possible means of casting doubt on my terrible conviction — the discovery that my vision of Prague had been false — and Prague was the next city on our route.

Meanwhile, I was no sooner in Bertha's society again than I was as completely under her sway as before. What if I saw into the heart of Bertha, the matured woman — Bertha, my wife? Bertha, the girl, was a fascinating secret to me still: I trembled under her touch; I felt the witchery of her presence; I yearned to be assured of her love. The fear of poison is feeble against the sense of thirst.

Nay, I was just as jealous of my brother as before — just as much irritated by his small patronizing ways; for my pride, my diseased sensibility, were there as they had always been, and winced as inevitably under every offence as my eye winced from an intruding mote. The future, even when brought within the compass of feeling by a vision that made me shudder, had still no more than the force of an idea, compared with the force of present emotion — of my love for Bertha, of my dislike and jealousy towards my brother.

It is an old story, that men sell themselves to the tempter, and sign a bond with

---

① tumult: a loud noise, especially that produced by an excited crowd, or a state of confusion, change, or uncertainty their blood, because it is only to take effect at a distant day; then rush on to snatch the cup their souls thirst after with an impulse not the less savage because there is a dark shadow beside them for evermore. There is no short cut, no patent tram-road, to wisdom: after all the centuries of invention, the soul's path lies through the thorny wilderness which must be still trodden in solitude, with bleeding feet, with sobs for help, as it was trodden by them of old time.

My mind speculated eagerly on the means by which I should become my brother's successful rival, for I was still too timid, in my ignorance of Bertha's actual feeling, to venture on any step that would urge from her an avowal of it. I thought I should gain confidence even for this, if my vision of Prague proved to have been veracious[①] ; and yet, the horror of that certitude! Behind the slim girl Bertha, whose words and looks I watched for, whose touch was bliss, there stood continually that Bertha with the fuller form, the harder eyes, the more rigid mouth — with the barren, selfish soul laid bare; no longer a fascinating secret, but a measured fact, urging itself perpetually on my unwilling sight.

Are you unable to give me your sympathy — you who read this? Are you unable to imagine this double consciousness at work within me, flowing on like two parallel streams which never mingle their waters and blend into a common hue? Yet you must have known something of the presentiments that spring from an insight at war with passion; and my visions were only like presentiments intensified to horror. You have known the powerlessness of ideas before the might of impulse; and my visions, when once they had passed into memory, were mere ideas — pale shadows that beckoned in vain, while my hand was grasped by the living and the loved.

In after-days I thought with bitter regret that if I had foreseen something more or something different — if instead of that hideous vision which poisoned the passion it could not destroy, or if even along with it I could have had a foreshadowing of

① veracious: real and exact

that moment when I looked on my brother's face for the last time, some softening influence would have been shed over my feeling towards him: pride and hatred would surely have been subdued into pity, and the record of those hidden sins would have been shortened. But this is one of the vain thoughts with which we men flatter ourselves. We try to believe that the egoism within us would have easily been melted, and that it was only the narrowness of our knowledge which hemmed in① our generosity, our awe, our human piety, and hindered them from submerging our hard indifference to the sensations and emotions of our fellows. Our tenderness and self-renunciation seem strong when our egoism has had its day — when, after our mean striving for a triumph that is to be another's loss, the triumph comes suddenly, and we shudder at it, because it is held out by the chill hand of death.

Our arrival in Prague happened at night, and I was glad of this, for it seemed like a deferring of a terribly decisive moment, to be in the city for hours without seeing it. As we were not to remain long in Prague, but to go on speedily to Dresden, it was proposed that we should drive out the next morning and take a general view of the place, as well as visit some of its specially interesting spots, before the heat became oppressive — for we were in August, and the season was hot and dry. But it happened that the ladies were rather late at their morning toilet, and to my father's politely-repressed but perceptible annoyance, we were not in the carriage till the morning was far advanced. I thought with a sense of relief, as we entered the Jews' quarter, where we were to visit the old synagogue, that we should be kept in this flat, shut-up part of the city, until we should all be too tired and too warm to go farther, and so we should return without seeing more than the streets through which we had already passed. That would give me another day's suspense — suspense, the only form in which a fearful spirit knows the solace of hope. But, as I stood under the blackened, groined arches of that old synagogue②, made dimly visible by the seven thin candles

---

① hem in: enclose, surround and immerse

② synagogue: a building in which Jewish people worship and study their religion in the sacred lamp, while our Jewish cicerone[①] reached down the Book of the Law, and read to us in its ancient tongue — I felt a shuddering impression that this strange building, with its shrunken lights, this surviving withered remnant of medieval Judaism, was of a piece with my vision. Those darkened dusty Christian saints, with their loftier arches and their larger candles, needed the consolatory scorn with which they might point to a more shrivelled death-in-life than their own.

As I expected, when we left the Jews' quarter the elders of our party wished to return to the hotel. But now, instead of rejoicing in this, as I had done beforehand, I felt a sudden overpowering impulse to go on at once to the bridge, and put an end to the suspense I had been wishing to protract. I declared, with unusual decision, that I would get out of the carriage and walk on alone; they might return without me. My father, thinking this merely a sample of my usual " poetic nonsense," objected that I should only do myself harm by walking in the heat; but when I persisted, he said angrily that I might follow my own absurd devices, but that Schmidt (our courier) must go with me. I assented to this, and set off with Schmidt towards the bridge. I had no sooner passed from under the archway of the grand old gate leading an to the bridge, than a trembling seized me, and I turned cold under the mid-day sun; yet I went on; I was in search of something--a small detail which I remembered with special intensity as part of my vision.

There it was — the patch of rainbow light on the pavement transmitted through a lamp in the shape of a star.

Chapter II

Before the autumn was at an end, and while the brown leaves still stood thick on the beeches in our park, my brother and Bertha were engaged to each other, and

① cicerone: a guide for sightseers

it was understood that their marriage was to take place early in the next spring. In spite of the certainty I had felt from that moment on the bridge at Prague, that Bertha would one day be my wife, my constitutional timidity and distrust had continued to benumb me, and the words in which I had sometimes premeditated a confession of my love, had died away unuttered. The same conflict had gone on within me as before — the longing for an assurance of love from Bertha's lips, the dread lest a word of contempt and denial should fall upon me like a corrosive acid. What was the conviction of a distant necessity to me? l trembled under a present glance, I hungered after a present joy, I was clogged and chilled by a present fear. And so the days passed on: I witnessed Bertha's engagement and heard her marriage discussed as if I were under a conscious nightmare — knowing it was a dream that would vanish, but feeling stifled under the grasp of hard-clutching fingers.

When I was not in Bertha's presence — and I was with her very often, for she continued to treat me with a playful patronage that wakened no jealousy in my brother — I spent my time chiefly in wandering, in strolling, or taking long rides while the daylight lasted, and then shutting myself up with my unread books; for books had lost the power of chaining my attention. My self-consciousness was heightened to that pitch of intensity in which our own emotions take the form of a drama which urges itself imperatively on our contemplation, and we begin to weep, less under the sense of our suffering than at the thought of it. I felt a sort of pitying anguish over the pathos of my own lot: the lot of a being finely organized for pain, but with hardly any fibres that responded to pleasure — to whom the idea of future evil robbed the present of its joy, and for whom the idea of future good did not still the uneasiness of a present yearning or a present dread. I went dumbly through that stage of the poet's suffering, in which he feels the delicious pang of utterance, and makes an image of his sorrows.

I was left entirely without remonstrance① concerning this dreamy wayward life: I knew my father's thought about me: " That lad will never be good for anything in life: he may waste his years in an insignificant way on the income that falls to him: I shall not trouble myself about a career for him."

One mild morning in the beginning of November, it happened that I was standing outside the portico patting lazy old Caesar, a Newfoundland almost blind with age, the only dog that ever took any notice of me — for the very dogs shunned me, and fawned on the happier people about me — when the groom brought up my brother's horse which was to carry him to the hunt, and my brother himself appeared at the door, florid, broad-chested, and self-complacent, feeling what a good-natured fellow he was not to behave insolently to us all on the strength of his great advantages.

" Latimer, old boy," he said to me in a tone of compassionate cordiality, " what a pity it is you don't have a run with the hounds now and then! The finest thing in the world for low spirits!"

" Low spirits!" I thought bitterly, as he rode away; " that is the sort of phrase with which coarse, narrow natures like yours think to describe experience of which you can know no more than your horse knows. It is to such as you that the good of this world falls: ready dulness, healthy selfishness, good-tempered conceit — these are the keys to happiness."

The quick thought came, that my selfishness was even stronger than his — it was only a suffering selfishness instead of an enjoying one. But then, again, my exasperating insight into Alfred's self-complacent soul, his freedom from all the doubts and fears, the unsatisfied yearnings, the exquisite tortures of sensitiveness, that had made the web of my life, seemed to absolve② me from all bonds towards him. This man needed no pity, no love; those fine influences would have been as little felt by him as the delicate white mist is felt by the rock it caresses. There was no evil

---

① remonstrance: complain

② absolve: to free someone from guilt, blame, or responsibility for something in store for him: if he was not to marry Bertha, it would be because he had found a lot pleasanter to himself.

Mr. Filmore's house lay not more than half a mile beyond our own gates, and whenever I knew my brother was gone in another direction, I went there for the chance of finding Bertha at home. Later on in the day I walked thither. By a rare accident she was alone, and we walked out in the grounds together, for she seldom went on foot beyond the trimly-swept gravel-walks. I remember what a beautiful sylph she looked to me as the low November sun shone on her blond hair, and she tripped along teasing me with her usual light banter, to which I listened half fondly, half moodily; it was all the sign Bertha's mysterious inner self ever made to me. To-day perhaps, the moodiness predominated, for I had not yet shaken off the access of jealous hate which my brother had raised in me by his parting patronage. Suddenly I interrupted and startled her by saying, almost fiercely, " Bertha, how can you love Alfred?"

She looked at me with surprise for a moment, but soon her light smile came again, and she answered sarcastically, " Why do you suppose I love him?"

" How can you ask that, Bertha?"

" What! your wisdom thinks I must love the man I'm going to marry? The most unpleasant thing in the world. I should quarrel with him; I should be jealous of him; our menage would be conducted in a very ill-bred manner. A little quiet contempt contributes greatly to the elegance of life."

" Bertha, that is not your real feeling. Why do you delight in trying to deceive me by inventing such cynical speeches?"

" I need never take the trouble of invention in order to deceive you, my small Tasso" — (that was the mocking name she usually gave me). " The easiest way to deceive a poet is to tell him the truth."

She was testing the validity of her epigram in a daring way, and for a moment the shadow of my vision — the Bertha whose soul was no secret to me — passed between me and the radiant girl, the playful sylph whose feelings were a fascinating mystery. I suppose I must have shuddered, or betrayed in some other way my momentary chill of horror.

" Tasso!" she said, seizing my wrist, and peeping round into my face, " are you really beginning to discern what a heartless girl I am? Why, you are not half the poet I thought you were; you are actually capable of believing the truth about me."

The shadow passed from between us, and was no longer the object nearest to me. The girl whose light fingers grasped me, whose elfish charming face looked into mine — who, I thought, was betraying an interest in my feelings that she would not have directly avowed, — this warm breathing presence again possessed my senses and imagination like a returning siren melody which had been overpowered for an instant by the roar of threatening waves. It was a moment as delicious to me as the waking up to a consciousness of youth after a dream of middle age. I forgot everything but my passion, and said with swimming eyes.

" Bertha, shall you love me when we are first married? I wouldn't mind if you really loved me only for a little while."

Her look of astonishment, as she loosed my hand and started away from me, recalled me to a sense of my strange, my criminal indiscretion.①

" Forgive me," I said, hurriedly, as soon as I could speak again; " I did not know what I was saying."

" Ah, Tasso's mad fit has come on, I see," she answered quietly, for she had recovered herself sooner than I had. " Let him go home and keep his head cool. I must go in, for the sun is setting."

I left her — full of indignation against myself. I had let slip words which, if she reflected on them, might rouse in her a suspicion of my abnormal mental condition — a suspicion which of all things I dreaded. And besides that, I was

① indiscretion: something, especially a sexual relationship, that is considered embarrassing or morally wrong.

ashamed of the apparent baseness I had committed in uttering them to my brother's betrothed wife. I wandered home slowly, entering our park through a private gate instead of by the lodges. As I approached the house, I saw a man dashing off at full speed from the stable-yard across the park. Had any accident happened at home? No; perhaps it was only one of my father's peremptory business errands that required this headlong haste.

Nevertheless, I quickened my pace without any distinct motive, and was soon at the house. I will not dwell on the scene I found there. My brother was dead — had been pitched from his horse, and killed on the spot by a concussion of the brain.

I went up to the room where he lay, and where my father was seated beside him with a look of rigid despair. I had shunned my father more than any one since our return home, for the radical antipathy between our natures made my insight into his inner self a constant affliction to me. But now, as I went up to him, and stood beside him in sad silence, I felt the presence of a new element that blended us as we had never been blent before. My father had been one of the most successful men in the money-getting world: he had had no sentimental sufferings, no illness. The heaviest trouble that had befallen him was the death of his first wife. But he married my mother soon after; and I remember he seemed exactly the same, to my keen childish observation, the week after her death as before. But now, at last, a sorrow had come — the sorrow of old age, which suffers the more from the crushing of its pride and its hopes, in proportion as the pride and hope are narrow and prosaic.

His son was to have been married soon — would probably have stood for the borough at the next election. That son's existence was the best motive that could be alleged for making new purchases of land every year to round off the estate. It is a dreary thing onto live on doing the same things year after year, without knowing why we do them. Perhaps the tragedy of disappointed youth and passion is less piteous than the tragedy of disappointed age and worldliness.

As I saw into the desolation of my father's heart, I felt a movement of deep pity towards him, which was the beginning of a new affection — an affection that grew and strengthened in spite of the strange bitterness with which he regarded me in the first month or two after my brother's death. If it had not been for the softening influence of my compassion for him — the first deep compassion I had ever felt — I should have been stung by the perception that my father transferred the inheritance of an eldest son to me with a mortified sense that fate had compelled him to the unwelcome course of caring for me as an important being. It was only in spite of himself that he began to think of me with anxious regard. There is hardly any neglected child for whom death has made vacant a more favoured place, who will not understand what I mean.

Gradually, however, my new deference to his wishes, the effect of that patience which was born of my pity for him, won upon his affection, and he began to please himself with the endeavour to make me fill any brother's place as fully as my feebler personality would admit. I saw that the prospect which by and by presented itself of my becoming Bertha's husband was welcome to him, and he even contemplated in my case what he had not intended in my brother's — that his son and daughter-in-law should make one household with him. My softened feelings towards my father made this the happiest time I had known since childhood; — these last months in which I retained the delicious illusion of loving Bertha, of longing and doubting and hoping that she might love me. She behaved with a certain new consciousness and distance towards me after my brother's death; and I too was under a double constraint — that of delicacy towards my brother's memory and of anxiety as to the impression my abrupt words had left on her mind. But the additional screen this mutual reserve erected between us only brought me more completely under her power: no matter how empty the adytum, so that the veil be thick enough. So absolute is our soul's need of something hidden and uncertain for the maintenance of that doubt and hope and effort which are the breath of its life, that if the whole future were laid bare to us beyond to-day, the interest of all mankind would be bent on the hours that lie between; we should pant after the uncertainties of our one morning and our one afternoon; we should rush fiercely to the Exchange for our last possibility of speculation, of success, of disappointment: we should have a glut of political prophets foretelling a crisis or a no-crisis within the only twenty-four hours left open to prophecy. Conceive the condition of the human mind if all propositions whatsoever were self-evident except one, which was to become self-evident at the close of a summer's day, but in the meantime might be the subject of question, of hypothesis, of debate. Art and philosophy, literature and science, would fasten like bees on that one proposition which had the honey of probability in it, and be the more eager because their enjoyment would end with sunset. Our impulses, our spiritual activities, no more adjust themselves to the idea of their future nullity① , than the beating of our heart, or the irritability of our muscles.

Bertha, the slim, fair-haired girl, whose present thoughts and emotions were an enigma to me amidst the fatiguing obviousness of the other minds around me, was as absorbing to me as a single unknown to-day — as a single hypothetic proposition to remain problematic till sunset; and all the cramped, hemmed-in belief and disbelief, trust and distrust, of my nature, welled out in this one narrow channel.

And she made me believe that she loved me. Without ever quitting her tone of badinage② and playful superiority, she intoxicated me with the sense that I was necessary to her, that she was never at ease, unless I was near her, submitting to her playful tyranny. It costs a woman so little effort to beset us in this way! A half-repressed word, a moment's unexpected silence, even an easy fit of petulance③ on our account, will serve us as hashish④ for a long while. Out of the subtlest web of scarcely perceptible signs, she set me weaving the fancy that she had always

① nullity: something such as an agreement or decision which no longer has legal force

② badinage: conversation or remarks that are joking and not serious

③ petulance: physically and mentally bad-tempered nature

④ hashish: a drug, illegal in many countries, made from the cannabis plant and usually smoked unconsciously loved me better than Alfred, but that, with the ignorant fluttered sensibility of a young girl, she had been imposed on by the charm that lay for her in the distinction of being admired and chosen by a man who made so brilliant a figure in the world as my brother. She satirized herself in a very graceful way for her vanity and ambition. What was it to me that I had the light of my wretched provision on the fact that now it was I who possessed at least all but the personal part of my brother's advantages? Our sweet illusions are half of them conscious illusions, like effects of colour that we know to be made up of tinsel, broken glass, and rags.

We were married eighteen months after Alfred's death, one cold, clear morning in April, when there came hail and sunshine both together; and Bertha, in her white silk and pale-green leaves, and the pale hues of her hair and face, looked like the spirit of the morning. My father was happier than he had thought of being again: my marriage, he felt sure, would complete the desirable modification of my character, and make me practical and worldly enough to take my place in society among sane men. For he delighted in Bertha's tact and acuteness, and felt sure she would be mistress of me, and make me what she chose: I was only twenty-one, and madly in love with her. Poor father! He kept that hope a little while after our first year of marriage, and it was not quite extinct when paralysis came and saved him from utter disappointment.

I shall hurry through the rest of my story, not dwelling so much as I have hitherto done on my inward experience. When people are well known to each other, they talk rather of what befalls them externally, leaving their feelings and sentiments to be inferred.

We lived in a round of visits for some time after our return home, giving splendid dinner-parties, and making a sensation in our neighbourhood by the new lustre of our equipage, for my father had reserved this display of his increased wealth for the period of his son's marriage; and we gave our acquaintances liberal opportunity for remarking that it was a pity I made so poor a figure as an heir and a bridegroom.

The nervous fatigue of this existence, the insincerities and platitudes which I had to live through twice over — through my inner and outward sense — would have been maddening to me, if I had not had that sort of intoxicated callousness which came from the delights of a first passion. A bride and bridegroom, surrounded by all the appliances of wealth, hurried through the day by the whirl of society, filling their solitary moments with hastily-snatched caresses, are prepared for their future life together as the novice is prepared for the cloister — by experiencing its utmost contrast.

Through all these crowded excited months, Bertha's inward self remained shrouded from me, and I still read her thoughts only through the language of her lips and demeanour① : I had still the human interest of wondering whether what I did and said pleased her, of longing to hear a word of affection, of giving a delicious exaggeration of meaning to her smile. But I was conscious of a growing difference in her manner towards me; sometimes strong enough to be called haughty coldness, cutting and chilling me as the hail had done that came across the sunshine on our marriage morning; sometimes only perceptible in the dexterous avoidance of a tete-a-tete② walk or dinner to which I had been looking forward. I had been deeply pained by this — had even felt a sort of crushing of the heart, from the sense that my brief day of happiness was near its setting; but still I remained dependent on Bertha, eager for the last rays of a bliss that would soon be gone for ever, hoping and watching for some after-glow more beautiful from the impending night.

I remember — how should I not remember? — the time when that dependence and hope utterly left me, when the sadness I had felt in Bertha's growing estrangement became a joy that I looked back upon with longing as a man might look back on the last pains in a paralysed limb. It was just after the close of my father's last illness, which had necessarily withdrawn us from society and thrown us more

① demeanour: a way of looking and behaving

② tete–a–tete: informal private conversation between two people, especially friends on each other. It was the evening of father's death. On that evening the veil which had shrouded Bertha's soul from me — had made me find in her alone among my fellow-beings the blessed possibility of mystery, and doubt, and expectation — was first withdrawn. Perhaps it was the first day since the beginning of my passion for her, in which that passion was completely neutralized by the presence of an absorbing feeling of another kind. I had been watching by my father's deathbed: I had been witnessing the last fitful yearning glance his soul had cast back on the spent inheritance of life — the last faint consciousness of love he had gathered from the pressure of my hand. What are all our personal loves when we have been sharing in that supreme agony? In the first moments when we come away from the presence of death, every other relation to the living is merged, to our feeling, in the great relation of a common nature and a common destiny.

In that state of mind I joined Bertha in her private sitting-room. She was seated in a leaning posture on a settee, with her back towards the door; the great rich coils of her pale blond hair surmounting her small neck, visible above the back of the settee. I remember, as I closed the door behind me, a cold tremulousness seizing me, and a vague sense of being hated and lonely — vague and strong, like a presentiment. I know how I looked at that moment, for I saw myself in Bertha's thought as she lifted her cutting grey eyes, and looked at me: a miserable ghost-seer, surrounded by phantoms in the noonday, trembling under a breeze when the leaves were still, without appetite for the common objects of human desires, but pining after the moon-beams. We were front to front with each other, and judged each other. The terrible moment of complete illumination had come to me, and I saw that the darkness had hidden no landscape from me, but only a blank prosaic wall: from that evening forth, through the sickening years which followed, I saw all round the narrow room of this woman's soul — saw petty artifice and mere negation where I had delighted to believe in coy sensibilities and in wit at war with latent feeling — saw the light floating vanities of the girl defining themselves into the systematic coquetry[①], the scheming selfishness, of the woman — saw repulsion and antipathy harden into cruel hatred, giving pain only for the sake of wreaking itself.

For Bertha too, after her kind, felt the bitterness of disillusion. She had believed that my wild poet's passion for her would make me her slave; and that, being her slave, I should execute her will in all things. With the essential shallowness of a negative, unimaginative nature, she was unable to conceive the fact that sensibilities were anything else than weaknesses. She had thought my weaknesses would put me in her power, and she found them unmanageable forces. Our positions were reversed. Before marriage she had completely mastered my imagination, for she was a secret to me; and I created the unknown thought before which I trembled as if it were hers. But now that her soul was laid open to me, now that I was compelled to share the privacy of her motives, to follow all the petty devices that preceded her words and acts, she found herself powerless with me, except to produce in me the chill shudder of repulsion — powerless, because I could be acted on by no lever within her reach. I was dead to worldly ambitions, to social vanities, to all the incentives within the compass of her narrow imagination, and I lived under influences utterly invisible to her.

She was really pitiable to have such a husband, and so all the world thought. A graceful, brilliant woman, like Bertha, who smiled on morning callers, made a figure in ball-rooms, and was capable of that light repartee which, from such a woman, is accepted as wit, was secure of carrying off all sympathy from a husband who was sickly, abstracted, and, as some suspected, crack- brained. Even the servants in our house gave her the balance of their regard and pity. For there were no audible quarrels between us; our alienation, our repulsion from each other, lay within the silence of our own hearts; and if the mistress went out a great deal, and seemed to dislike the

---

① coquetry: a woman who likes to attract attention by behaving as if she is sexually interested in people, in a pleasant but not serious way master's society, was it not natural, poor thing? The master was odd. I was kind and just to my dependants, but I excited in them a shrinking, half-contemptuous pity; for this class of men and women are but slightly determined in their estimate of others by general considerations, or even experience, of character. They judge of persons as they judge of coins, and value those who pass current at a high rate.

After a time I interfered so little with Bertha's habits that it might seem wonderful how her hatred towards me could grow so intense and active as it did. But she had begun to suspect, by some involuntary betrayal of mine, that there was an abnormal power of penetration in me — that fitfully, at least, I was strangely cognizant of her thoughts and intentions, and she began to be haunted by a terror of me, which alternated every now and then with defiance. She meditated continually how the incubus could be shaken off her life — how she could be freed from this hateful bond to a being whom she at once despised as an imbecile[①], and dreaded as an inquisitor. For a long while she lived in the hope that my evident wretchedness would drive me to the commission of suicide; but suicide was not in my nature. I was too completely swayed by the sense that I was in the grasp of unknown forces, to believe in my power of self-release. Towards my own destiny I had become entirely passive; for my one ardent desire had spent itself, and impulse no longer predominated over knowledge. For this reason I never thought of taking any steps towards a complete separation, which would have made our alienation evident to the world. Why should I rush for help to a new course, when I was only suffering from the consequences of a deed which had been the act of my intensest will? That would have been the logic of one who had desires to gratify, and I had no desires. But Bertha and I lived more and more aloof from each other. The rich find it easy to live married and apart.

That course of our life which I have indicated in a few sentences filled the

① imbecile: a person who behaves in a stupid way

space of years. So much misery — so slow and hideous a growth of hatred and sin, may be compressed into a sentence! And men judge of each other's lives through this summary medium. They epitomize① the experience of their fellow-mortal, and pronounce judgment on him in neat syntax, and feel themselves wise and virtuous — conquerors over the temptations they define in well-selected predicates. Seven years of wretchedness glide glibly② over the lips of the man who has never counted them out in moments of chill disappointment, of head and heart throbbings, of dread and vain wrestling, of remorse and despair. We learn words by rote, but not their meaning; that must be paid for with our life-blood, and printed in the subtle fibres of our nerves.

But I will hasten to finish my story. Brevity is justified at once to those who readily understand, and to those who will never understand.

Some years after my father's death, I was sitting by the dim firelight in my library one January evening — sitting in the leather chair that used to be my father's — when Bertha appeared at the door, with a candle in her hand, and advanced towards me. I knew the ball-dress she had on — the white ball-dress, with the green jewels, shone upon by the light of the wax candle which lit up the medallion of the dying Cleopatra on the mantelpiece. Why did she come to me before going out? I had not seen her in the library, which was my habitual place for months. Why did she stand before me with the candle in her hand, with her cruel contemptuous eyes fixed on me, and the glittering serpent, like a familiar demon, on her breast? For a moment I thought this fulfilment of my vision at Vienna marked some dreadful crisis in my fate, but I saw nothing in Bertha's mind, as she stood before me, except scorn for the look of overwhelming misery with which I sat before her... "Fool, idiot, why don't you kill yourself, then?" — that was her thought. But at length her thoughts reverted to her errand, and she spoke aloud. The apparently indifferent nature of the errand seemed to make a ridiculous anticlimax to my prevision and my agitation.

---

① epitomize: typify, illustrate and exemplify of meaning and significance of something

② glibly: speaking or spoken in a confident way, but without careful thought or honesty

" I have had to hire a new maid. Fletcher is going to be married, and she wants me to ask you to let her husband have the public-house and farm at Molton. I wish him to have it. You must give the promise now, because Fletcher is going to-morrow morning — and quickly, because I'm in a hurry."

" Very well; you may promise her," I said, indifferently, and Bertha swept out of the library again.

I always shrank from the sight of a new person, and all the more when it was a person whose mental life was likely to weary my reluctant insight with worldly ignorant trivialities. But I shrank especially from the sight of this new maid, because her advent had been announced to me at a moment to which I could not cease to attach some fatality: I had a vague dread that I should find her mixed up with the dreary drama of my life — that some new sickening vision would reveal her to me as an evil genius. When at last I did unavoidably meet her, the vague dread was changed into definite disgust. She was a tall, wiry, dark-eyed woman, this Mrs. Archer, with a face handsome enough to give her coarse hard nature the odious finish of bold, self-confident coquetry. That was enough to make me avoid her, quite apart from the contemptuous feeling with which she contemplated me. I seldom saw her; but I perceived that she rapidly became a favourite with her mistress, and, after the lapse of eight or nine months, I began to be aware that there had arisen in Bertha's mind towards this woman a mingled feeling of fear and dependence, and that this feeling was associated with ill-defined images of candle-light scenes in her dressing-room, and the locking-up of something in Bertha's cabinet. My interviews with my wife had become so brief and so rarely solitary, that I had no opportunity of perceiving these images in her mind with more definiteness. The recollections of the past become contracted in the rapidity of thought till they sometimes bear hardly a more distinct resemblance to the external reality than the forms of an oriental alphabet to the objects that suggested them.

Besides, for the last year or more a modification had been going forward in my mental condition, and was growing more and more marked. My insight into the minds of those around me was becoming dimmer and more fitful, and the ideas that crowded my double consciousness became less and less dependent on any personal contact. All that was personal in me seemed to be suffering a gradual death, so that I was losing the organ through which the personal agitations and projects of others could affect me. But along with this relief from wearisome insight, there was a new development of what I concluded — as I have since found rightly — to be a provision of external scenes. It was as if the relation between me and my fellow-men was more and more deadened, and my relation to what we call the inanimate was quickened into new life.

The more I lived apart from society, and in proportion as my wretchedness subsided from the violent throb of agonized passion into the dulness of habitual pain, the more frequent and vivid became such visions as that I had had of Prague — of strange cities, of sandy plains, of gigantic ruins, of midnight skies with strange bright constellations, of mountain-passes, of grassy nooks flecked with the afternoon sunshine through the boughs: I was in the midst of such scenes, and in all of them one presence seemed to weigh on me in all these mighty shapes — the presence of something unknown and pitiless. For continual suffering had annihilated religious faith within me: to the utterly miserable — the unloving and the unloved — there is no religion possible, no worship but a worship of devils. And beyond all these, and continually recurring, was the vision of my death — the pangs, the suffocation, the last struggle, when life would be grasped at in vain.

Things were in this state near the end of the seventh year. I had become entirely free from insight, from my abnormal cognizance of any other consciousness than my own, and instead of intruding involuntarily into the world of other minds, was living continually in my own solitary future. Bertha was aware that I was greatly changed. To my surprise she had of late seemed to seek opportunities of remaining in my society, and had cultivated that kind of distant yet familiar talk which is customary between a husband and wife who live in polite and irrevocable alienation. I bore this with languid submission, and without feeling enough interest in her motives to be roused into keen observation; yet I could not help perceiving something triumphant and excited in her carriage and the expression of her face — something too subtle to express itself in words or tones, but giving one the idea that she lived in a state of expectation or hopeful suspense. My chief feeling was satisfaction that her inner self was once more shut out from me; and I almost revelled for the moment in the absent melancholy that made me answer her at cross purposes, and betray utter ignorance of what she had been saying. I remember well the look and the smile with which she one day said, after a mistake of this kind on my part: " I used to think you were a clairvoyant, and that was the reason why you were so bitter against other clairvoyants, wanting to keep your monopoly; but I see now you have become rather duller than the rest of the world."

I said nothing in reply. It occurred to me that her recent obtrusion of herself upon me might have been prompted by the wish to test my power of detecting some of her secrets; but I let the thought drop again at once: her motives and her deeds had no interest for me, and whatever pleasures she might be seeking, I had no wish to baulk her. There was still pity in my soul for every living thing, and Bertha was living — was surrounded with possibilities of misery.

Just at this time there occurred an event which roused me somewhat from my inertia, and gave me an interest in the passing moment that I had thought impossible for me. It was a visit from Charles Meunier, who had written me word that he was coming to England for relaxation from too strenuous labour, and would like too see me. Meunier had now a European reputation; but his letter to me expressed that keen remembrance of an early regard, an early debt of sympathy, which is inseparable from nobility of character: and I too felt as if his presence would be to me like a transient resurrection into a happier pre-existence.

He came, and as far as possible, I renewed our old pleasure of making tete-a-tete excursions, though, instead of mountains and glacers and the wide blue lake, we had to content ourselves with mere slopes and ponds and artificial plantations. The years had changed us both, but with what different result! Meunier was now a brilliant figure in society, to whom elegant women pretended to listen, and whose acquaintance was boasted of by noblemen ambitious of brains. He repressed with the utmost delicacy all betrayal of the shock which I am sure he must have received from our meeting, or of a desire to penetrate into my condition and circumstances, and sought by the utmost exertion of his charming social powers to make our reunion agreeable. Bertha was much struck by the unexpected fascinations of a visitor whom she had expected to find presentable only on the score of his celebrity, and put forth all her coquetries and accomplishments. Apparently she succeeded in attracting his admiration, for his manner towards her was attentive and flattering. The effect of his presence on me was so benignant, especially in those renewals of our old tete-a-tete wanderings, when he poured forth to me wonderful narratives of his professional experience, that more than once, when his talk turned on the psychological relations of disease, the thought crossed my mind that, if his stay with me were long enough, I might possibly bring myself to tell this man the secrets of my lot. Might there not lie some remedy for me, too, in his science? Might there not at least lie some comprehension and sympathy ready for me in his large and susceptible mind? But the thought only flickered feebly now and then, and died out before it could become a wish. The horror I had of again breaking in on the privacy of another soul, made me, by an irrational instinct, draw the shroud of concealment more closely around my own, as we automatically perform the gesture we feel to be wanting in another.

When Meunier's visit was approaching its conclusion, there happened an event which caused some excitement in our household, owing to the surprisingly strong effect it appeared to produce on Bertha — on Bertha, the self-possessed, who usually seemed inaccessible to feminine agitations, and did even her hate in a self-restrained hygienic manner. This event was the sudden severe illness of her maid, Mrs. Archer.

I have reserved to this moment the mention of a circumstance which had forced itself on my notice shortly before Meunier's arrival, namely, that there had been some quarrel between Bertha and this maid, apparently during a visit to a distant family, in which she had accompanied her mistress. I had overheard Archer speaking in a tone of bitter insolence① , which I should have thought an adequate reason for immediate dismissal. No dismissal followed; on the contrary, Bertha seemed to be silently putting up with personal inconveniences from the exhibitions of this woman's temper. I was the more astonished to observe that her illness seemed a cause of strong solicitude② to Bertha; that she was at the bedside night and day, and would allow no one else to officiate as head-nurse. It happened that our family doctor was out on a holiday, an accident which made Meunier's presence in the house doubly welcome, and he apparently entered into the case with an interest which seemed so much stronger than the ordinary professional feeling, that one day when he had fallen into a long fit of silence after visiting her, I said to him —

" Is this a very peculiar case of disease, Meunier?"

" No," he answered, " it is an attack of peritonitis, which will bc fatal, but which does not differ physically from many other cases that have come under my observation. But I'll tell you what I have on my mind. I want to make an experiment on this woman, if you will give me permission. It can do her no harm — will give her no pain — for I shall not make it until life is extinct to all purposes of sensation. I want to try the effect of transfusing blood into her arteries after the heart has ceased to beat for some minutes. I have tried the experiment again and again with animals that have died of this disease, with astounding results, and I want to try it on a human subject. I have the small tubes necessary, in a case I have with me, and the rest of the apparatus could be prepared readily. I should use my own blood — take it from my own arm. This woman won't live through the night, I'm convinced, and I want you

① insolence: rude and not showing respect

② solicitude: showing care and helpful attention to someone

to promise me your assistance in making the experiment. I can't do without another hand, but it would perhaps not be well to call in a medical assistant from among your provincial doctors. A disagreeable foolish version of the thing might get abroad."

" Have you spoken to my wife on the subject?" I said, " because she appears to be peculiarly sensitive about this woman: she has been a favourite maid."

" To tell you the truth," said Meunier, " I don't want her to know about it. There are always insuperable difficulties with women in these matters, and the effect on the supposed dead body may be startling. You and I will sit up together, and be in readiness. When certain symptoms appear I shall take you in, and at the right moment we must manage to get every one else out of the room."

I need not give our farther conversation on the subject. He entered very fully into the details, and overcame my repulsion from them, by exciting in me a mingled awe and curiosity concerning the possible results of his experiment.

We prepared everything, and he instructed me in my part as assistant. He had not told Bertha of his absolute conviction that Archer would not survive through the night, and endeavoured to persuade her to leave the patient and take a night's rest. But she was obstinate[①] , suspecting the fact that death was at hand, and supposing that he wished merely to save her nerves. She refused to leave the sick-room. Meunier and I sat up together in the library, he making frequent visits to the sick-room, and returning with the information that the case was taking precisely the course he expected.

Once he said to me, " Can you imagine any cause of ill-feeling this woman has against her mistress, who is so devoted to her?"

" I think there was some misunderstanding between them before her illness. Why do you ask?"

" Because I have observed for the last five or six hours — since, I fancy, she has

① obstinate: unreasonably determined, especially to act in a particular way and not to change at all, despite what anyone else says lost all hope of recovery — there seems a strange prompting in her to say something which pain and failing strength forbid her to utter; and there is a look of hideous meaning in her eyes, which she turns continually towards her mistress. In this disease the mind often remains singularly clear to the last."

" I am not surprised at an indication of malevolent feeling in her," I said. " She is a woman who has always inspired me with distrust and dislike, but she managed to insinuate herself into her mistress's favour." He was silent after this, looking at the fire with an air of absorption, till he went upstairs again. He stayed away longer than usual, and on returning, said to me quietly, " Come now."

I followed him to the chamber where death was hovering. The dark hangings of the large bed made a background that gave a strong relief to Bertha's pale face as I entered. She started forward as she saw me enter, and then looked at Meunier with an expression of angry inquiry; but he lifted up his hand as it to impose silence, while he fixed his glance on the dying woman and felt her pulse. The face was pinched and ghastly, a cold perspiration was on the forehead, and the eyelids were lowered so as to conceal the large dark eyes. After a minute or two, Meunier walked round to the other side of the bed where Bertha stood, and with his usual air of gentle politeness towards her begged her to leave the patient under our care — everything should be done for her — she was no longer in a state to be conscious of an affectionate presence. Bertha was hesitating, apparently almost willing to believe his assurance and to comply. She looked round at the ghastly dying face, as if to read the confirmation of that assurance, when for a moment the lowered eyelids were raised again, and it seemed as if the eyes were looking towards Bertha, but blankly. A shudder passed through Bertha's frame, and she returned to her station near the pillow, tacitly implying that she would not leave the room.

The eyelids were lifted no more. Once I looked at Bertha as she watched the face of the dying one. She wore a rich peignoir, and her blond hair was half covered by a lace cap: in her attire she was, as always, an elegant woman, fit to figure in a picture of modern aristocratic life: but I asked myself how that face of hers could ever have seemed to me the face of a woman born of woman, with memories of childhood, capable of pain, needing to be fondled? The features at that moment seemed so preternaturally sharp, the eyes were so hard and eager — she looked like a cruel immortal, finding her spiritual feast in the agonies of a dying race. For across those hard features there came something like a flash when the last hour had been breathed out, and we all felt that the dark veil had completely fallen. What secret was there between Bertha and this woman? I turned my eyes from her with a horrible dread lest my insight should return, and I should be obliged to see what had been breeding about two unloving women's hearts. I felt that Bertha had been watching for the moment of death as the sealing of her secret: I thanked Heaven it could remain sealed for me.

Meunier said quietly, " She is gone." He then gave his arm to Bertha, and she submitted to be led out of the room.

I suppose it was at her order that two female attendants came into the room, and dismissed the younger one who had been present before. When they entered, Meunier had already opened the artery in the long thin neck that lay rigid on the pillow, and I dismissed them, ordering them to remain at a distance till we rang: the doctor, I said, had an operation to perform — he was not sure about the death. For the next twenty minutes I forgot everything but Meunier and the experiment in which he was so absorbed, that I think his senses would have been closed against all sounds or sights which had no relation to it. It was my task at first to keep up the artificial respiration in the body after the transfusion had been effected, but presently Meunier relieved me, and I could see the wondrous slow return of life; the breast began to heave, the inspirations became stronger, the eyelids quivered, and the soul seemed to have returned beneath them. The artificial respiration was withdrawn: still the breathing continued, and there was a movement of the lips.

Just then I heard the handle of the door moving: I suppose Bertha had heard from the women that they had been dismissed: probably a vague fear had arisen in her mind, for she entered with a look of alarm. She came to the foot of the bed and gave a stifled cry.

The dead woman's eyes were wide open, and met hers in full recognition — the recognition of hate. With a sudden strong effort, the hand that Bertha had thought for ever still was pointed towards her, and the haggard face moved. The gasping eager voice said —

" You mean to poison your husband...the poison is in the black cabinet...I got it for you...you laughed at me, and told lies about me behind my back, to make me disgusting...because you were jealous ...are you sorry ...now?"

The lips continued to murmur, but the sounds were no longer distinct. Soon there was no sound — only a slight movement: the flame had leaped out, and was being extinguished the faster. The wretched woman's heart-strings had been set to hatred and vengeance; the spirit of life had swept the chords for an instant, and was gone again for ever. Great God! Is this what it is to live again... to wake up with our unstilled thirst upon us, with our unuttered curses rising to our lips, with our muscles ready to act out their half-committed sins?

Bertha stood pale at the foot of the bed, quivering and helpless, despairing of devices, like a cunning animal whose hiding-places are surrounded by swift-advancing flame. Even Meunier looked paralysed; life for that moment ceased to be a scientific problem to him. As for me, this scene seemed of one texture with the rest of my existence: horror was my familiar, and this new revelation was only like an old pain recurring with new circumstances.

* * *

Since then Bertha and I have lived apart — she in her own neighbourhood, the mistress of half our wealth, I as a wanderer in foreign countries, until I came to this Devonshire nest to die.

Bertha lives pitied and admired; for what had I against that charming woman, whom everyone but myself could have been happy with? There had been no witness of the scene in the dying room except Meunier, and while Meunier lived his lips were sealed by a promise to me.

Once or twice, weary of wandering, I rested in a favourite spot, and my heart went out towards the men and women and children whose faces were becoming familiar to me; but I was driven away again in terror at the approach of my old insight — driven away to live continually with the one Unknown Presence revealed and yet hidden by the moving curtain of the earth and sky. Till at last disease took hold of me and forced me to rest here — forced me to live in dependence on my servants. And then the curse of insight — of my double consciousness, came again, and has never left me. I know all their narrow thoughts, their feeble regard, their half-wearied pity.

* * *

It is the 20th of September, 1850. I know these figures I have just written, as if they were a long familiar inscription. I have seen them on this pace in my desk unnumbered times, when the scene of my dying struggle has opened upon me...

(1859)

Topics for discussion

1. George Eliot's " The Lifted Veil" is regarded as Gothic fiction of the 19th century, and could you talk about the supernatural elements in it?

2. Could you think the character of Latimer as a masochist? Please make some explanation about it?

3. Is there some impact of Charles Darwin's *On the Origin of Species* on George Eliot's " The Lifted Veil"?

References for further reading

[1] Ashton, Rosemary. *George Eliot: A Life*, New York: Penguin Press, 1996.

[2] Chapman, Raymond, *The Sense of the Past in Victorian Literature*, London: CroomHelm, 1986.

[3] Haight, Gordon S., ed. *Selections from George Eliot's Letters*. New Haven: Yale University Press, 1985.

[4] Hughes, Kathryn. *George Eliot: The Last Victorian*, New York: Farrar Straus Giroux, 1998.

Joseph Conrad (1857 — 1924)

The Secret Sharer

Introduction to the author

Joseph Conrad (December 3, 1857 — August 3, 1924) was a Polish-born English author who wrote in English after settling in England. He is chiefly remembered for such novels as *Heart of Darkness* which contains bitter reflections on colonialism and as a master prose stylist and a representative of modernist literature. His narrative style and characterization have influenced many authors, including D. H. Lawrence, F. Scott Fitzgerald, William Faulkner, Ernest Hemingway, George Orwell and Joseph Heller. The native Poland's experiences, the merchant navies and a European-dominated world in Conrad's works explore human soul profoundly and deeply. He is regarded as one of the greatest novelists in English.

Joseph Conrad was born to Apollo Korzeniowski and Ewa Bobrowska on December 3, 1857 in Berdychiv, Poland, the only child of the couple. Conrad was born Jozef Teodor Konrad Korzeniowski. His father was a writer, translator, political activist and revolutionary. His parents were exiled to Russia in 1862 and both of them died before Conrad was 11 years old. Conrad did not speak English fluently until he was in his twenties. He joined the merchant marines and travelled to Africa, Australia, India and the Orient. These experiences as a sailor became an integrated part in his writing, producing many characters of his stories and novels from the authentic names of actual persons. Eventually Conrad settled in England and was granted British nationality in 1886. Although he always regarded himself as a Pole all his life. Conrad wrote all his books in English.

In 1896, Conrad married an English woman, Jessie George. The couple had two sons, Borys and John. The family rented a long series of successive homes, occasionally in France, sometimes briefly in London, but mostly in the English countryside. Conrad suffered from poor health, physical and mental, all his life, due to which Conrad reluctantly gave up the sea to start his literary career. On August 3, 1924, Conrad died of a heart attack, aged 66. He was buried at Canterbury Cemetery, Canterbury.

Major works by Joseph Conrad

Novels

Almayer's Folly, 1895
An Outcast of the Islands, 1896
The Nigger of the "Narcissus", 1897
Heart of Darkness, 1899
Lord Jim, 1900
Typhoon, 1902, (began in 1899)
The Secret Agent, 1907
Under Western Eyes, 1911
Chance, 1913
Victory, 1915
The Shadow Line, 1917
The Arrow of Gold, 1919
The Rescue, 1920
The Rover, 1923

Essays

The Mirror of the Sea, 1906
A Personal Record, 1912

The First News, 1918

The Shock of War, 1919

The Polish Question, 1919

Notes on Life and Letters, 1921

Appreciation

" The Secret Sharer" was written in 1909 and became a part of the short-story collection *Twixt Land and Sea* which was first published in 1912. The story takes place at sea, near the Gulf of Siam, a psychological tale told by a young nameless Captain. As the story begins, the captain has just taken command of his first ship a fortnight earlier and he is familiar with neither the ship nor the crew. Knowing that he is facing a considerably older and more experienced crew, the captain can feel a strong sense of insecurity and uncertainty. The captain offered to be on look-out duty the first night when they are waiting for enough wind to sail, which shocked his crew. When on duty, the captain discovers a naked body of a man clutching bottom ring of the side ladder of the ship. He helps the person onto the boat and hides him in his cabin without the knowledge of the rest of the crew. The mysterious swimmer tells the captain his story. His name is Leggatt, and he swam away from the " Sephora", a nearby ship to escape a trial. He has been accused of killing another crew member during a storm. The man further explained that he killed the man because the man refuses to carry out an order, which may endanger the ship and the lives of the people on the ship. Seeing so much of himself in the man, the captain keeps Leggatt hidden in his quarters and they become the sharers of the secret. In order to hide the fugitive, the captain has to deceive his crew and those from the " Sephora", even the old captain of the " Sephora" when he boards the ship to ask about the escaped man. Eventually they contrive a plan, allowing Leggatt to escape by bringing the ship perilously close to land so that Leggatt can slip out without being detected. They succeed.

The story was based on a true story about a murder on a ship in 1880. It was created in just two weeks, while Conrad was writing *Under Western Eyes*. He wrote " The Secret Sharer" as a break from his much larger novel that was emotionally difficult for him. The story originally appeared in *Harper's Magazine*, under the title " The Secret-Sharer", but Conrad revised the title to make it more ambiguous, making Leggatt secretly share with the captain, rather than merely sharing a secret. In this way, the writer employs mirror images to indicate a symbolic relationship between the captain and Leggatt. It is one of Conrad's best short stories, a psychological and autobiographical masterpiece of writing, including the elements of real events. Looking for identity and understanding, the nameless narrator can be viewed as a representation of the rite of initiation that every person is to experience in his or her life.

Selected Reading

The Secret Sharer

I

On my right hand there were lines of fishing stakes resembling a mysterious system of half-submerged bamboo fences, incomprehensible in its division of the domain of tropical fishes, and crazy of aspect as if abandoned forever by some nomad tribe of fishermen now gone to the other end of the ocean; for there was no sign of human habitation as far as the eye could reach. To the left a group of barren islets, suggesting ruins of stone walls, towers, and blockhouses, had its foundations set in a blue sea that itself looked solid, so still and stable did it lie below my feet; even the track of light from the westering sun shone smoothly, without that animated glitter which tells of an imperceptible① ripple. And when I turned my head to take

① imperceptible: unable to be noticed or felt because of being very slight a parting glance at the tug which had just left us anchored outside the bar, I saw the straight line of the flat shore joined to the stable sea, edge to edge, with a perfect and unmarked closeness, in one leveled floor half brown, half blue under the enormous dome of the sky. Corresponding in their insignificance to the islets① of the sea, two small clumps of trees, one on each side of the only fault in the impeccable joint, marked the mouth of the river Meinam we had just left on the first preparatory stage of our homeward journey; and, far back on the inland level, a larger and loftier mass, the grove surrounding the great Paknam pagoda, was the only thing on which the eye could rest from the vain task of exploring the monotonous sweep of the horizon. Here and there gleams as of a few scattered pieces of silver marked the windings of the great river; and on the nearest of them, just within the bar, the tug steaming right into the land became lost to my sight, hull and funnel and masts, as though the impassive earth had swallowed her up without an effort, without a tremor. My eye followed the light cloud of her smoke, now here, now there, above the plain, according to the devious curves of the stream, but always fainter and farther away, till I lost it at last behind the miter-shaped hill of the great pagoda. And then I was left alone with my ship, anchored at the head of the Gulf of Siam. She floated at the starting point of a long journey, very still in an immense stillness, the shadows of her spars flung far to the eastward by the setting sun. At that moment I was alone on her decks. There was not a sound in her — and around us nothing moved, nothing lived, not a canoe on the water, not a bird in the air, not a cloud in the sky. In this breathless pause at the threshold of a long passage we seemed to be measuring our fitness for a long and arduous enterprise, the appointed task of both our existences to be carried out, far from all human eyes, with only sky and sea for spectators and for judges.

There must have been some glare in the air to interfere with one's sight, because it was only just before the sun left us that my roaming eyes made out beyond the

① islet: small island

highest ridges of the principal islet of the group something which did away with the solemnity of perfect solitude. The tide of darkness flowed on swiftly; and with tropical suddenness a swarm of stars came out above the shadowy earth, while I lingered yet, my hand resting lightly on my ship's rail as if on the shoulder of a trusted friend. But, with all that multitude of celestial bodies staring down at one, the comfort of quiet communion with her was gone for good. And there were also disturbing sounds by this time — voices, footsteps forward; the steward flitted along the main-deck, a busily ministering spirit; a hand bell tinkled urgently under the poop deck....

I found my two officers waiting for me near the supper table, in the lighted cuddy. We sat down at once, and as I helped the chief mate, I said:

" Are you aware that there is a ship anchored inside the islands? I saw her mastheads above the ridge as the sun went down."

He raised sharply his simple face, overcharged by a terrible growth of whisker, and emitted his usual ejaculations: " Bless my soul, sir! You don't say so!"

My second mate was a round-cheeked, silent young man, grave beyond his years, I thought; but as our eyes happened to meet I detected a slight quiver on his lips. I looked down at once. It was not my part to encourage sneering on board my ship. It must be said, too, that I knew very little of my officers. In consequence of certain events of no particular significance, except to myself, I had been appointed to the command only a fortnight before. Neither did I know much of the hands forward. All these people had been together for eighteen months or so, and my position was that of the only stranger on board. I mention this because it has some bearing on what is to follow. But what I felt most was my being a stranger to the ship; and if all the truth must be told, I was somewhat of a stranger to myself. The youngest man on board (barring the second mate), and untried as yet by a position of the fullest responsibility, I was willing to take the adequacy of the others for granted. They had simply to be equal to their tasks; but I wondered how far I should turn out faithful to that ideal conception of one's own personality every man sets up for himself secretly.

Meantime the chief mate, with an almost visible effect of collaboration on the part of his round eyes and frightful whiskers, was trying to evolve a theory of the anchored ship. His dominant trait was to take all things into earnest consideration. He was of a painstaking turn of mind. As he used to say, he " liked to account to himself" for practically everything that came in his way, down to a miserable scorpion he had found in his cabin a week before. The why and the wherefore of that scorpion — how it got on board and came to select his room rather than the pantry (which was a dark place and more what a scorpion would be partial to), and how on earth it managed to drown itself in the inkwell of his writing desk — had exercised him infinitely. The ship within the islands was much more easily accounted for; and just as we were about to rise from table he made his pronouncement. She was, he doubted not, a ship from home lately arrived. Probably she drew too much water to cross the bar except at the top of spring tides. Therefore she went into that natural harbor to wait for a few days in preference to remaining in an open roadstead.

" That's so," confirmed the second mate, suddenly, in his slightly hoarse voice. " She draws over twenty feet. She's the Liverpool ship Sephora with a cargo of coal. Hundred and twenty-three days from Cardiff."

We looked at him in surprise.

" The tugboat skipper told me when he came on board for your letters, sir," explained the young man. " He expects to take her up the river the day after tomorrow."

After thus overwhelming us with the extent of his information he slipped out of the cabin. The mate observed regretfully that he " could not account for that young fellow's whims." What prevented him telling us all about it at once, he wanted to know.

I detained him as he was making a move. For the last two days the crew had had plenty of hard work, and the night before they had very little sleep. I felt painfully that I — a stranger — was doing something unusual when I directed him to let all hands turn in without setting an anchor watch. I proposed to keep on deck myself till one o'clock or thereabouts. I would get the second mate to relieve me at that hour.

" He will turn out the cook and the steward at four," I concluded, " and then give you a call. Of course at the slightest sign of any sort of wind we'll have the hands up and make a start at once."

He concealed his astonishment. " Very well, sir." Outside the cuddy he put his head in the second mate's door to inform him of my unheard-of caprice to take a five hours' anchor watch on myself. I heard the other raise his voice incredulously — " What? The Captain himself ?" Then a few more murmurs, a door closed, then another. A few moments later I went on deck.

My strangeness, which had made me sleepless, had prompted that unconventional arrangement, as if I had expected in those solitary hours of the night to get on terms with the ship of which I knew nothing, manned by men of whom I knew very little more. Fast alongside a wharf, littered like any ship in port with a tangle of unrelated things, invaded by unrelated shore people, I had hardly seen her yet properly. Now, as she lay cleared for sea, the stretch of her main-deck seemed to me very find under the stars. Very fine, very roomy for her size, and very inviting. I descended the poop and paced the waist, my mind picturing to myself the coming passage through the Malay Archipelago, down the Indian Ocean, and up the Atlantic. All its phases were familiar enough to me, every characteristic, all the alternatives which were likely to face me on the high seas — everything!... except the novel responsibility of command. But I took heart from the reasonable thought that the ship was like other ships, the men like other men, and that the sea was not likely to keep any special surprises expressly for my discomfiture.

Arrived at that comforting conclusion, I bethought myself of a cigar and went below to get it. All was still down there. Everybody at the after end of the ship was sleeping profoundly. I came out again on the quarter-deck, agreeably at ease in my sleeping suit on that warm breathless night, barefooted, a glowing cigar in my teeth, and, going forward, I was met by the profound silence of the fore end of the ship. Only as I passed the door of the forecastle, I heard a deep, quiet, trustful sigh of some sleeper inside. And suddenly I rejoiced in the great security of the sea as compared with the unrest of the land, in my choice of that untempted life presenting no disquieting problems, invested with an elementary moral beauty by the absolute straightforwardness of its appeal and by the singleness of its purpose.

The riding light in the forerigging burned with a clear, untroubled, as if symbolic, flame, confident and bright in the mysterious shades of the night. Passing on my way aft along the other side of the ship, I observed that the rope side ladder, put over, no doubt, for the master of the tug when he came to fetch away our letters, had not been hauled in as it should have been. I became annoyed at this, for exactitude in some small matters is the very soul of discipline. Then I reflected that I had myself peremptorily① dismissed my officers from duty, and by my own act had prevented the anchor watch being formally set and things properly attended to. I asked myself whether it was wise ever to interfere with the established routine of duties even from the kindest of motives. My action might have made me appear eccentric. Goodness only knew how that absurdly whiskered mate would " account" for my conduct, and what the whole ship thought of that informality of their new captain. I was vexed with myself.

Not from compunction certainly, but, as it were mechanically, I proceeded to get the ladder in myself. Now a side ladder of that sort is a light affair and comes in easily, yet my vigorous tug, which should have brought it flying on board, merely recoiled upon my body in a totally unexpected jerk. What the devil!... I was so astounded by the immovableness of that ladder that I remained stockstill, trying to account for it to myself like that imbecile mate of mine. In the end, of course, I put

---

① peremptory: expecting to be obeyed immediately and without asking questions my head over the rail.

The side of the ship made an opaque belt of shadow on the darkling glassy shimmer of the sea. But I saw at once something elongated and pale floating very close to the ladder. Before I could form a guess a faint flash of phosphorescent[①] light, which seemed to issue suddenly from the naked body of a man, flickered in the sleeping water with the elusive, silent play of summer lightning in a night sky. With a gasp I saw revealed to my stare a pair of feet, the long legs, a broad livid back immersed right up to the neck in a greenish cadaverous glow. One hand, awash, clutched the bottom rung of the ladder. He was complete but for the head. A headless corpse! The cigar dropped out of my gaping mouth with a tiny plop and a short hiss quite audible in the absolute stillness of all things under heaven. At that I suppose he raised up his face, a dimly pale oval in the shadow of the ship's side. But even then I could only barely make out down there the shape of his black-haired head. However, it was enough for the horrid, frost-bound sensation which had gripped me about the chest to pass off. The moment of vain exclamations was past, too. I only climbed on the spare spar and leaned over the rail as far as I could, to bring my eyes nearer to that mystery floating alongside.

As he hung by the ladder, like a resting swimmer, the sea lightning played about his limbs at every stir; and he appeared in it ghastly, silvery, fishlike. He remained as mute as a fish, too. He made no motion to get out of the water, either. It was inconceivable that he should not attempt to come on board, and strangely troubling to suspect that perhaps he did not want to. And my first words were prompted by just that troubled incertitude.

"What's the matter?" I asked in my ordinary tone, speaking down to the face upturned exactly under mine.

"Cramp," it answered, no louder. Then slightly anxious, "I say, no need to call

---

① phosphorescent: giving off light after radiation has hit

anyone."

" I was not going to," I said.

" Are you alone on deck?"

" Yes."

I had somehow the impression that he was on the point of letting go the ladder to swim away beyond my ken — mysterious as he came. But, for the moment, this being appearing as if he had risen from the bottom of the sea (it was certainly the nearest land to the ship) wanted only to know the time. I told him. And he, down there, tentatively:

" I suppose your captain's turned in?"

" I am sure he isn't," I said.

He seemed to struggle with himself, for I heard something like the low, bitter murmur of doubt. " What's the good?" His next words came out with a hesitating effort.

" Look here, my man. Could you call him out quietly?"

I thought the time Had come to declare myself.

" I am the captain."

I heard a " By Jove!" whispered at the level of the water. The phosphorescence flashed in the swirl of the water all about his limbs, his other hand seized the ladder.

" My name's Leggatt."

The voice was calm and resolute. A good voice. The self-possession of that man had somehow induced a corresponding state in myself. It was very quietly that I remarked:

" You must be a good swimmer."

" Yes. I've been in the water practically since nine o'clock. The question for me now is whether I am to let go this ladder and go on swimming till I sink from exhaustion, or — to come on board here."

I felt this was no mere formula of desperate speech, but a real alternative in the view of a strong soul. I should have gathered from this that he was young; indeed, it is only the young who are ever confronted by such clear issues. But at the time it was pure intuition on my part. A mysterious communication was established already between us two — in the face of that silent, darkened tropical sea. I was young, too; young enough to make no comment. The man in the water began suddenly to climb up the ladder, and I hastened away from the rail to fetch some clothes.

Before entering the cabin I stood still, listening in the lobby at the foot of the stairs. A faint snore came through the closed door of the chief mate's room. The second mate's door was on the hook, but the darkness in there was absolutely soundless. He, too, was young and could sleep like a stone. Remained the steward, but he was not likely to wake up before he was called. I got a sleeping suit out of my room and, coming back on deck, saw the naked man from the sea sitting on the main hatch, glimmering white in the darkness, his elbows on his knees and his head in his hands. In a moment he had concealed his damp body in a sleeping suit of the same gray-stripe pattern as the one I was wearing and followed me like my double on the poop. Together we moved right aft, barefooted, silent.

" What is it?" I asked in a deadened voice, taking the lighted lamp out of the binnacle, and raising it to his face.

" An ugly business."

He had rather regular features; a good mouth; light eyes under somewhat heavy, dark eyebrows; a smooth, square forehead; no growth on his cheeks; a small, brown mustache, and a well-shaped, round chin. His expression was concentrated, meditative, under the inspecting light of the lamp I held up to his face; such as a man thinking hard in solitude might wear. My sleeping suit was just right for his size. A well-knit young fellow of twenty-five at most. He caught his lower lip with the edge of white, even teeth.

" Yes," I said, replacing the lamp in the binnacle. The warm, heavy tropical night closed upon his head again.

" There's a ship over there," he murmured.

" Yes, I know. The Sephora. Did you know of us?"

" Hadn't the slightest idea. I am the mate of her — ". He paused and corrected himself. " I should say I was."

" Aha! Something wrong?"

" Yes. Very wrong indeed. I've killed a man."

" What do you mean? Just now?"

" No, on the passage. Weeks ago. Thirty-nine south. When I say a man — "

" Fit of temper," I suggested, confidently.

The shadowy, dark head, like mine, seemed to nod imperceptibly above the ghostly gray of my sleeping suit. It was, in the night, as though I had been faced by my own reflection in the depths of a somber and immense mirror.

" A pretty thing to have to own up to for a Conway boy," murmured my double, distinctly.

" You're a Conway boy?"

" I am," he said, as if startled. Then, slowly... " Perhaps you too — "

It was so; but being a couple of years older I had left before he joined. After a quick interchange of dates a silence fell; and I thought suddenly of my absurd mate with his terrific whiskers and the " Bless my soul — you don't say so" type of intellect. My double gave me an inkling of his thoughts by saying: " My father's a parson in Norfolk. Do you see me before a judge and jury on that charge? For myself I can't see the necessity. There are fellows that an angel from heaven — And I am not that. He was one of those creatures that are just simmering all the time with a silly sort of wickedness. Miserable devils that have no business to live at all. He wouldn't do his duty and wouldn't let anybody else do theirs. But what's the good of talking! You know well enough the sort of ill-conditioned snarling cur — "

He appealed to me as if our experiences had been as identical as our clothes. And I knew well enough the pestiferous danger of such a character where there are no means of legal repression. And I knew well enough also that my double there was no homicidal ruffian[1]. I did not think of asking him for details, and he told me the story roughly in brusque, disconnected sentences. I needed no more. I saw it all going on as though I were myself inside that other sleeping suit.

" It happened while we were setting a reefed foresail, at dusk. Reefed foresail! You understand the sort of weather. The only sail we had left to keep the ship running; so you may guess what it had been like for days. Anxious sort of job, that. He gave me some of his cursed insolence at the sheet. I tell you I was overdone with this terrific weather that seemed to have no end to it. Terrific, I tell you — and a deep ship. I believe the fellow himself was half crazed with funk. It was no time for gentlemanly reproof, so I turned round and felled him like an ox. He up and at me. We closed just as an awful sea made for the ship. All hands saw it coming and took to the rigging, but I had him by the throat, and went on shaking him like a rat, the men above us yelling, 'Look out! look out!' Then a crash as if the sky had fallen on my head. They say that for over ten minutes hardly anything was to be seen of the ship — just the three masts and a bit of the forecastle head and of the poop all awash driving along in a smother of foam. It was a miracle that they found us, jammed together behind the forebitts. It's clear that I meant business, because I was holding him by the throat still when they picked us up. He was black in the face. It was too much for them. It seems they rushed us aft together, gripped as we were, screaming 'Murder!' like a lot of lunatics, and broke into the cuddy. And the ship running for her life, touch and go all the time, any minute her last in a sea fit to turn your hair gray only a-looking at it. I understand that the skipper, too, started raving like the rest of them. The man had been deprived of sleep for more than a week, and to have this sprung on him at the height of a furious gale nearly drove him out of his mind. I wonder they didn't fling me overboard after getting the carcass of their precious

① ruffian: a violent, wild, and unpleasant person, usually a man shipmate out of my fingers. They had rather a job to separate us, I've been told. A sufficiently fierce story to make an old judge and a respectable jury sit up a bit. The first thing I heard when I came to myself was the maddening howling of that endless gale, and on that the voice of the old man. He was hanging on to my bunk, staring into my face out of his sou'wester.

" 'Mr. Leggatt, you have killed a man. You can act no longer as chief mate of this ship.' "

His care to subdue his voice made it sound monotonous. He rested a hand on the end of the skylight to steady himself with, and all that time did not stir a limb, so far as I could see. " Nice little tale for a quiet tea party," he concluded in the same tone.

One of my hands, too, rested on the end of the skylight; neither did I stir a limb, so far as I knew. We stood less than a foot from each other. It occurred to me that if old " Bless my soul — you don't say so" were to put his head up the companion and catch sight of us, he would think he was seeing double, or imagine himself come upon a scene of weird witchcraft; the strange captain having a quiet confabulation by the wheel with his own gray ghost. I became very much concerned to prevent anything of the sort. I heard the other's soothing undertone.

" My father's a parson in Norfolk," it said. Evidently he had forgotten he had told me this important fact before. Truly a nice little tale.

" You had better slip down into my stateroom now," I said, moving off stealthily① . My double followed my movements; our bare feet made no sound; I let him in, closed the door with care, and, after giving a call to the second mate, returned on deck for my relief.

" Not much sign of any wind yet," I remarked when he approached.

" No, sir. Not much," he assented, sleepily, in his hoarse voice, with just enough deference, no more, and barely suppressing a yawn.

---

① stealthily: moving to avoid being seen

" Well, that's all you have to look out for. You have got your orders."

" Yes, sir."

I paced a turn or two on the poop and saw him take up his position face forward with his elbow in the ratlines of the mizzen rigging before I went below. The mate's faint snoring was still going on peacefully. The cuddy lamp was burning over the table on which stood a vase with flowers, a polite attention from the ship's provision merchant — the last flowers we should see for the next three months at the very least. Two bunches of bananas hung from the beam symmetrically, one on each side of the rudder casing. Everything was as before in the ship — except that two of her captain's sleeping suits were simultaneously in use, one motionless in the cuddy, the other keeping very still in the captain's stateroom.

It must be explained here that my cabin had the form of the capital letter L, the door being within the angle and opening into the short part of the letter. A couch was to the left, the bed place to the right; my writing desk and the chronometers' table faced the door. But anyone opening it, unless he stepped right inside, had no view of what I call the long (or vertical) part of the letter. It contained some lockers surmounted by a bookcase; and a few clothes, a thick jacket or two, caps, oilskin coat, and such like, hung on hooks. There was at the bottom of that part a door opening into my bathroom, which could be entered also directly from the saloon. But that way was never used.

The mysterious arrival had discovered the advantage of this particular shape. Entering my room, lighted strongly by a big bulkhead lamp swung on gimbals above my writing desk, I did not see him anywhere till he stepped out quietly from behind the coats hung in the recessed part.

" I heard somebody moving about, and went in there at once," he whispered.

I, too, spoke under my breath.

" Nobody is likely to come in here without knocking and getting permission."

He nodded. His face was thin and the sunburn faded, as though he had been ill.

And no wonder. He had been, I heard presently, kept under arrest in his cabin for nearly seven weeks. But there was nothing sickly in his eyes or in his expression. He was not a bit like me, really; yet, as we stood leaning over my bed place, whispering side by side, with our dark heads together and our backs to the door, anybody bold enough to open it stealthily would have been treated to the uncanny sight of a double captain busy talking in whispers with his other self.

"But all this doesn't tell me how you came to hang on to our side ladder," I inquired, in the hardly audible murmurs we used, after he had told me something more of the proceedings on board the Sephora once the bad weather was over.

"When we sighted Java Head I had had time to think all those matters out several times over. I had six weeks of doing nothing else, and with only an hour or so every evening for a tramp on the quarter-deck."

He whispered, his arms folded on the side of my bed place, staring through the open port. And I could imagine perfectly the manner of this thinking out — a stubborn if not a steadfast operation; something of which I should have been perfectly incapable.

"I reckoned it would be dark before we closed with the land," he continued, so low that I had to strain my hearing near as we were to each other, shoulder touching shoulder almost. "So I asked to speak to the old man. He always seemed very sick when he came to see me — as if he could not look me in the face. You know, that foresail saved the ship. She was too deep to have run long under bare poles. And it was I that managed to set it for him. Anyway, he came. When I had him in my cabin — he stood by the door looking at me as if I had the halter① round my neck already — I asked him right away to leave my cabin door unlocked at night while the ship was going through Sunda Straits. There would be the Java coast within two or three miles, off Angier Point. I wanted nothing more. I've had a prize for swimming

① halter: piece of rope or a leather strap that is tied around an animal's head so that it can be led by someone or tied to something my second year in the Conway."

" I can believe it," I breathed out.

" God only knows why they locked me in every night. To see some of their faces you'd have thought they were afraid I'd go about at night strangling people. Am I a murdering brute? Do I look it? By Jove! If I had been he wouldn't have trusted himself like that into my room. You'll say I might have chucked him aside and bolted out, there and then — it was dark already. Well, no. And for the same reason I wouldn't think of trying to smash the door. There would have been a rush to stop me at the noise, and I did not mean to get into a confounded scrimmage. Somebody else might have got killed — for I would not have broken out only to get chucked back, and I did not want any more of that work. He refused, looking more sick than ever. He was afraid of the men, and also of that old second mate of his who had been sailing with him for years — a gray-headed old humbug; and his steward, too, had been with him devil knows how long — seventeen years or more — a dogmatic sort of loafer who hated me like poison, just because I was the chief mate. No chief mate ever made more than one voyage in the Sephora, you know. Those two old chaps ran the ship. Devil only knows what the skipper wasn't afraid of (all his nerve went to pieces altogether in that hellish spell of bad weather we had) — of what the law would do to him — of his wife, perhaps. Oh, yes! she's on board. Though I don't think she would have meddled. She would have been only too glad to have me out of the ship in any way. The 'brand of Cain' business, don't you see. That's all right. I was ready enough to go off wandering on the face of the earth — and that was price enough to pay for an Abel of that sort. Anyhow, he wouldn't listen to me. 'This thing must take its course. I represent the law here.' He was shaking like a leaf. 'So you won't?' 'No!' 'Then I hope you will be able to sleep on that,' I said, and turned my back on him. 'I wonder that you can,' cries he, and locks the door.

" Well after that, I couldn't. Not very well. That was three weeks ago. We have had a slow passage through the Java Sea; drifted about Carimata for ten days. When we anchored here they thought, I suppose, it was all right. The nearest land (and that's five miles) is the ship's destination; the consul would soon set about catching me; and there would have been no object in bolding to these islets there. I don't suppose there's a drop of water on them. I don't know how it was, but tonight that steward, after bringing me my supper, went out to let me eat it, and left the door unlocked. And I ate it — all there was, too. After I had finished I strolled out on the quarter-deck. I don't know that I meant to do anything. A breath of fresh air was all I wanted, I believe. Then a sudden temptation came over me. I kicked off my slippers and was in the water before I had made up my mind fairly. Somebody heard the splash and they raised an awful hullabaloo① . 'He's gone! Lower the boats! He's committed suicide! No, he's swimming.' Certainly I was swimming. It's not so easy for a swimmer like me to commit suicide by drowning. I landed on the nearest islet before the boat left the ship's side. I heard them pulling about in the dark, hailing, and so on, but after a bit they gave up. Everything quieted down and the anchorage became still as death. I sat down on a stone and began to think. I felt certain they would start searching for me at daylight. There was no place to hide on those stony things — and if there had been, what would have been the good? But now I was clear of that ship, I was not going back. So after a while I took off all my clothes, tied them up in a bundle with a stone inside, and dropped them in the deep water on the outer side of that islet. That was suicide enough for me. Let them think what they liked, but I didn't mean to drown myself. I meant to swim till I sank — but that's not the same thing. I struck out for another of these little islands, and it was from that one that I first saw your riding light. Something to swim for. I went on easily, and on the way I came upon a flat rock a foot or two above water. In the daytime, I dare say, you might make it out with a glass from your poop. I scrambled up on it and rested myself for a bit. Then I made another start. That last spell must have been over a mile."

---

① hullabaloo: a loud noise made by people, often because they are angry, or a situation in which many people are angry or upset

His whisper was getting fainter and fainter, and all the time he stared straight out through the porthole, in which there was not even a star to be seen. I had not interrupted him. There was something that made comment impossible in his narrative, or perhaps in himself; a sort of feeling, a quality, which I can't find a name for. And when he ceased, all I found was a futile whisper: " So you swam for our light?"

" Yes — straight for it. It was something to swim for. I couldn't see any stars low down because the coast was in the way, and I couldn't see the land, either. The water was like glass. One might have been swimming in a confounded thousand-feet deep cistern① with no place for scrambling out anywhere; but what I didn't like was the notion of swimming round and round like a crazed bullock before I gave out; and as I didn't mean to go back...No. Do you see me being hauled back, stark naked, off one of these little islands by the scruff of the neck and fighting like a wild beast? Somebody would have got killed for certain, and I did not want any of that. So I went on. Then your ladder — ."

" Why didn't you hail the ship?" I asked, a little louder.

He touched my shoulder lightly. Lazy footsteps came right over our heads and stopped. The second mate had crossed from the other side of the poop and might have been hanging over the rail for all we knew.

" He couldn't hear us talking — could he?" My double breathed into my very ear, anxiously.

His anxiety was in answer, a sufficient answer, to the question I had put to him. An answer containing all the difficulty of that situation. I closed the porthole quietly, to make sure. A louder word might have been overheard.

" Who's that?" he whispered then.

" My second mate. But I don't know much more of the fellow than you do."

And I told him a little about myself. I had been appointed to take charge while I

---

① cistern: a container in which water is stored, especially one connected to a toilet or in the roof of a house least expected anything of the sort, not quite a fortnight ago. I didn't know either the ship or the people. Hadn't had the time in port to look about me or size anybody up. And as to the crew, all they knew was that I was appointed to take the ship home. For the rest, I was almost as much of a stranger on board as himself, I said. And at the moment I felt it most acutely. I felt that it would take very little to make me a suspect person in the eyes of the ship's company.

He had turned about meantime; and we, the two strangers in the ship, faced each other in identical attitudes.

" Your ladder — ", he murmured, after a silence. " Who'd have thought of finding a ladder hanging over at night in a ship anchored out here! I felt just then a very unpleasant faintness. After the life I've been leading for nine weeks, anybody would have got out of condition. I wasn't capable of swimming round as far as your rudder chains. And, lo and behold① ! there was a ladder to get hold of. After I gripped it I said to myself, 'What's the good?' When I saw a man's head looking over I thought I would swim away presently and leave him shouting — in whatever language it was. I didn't mind being looked at. I — I liked it. And then you speaking to me so quietly — as if you had expected me — made me hold on a little longer. It had been a confounded lonely time — I don't mean while swimming. I was glad to talk a little to somebody that didn't belong to the Sephora. As to asking for the captain, that was a mere impulse. It could have been no use, with all the ship knowing about me and the other people pretty certain to be round here in the morning. I don't know — I wanted to be seen, to talk with somebody, before I went on. I don't know what I would have said.... 'Fine night, isn't it?' or something of the sort."

" Do you think they will be round here presently?" I asked with some incredulity.

" Quite likely," he said, faintly.

" He looked extremely haggard all of a sudden. His head rolled on his shoulders.

① lo and behold: something that you say when you tell someone about something surprising that happened

" H'm. We shall see then. Meantime get into that bed," I whispered. " Want help? There."

It was a rather high bed place with a set of drawers underneath. This amazing swimmer really needed the lift I gave him by seizing his leg. He tumbled in, rolled over on his back, and flung one arm across his eyes. And then, with his face nearly hidden, he must have looked exactly as I used to look in that bed. I gazed upon my other self for a while before drawing across carefully the two green serge curtains which ran on a brass rod. I thought for a moment of pinning them together for greater safety, but I sat down on the couch, and once there I felt unwilling to rise and hunt for a pin. I would do it in a moment. I was extremely tired, in a peculiarly intimate way, by the strain of stealthiness, by the effort of whispering and the general secrecy of this excitement. It was three o'clock by now and I had been on my feet since nine, but I was not sleepy; I could not have gone to sleep. I sat there, fagged out, looking at the curtains, trying to clear my mind of the confused sensation of being in two places at once, and greatly bothered by an exasperating knocking in my head. It was a relief to discover suddenly that it was not in my head at all, but on the outside of the door. Before I could collect myself the words " Come in" were out of my mouth, and the steward entered with a tray, bringing in my morning coffee. I had slept, after all, and I was so frightened that I shouted, " This way! I am here, steward," as though he had been miles away. He put down the tray on the table next the couch and only then said, very quietly, " I can see you are here, sir." I felt him give me a keen look, but I dared not meet his eyes just then. He must have wondered why I had drawn the curtains of my bed before going to sleep on the couch. He went out, hooking the door open as usual.

I heard the crew washing decks above me. I knew I would have been told at once if there had been any wind. Calm, I thought, and I was doubly vexed① . Indeed,

① vexed: troubling and difficult

I felt dual more than ever. The steward reappeared suddenly in the doorway. I jumped up from the couch so quickly that he gave a start.

" What do you want here?"

" Close your port, sir — they are washing decks."

" It is closed," I said, reddening.

" Very well, sir." But he did not move from the doorway and returned my stare in an extraordinary, equivocal manner for a time. Then his eyes wavered, all his expression changed, and in a voice unusually gentle, almost coaxingly:

" May I come in to take the empty cup away, sir?"

" Of course!" I turned my back on him while he popped in and out. Then I unhooked and closed the door and even pushed the bolt. This sort of thing could not go on very long. The cabin was as hot as an oven, too. I took a peep at my double, and discovered that he had not moved, his arm was still over his eyes; but his chest heaved; his hair was wet; his chin glistened with perspiration. I reached over him and opened the port.

" I must show myself on deck," I reflected.

Of course, theoretically, I could do what I liked, with no one to say nay to me within the whole circle of the horizon; but to lock my cabin door and take the key away I did not dare. Directly I put my head out of the companion I saw the group of my two officers, the second mate barefooted, the chief mate in long India-rubber boots, near the break of the poop, and the steward halfway down the poop ladder talking to them eagerly. He happened to catch sight of me and dived, the second ran down on the main-deck shouting some order or other, and the chief mate came to meet me, touching his cap.

There was a sort of curiosity in his eye that I did not like. I don't know whether the steward had told them that I was " queer" only, or downright drunk, but I know the man meant to have a good look at me. I watched him coming with a smile which, as he got into point-blank range, took effect and froze his very whiskers. I did not give him time to open his lips.

" Square the yards by lifts and braces before the hands go to breakfast."

It was the first particular order I had given on board that ship; and I stayed on deck to see it executed, too. I had felt the need of asserting myself without loss of time. That sneering young cub got taken down a peg or two on that occasion, and I also seized the opportunity of having a good look at the face of every foremast man as they filed past me to go to the after braces. At breakfast time, eating nothing myself, I presided with such frigid dignity that the two mates were only too glad to escape from the cabin as soon as decency permitted; and all the time the dual working of my mind distracted me almost to the point of insanity. I was constantly watching myself, my secret self, as dependent on my actions as my own personality, sleeping in that bed, behind that door which faced me as I sat at the head of the table. It was very much like being mad, only it was worse because one was aware of it.

I had to shake him for a solid minute, but when at last he opened his eyes it was in the full possession of his senses, with an inquiring look.

" All's well so far," I whispered. " Now you must vanish into the bathroom."

He did so, as noiseless as a ghost, and then I rang for the steward, and facing him boldly, directed him to tidy up my stateroom while I was having my bath — " and be quick about it." As my tone admitted of no excuses, he said, " Yes, sir," and ran off to fetch his dustpan① and brushes. I took a bath and did most of my dressing, splashing, and whistling softly for the steward's edification②, while the secret sharer of my life stood drawn up bolt upright in that little space, his face looking very sunken in daylight, his eyelids lowered under the stern, dark line of his eyebrows drawn together by a slight frown.

When I left him there to go back to my room the steward was finishing dusting. I sent for the mate and engaged him in some insignificant conversation. It was, as it

① dustpan: a flat container with a handle into which you brush dust and dirt

② edification: the improvement of the mind and understanding, especially by learning were, trifling with the terrific character of his whiskers; but my object was to give him an opportunity for a good look at my cabin. And then I could at last shut, with a clear conscience, the door of my stateroom and get my double back into the recessed part. There was nothing else for it. He had to sit still on a small folding stool, half smothered by the heavy coats hanging there. We listened to the steward going into the bathroom out of the saloon, filling the water bottles there, scrubbing the bath, setting things to rights, whisk, bang, clatter — out again into the saloon — turn the key — click. Such was my scheme for keeping my second self invisible. Nothing better could be contrived under the circumstances. And there we sat; I at my writing desk ready to appear busy with some papers, he behind me out of sight of the door. It would not have been prudent to talk in daytime; and I could not have stood the excitement of that queer sense of whispering to myself. Now and then, glancing over my shoulder, I saw him far back there, sitting rigidly on the low stool, his bare feet close together, his arms folded, his head hanging on his breast — and perfectly still. Anybody would have taken him for me.

I was fascinated by it myself. Every moment I had to glance over my shoulder. I was looking at him when a voice outside the door said:

" Beg pardon, sir."

" Well!... I kept my eyes on him, and so when the voice outside the door announced, " There's a ship's boat coming our way, sir," I saw him give a start — the first movement he had made for hours. But he did not raise his bowed head.

" All right. Get the ladder over."

I hesitated. Should I whisper something to him? But what? His immobility seemed to have been never disturbed. What could I tell him he did not know already?... Finally I went on deck.

II

The skipper of the Sephora had a thin red whisker all round his face, and the sort of complexion that goes with hair of that color; also the particular, rather smeary shade of blue in the eyes. He was not exactly a showy figure; his shoulders were high, his stature but middling — one leg slightly more bandy than the other. He shook hands, looking vaguely around. A spiritless tenacity was his main characteristic, I judged. I behaved with a politeness which seemed to disconcert him. Perhaps he was shy. He mumbled to me as if he were ashamed of what he was saying; gave his name (it was something like Archbold — but at this distance of years I hardly am sure), his ship's name, and a few other particulars of that sort, in the manner of a criminal making a reluctant and doleful confession. He had had terrible weather on the passage out — terrible — terrible — wife aboard, too.

By this time we were seated in the cabin and the steward brought in a tray with a bottle and glasses. " Thanks! No." Never took liquor. Would have some water, though. He drank two tumblerfuls. Terrible thirsty work. Ever since daylight had been exploring the islands round his ship.

" What was that for — fun?" I asked, with an appearance of polite interest.

" No!" He sighed. " Painful duty."

As he persisted in his mumbling and I wanted my double to hear every word, I hit upon the notion of informing him that I regretted to say I was hard of hearing.

" Such a young man, too!" he nodded, keeping his smeary blue, unintelligent eyes fastened upon me. " What was the cause of it — some disease? " he inquired, without the least sympathy and as if he thought that, if so, I'd got no more than I deserved.

" Yes; disease," I admitted in a cheerful tone which seemed to shock him. But my point was gained, because he had to raise his voice to give me his tale. It is not worth while to record his version. It was just over two months since all this had happened, and he had thought so much about it that he seemed completely muddled as to its bearings, but still immensely impressed.

" What would you think of such a thing happening on board your own ship? I've had the Sephora for these fifteen years. I am a well-known shipmaster."

He was densely distressed — and perhaps I should have sympathized with him if I had been able to detach my mental vision from the unsuspected sharer of my cabin as though he were my second self. There he was on the other side of the bulkhead, four or five feet from us, no more, as we sat in the saloon. I looked politely at Captain Archbold (if that was his name), but it was the other I saw, in a gray sleeping suit, seated on a low stool, his bare feet close together, his arms folded, and every word said between us falling into the ears of his dark head bowed on his chest.

" I have been at sea now, man and boy, for seven-and-thirty years, and I've never heard of such a thing happening in an English ship. And that it should be my ship. Wife on board, too."

I was hardly listening to him.

" Don't you think," I said, " that the heavy sea which, you told me, came aboard just then might have killed the man? I have seen the sheer weight of a sea kill a man very neatly, by simply breaking his neck."

" Good God!" he uttered, impressively, fixing his smeary blue eyes on me. " The sea! No man killed by the sea ever looked like that." He seemed positively scandalized at my suggestion. And as I gazed at him certainly not prepared for anything original on his part, he advanced his head close to mine and thrust his tongue out at me so suddenly that I couldn't help starting back.

After scoring over my calmness in this graphic way he nodded wisely. If I had seen the sight, he assured me, I would never forget it as long as I lived. The weather was too bad to give the corpse a proper sea burial. So next day at dawn they took it up on the poop, covering its face with a bit of bunting; he read a short prayer, and then, just as it was, in its oilskins and long boots, they launched it amongst those mountainous seas that seemed ready every moment to swallow up the ship herself and the terrified lives on board of her.

" That reefed foresail saved you," I threw in.

" Under God — it did," he exclaimed fervently. " It was by a special mercy, I firmly believe, that it stood some of those hurricane squalls."

" It was the setting of that sail which — ," I began.

" God's own hand in it," he interrupted me. " Nothing less could have done it. I don't mind telling you that I hardly dared give the order. It seemed impossible that we could touch anything without losing it, and then our last hope would have been gone."

The terror of that gale was on him yet. I let him go on for a bit, then said, casually — as if returning to a minor subject:

" You were very anxious to give up your mate to the shore people, I believe?"

He was. To the law. His obscure tenacity on that point had in it something incomprehensible and a little awful; something, as it were, mystical, quite apart from his anxiety that he should not be suspected of " countenancing any doings of that sort." Seven-and-thirty virtuous years at sea, of which over twenty of immaculate command, and the last fifteen in the Sephora, seemed to have laid him under some pitiless obligation.

" And you know," he went on, groping shame-facedly amongst his feelings, " I did not engage that young fellow. His people had some interest with my owners. I was in a way forced to take him on. He looked very smart, very gentlemanly, and all that. But do you know — I never liked him, somehow. I am a plain man. You see, he wasn't exactly the sort for the chief mate of a ship like the Sephora."

I had become so connected in thoughts and impressions with the secret sharer of my cabin that I felt as if I, personally, were being given to understand that I, too, was not the sort that would have done for the chief mate of a ship like the Sephora. I had no doubt of it in my mind.

" Not at all the style of man. You understand," he insisted, superfluously, looking hard at me.

I smiled urbanely[①]. He seemed at a loss for a while.

" I suppose I must report a suicide."

" Beg pardon?"

" Suicide! That's what I'll have to write to my owners directly I get in."

" Unless you manage to recover him before tomorrow," I assented, dispassionately... " I mean, alive."

He mumbled something which I really did not catch, and I turned my ear to him in a puzzled manner. He fairly bawled:

" The land — I say, the mainland is at least seven miles off my anchorage."

" About that."

My lack of excitement, of curiosity, of surprise, of any sort of pronounced interest, began to arouse his distrust. But except for the felicitous[②] pretense of deafness I had not tried to pretend anything. I had felt utterly incapable of playing the part of ignorance properly, and therefore was afraid to try. It is also certain that he had brought some ready-made suspicions with him, and that he viewed my politeness as a strange and unnatural phenomenon. And yet how else could I have received him? Not heartily! That was impossible for psychological reasons, which I need not state here. My only object was to keep off his inquiries. Surlily[③]? Yes, but surliness might have provoked a point — blank question. From its novelty to him and from its nature, punctilious courtesy was the manner best calculated to restrain the man. But there was the danger of his breaking through my defense bluntly. I could not, I think, have met him by a direct lie, also for psychological (not moral) reasons. If he had only known how afraid I was of his putting my feeling of identity with the other to the test! But, strangely enough — (I thought of it only afterwards) — I believe that he

---

① urbanely: (especially of a man) confident, comfortable, and polite in social situations: Herschel was an urbane, kindly, and generous man

② felicitous: suitable or right and expressing well the intended thought or feeling

③ surlily: often in a bad mood, unfriendly, and not polite

was not a little disconcerted by the reverse side of that weird situation, by something in me that reminded him of the man he was seeking — suggested a mysterious similitude to the young fellow he had distrusted and disliked from the first.

However that might have been, the silence was not very prolonged. He took another oblique step.

" I reckon I had no more than a two-mile pull to your ship. Not a bit more."

" And quite enough, too, in this awful heat," I said.

Another pause full of mistrust followed. Necessity, they say, is mother of invention, but fear, too, is not barren of ingenious suggestions. And I was afraid he would ask me point-blank for news of my other self.

" Nice little saloon, isn't it?" I remarked, as if noticing for the first time the way his eyes roamed from one closed door to the other. " And very well fitted out, too. Here, for instance," I continued, reaching over the back of my seat negligently and flinging the door open, " is my bathroom."

He made an eager movement, but hardly gave it a glance. I got up, shut the door of the bathroom, and invited him to have a look round, as if I were very proud of my accommodation. He had to rise and be shown round, but he went through the business without any raptures whatever.

" And now we'll have a look at my stateroom," I declared, in a voice as loud as I dared to make it, crossing the cabin to the starboard side with purposely heavy steps.

He followed me in and gazed around. My intelligent double had vanished. I played my part.

" Very convenient — isn't it?"

" Very nice. Very comf..." He didn't finish and went out brusquely as if to escape from some unrighteous wiles of mine. But it was not to be. I had been too frightened not to feel vengeful; I felt I had him on the run, and I meant to keep him on the run. My polite insistence must have had something menacing in it, because he gave in suddenly. And I did not let him off a single item; mate's room, pantry, storerooms, the very sail locker which was also under the poop — he had to look into them all. When at last I showed him out on the quarter-deck he drew a long, spiritless sigh, and mumbled dismally that he must really be going back to his ship now. I desired my mate, who had joined us, to see to the captain's boat.

The man of whiskers gave a blast on the whistle which he used to wear hanging round his neck, and yelled, " Sephora's away!" My double down there in my cabin must have heard, and certainly could not feel more relieved than I. Four fellows came running out from somewhere forward and went over the side, while my own men, appearing on deck too, lined the rail. I escorted my visitor to the gangway ceremoniously, and nearly overdid it. He was a tenacious① beast. On the very ladder he lingered, and in that unique, guiltily conscientious manner of sticking to the point:

" I say... you... you don't think that — "

I covered his voice loudly:

" Certainly not.... I am delighted. Good-by."

I had an idea of what he meant to say, and just saved myself by the privilege of defective hearing. He was too shaken generally to insist, but my mate, close witness of that parting, looked mystified and his face took on a thoughtful cast. As I did not want to appear as if I wished to avoid all communication with my officers, he had the opportunity to address me.

" Seems a very nice man. His boat's crew told our chaps a very extraordinary story, if what I am told by the steward is true. I suppose you had it from the captain, sir?"

" Yes. I had a story from the captain."

" A very horrible affair — isn't it, sir?"

" It is."

" Beats all these tales we hear about murders in Yankee ships."

---

① tenacious: strong-willed

“ I don’t think it beats them. I don’t think it resembles them in the least.”

“ Bless my soul — you don’t say so! But of course I’ve no acquaintance whatever with American ships, not I so I couldn’t go against your knowledge. It’s horrible enough for me.... But the queerest part is that those fellows seemed to have some idea the man was hidden aboard here. They had really. Did you ever hear of such a thing?”

“ Preposterous - isn’t it?”

We were walking to and fro athwart the quarter-deck. No one of the crew forward could be seen (the day was Sunday), and the mate pursued:

“ There was some little dispute about it. Our chaps took offense. ‘As if we would harbor a thing like that,’ they said. ‘Wouldn’t you like to look for him in our coal-hole?’ Quite a tiff. But they made it up in the end. I suppose he did drown himself. Don’t you, sir?”

“ I don’t suppose anything.”

“ You have no doubt in the matter, sir?”

“ None whatever.”

I left him suddenly. I felt I was producing a bad impression, but with my double down there it was most trying to be on deck. And it was almost as trying to be below. Altogether a nerve-trying situation. But on the whole I felt less torn in two when I was with him. There was no one in the whole ship whom I dared take into my confidence. Since the hands had got to know his story, it would have been impossible to pass him off for anyone else, and an accidental discovery was to be dreaded now more than ever....

The steward being engaged in laying the table for dinner, we could talk only with our eyes when I first went down. Later in the afternoon we had a cautious try at whispering. The Sunday quietness of the ship was against us; the stillness of air and water around her was against us; the elements, the men were against us — everything was against us in our secret partnership; time itself — for this could not go on forever. The very trust in Providence was, I suppose, denied to his guilt. Shall I confess that this thought cast me down very much? And as to the chapter of accidents which counts for so much in the book of success, I could only hope that it was closed. For what favorable accident could be expected?

" Did you hear everything?" were my first words as soon as we took up our position side by side, leaning over my bed place.

He had. And the proof of it was his earnest whisper, " The man told you he hardly dared to give the order."

I understood the reference to be to that saving foresail.

" Yes. He was afraid of it being lost in the setting."

" I assure you he never gave the order. He may think he did, but he never gave it. He stood there with me on the break of the poop after the main topsail blew away, and whimpered about our last hope — positively whimpered about it and nothing else — and the night coming on! To hear one's skipper go on like that in such weather was enough to drive any fellow out of his mind. It worked me up into a sort of desperation. I just took it into my own hands and went away from him, boiling, and — But what's the use telling you? You know!... Do you think that if I had not been pretty fierce with them I should have got the men to do anything? Not It! The bo's'n perhaps? Perhaps! It wasn't a heavy sea — it was a sea gone mad! I suppose the end of the world will be something like that; and a man may have the heart to see it coming once and be done with it — but to have to face it day after day — I don't blame anybody. I was precious little better than the rest. Only — I was an officer of that old coal wagon, anyhow — ."

" I quite understand," I conveyed that sincere assurance into his ear. He was out of breath with whispering; I could hear him pant slightly. It was all very simple. The same strung-up force which had given twenty-four men a chance, at least, for their lives, had, in a sort of recoil, crushed an unworthy mutinous[①] existence.

But I had no leisure to weigh the merits of the matter — footsteps in the saloon, a heavy knock. " There's enough wind to get under way with, sir." Here was the call of a new claim upon my thoughts and even upon my feelings.

" Turn the hands up," I cried through the door. " I'll be on deck directly."

I was going out to make the acquaintance of my ship. Before I left the cabin our eyes met — the eyes of the only two strangers on board. I pointed to the recessed part where the little campstool awaited him and laid my finger on my lips. He made a gesture — somewhat vague — a little mysterious, accompanied by a faint smile, as if of regret.

This is not the place to enlarge upon the sensations of a man who feels for the first time a ship move under his feet to his own independent word. In my case they were not unalloyed. I was not wholly alone with my command; for there was that stranger in my cabin. Or rather, I was not completely and wholly with her. Part of me was absent. That mental feeling of being in two places at once affected me physically as if the mood of secrecy had penetrated my very soul. Before an hour had elapsed since the ship had begun to move, having occasion to ask the mate (he stood by my side) to take a compass bearing of the pagoda, I caught myself reaching up to his ear in whispers. I say I caught myself, but enough had escaped to startle the man. I can't describe it otherwise than by saying that he shied. A grave, preoccupied manner, as though he were in possession of some perplexing intelligence, did not leave him henceforth. A little later I moved away from the rail to look at the compass with such a stealthy gait that the helmsman noticed it - and I could not help noticing the unusual roundness of his eyes. These are trifling instances, though it's to no commander's advantage to be suspected of ludicrous eccentricities. But I was also more seriously affected. There are to a seaman certain words, gestures, that should in

① mutinous: an occasion when a group of people, especially soldiers or sailors, refuses to obey orders and/or attempts to take control from people in authority given conditions come as naturally, as instinctively as the winking of a menaced eye. A certain order should spring on to his lips without thinking; a certain sign should get itself made, so to speak, without reflection. But all unconscious alertness had abandoned me. I had to make an effort of will to recall myself back (from the cabin) to the conditions of the moment. I felt that I was appearing an irresolute commander to those people who were watching me more or less critically.

And, besides, there were the scares. On the second day out, for instance, coming off the deck in the afternoon (I had straw slippers on my bare feet) I stopped at the open pantry door and spoke to the steward. He was doing something there with his back to me. At the sound of my voice he nearly jumped out of his skin, as the saying is, and incidentally broke a cup.

" What on earth's the matter with you?" I asked, astonished.

He was extremely confused. " Beg your pardon, sir. I made sure you were in your cabin."

" You see I wasn't."

" No, sir. I could have sworn I had heard you moving in there not a moment ago. It's most extraordinary... very sorry, sir."

I passed on with an inward shudder. I was so identified with my secret double that I did not even mention the fact in those scanty, fearful whispers we exchanged. I suppose he had made some slight noise of some kind or other. It would have been miraculous if he hadn't at one time or another. And yet, haggard as he appeared, he looked always perfectly self-controlled, more than calm — almost invulnerable. On my suggestion he remained almost entirely in the bathroom, which, upon the whole, was the safest place. There could be really no shadow of an excuse for anyone ever wanting to go in there, once the steward had done with it. It was a very tiny place. Sometimes he reclined on the floor, his legs bent, his head sustained on one elbow. At others I would find him on the campstool, sitting in his gray sleeping suit and with his cropped dark hair like a patient, unmoved convict. At night I would smuggle him into my bed place, and we would whisper together, with the regular footfalls of the officer of the watch passing and repassing over our heads. It was an infinitely miserable time. It was lucky that some tins of fine preserves were stowed in a locker in my stateroom; hard bread I could always get hold of; and so he lived on stewed chicken, PATE DE FOIE GRAS, asparagus, cooked oysters, sardines — on all sorts of abominable① sham delicacies out of tins. My early-morning coffee he always drank; and it was all I dared do for him in that respect.

Every day there was the horrible maneuvering to go through so that my room and then the bathroom should be done in the usual way. I came to hate the sight of the steward, to abhor the voice of that harmless man. I felt that it was he who would bring on the disaster of discovery. It hung like a sword over our heads.

The fourth day out, I think (we were then working down the east side of the Gulf of Siam, tack for tack, in light winds and smooth water) — the fourth day, I say, of this miserable juggling with the unavoidable, as we sat at our evening meal, that man, whose slightest movement I dreaded, after putting down the dishes ran up on deck busily. This could not be dangerous. Presently he came down again; and then it appeared that he had remembered a coat of mine which I had thrown over a rail to dry after having been wetted in a shower which had passed over the ship in the afternoon. Sitting stolidly at the head of the table I became terrified at the sight of the garment on his arm. Of course he made for my door. There was no time to lose.

" Steward," I thundered. My nerves were so shaken that I could not govern my voice and conceal my agitation. This was the sort of thing that made my terrifically whiskered mate tap his forehead with his forefinger. I had detected him using that gesture while talking on deck with a confidential air to the carpenter. It was too far to hear a word, but I had no doubt that this pantomime② could only refer to the strange new captain.

---

① abominable: very bad or unpleasant

② pantomime: gesture

" Yes, sir," the pale-faced steward turned resignedly to me. It was this maddening course of being shouted at, checked without rhyme or reason, arbitrarily chased out of my cabin, suddenly called into it, sent flying out of his pantry on incomprehensible errands, that accounted for the growing wretchedness of his expression.

" Where are you going with that coat?"

" To your room, sir."

" Is there another shower coming?"

" I'm sure I don't know, sir. Shall I go up again and see, sir?"

" No! never mind."

My object was attained, as of course my other self in there would have heard everything that passed. During this interlude my two officers never raised their eyes off their respective plates; but the lip of that confounded cub, the second mate, quivered visibly.

I expected the steward to hook my coat on and come out at once. He was very slow about it; but I dominated my nervousness sufficiently not to shout after him. Suddenly I became aware (it could be heard plainly enough) that the fellow for some reason or other was opening the door of the bathroom. It was the end. The place was literally not big enough to swing a cat in. My voice died in my throat and I went stony all over. I expected to hear a yell of surprise and terror, and made a movement, but had not the strength to get on my legs. Everything remained still. Had my second self taken the poor wretch by the throat? I don't know what I could have done next moment if I had not seen the steward come out of my room, close the door, and then stand quietly by the sideboard.

" Saved," I thought. " But, no! Lost! Gone! He was gone!"

I laid my knife and fork down and leaned back in my chair. My head swam. After a while, when sufficiently recovered to speak in a steady voice, I instructed my mate to put the ship round at eight o'clock himself.

" I won't come on deck," I went on. " I think I'll turn in, and unless the wind shifts I don't want to be disturbed before midnight. I feel a bit seedy."

" You did look middling bad a little while ago," the chief mate remarked without showing any great concern.

They both went out, and I stared at the steward clearing the table. There was nothing to be read on that wretched man's face. But why did he avoid my eyes, I asked myself. Then I thought I should like to hear the sound of his voice.

" Steward!"

" Sir!" Startled as usual.

" Where did you hang up that coat?"

" In the bathroom, sir." The usual anxious tone. " It's not quite dry yet, sir."

For some time longer I sat in the cuddy. Had my double vanished as he had come? But of his coming there was an explanation, whereas his disappearance would be inexplicable.... I went slowly into my dark room, shut the door, lighted the lamp, and for a time dared not turn round. When at last I did I saw him standing bolt-upright in the narrow recessed part. It would not be true to say I had a shock, but an irresistible doubt of his bodily existence flitted through my mind. Can it be, I asked myself, that he is not visible to other eyes than mine? It was like being haunted. Motionless, with a grave face, he raised his hands slightly at me in a gesture which meant clearly, " Heavens! what a narrow escape!" Narrow indeed. I think I had come creeping quietly as near insanity as any man who has not actually gone over the border. That gesture restrained me, so to speak.

The mate with the terrific whiskers was now putting the ship on the other tack. In the moment of profound silence which follows upon the hands going to their stations I heard on the poop his raised voice: " Hard alee!" and the distant shout of the order repeated on the main-deck. The sails, in that light breeze, made but a faint fluttering noise. It ceased. The ship was coming round slowly: I held my breath in the renewed stillness of expectation; one wouldn't have thought that there was a single living soul on her decks. A sudden brisk shout, " Mainsail haul!" broke the spell, and in the noisy cries and rush overhead of the men running away with the main brace we two, down in my cabin, came together in our usual position by the bed place.

He did not wait for my question. " I heard him fumbling here and just managed to squat myself down in the bath," he whispered to me. " The fellow only opened the door and put his arm in to hang the coat up. All the same — "

" I never thought of that," I whispered back, even more appalled than before at the closeness of the shave, and marveling at that something unyielding in his character which was carrying him through so finely. There was no agitation in his whisper. Whoever was being driven distracted, it was not he. He was sane. And the proof of his sanity was continued when he took up the whispering again.

" It would never do for me to come to life again."

It was something that a ghost might have said. But what he was alluding to was his old captain's reluctant admission of the theory of suicide. It would obviously serve his turn — if I had understood at all the view which seemed to govern the unalterable purpose of his action.

" You must maroon me as soon as ever you can get amongst these islands off the Cambodge shore," he went on.

" Maroon you! We are not living in a boy's adventure tale," I protested. His scornful whispering took me up.

" We aren't indeed! There's nothing of a boy's tale in this. But there's nothing else for it. I want no more. You don't suppose I am afraid of what can be done to me? Prison or gallows or whatever they may please. But you don't see me coming back to explain such things to an old fellow in a wig and twelve respectable tradesmen, do you? What can they know whether I am guilty or not — or of WHAT I am guilty, either? That's my affair. What does the Bible say? 'Driven off the face of the earth.' Very well, I am off the face of the earth now. As I came at night so I shall go."

" Impossible!" I murmured. " You can't."

" Can't?... Not naked like a soul on the Day of Judgment. I shall freeze on to this sleeping suit. The Last Day is not yet — and...you have understood thoroughly. Didn't you?"

I felt suddenly ashamed of myself. I may say truly that I understood — and my hesitation in letting that man swim away from my ship's side had been a mere sham sentiment, a sort of cowardice.

" It can't be done now till next night," I breathed out. " The ship is on the off-shore tack and the wind may fail us."

" As long as I know that you understand," he whispered. " But of course you do. It's a great satisfaction to have got somebody to understand. You seem to have been there on purpose." And in the same whisper, as if we two whenever we talked had to say things to each other which were not fit for the world to hear, he added, " It's very wonderful."

We remained side by side talking in our secret way — but sometimes silent or just exchanging a whispered word or two at long intervals. And as usual he stared through the port. A breath of wind came now and again into our faces. The ship might have been moored in dock, so gently and on an even keel she slipped through the water, that did not murmur even at our passage, shadowy and silent like a phantom① sea.

At midnight I went on deck, and to my mate's great surprise put the ship round on the other tack. His terrible whiskers flitted round me in silent criticism. I certainly should not have done it if it had been only a question of getting out of that sleepy gulf as quickly as possible. I believe he told the second mate, who relieved him, that it was a great want of judgment. The other only yawned. That intolerable cub shuffled about so sleepily and lolled against the rails in such a slack, improper fashion that I came down on him sharply.

" Aren't you properly awake yet?"

---

① phantom: almost transparent form of a person, animal, or other object

" Yes, sir! I am awake."

" Well, then, be good enough to hold yourself as if you were. And keep a lookout. If there's any current we'll be closing with some islands before daylight."

The east side of the gulf is fringed with islands, some solitary, others in groups. One the blue background of the high coast they seem to float on silvery patches of calm water, arid and gray, or dark green and rounded like clumps of evergreen bushes, with the larger ones, a mile or two long, showing the outlines of ridges, ribs of gray rock under the dark mantle of matted leafage. Unknown to trade, to travel, almost to geography, the manner of life they harbor is an unsolved secret. There must be villages — settlements of fishermen at least — on the largest of them, and some communication with the world is probably kept up by native craft. But all that forenoon, as we headed for them, fanned along by the faintest of breezes, I saw no sign of man or canoe in the field of the telescope I kept on pointing at the scattered group.

At noon I have no orders for a change of course, and the mate's whiskers became much concerned and seemed to be offering themselves unduly to my notice. At last I said:

" I am going to stand right in. Quite in — as far as I can take her."

The stare of extreme surprise imparted an air of ferocity also to his eyes, and he looked truly terrific for a moment.

" We're not doing well in the middle of the gulf," I continued, casually. " I am going to look for the land breezes tonight."

" Bless my soul! Do you mean, sir, in the dark amongst the lot of all them islands and reefs and shoals?"

" Well — if there are any regular land breezes at all on this coast one must get close inshore to find them, mustn't one?"

" Bless my soul!" he exclaimed again under his breath. All that afternoon he wore a dreamy, contemplative appearance which in him was a mark of perplexity.

After dinner I went into my stateroom as if I meant to take some rest. There we two bent our dark heads over a half-unrolled chart lying on my bed.

" There," I said. " It's got to be Koh-ring. I've been looking at it ever since sunrise. It has got two hills and a low point. It must be inhabited. And on the coast opposite there is what looks like the mouth of a biggish river — with some towns, no doubt, not far up. It's the best chance for you that I can see."

" Anything. Koh-ring let it be."

He looked thoughtfully at the chart as if surveying chances and distances from a lofty height and following with his eyes his own figure wandering on the blank land of Cochin-China, and then passing off that piece of paper clean out of sight into uncharted regions. And it was as if the ship had two captains to plan her course for her. I had been so worried and restless running up and down that I had not had the patience to dress that day. I had remained in my sleeping suit, with straw slippers and a soft floppy hat. The closeness of the heat in the gulf had been most oppressive, and the crew were used to seeing me wandering in that airy attire.

" She will clear the south point as she heads now," I whispered into his ear. " Goodness only knows when, though, but certainly after dark. I'll edge her in to half a mile, as far as I may be able to judge in the dark — ."

" Be careful," he murmured, warningly — and I realized suddenly that all my future, the only future for which I was fit, would perhaps go irretrievably to pieces in any mishap to my first command.

I could not stop a moment longer in the room. I motioned him to get out of sight and made my way on the poop. That unplayful cub had the watch. I walked up and down for a while thinking things out, then beckoned him over.

" Send a couple of hands to open the two quarter-deck ports," I said, mildly.

He actually had the impudence, or else so forgot himself in his wonder at such an incomprehensible order, as to repeat:

" Open the quarter-deck ports! What for, sir?"

" The only reason you need concern yourself about is because I tell you to do so. Have them open wide and fastened properly."

He reddened and went off, but I believe made some jeering remark to the carpenter as to the sensible practice of ventilating a ship's quarter-deck. I know he popped into the mate's cabin to impart the fact to him because the whiskers came on deck, as it were by chance, and stole glances at me from below — for signs of lunacy① or drunkenness, I suppose.

A little before supper, feeling more restless than ever, I rejoined, for a moment, my second self. And to find him sitting so quietly was surprising, like something against nature, inhuman.

I developed my plan in a hurried whisper.

" I shall stand in as close as I dare and then put her round. I will presently find means to smuggle you out of here into the sail locker, which communicates with the lobby. But there is an opening, a sort of square for hauling the sails out, which gives straight on the quarter-deck and which is never closed in fine weather, so as to give air to the sails. When the ship's way is deadened in stays and all the hands are aft at the main braces you will have a clear road to slip out and get overboard through the open quarter-deck port. I've had them both fastened up. Use a rope's end to lower yourself into the water so as to avoid a splash — you know. It could be heard and cause some beastly complication."

He kept silent for a while, then whispered, " I understand."

" I won't be there to see you go," I began with an effort. " The rest…I only hope I have understood, too."

" You have. From first to last" — and for the first time there seemed to be a faltering, something strained in his whisper. He caught hold of my arm, but the ringing of the supper bell made me start. He didn't though; he only released his grip.

---

① lunacy: stupid behaviour that will have bad results

After supper I didn't come below again till well past eight o'clock. The faint, steady breeze was loaded with dew; and the wet, darkened sails held all there was of propelling power in it. The night, clear and starry, sparkled darkly, and the opaque, lightless patches shifting slowly against the low stars were the drifting islets. On the port bow there was a big one more distant and shadowily imposing by the great space of sky it eclipsed.

On opening the door I had a back view of my very own self looking at a chart. He had come out of the recess and was standing near the table.

" Quite dark enough," I whispered.

He stepped back and leaned against my bed with a level, quiet glance. I sat on the couch. We had nothing to say to each other. Over our heads the officer of the watch moved here and there. Then I heard him move quickly. I knew what that meant. He was making for the companion; and presently his voice was outside my door.

" We are drawing in pretty fast, sir. Land looks rather close."

" Very well," I answered. " I am coming on deck directly."

I waited till he was gone out of the cuddy, then rose. My double moved too. The time had come to exchange our last whispers, for neither of us was ever to hear each other's natural voice.

" Look here!" I opened a drawer and took out three sovereigns. " Take this anyhow. I've got six and I'd give you the lot, only I must keep a little money to buy some fruit and vegetables for the crew from native boats as we go through Sunda Straits."

He shook his head.

" Take it," I urged him, whispering desperately. " No one can tell what — "

He smiled and slapped meaningly the only pocket of the sleeping jacket. It was not safe, certainly. But I produced a large old silk handkerchief of mine, and tying the three pieces of gold in a corner, pressed it on him. He was touched, I supposed, because he took it at last and tied it quickly round his waist under the jacket, on his bare skin.

Our eyes met; several seconds elapsed, till, our glances still mingled, I extended my hand and turned the lamp out. Then I passed through the cuddy, leaving the door of my room wide open.... " Steward!"

He was still lingering in the pantry in the greatness of his zeal, giving a rub-up to a plated cruet stand the last thing before going to bed. Being careful not to wake up the mate, whose room was opposite, I spoke in an undertone.

He looked round anxiously. " Sir!"

" Can you get me a little hot water from the galley?"

" I am afraid, sir, the galley fire's been out for some time now."

" Go and see."

He flew up the stairs.

" Now," I whispered, loudly, into the saloon — too loudly, perhaps, but I was afraid I couldn't make a sound. He was by my side in an instant — the double captain slipped past the stairs — through a tiny dark passage... a sliding door. We were in the sail locker, scrambling on our knees over the sails. A sudden thought struck me. I saw myself wandering barefooted, bareheaded, the sun beating on my dark poll. I snatched off my floppy hat and tried hurriedly in the dark to ram it on my other self. He dodged and fended off silently. I wonder what he thought had come to me before he understood and suddenly desisted. Our hands met gropingly, lingered united in a steady, motionless clasp for a second.... No word was breathed by either of us when they separated.

I was standing quietly by the pantry door when the steward returned.

" Sorry, sir. Kettle barely warm. Shall I light the spirit lamp?"

" Never mind."

I came out on deck slowly. It was now a matter of conscience to shave the land as close as possible — for now he must go overboard whenever the ship was put in stays. Must! There could be no going back for him. After a moment I walked over to leeward[1] and my heart flew into my mouth at the nearness of the land on the bow. Under any other circumstances I would not have held on a minute longer. The second mate had followed me anxiously.

I looked on till I felt I could command my voice.

" She will weather," I said then in a quiet tone.

" Are you going to try that, sir?" he stammered out incredulously.

I took no notice of him and raised my tone just enough to be heard by the helmsman.

" Keep her good full."

" Good full, sir."

The wind fanned my cheek, the sails slept, the world was silent. The strain of watching the dark loom of the land grow bigger and denser was too much for me. I had shut my eyes — because the ship must go closer. She must! The stillness was intolerable. Were we standing still?

When I opened my eyes the second view started my heart with a thump. The black southern hill of Koh-ring seemed to hang right over the ship like a towering fragment of everlasting night. On that enormous mass of blackness there was not a gleam to be seen, not a sound to be heard. It was gliding irresistibly towards us and yet seemed already within reach of the hand. I saw the vague figures of the watch grouped in the waist, gazing in awed silence.

" Are you going on, sir?" inquired an unsteady voice at my elbow.

I ignored it. I had to go on.

" Keep her full. Don't check her way. That won't do now," I said warningly.

" I can't see the sails very well," the helmsman answered me, in strange, quavering tones.

---

① leeward: in the direction toward which the wind is blowing

Was she close enough? Already she was, I won't say in the shadow of the land, but in the very blackness of it, already swallowed up as it were, gone too close to be recalled, gone from me altogether.

" Give the mate a call," I said to the young man who stood at my elbow as still as death. " And turn all hands up."

My tone had a borrowed loudness reverberated from the height of the land. Several voices cried out together: " We are all on deck, sir."

Then stillness again, with the great shadow gliding closer, towering higher, without a light, without a sound. Such a hush had fallen on the ship that she might have been a bark of the dead floating in slowly under the very gate of Erebus.

" My God! Where are we?"

It was the mate moaning at my elbow. He was thunderstruck, and as it were deprived of the moral support of his whiskers. He clapped his hands and absolutely cried out, " Lost!"

" Be quiet," I said, sternly.

He lowered his tone, but I saw the shadowy gesture of his despair. " What are we doing here?"

" Looking for the land wind."

He made as if to tear his hair, and addressed me recklessly.

" She will never get out. You have done it, sir. I knew it'd end in something like this. She will never weather, and you are too close now to stay. She'll drift ashore before she's round. O my God!"

I caught his arm as he was raising it to batter his poor devoted head, and shook it violently.

" She's ashore already," he wailed, trying to tear himself away.

" Is she?... Keep good full there!"

" Good full, sir," cried the helmsman in a frightened, thin, childlike voice.

I hadn't let go the mate's arm and went on shaking it. " Ready about, do you hear? You go forward" — shake — "and stop there" — shake — "and hold your noise" — shake — "and see these head-sheets properly overhauled" — shake, shake — shake.

And all the time I dared not look towards the land lest my heart should fail me. I released my grip at last and he ran forward as if fleeing for dear life.

I wondered what my double there in the sail locker thought of this commotion. He was able to hear everything — and perhaps he was able to understand why, on my conscience, it had to be thus close — no less. My first order " Hard alee!" re-echoed ominously under the towering shadow of Koh-ring as if I had shouted in a mountain gorge. And then I watched the land intently. In that smooth water and light wind it was impossible to feel the ship coming-to. No! I could not feel her. And my second self was making now ready to ship out and lower himself overboard. Perhaps he was gone already…?

The great black mass brooding over our very mastheads began to pivot away from the ship's side silently. And now I forgot the secret stranger ready to depart, and remembered only that I was a total stranger to the ship. I did not know her. Would she do it? How was she to be handled?

I swung the mainyard and waited helplessly. She was perhaps stopped, and her very fate hung in the balance, with the black mass of Koh-ring like the gate of the everlasting night towering over her taffrail. What would she do now? Had she way on her yet? I stepped to the side swiftly, and on the shadowy water I could see nothing except a faint phosphorescent flash revealing the glassy smoothness of the sleeping surface. It was impossible to tell — and I had not learned yet the feel of my ship. Was she moving? What I needed was something easily seen, a piece of paper, which I could throw overboard and watch. I had nothing on me. To run down for it I didn't dare. There was no time. All at once my strained, yearning stare distinguished a white object floating within a yard of the ship's side. White on the black water. A phosphorescent flash passed under it. What was that thing?... I recognized my own floppy hat. It must have fallen off his head... and he didn't bother. Now I had what I wanted — the saving mark for my eyes. But I hardly thought of my other self, now gone from the ship, to be hidden forever from all friendly faces, to be a fugitive and a vagabond on the earth, with no brand of the curse on his sane forehead to stay a slaying hand... too proud to explain.

And I watched the hat — the expression of my sudden pity for his mere flesh. It had been meant to save his homeless head from the dangers of the sun. And now — behold — it was saving the ship, by serving me for a mark to help out the ignorance of my strangeness. Ha! It was drifting forward, warning me just in time that the ship had gathered sternaway.

" Shift the helm," I said in a low voice to the seaman standing still like a statue.

The man's eyes glistened wildly in the binnacle light as he jumped round to the other side and spun round the wheel.

I walked to the break of the poop. On the over-shadowed deck all hands stood by the forebraces waiting for my order. The stars ahead seemed to be gliding from right to left. And all was so still in the world that I heard the quiet remark, " She's round," passed in a tone of intense relief between two seamen.

" Let go and haul."

The foreyards ran round with a great noise, amidst cheery cries. And now the frightful whiskers made themselves heard giving various orders. Already the ship was drawing ahead. And I was alone with her. Nothing! no one in the world should stand now between us, throwing a shadow on the way of silent knowledge and mute affection, the perfect communion of a seaman with his first command.

Walking to the taffrail, I was in time to make out, on the very edge of a darkness thrown by a towering black mass like the very gateway of Erebus — yes, I was in time to catch an evanescent glimpse of my white hat left behind to mark the spot where the secret sharer of my cabin and of my thoughts, as though he were my second self, had lowered himself into the water to take his punishment: a free man, a proud swimmer striking out for a new destiny.

Topics for discussion

1. How do you make comment on Joseph Conrad's concept of the dark side of man in *The Secret Sharer*?

2. Discuss how Leggatt and the captain are related. Is Leggatt a double for the captain?

3. How do you understand the statement " Conrad establishes this psychological state of identification between the captain and Leggatt so that Leggatt's moral crisis becomes metaphorically the captain's moral crisis"?

References for further reading

[1] Curle, Richard. *Joseph Conrad: A Study*, New York, Doubleday: Page & Company, 1914.

[2] Gurko, Leo. *Joseph Conrad: Giant in Exile*, New York: The MacMillan Company, 1962.

[3] Meyers, Jeffrey. *Joseph Conrad: A Biography*, New York: Charles Scribner's Sons, 1991.

[4] Najder, Zdzisław. *Conrad under Familial Eyes*, Cambridge: Cambridge University Press, 1984.

[5] Stape, J. H. ed. *The Cambridge Companion to Joseph Conrad*, Cambridge: Cambridge University Press, 2006.

[6] Stape, John. *The Several Lives of Joseph Conrad*, New York: Pantheon, 2007.

W. W. Jacobs (1863 — 1943)

The Monkey's Paw

Introduction to the author

William Wymark Jacobs (September 8, 1863 — September 1, 1943), was an English author of short stories and novels. He was one of the most popular humorists of the early 1900s, but his most famous story "The Monkey's Paw" is a horror classic. Jacobs was born in Wapping, London. His father was a wharf manager at the South Devon wharf at Lower East Smithfield. He grew up in Wapping, a seaport section of London. He attended a private school in London and later Birkbeck College (now part of the University of London). In 1879, Jacobs began work as a clerk in the civil service. Jacobs published his stories and articles in magazines. His first collection of stories is *Many Cargoes*, followed by the novellas — *The Skipper's Wooing and The Brown Man's Servant*. Since his third book — *Sea Urchins* he begins his true devotion to writing.

In 1900, Jacobs married Agnes Eleanor Williams, a famous suffragette and socialist. They lived in Kings Place Road, Buckhurst Hill, Essex. But his marriage was not happy one, which maybe caused that most women in his fiction are negative. Jacobs was prolific during the early years of his career but his writing output declined somewhat around the First World War. In his later years, he devoted himself to the adaptations of his own short stories for the stage. Jacobs died at Hornsey Lane, Islington, London.

Jacobs is now noted for his macabre tale " The Monkey's Paw" and some ghost stories, including " The Toll House". However, most of his works was humorous in tone, and most of his fiction concerns Marine life.

Major works by W. W Jacobs

Stories

Deep Waters, 1919

The Lady of the Barge, 1902 (Contains The Monkey's Paw.)

Light Freights, 1901

Many Cargoes, 1896

Night Watches, 1914

Odd Craft, 1903 (Contains Thc Money Box.)

Sailors' Knots, 1909

Sea Urchins, 1898

Sea Whispers, 1926

Ship's Company, 1911

Short Cruises, 1907

Novels

At Sunwich Port, 1902

The Castaways, 1916

Dialstone Lane, 1902

A Master of Craft, 1900

Salthaven, 1908

The Skipper's Wooing and The Brown Man's Servant, 1897

Appreciation

" The Monkey's Paw" is a classic of horror fiction. The story opens with Mr. White and his son playing a game of chess. Mrs. White is knitting by the fire. The family spends a cozy evening. The Sergeant-Major Morris, an old friend of Mr. White's, comes to visit them. The Sergeant-Major tells the White some tale about his trip to India. He tells them of a magical monkey's paw, which allowing three man three wishes each. Morris warns the Whites not to wish on the paw at all. However, Herbert coaxes his father to wish for 200 pounds. As a result, Herbert was caught in some machinery, and died. The Whites got the 200 pounds from a company as compensation. Mrs. White pleads her husband makes a wish that Herbert would be alive again. They wait for his son's coming back, but no one comes. Suddenly, a slight knock is heard at the door. The knocking develops into rapid bangings on the door. Mrs. White desires to open the door. At that time, Mr. White asks his third wish. What they see outside the door is still and empty street, dim streetlight flickering.

Jacobs uses foreshadowing, imagery and symbolism in the story to explore the consequences of tempting fate. The story is tightly constructed so that it revolves around simple surprising ending. In language, the writer uses dialogue and slang to show the genuine characters.

Selected Reading

The Monkey's Paw

I

Without, the night was cold and wet, but in the small parlour[①] of Laburnam

① parlour: a store that sells a stated product, or a business that provides a stated service

Villa the blinds were drawn and the fire burned brightly. Father and son were at chess, the former, who possessed ideas about the game involving radical changes, putting his king into such sharp and unnecessary perils that it even provoked comment from the white-haired old lady knitting placidly by the fire.

" Hark at the wind," said Mr. White, who, having seen a fatal mistake after it was too late, was amiably desirous of preventing his son from seeing it.

" I'm listening," said the latter, grimly surveying the board as he stretched out his hand. " Check."

" I should hardly think that he'd come to-night," said his father, with his hand poised① over the board.

" Mate," replied the son.

" That's the worst of living so far out," bawled Mr. White, with sudden and unlooked-for violence; " of all the beastly, slushy,② out-of-the-way places to live in, this is the worst. Pathway's a bog, and the road's a torrent. I don't know what people are thinking about. I suppose because only two houses on the road are let, they think it doesn't matter."

" Never mind, dear," said his wife soothingly; " perhaps you'll win the next one."

Mr. White looked up sharply, just in time to intercept a knowing glance between mother and son. The words died away on his lips, and he hid a guilty grin in his thin grey beard.

" There he is," said Herbert White, as the gate banged to loudly and heavy footsteps came toward the door.

The old man rose with hospitable haste, and opening the door, was heard condoling with the new arrival. The new arrival also condoled with himself, so that

① poise: balance in the way a person holds or moves their body

② slushy: partly melted

Mrs. White said, " Tut,[①] tut!" and coughed gently as her husband entered the room, followed by a tall burly man, beady of eye and rubicund of visage.

" Sergeant-Major Morris," he said, introducing him.

The sergeant-major shook hands, and taking the proffered seat by the fire, watched contentedly while his host got out whisky and tumblers and stood a small copper kettle on the fire.

At the third glass his eyes got brighter, and he began to talk, the little family circle regarding with eager interest this visitor from distant parts, as he squared his broad shoulders in the chair and spoke of strange scenes and doughty deeds; of wars and plagues and strange peoples.

" Twenty-one years of it," said Mr. White, nodding at his wife and son. " When he went away he was a slip of a youth in the warehouse. Now look at him."

" He don't look to have taken much harm," said Mrs. White, politely.

" I'd like to go to India myself," said the old man, " just to look round a bit, you know."

" Better where you are," said the sergeant-major, shaking his head. He put down the empty glass, and sighing softly, shook it again.

" I should like to see those old temples and fakirs[②] and jugglers[③] ," said the old man. " What was that you started telling me the other day about a monkey's paw or something, Morris?"

" Nothing," said the soldier hastily. " Leastways, nothing worth hearing."

" Monkey's paw?" said Mrs. White curiously.

" Well, it's just a bit of what you might call magic, perhaps," said the sergeant-major off-handedly.

---

① tut: (exclamation) used in writing to represent the sound made to show you disapprove of something

② Fakirs: a member of an Islamic religious group, or a Hindu holy man

③ juggler: a person who juggles objects in order to entertain people

His three listeners leaned forward eagerly. The visitor absentmindedly put his empty glass to his lips and then set it down again. His host filled it for him.

" To look at," said the sergeant-major, fumbling in his pocket, " it's just an ordinary little paw, dried to a mummy."

He took something out of his pocket and proffered it. Mrs. White drew back with a grimace, but her son, taking it, examined it curiously.

" And what is there special about it?" inquired Mr. White, as he took it from his son and, having examined it, placed it upon the table.

" It had a spell put on it by an old fakir," said the sergeant-major, " a very holy man. He wanted to show that fate ruled people's lives, and that those who interfered with it did so to their sorrow. He put a spell on it so that three separate men could each have three wishes from it."

His manner was so impressive that his hearers were conscious that their light laughter jarred somewhat.

" Well, why don't you have three, sir?" said Herbert White cleverly.

The soldier regarded him in the way that middle age is wont to regard presumptuous youth. " I have," he said quietly, and his blotchy face whitened.

" And did you really have the three wishes granted?" asked Mrs. White.

" I did," said the sergeant-major, and his glass tapped against his strong teeth.

" And has anybody else wished?" inquired the old lady.

" The first man had his three wishes, yes," was the reply. " I don't know what the first two were, but the third was for death. That's how I got the paw."

His tones were so grave that a hush fell upon the group.

" If you've had your three wishes, it's no good to you now, then, Morris," said the old man at last. " What do you keep it for?"

The soldier shook his head. " Fancy, I suppose," he said slowly.

" If you could have another three wishes," said the old man, eyeing him keenly, " would you have them?"

“ I don’t know,” said the other. “ I don’t know.”

He took the paw, and dangling it between his front finger and thumb, suddenly threw it upon the fire. White, with a slight cry, stooped down and snatched it off.

“ Better let it burn,” said the soldier solemnly.

“ If you don’t want it, Morris,” said the old man, “ give it to me.”

“ I won’t,” said his friend doggedly. “ I threw it on the fire. If you keep it, don’t blame me for what happens. Pitch it on the fire again, like a sensible man.”

The other shook his head and examined his new possession closely. “ How do you do it?” he inquired.

“ Hold it up in your right hand and wish aloud,” said the sergeant-major, “ but I warn you of the consequences.”

“ Sounds like the Arabian Nights,” said Mrs White, as she rose and began to set the supper. “ Don’t you think you might wish for four pairs of hands for me?”

Her husband drew the talisman① from his pocket and then all three burst into laughter as the sergeant-major, with a look of alarm on his face, caught him by the arm.

“ If you must wish,” he said gruffly, “ wish for something sensible.”

Mr. White dropped it back into his pocket, and placing chairs, motioned his friend to the table. In the business of supper the talisman was partly forgotten, and afterward the three sat listening in an enthralled fashion to a second instalment of the soldier’s adventures in India.

“ If the tale about the monkey paw is not more truthful than those he has been telling us,” said Herbert, as the door closed behind their guest, just in time for him to catch the last train, “ we shan’t make much out of it.”

“ Did you give him anything for it, father?” inquired Mrs. White, regarding her husband closely.

---

① talisman: an object believed to bring good luck or to keep its owner safe from harm

" A trifle," said he, colouring slightly. " He didn't want it, but I made him take it. And he pressed me again to throw it away."

" Likely," said Herbert, with pretended horror. " Why, we're going to be rich, and famous, and happy. Wish to be an emperor, father, to begin with; then you can't be henpecked."

He darted round the table, pursued by the maligned Mrs. White armed with an antimacassar.①

Mr. White took the paw from his pocket and eyed it dubiously. " I don't know what to wish for, and that's a fact," he said slowly. " It seems to me I've got all I want."

" If you only cleared the house, you'd be quite happy, wouldn't you?" said Herbert, with his hand on his shoulder. " Well, wish for two hundred pounds, then; that'll just do it."

His father, smiling shamefacedly at his own credulity, held up the talisman, as his son, with a solemn face somewhat marred by a wink at his mother, sat down at the piano and struck a few impressive chords.

" I wish for two hundred pounds," said the old man distinctly.

A fine crash from the piano greeted the words, interrupted by a shuddering cry from the old man. His wife and son ran toward him.

" It moved," he cried, with a glance of disgust at the object as it lay on the floor. " As I wished it twisted in my hands like a snake."

" Well, I don't see the money," said his son, as he picked it up and placed it on the table, " and I bet I never shall."

" It must have been your fancy, father," said his wife, regarding him anxiously.

He shook his head. " Never mind, though; there's no harm done, but it gave me a shock all the same."

---

① antimacassar: a cloth, used mainly in the past, for putting over the back of a chair in order to keep it clean or to decorate it

They sat down by the fire again while the two men finished their pipes. Outside, the wind was higher than ever, and the old man started nervously at the sound of a door banging upstairs. A silence unusual and depressing settled upon all three, which lasted until the old couple rose to retire for the night.

" I expect you'll find the cash tied up in a big bag in the middle of your bed," said Herbert, as he bade them good-night, " and something horrible squatting up on top of the wardrobe watching you as you pocket your ill-gotten gains."

He sat alone in the darkness, gazing at the dying fire, and seeing faces in it. The last face was so horrible and so simian that he gazed at it in amazement. It got so vivid that, with a little uneasy laugh, he felt on the table for a glass containing a little water to throw over it. His hand grasped the monkey's paw, and with a little shiver he wiped his hand on his coat and went up to bed.

II

In the brightness of the wintry sun next morning as it streamed over the breakfast table Herbert laughed at his fears. There was an air of prosaic wholesomeness about the room which it had lacked on the previous night, and the dirty, shrivelled little paw was pitched on the sideboard with a carelessness which betokened no great belief in its virtues.

" I suppose all old soldiers are the same," said Mrs White. " The idea of our listening to such nonsense! How could wishes be granted in these days? And if they could, how could two hundred pounds hurt you, father?"

" Might drop on his head from the sky," said the frivolous Herbert.

" Morris said the things happened so naturally," said his father, " that you might if you so wished attribute it to coincidence."

" Well, don't break into the money before I come back," said Herbert, as he rose from the table. " I'm afraid it'll turn you into a mean, avaricious[1] man, and we shall have to disown you."

His mother laughed, and following him to the door, watched him down the road, and returning to the breakfast table, was very happy at the expense of her husband's credulity.[2] All of which did not prevent her from scurrying to the door at the postman's knock, nor prevent her from referring somewhat shortly to retired sergeant-majors of bibulous habits when she found that the post brought a tailor's bill.

" Herbert will have some more of his funny remarks, I expect, when he comes home," she said, as they sat at dinner.

" I dare say," said Mr. White, pouring himself out some beer; " but for all that, the thing moved in my hand; that I'll swear to."

" You thought it did," said the old lady soothingly.

" I say it did," replied the other. " There was no thought about it; I had just — What's the matter?"

His wife made no reply. She was watching the mysterious movements of a man outside, who, peering in an undecided fashion at the house, appeared to be trying to make up his mind to enter. In mental connection with the two hundred pounds, she noticed that the stranger was well dressed and wore a silk hat of glossy newness. Three times he paused at the gate, and then walked on again. The fourth time he stood with his hand upon it, and then with sudden resolution flung it open and walked up the path. Mrs. White at the same moment placed her hands behind her, and hurriedly unfastening the strings of her apron, put that useful article of apparel[3] beneath the cushion of her chair.

She brought the stranger, who seemed ill at ease, into the room. He gazed at her

① avaricious: greedy

② credulity: willingness to believe that something is real or true

③ apparel: clothes of a particular type when they are being sold in a shop furtively, and listened in a preoccupied fashion as the old lady apologized for the appearance of the room, and her husband's coat, a garment which he usually reserved for the garden. She then waited as patiently as her sex would permit, for him to broach① his business, but he was at first strangely silent.

" I — was asked to call," he said at last, and stooped and picked a piece of cotton from his trousers. " I come from Maw and Meggins."

The old lady started. " Is anything the matter?" she asked breathlessly. " Has anything happened to Herbert? What is it? What is it?"

Her husband interposed. " There, there, mother," he said hastily. " Sit down, and don't jump to conclusions. You've not brought bad news, I'm sure, sir" and he eyed the other wistfully.

" I'm sorry — " began the visitor.

" Is he hurt?" demanded the mother.

The visitor bowed in assent. " Badly hurt," he said quietly, " but he is not in any pain."

" Oh, thank God!" said the old woman, clasping her hands. " Thank God for that! Thank — "

She broke off suddenly as the sinister meaning of the assurance dawned upon her and she saw the awful confirmation of her fears in the other's averted face. She caught her breath, and turning to her slower-witted husband, laid her trembling old hand upon his. There was a long silence.

" He was caught in the machinery," said the visitor at length, in a low voice.

" Caught in the machinery," repeated Mr. White, in a dazed fashion, " yes."

He sat staring blankly out at the window, and taking his wife's hand between his own, pressed it as he had been wont to do in their old courting days nearly forty years before.

---

① broach: to begin a discussion of something difficult

" He was the only one left to us," he said, turning gently to the visitor. " It is hard."

The other coughed, and rising, walked slowly to the window. " The firm wished me to convey their sincere sympathy with you in your great loss," he said, without looking round. " I beg that you will understand I am only their servant and merely obeying orders."

There was no reply; the old woman's face was white, her eyes staring, and her breath inaudible; on the husband's face was a look such as his friend the sergeant might have carried into his first action.

" I was to say that Maw and Meggins disclaim all responsibility," continued the other. " They admit no liability at all, but in consideration of your son's services they wish to present you with a certain sum as compensation."

Mr. White dropped his wife's hand, and rising to his feet, gazed with a look of horror at his visitor. His dry lips shaped the words, " How much?"

" Two hundred pounds," was the answer.

Unconscious of his wife's shriek, the old man smiled faintly, put out his hands like a sightless man, and dropped, a senseless heap, to the floor.

III

In the huge new cemetery, some two miles distant, the old people buried their dead, and came back to a house steeped in shadow and silence. It was all over so quickly that at first they could hardly realize it, and remained in a state of expectation as though of something else to happen — something else which was to lighten this load, too heavy for old hearts to bear.

But the days passed, and expectation gave place to resignation — the hopeless resignation of the old, sometimes miscalled, apathy. Sometimes they hardly exchanged a word, for now they had nothing to talk about, and their days were long to weariness.

It was about a week after that that the old man, waking suddenly in the night, stretched out his hand and found himself alone. The room was in darkness, and the sound of subdued weeping came from the window. He raised himself in bed and listened.

" Come back," he said tenderly. " You will be cold."

" It is colder for my son," said the old woman, and wept afresh.

The sound of her sobs died away on his ears. The bed was warm, and his eyes heavy with sleep. He dozed fitfully, and then slept until a sudden wild cry from his wife awoke him with a start.

" The paw!" she cried wildly. " The monkey's paw!"

He started up in alarm. " Where? Where is it? What's the matter?"

She came stumbling across the room toward him. " I want it," she said quietly. " You've not destroyed it?"

" It's in the parlour, on the bracket," he replied, marvelling. " Why?"

She cried and laughed together, and bending over, kissed his cheek.

" I only just thought of it," she said hysterically. " Why didn't I think of it before? Why didn't you think of it?"

" Think of what?" he questioned.

" The other two wishes," she replied rapidly. " We've only had one."

" Was not that enough?" he demanded fiercely.

" No," she cried, triumphantly; " we'll have one more. Go down and get it quickly, and wish our boy alive again."

The man sat up in bed and flung the bedclothes from his quaking limbs. " Good God, you are mad!" he cried aghast.

" Get it," she panted; " get it quickly, and wish — Oh, my boy, my boy!"

Her husband struck a match and lit the candle. " Get back to bed," he said, unsteadily. " You don't know what you are saying."

" We had the first wish granted," said the old woman, feverishly[①] ; " why not the second."

" A coincidence," stammered the old man.

" Go and get it and wish," cried the old woman, quivering with excitement.

The old man turned and regarded her, and his voice shook. " He has been dead ten days, and besides he — I — would not tell you else, but — I could only recognize him by his clothing. If he was too terrible for you to see then, how now?"

" Bring him back," cried the old woman, and dragged him toward the door. " Do you think I fear the child I have nursed?"

He went down in the darkness, and felt his way to the parlour, and then to the mantelpiece. The talisman was in its place, and a horrible fear that the unspoken wish might bring his mutilated son before him ere[②] he could escape from the room seized upon him, and he caught his breath as he found that he had lost the direction of the door. His brow cold with sweat, he felt his way round the table, and groped along the wall until he found himself in the small passage with the unwholesome thing in his hand.

Even his wife's face seemed changed as he entered the room. It was white and expectant, and to his fears seemed to have an unnatural look upon it. He was afraid of her.

" Wish!" she cried, in a strong voice.

" It is foolish and wicked," he faltered.

" Wish!" repeated his wife.

He raised his hand. " I wish my son alive again."

The talisman fell to the floor, and he regarded it fearfully. Then he sank trembling into a chair as the old woman, with burning eyes, walked to the window and raised the blind.

---

① feverishly: unnaturally excited or active

② ere (literary or old use): before, after and already

He sat until he was chilled with the cold, glancing occasionally at the figure of the old woman peering through the window. The candle end, which had burnt below the rim of the china candlestick, was throwing pulsating shadows on the ceiling and walls, until, with a flicker larger than the rest, it expired. The old man, with an unspeakable sense of relief at the failure of the talisman, crept back to his bed, and a minute or two afterward the old woman came silently and apathetically beside him.

Neither spoke, but both lay silently listening to the ticking of the clock. A stair creaked, and a squeaky mouse scurried noisily through the wall. The darkness was oppressive, and after lying for some time screwing up his courage, the husband took the box of matches, and striking one, went downstairs for a candle.

At the foot of the stairs the match went out, and he paused to strike another, and at the same moment a knock, so quiet and stealthy as to be scarcely audible, sounded on the front door.

The matches fell from his hand. He stood motionless, his breath suspended until the knock was repeated. Then he turned and fled swiftly back to his room, and closed the door behind him. A third knock sounded through the house.

" What's that?" cried the old woman, starting up.

" A rat," said the old man, in shaking tones — " a rat. It passed me on the stairs."

His wife sat up in bed listening. A loud knock resounded through the house.

" It's Herbert!" she screamed. " It's Herbert!"

She ran to the door, but her husband was before her, and catching her by the arm, held her tightly.

" What are you going to do?" he whispered hoarsely.

" It's my boy; it's Herbert!" she cried, struggling mechanically. " I forgot it was two miles away. What are you holding me for? Let go. I must open the door."

" For God's sake, don't let it in," cried the old man trembling.

" You're afraid of your own son," she cried, struggling. " Let me go. I'm coming, Herbert; I'm coming."

There was another knock, and another. The old woman with a sudden wrench broke free and ran from the room. Her husband followed to the landing, and called after her appealingly as she hurried downstairs. He heard the chain rattle back and the bottom bolt drawn slowly and stiffly from the socket. Then the old woman's voice, strained and panting.

" The bolt," she cried loudly. " Come down. I can't reach it."

But her husband was on his hands and knees groping wildly on the floor in search of the paw. If he could only find it before the thing outside got in. A perfect fusillade① of knocks reverberated through the house, and he heard the scraping of a chair as his wife put it down in the passage against the door. He heard the creaking of the bolt as it came slowly back, and at the same moment he found the monkey's paw, and frantically② breathed his third and last wish.

The knocking ceased suddenly, although the echoes of it were still in the house. He heard the chair drawn back and the door opened. A cold wind rushed up the staircase, and a long loud wail of disappointment and misery from his wife gave him courage to run down to her side, and then to the gate beyond. The street lamp flickering opposite shone on a quiet and deserted road.

Topics for discussion

1. What do you think of the narrative structure in " The Monkey's Paw"?

2. Discuss the foreshadowing in Jacobs's " The Monkey's Paw" with your classmates.

3. How did the Industrial Revolution affect families like Whites in Jacobs' story?

---

① fusillade: a large number of bullets fired at the same time or one after another very quickly

② frantically: done in a hurried way and in a state of excitement or confusion

References for further reading

[1] Cloy, John D. *Pensive jester: the literary career of W.W. Jacobs*. Lanham, Md. : University Press of America, 1996.

[2] Donaldson, " W.W. Jacobs", in E.F. Bleider. Ed. *Supernatural Fiction Writers*. New York: Scribner's, 1985.

Rudyard Kipling (1865 — 1936)

Mrs. Bathurst

Introduction to the author

Joseph Rudyard Kipling (December 30, 1865 — January 18, 1936) was an English author of short-story, poem, novel, literature for children, travel literature and science fiction novels, chiefly remembered for his tales and poems of British soldiers in India and his tales for children. Kipling is best known for his works of fiction, including *The Jungle Book, Just So Stories*, *Kim* and many short stories. Kipling is regarded as a major innovator in the art of the short story. Kipling was the recipient of many honorary degrees and other awards. In 1907, he was awarded the Nobel Prize in Literature, making him the first English-language writer to receive the prize. Kipling is also remembered for his British Poet Laureateship. In 1926, he received the Gold Medal of the Royal Society of Literature, an honor which only Scott, Meredith, and Hardy had been awarded before him.

Rudyard Kipling was born on December 30, 1865 in Bombay, British India, to Alice and Lockwood Kipling. His father was a sculptor and pottery designer and once served as the Principal and Professor of Architectural Sculpture at Sir Jamsetjee Jeejebhoy School of Art in Bombay. Among his famous relatives, the most eminent was his first cousin, Stanley Baldwin. Baldwin was Conservative Prime Minister of the U.K three times in the 1920s and 1930s. when he was five years old, Kipling was taken to England for education. In January 1878, Kipling was admitted to the United Services College at Westward Ho, Devon, a school to prepare boys for the British Army. In 1882, he returned to India and worked for two Anglo-Indian newspapers, the *Civil and Military Gazette* and the *Pioneer*. His literary career started with *Departmental Ditties* (1886), but subsequently he became chiefly known as a writer of short stories. As a prolific writer, he produced a great number of short stories, sketches, poems and four novels.

In 1892, Kipling married Carrie Balestier in London. At the wedding, Henry James gave the bride away. The couple first lived in Vermont, America. Then, they returned to England in 1896. during the Boer War between 1899 to 1902, Kipling visited South Africa several times. Due to the trips, Kipling became familiar with the life and people in South Africa and South African culture provides important features for his writings such as " Mrs. Bathurst". On the night of January 12, 1936, Kipling suffered a haemorrhage in his small intestine. He was given a surgery, but died of a perforated duodenal ulcer soon on January 18, 1936, aged 70. Kipling's cremated ashes were buried in Poets' Corner, Westminster Abbey, next to the graves of Charles Dickens and Thomas Hardy.

Major works by Rudyard Kipling

Collections of short stories

Plain Tales from the Hills, 1888

In Black and White, 1888

The Story of the Gadsbys, 1888

Wee Willie Winkie and Other Child Stories, 1888

From Sea to Sea and Other Sketches, Letters of Travel, 1889

The Light that Failed, 1891

Jungle Books, 1894

The Second Jungle Book, 1895

Stalky & Co.,1899

Just So Stories for Little Children, 1902

With the Night Mail,1905

Puck of Pook's Hill, 1906

Puck of Pook's Hill, 1906

Rewards and Fairies, 1910

As Easy As A. B. C, 1912

Poetry

Barrack-Room Ballads, 1892

Non-fiction

The Fringes of the Fleet, 1915

Appreciation

The story takes place in Glengariff, South Africa, after the Boer War. It is about the tragic story of Mrs. Bathurst, a hotel owner in New Zealand, and her lover, Mr. Vickery. It is suggested that Mr. Vickery deserted the navy because of the hotel owner, Mrs. Bathurst, a widow. She was very generous and courageous, and she often let soldiers rent rooms on credit. The main part of the story relates to Pyecroft's recent encounter with Vickery. Vickery asked him to see a movie again and again and pay special attention to the portion of " Home an' Friends", which contains a scene about Mrs. Bathurst. Vickery urged Pyecroft to return to the theatre for five nights, which made him fear for his safety, because he was afraid that Vickery would become violent when the cinema left town and he could no long access to the stimulant of seeing Mrs. Bathurst on film. Then, after Pyecroft's account, Hooper speaks up to tell that a month ago he discovered two tramps who had been living in the forest and they had been killed by lightening. One of the two men had false teeth and tattoos on his arms and chest, including the letters " M.V.". The death of Mr. Vickery made Pyecroft relieved finally.

" Mrs. Bathurst" is one of Kipling's most popular short stories. The story was positively received by the readers. Its use of the dialect, the complex structure, and the images of the sea, South African culture and nautical life are typical aspects of Kipling's fiction works.

Selected Reading

Mrs. Bathurst

The day that I chose to visit H.M.S. _Peridot_ in Simon's Bay was the day that the Admiral had chosen to send her up the coast. She was just steaming out to sea as my train came in, and since the rest of the Fleet were either coaling or busy at the rifle-ranges a thousand feet up the hill, I found myself stranded①, lunchless, on the sea-front with no hope of return to Cape Town before five P.M. At this crisis I had the luck to come across my friend Inspector Hooper, Cape Government Railways, in command of an engine and a brake-van chalked② for repair.

" If you get something to eat," he said, " I'll run you down to Glengariff siding till the goods comes along. It's cooler there than here, you see."

I got food and drink from the Greeks who sell all things at a price, and the engine trotted③ us a couple of miles up the line to a bay of drifted sand and a plank-platform half buried in sand not a hundred yards from the edge of the surf. Moulded dunes④,

① strand: (usually used in the passive) to bring into or leave in a helpless position

② chalk: to mark or write with chalk

③ trot: to go at a quick, steady pace; move briskly; bustle; hurry

④ dune: a sand hill or sand ridge formed by the wind, usually in desert regions ornear lakes and o ceans whiter than any snow, rolled far inland up a brown and purple valley of splintered[①] rocks and dry scrub[②] . A crowd of Malays hauled at a net beside two blue and green boats on the beach; a picnic party danced and shouted barefoot where a tiny river trickled across the flat, and a circle of dry hills, whose feet were set in sands of silver, locked us in against a seven-coloured sea. At either horn of the bay the railway line, cut just above high water-mark, ran round a shoulder of piled rocks, and disappeared.

" You see there's always a breeze here," said Hooper, opening the door as the engine left us in the siding on the sand, and the strong south-easter buffeting under Elsie's Peak dusted sand into our tickey beer. Presently he sat down to a file full of spiked documents. He had returned from a long trip up-country, where he had been reporting on damaged rolling- stock, as far away as Rhodesia. The weight of the bland wind on my eyelids; the song of it under the car roof, and high up among the rocks; the drift of fine grains chasing each other musically ashore; the tramp of the surf; the voices of the picnickers; the rustle of Hooper's file, and the presence of the assured sun, joined with the beer to cast me into magical slumber. The hills of False Bay were just dissolving into those of fairyland when I heard footsteps on the sand outside, and the clink of our couplings.

" Stop that!" snapped Hooper, without raising his head from his work. " It's those dirty little Malay boys, you see: they're always playing with the trucks...."

" Don't be hard on 'em. The railway's a general refuge in Africa," I replied.

" 'Tis — up-country at any rate. That reminds me," he felt in his waistcoat-pocket, " I've got a curiosity for you from Wankies — beyond Buluwayo. It's more of a souvenir perhaps than — "

" The old hotel's inhabited," cried a voice. " White men from the language. Marines to the front! Come on, Pritch. Here's your Belmont. Wha — i — i!"

---

① splinter: to split or break into a small sharp broken piece of wood, glass, plastic or similarmate rial

② scrub: scrub consists of low trees and bushes, especially in an area that has very little rain

The last word dragged like a rope as Mr. Pyecroft ran round to the open door, and stood looking up into my face. Behind him an enormous Sergeant of Marines trailed a stalk of dried seaweed, and dusted the sand nervously from his fingers.

" What are you doing here?" I asked. " I thought the _Hierophant_ was down the coast?"

" We came in last Tuesday — from Tristan D'Acunha — for overhaul, and we shall be in dockyard hands for two months, with boiler-seatings."

" Come and sit down," Hooper put away the file.

" This is Mr. Hooper of the Railway," I exclaimed, as Pyecroft turned to haul up the black-moustached sergeant.

" This is Sergeant Pritchard, of the _Agaric_, an old shipmate," said he. " We were strollin' on the beach." The monster blushed and nodded. He filled up one side of the van when he sat down.

" And this is my friend, Mr. Pyecroft," I added to Hooper, already busy with the extra beer which my prophetic soul had bought from the Greeks.

" _Moi aussi_" quoth Pyecroft, and drew out beneath his coat a labelled quart bottle.

" Why, it's Bass," cried Hooper.

" It was Pritchard," said Pyecroft. " They can't resist him."

" That's not so," said Pritchard, mildly.

" Not _verbatim① _ per'aps, but the look in the eye came to the same thing."

" Where was it?" I demanded.

" Just on beyond here — at Kalk Bay. She was slappin' a rug in a back verandah② . Pritch hadn't more than brought his batteries to bear, before she stepped

① verbatim: in exactly the same words; word for word

② verandah: also veranda, a large, open porch, usually roofed and partly enclosed, as by a railing, often extending across the front and sides of a house; gallery. (Chiefly South Midland and Southern U.S.)

indoors an' sent it flyin' over the wall."

Pyecroft patted the warm bottle.

" It was all a mistake," said Pritchard. " I shouldn't wonder if she mistook me for Maclean. We're about of a size."

I had heard householders of Muizenburg, St. James's, and Kalk Bay complain of the difficulty of keeping beer or good servants at the seaside, and I began to see the reason. None the less, it was excellent Bass, and I too drank to the health of that large-minded① maid.

" It's the uniform that fetches 'em, an' they fetch it," said Pyecroft. " My simple navy blue is respectable, but not fascinatin'. Now Pritch in 'is Number One rig is always 'purr Mary, on the terrace' — _ex officio_ as you might say."

" She took me for Maclean, I tell you," Pritchard insisted. " Why — why — to listen to him you wouldn't think that only yesterday — "

" Pritch," said Pyecroft, " be warned in time. If we begin tellin' what we know about each other we'll be turned out of the pub. Not to mention aggravated desertion on several occasions — "

" Never anything more than absence without leaf — I defy you to prove it," said the Sergeant hotly. " An' if it comes to that how about Vancouver in' 87?"

" How about it? Who pulled bow in the gig going ashore? Who told Boy Niven...?"

" Surely you were court martialled for that?" I said. The story of Boy Niven who lured seven or eight able-bodied seamen and marines into the woods of British Columbia used to be a legend of the Fleet.

" Yes, we were court-martialled to rights," said Pritchard, " but we should have been tried for murder if Boy Niven ' adn't been unusually tough. He told us he had an uncle 'oo'd give us land to farm. 'E said he was born at the back o' Vancouver Island,

① large-minded: having tolerant views or liberal ideas; broad-minded and _all_ the time the beggar was a balmy Barnado Orphan!"

" _But_ we believed him," said Pyecroft. " I did — you did — Paterson did — an' 'oo was the Marine that married the cocoanut-woman afterwards — him with the mouth?"

" Oh, Jones, Spit-Kid Jones. I 'aven't thought of 'im in years," said Pritchard. " Yes, Spit-Kid believed it, an' George Anstey and Moon. We were very young an' very curious."

" _But_ lovin' an' trustful to a degree," said Pyecroft.

" Remember when 'e told us to walk in single file for fear o' bears? 'Remember, Pye, when 'e 'opped about in that bog full o' ferns an' sniffed an' said 'e could smell the smoke of 'is uncle's farm? An' _all_ the time it was a dirty little out-lyin' uninhabited island. We walked round it in a day, an' come back to our boat lyin' on the beach. A whole day Boy Niven kept us walkin' in circles lookin' for 'is uncle's farm! He said his uncle was compelled by the law of the land to give us a farm!"

" Don't get hot, Pritch. We believed," said Pyecroft.

" He'd been readin' books. He only did it to get a run ashore an' have himself talked of. A day an' a night — eight of us — followin' Boy Niven round an uninhabited island in the Vancouver archipelago① ! Then the picket came for us an' a nice pack o' idiots we looked!"

" What did you get for it?" Hooper asked.

" Heavy thunder with continuous lightning for two hours. Thereafter sleet-squalls, a confused sea, and cold, unfriendly weather till conclusion o' cruise," said Pyecroft. " It was only what we expected, but what we felt, an' I assure you, Mr. Hooper, even a sailor-man has a heart to break, was bein' told that we able seamen an' promisin' marines 'ad misled Boy Niven. Yes, we poor back-to-the-landers was supposed to 'ave misled him! He rounded on② us, o' course, an' got off easy."

---

① archipelago: a large group or chain of islands

② round on: to attack or reply to (someone) with sudden irritation or anger

" Excep' for what we gave him in the steerin'-flat when we came out o' cells. 'Eard anything of 'im lately, Pye?"

" Signal Boatswain in the Channel Fleet, I believe — Mr. L.L. Niven is."

" An' Anstey died o' fever in Benin," Pritchard mused. " What come to Moon? Spit-Kid we know about."

" Moon — Moon! Now where did I last...? Oh yes, when I was in the _ Palladium_! I met Quigley at Buncrana Station. He told me Moon 'ad run when the _Astrild_ sloop was cruising among the South Seas three years back. He always showed signs o' bein' a Mormonastic beggar. Yes, he slipped off quietly an' they 'adn't time to chase 'im round the islands even if the navigatin' officer 'ad been equal to the job."

" Wasn't he?" said Hooper.

" Not so. Accordin' to Quigley the _Astrild_ spent half her commission rompin' ① up the beach like a she-turtle, an' the other half hatching turtles' eggs on the top o' numerous reefs. When she was docked at Sydney her copper looked like Aunt Maria's washing on the line an' her 'midship frames was sprung. The commander swore the dockyard 'ad done it haulin' the pore thing on to the slips. They _do_ do strange things at sea, Mr. Hooper."

" Ah! I'm not a tax-payer," said Hooper, and opened a fresh bottle. The Sergeant seemed to be one who had a difficulty in dropping subjects.

" How it all comes back, don't it?" he said. " Why Moon must 'ave 'ad sixteen years' service before he ran."

" It takes 'em at all ages. Look at — you know," said Pyecroft.

" Who?" I asked.

" A service man within eighteen months of his pension, is the party you're thinkin' of," said Pritchard. " A warrant 'oose name begins with a V., isn't it?"

① romp: to run or go rapidly and without effort, as in racing

" But, in a way o' puttin' it, we can't say that he actually did desert," Pyecroft suggested.

" Oh, no," said Pritchard. " It was only permanent absence up country without leaf. That was all."

" Up country?" said Hooper. " Did they circulate his description?"

" What for?" said Pritchard, most impolitely.

" Because deserters are like columns in the war. They don't move away from the line, you see. I've known a chap caught at Salisbury that way tryin' to get to Nyassa. They tell me, but o' course I don't know, that they don't ask questions on the Nyassa Lake Flotilla up there. I've heard of a P. and O. quartermaster ① in full command of an armed launch there."

" Do you think Click 'ud ha' gone up that way?" Pritchard asked.

" There's no saying. He was sent up to Bloemfontein to take over some Navy ammunition left in the fort. We know he took it over and saw it into the trucks. Then there was no more Click--then or thereafter. Four months ago it transpired, and thus the _casus belli_ stands at present," said Pyecroft.

" What were his marks?" said Hooper again.

" Does the Railway get a reward for returnin' 'em, then?" said Pritchard.

" If I did d'you suppose I'd talk about it?" Hooper retorted angrily.

" You seemed so very interested," said Pritchard with equal crispness.

" Why was he called Click?" I asked to tide over an uneasy little break in the conversation. The two men were staring at each other very fixedly.

" Because of an ammunition hoist carryin' away," said Pyecroft. " And it carried away four of 'is teeth--on the lower port side, wasn't it, Pritch? The substitutes which he bought weren't screwed home in a manner o' sayin'. When he talked fast they used to lift a little on the bed plate. 'Ence, 'Click.' They called 'im a superior man

① quartermaster: an officer charged with providing quarters, clothing, fuel, transportation, etc. for a body of troops.

which is what we'd call a long, black-'aired, genteely speakin', 'alf-bred beggar on the lower deck."

" Four false teeth on the lower left jaw," said Hooper, his hand in his waistcoat pocket. " What tattoo marks?"

" Look here," began Pritchard, half rising. " I'm sure we're very grateful to you as a gentleman for your 'orspitality, but per'aps we may 'ave made an error in — "

I looked at Pyecroft for aid, Hooper was crimsoning rapidly.

" If the fat marine now occupying the foc'sle will kindly bring 'is _status quo_ to an anchor yet once more, we may be able to talk like gentlemen — not to say friends," said Pyecroft. " He regards you, Mr. Hooper, as a emissary of the Law."

" I only wish to observe that when a gentleman exhibits such a peculiar, or I should rather say, such a _bloomin'_ curiosity in identification marks as our friend here — "

" Mr. Pritchard," I interposed, " I'll take all the responsibility for Mr. Hooper."

" An' _you_'ll apologise all round," said Pyecroft. " You're a rude little man, Pritch."

" But how was I — " he began, wavering.

" I don't know an' I don't care. Apologise!"

The giant looked round bewildered and took our little hands into his vast grip, one by one. " I was wrong," he said meekly as a sheep. " My suspicions was unfounded. Mr. Hooper, I apologise."

" You did quite right to look out for your own end o' the line," said Hooper. " I'd ha' done the same with a gentleman I didn't know, you see. If you don't mind I'd like to hear a little more o' your Mr. Vickery. It's safe with me, you see."

" Why did Vickery run," I began, but Pyecroft's smile made me turn my question to " Who was she?"

" She kep' a little hotel at Hauraki — near Auckland," said Pyecroft.

" By Gawd!" roared Pritchard, slapping his hand on his leg. " Not Mrs.

Bathurst!"

Pyecroft nodded slowly, and the Sergeant called all the powers of darkness to witness his bewilderment.

" So far as I could get at it Mrs. B. was the lady in question."

" But Click was married," cried Pritchard.

" An' 'ad a fifteen year old daughter. 'E's shown me her photograph. Settin' that aside, so to say, 'ave you ever found these little things make much difference? Because I haven't."

" Good Lord Alive an' Watchin'!... Mrs. Bathurst...." Then with another roar: " You can say what you please, Pye, but you don't make me believe it was any of 'er fault. She wasn't _that!_"

" If I was going to say what I please, I'd begin by callin' you a silly ox an' work up to the higher pressures at leisure. I'm trying to say solely what transpired[①] . M'rover, for once you're right. It wasn't her fault."

" You couldn't 'aven't made me believe it if it 'ad been," was the answer.

Such faith in a Sergeant of Marines interested me greatly. " Never mind about that," I cried. " Tell me what she was like."

" She was a widow," said Pyecroft. " Left so very young and never re-spliced. She kep' a little hotel for warrants and non-coms close to Auckland, an' she always wore black silk, and 'er neck--"

" You ask what she was like," Pritchard broke in. " Let me give you an instance. I was at Auckland first in '97, at the end o' the _Marroquin's_ commission, an' as I'd been promoted I went up with the others. She used to look after us all, an' she never lost by it--not a penny! 'Pay me now,' she'd say, 'or settle later. I know you won't let me suffer. Send the money from home if you like,' Why, gentlemen all, I tell you I've seen that lady take her own gold watch an' chain off her neck in the bar an' pass it to

① transpire: to occur; happen; take place

a bosun 'oo'd come ashore without 'is ticker an' 'ad to catch the last boat. 'I don't know your name,' she said, 'but when you've done with it, you'll find plenty that know me on the front. Send it back by one o' them.' And it was worth thirty pounds if it was worth 'arf a crown. The little gold watch, Pye, with the blue monogram① at the back. But, as I was sayin', in those days she kep' a beer that agreed with me--Slits it was called. One way an' another I must 'ave punished a good few bottles of it while we was in the bay — comin' ashore every night or so. Chaffin across the bar like, once when we were alone, 'Mrs. B.,' I said, 'when next I call I want you to remember that this is my particular — just as you're my particular?' (She'd let you go _that_ far!) 'Just as you're my particular,' I said. 'Oh, thank you, Sergeant Pritchard,' she says, an' put 'er hand up to the curl be'ind 'er ear. Remember that way she had, Pye?"

" I think so," said the sailor.

" Yes, 'Thank you, Sergeant Pritchard,' she says. 'The least I can do is to mark it for you in case you change your mind. There's no great demand for it in the Fleet,' she says, 'but to make sure I'll put it at the back o' the shelf,' an' she snipped off a piece of her hair ribbon with that old dolphin cigar cutter on the bar — remember it, Pye? — an' she tied a bow round what was left — just four bottles. That was '97 — no, '96. In '98 I was in the _Resiliant_ — China station — full commission. In Nineteen One, mark you, I was in the _Carthusian_, back in Auckland Bay again. Of course I went up to Mrs. B.'s with the rest of us to see how things were goin'. They were the same as ever. (Remember the big tree on the pavement by the side-bar, Pye?) I never said anythin' in special (there was too many of us talkin' to her), but she saw me at once."

" That wasn't difficult?" I ventured.

" Ah, but wait. I was comin' up to the bar, when, 'Ada,' she says to her niece, 'get me Sergeant Pritchard's particular,' and, gentlemen all, I tell you before I could

① monogram: a symbol, usually formed from the first letters of a person's names joined together, which is sewn or printed on clothes or other possessions shake 'ands with the lady, there were those four bottles o' Slits, with 'er 'air ribbon in a bow round each o' their necks, set down in front o' me, an' as she drew the cork she looked at me under her eyebrows in that blindish way she had o' lookin', an', 'Sergeant Pritchard,' she says, 'I do 'ope you 'aven't changed your mind about your particulars.' That's the kind o' woman she was — after five years!"

" I don't _see_ her yet somehow," said Hooper, but with sympathy.

" She — she never scrupled to feed a lame duck or set 'er foot on a scorpion① at any time of 'er life," Pritchard added valiantly.

" That don't help me either. My mother's like that for one."

The giant heaved inside his uniform and rolled his eyes at the car-roof. Said Pyecroft suddenly: —

" How many women have you been intimate with all over the world, Pritch?"

Pritchard blushed plum colour to the short hairs of his seventeen-inch neck.

" 'Undreds," said Pyecroft. " So've I. How many of 'em can you remember in your own mind, settin' aside the first — an' per'aps the last — _and one more_?"

" Few, wonderful few, now I tax myself," said Sergeant Pritchard, relievedly.

" An' how many times might you 'ave been at Aukland?"

" One — two," he began. " Why, I can't make it more than three times in ten years. But I can remember every time that I ever saw Mrs. B."

" So can I — an' I've only been to Auckland twice--how she stood an' what she was sayin' an' what she looked like. That's the secret. 'Tisn't beauty, so to speak, nor good talk necessarily. It's just It. Some women'll stay in a man's memory if they once walked down a street, but most of 'em you can live with a month on end, an' next commission you'd be put to it to certify whether they talked in their sleep or not, as one might say."

" Ah," said Hooper. " That's more the idea. I've known just two women of that

① scorpion: any of various harmless lizards, especially the red–or orange–headed males of certain Nort American skinks.

nature."

" An' it was no fault o' theirs?" asked Pritchard.

" None whatever. I know that!"

" An' if a man gets struck with that kind o' woman, Mr. Hooper?" Pritchard went on.

" He goes crazy — or just saves himself," was the slow answer.

" You've hit it," said the Sergeant. " You've seen an' known somethin' in the course o' your life, Mr. Hooper. I'm lookin' at you!" He set down his bottle.

" And how often had Vickery seen her?" I asked.

" That's the dark an' bloody mystery," Pyecroft answered. " I'd never come across him till I come out in the _Hierophant_ just now, an' there wasn't any one in the ship who knew much about him. You see, he was what you call a superior man. 'E spoke to me once or twice about Auckland and Mrs. B. on the voyage out. I called that to mind subsequently. There must 'ave been a good deal between 'em, to my way o' thinkin'. Mind you I'm only giving you my _sum_ of it all, because all I know is second-hand so to speak, or rather I should say more than second-'and."

" How?" said Hooper peremptorily①. " You must have seen it or heard it."

" Yes," said Pyecroft. " I used to think seein' and hearin' was the only regulation aids to ascertainin' facts, but as we get older we get more accommodatin'. The cylinders work easier, I suppose.... Were you in Cape Town last December when Phyllis's Circus came?"

" No — up country," said Hooper, a little nettled at the change of venue.

" I ask because they had a new turn of a scientific nature called 'Home and Friends for a Tickey.' "

" Oh, you mean the cinematograph — the pictures of prize-fights and steamers.

① peremptorily: leaving no opportunity for denial or refusal; imperative

I've seen 'em up country."

" Biograph or cinematograph was what I was alludin' to. London Bridge with the omnibuses — a troopship goin' to the war — marines on parade at Portsmouth an' the Plymouth Express arrivin' at Paddin'ton."

" Seen 'em all. Seen 'em all," said Hooper impatiently.

" We _Hierophants_ came in just before Christmas week an' leaf was easy."

" I think a man gets fed up with Cape Town quicker than anywhere else on the station. Why, even Durban's more like Nature. We was there for Christmas," Pritchard put in.

" Not bein' a devotee of Indian _peeris_, as our Doctor said to the Pusser, I can't exactly say. Phyllis's was good enough after musketry practice at Mozambique. I couldn't get off the first two or three nights on account of what you might call an imbroglio with our Torpedo Lieutenant in the submerged flat, where some pride of the West country had sugared up a gyroscope; but I remember Vickery went ashore with our Carpenter Rigdon — old Crocus we called him. As a general rule Crocus never left 'is ship unless an' until he was 'oisted out with a winch, but _when_ 'e went 'e would return noddin' like a lily gemmed with dew. We smothered him down below that night, but the things 'e said about Vickery as a fittin' playmate for a Warrant Officer of 'is cubic capacity, before we got him quiet, was what I should call pointed."

" I've been with Crocus--in the _Redoubtable_," said the Sergeant. " He's a character if there is one."

" Next night I went into Cape Town with Dawson and Pratt; but just at the door of the Circus I came across Vickery. 'Oh!' he says, 'you're the man I'm looking for. Come and sit next me. This way to the shillin' places!' I went astern at once, protestin' because tickey seats better suited my so-called finances. 'Come on,' says Vickery, 'I'm payin'.' Naturally I abandoned Pratt and Dawson in anticipation o' drinks to match the seats. 'No,' he says, when this was 'inted — 'not now. Not now.

As many as you please afterwards, but I want you sober for the occasion.' I caught 'is face under a lamp just then, an' the appearance of it quite cured me of my thirsts. Don't mistake. It didn't frighten me. It made me anxious. I can't tell you what it was like, but that was the effect which it 'ad on me. If you want to know, it reminded me of those things in bottles in those herbalistic shops at Plymouth — preserved in spirits of wine. White an' crumply things — previous to birth as you might say."

" You 'ave a beastial mind, Pye," said the Sergeant, relighting his pipe.

" Perhaps. We were in the front row, an' 'Home an' Friends' came on early. Vickery touched me on the knee when the number went up. 'If you see anything that strikes you,' he says, 'drop me a hint'; then he went on clicking. We saw London Bridge an' so forth an' so on, an' it was most interestin'. I'd never seen it before. You 'eard a little dynamo like buzzin', but the pictures were the real thing — alive an' movin'."

" I've seen 'em," said Hooper. " Of course they are taken from the very thing itself — you see."

" Then the Western Mail came in to Paddin'ton on the big magic lantern sheet. First we saw the platform empty an' the porters standin' by. Then the engine come in, head on, an' the women in the front row jumped: she headed so straight. Then the doors opened and the passengers came out and the porters got the luggage — just like life. Only--only when any one came down too far towards us that was watchin', they walked right out o' the picture, so to speak. I was 'ighly interested, I can tell you. So were all of us. I watched an old man with a rug 'oo'd dropped a book an' was tryin' to pick it up, when quite slowly, from be'ind two porters — carryin' a little reticule an' lookin' from side to side--comes out Mrs. Bathurst. There was no mistakin' the walk in a hundred thousand. She come forward — right forward — she looked out straight at us with that blindish look which Pritch alluded to. She walked on and on till she melted out of the picture — like — like a shadow jumpin' over a candle, an' as she went I 'eard Dawson in the ticky seats be'ind sing out: 'Christ! There's Mrs.

B.!' "

Hooper swallowed his spittle and leaned forward intently.

" Vickery touched me on the knee again. He was clickin' his four false teeth with his jaw down like an enteric at the last kick. 'Are you sure?' says he. 'Sure,' I says, 'didn't you 'ear Dawson give tongue? Why, it's the woman herself.' 'I was sure before,' he says, 'but I brought you to make sure. Will you come again with me to-morrow?' "

" 'Willingly,' I says, 'it's like meetin' old friends.' "

" 'Yes,' he says, openin' his watch, 'very like. It will be four-and-twenty hours less four minutes before I see her again. Come and have a drink,' he says. 'It may amuse you, but it's no sort of earthly use to me.' He went out shaking his head an' stumblin' over people's feet as if he was drunk already. I anticipated a swift drink an' a speedy return, because I wanted to see the performin' elephants. Instead o' which Vickery began to navigate the town at the rate o' knots[①], lookin' in at a bar every three minutes approximate Greenwich time. I'm not a drinkin' man, though there are those present" — he cocked his unforgetable eye at me — " who may have seen me more or less imbued with the fragrant spirit. None the less, when I drink I like to do it at anchor an' not at an average speed of eighteen knots on the measured mile. There's a tank as you might say at the back o' that big hotel up the hill — what do they call it?"

" The Molteno Reservoir," I suggested, and Hooper nodded.

" That was his limit o' drift. We walked there an' we come down through the Gardens — there was a South-Easter blowin' — an' we finished up by the Docks. Then we bore up the road to Salt River, and wherever there was a pub Vickery put in sweatin'. He didn't look at what he drunk — he didn't look at the change. He walked an' he drunk an' he perspired in rivers. I understood why old Crocus 'ad come back

---

① at the rate o' knots: if someone does something at a rate of knots, they do it very quickly in the condition 'e did, because Vickery an' I 'ad two an' a half hours o' this gipsy manoeuvre an' when we got back to the station there wasn't a dry atom on or in me."

" Did he say anything?" Pritchard asked.

" The sum total of 'is conversation from 7.45 P.M. till 11.15 P.M. was 'Let's have another.' Thus the mornin' an' the evenin' were the first day, as Scripture says.... To abbreviate a lengthy narrative, I went into Cape Town for five consecutive nights with Master Vickery, and in that time I must 'ave logged about fifty knots over the ground an' taken in two gallon o' all the worst spirits south the Equator. The evolution never varied. Two shilling seats for us two; five minutes o' the pictures, an' perhaps forty-five seconds o' Mrs. B. walking down towards us with that blindish look in her eyes an' the reticule[①] in her hand. Then out walk — and drink till train time."

" What did you think?" said Hooper, his hand fingering his waistcoat pocket.

" Several things," said Pyecroft. " To tell you the truth, I aren't quite done thinkin' about it yet. Mad? The man was a dumb lunatic — must 'ave been for months — years p'raps. I know somethin' o' maniacs, as every man in the Service must. I've been shipmates with a mad skipper — an' a lunatic Number One, but never both together I thank 'Eaven. I could give you the names o' three captains now 'oo ought to be in an asylum, but you don't find me interferin' with the mentally afflicted till they begin to lay about 'em with rammers an' winch-handles. Only once I crept up a little into the wind towards Master Vickery. 'I wonder what she's doin' in England,' I says. 'Don't it seem to you she's lookin' for somebody?' That was in the Gardens again, with the South-Easter blowin' as we were makin' our desperate round. 'She's lookin' for me,' he says, stoppin' dead under a lamp an' clickin'. When he wasn't drinkin', in which case all 'is teeth clicked on the glass, 'e was clickin' 'is four false teeth like a Marconi ticker. 'Yes! lookin' for me,' he said, an' he went on

① reticule: A drawstring handbag or purse

very softly an' as you might say affectionately. '_But?_ he went on, 'in future, Mr. Pyecroft, I should take it kindly of you if you'd confine your remarks to the drinks set before you. Otherwise,' he says, 'with the best will in the world towards you, I may find myself guilty of murder! Do you understand?' he says. 'Perfectly,' I says, 'but would it at all soothe you to know that in such a case the chances o' your being killed are precisely equivalent to the chances o' me being outed.' 'Why, no,' he says, 'I'm almost afraid that 'ud be a temptation."

" Then I said — we was right under the lamp by that arch at the end o' the Gardens where the trams came round — 'Assumin' murder was done — or attempted murder — I put it to you that you would still be left so badly crippled, as one might say, that your subsequent capture by the police — to 'oom you would 'ave to explain — would be largely inevitable.' 'That's better,' 'e says, passin' 'is hands over his forehead. 'That's much better, because,' he says, 'do you know, as I am now, Pye, I'm not so sure if I could explain anything much.' Those were the only particular words I had with 'im in our walks as I remember."

" What walks!" said Hooper. " Oh my soul, what walks!"

" They were chronic," said Pyecroft gravely, " but I didn't anticipate any danger till the Circus left. Then I anticipated that, bein' deprived of 'is stimulant, he might react on me, so to say, with a hatchet. Consequently, after the final performance an' the ensuin' wet walk, I kep' myself aloof from my superior officer on board in the execution of 'is duty as you might put it. Consequently, I was interested when the sentry informs me while I was passin' on my lawful occasions that Click had asked to see the captain. As a general rule warrant officers don't dissipate much of the owner's time, but Click put in an hour and more be'ind that door. My duties kep' me within eyeshot of it. Vickery came out first, an' 'e actually nodded at me an' smiled. This knocked me out o' the boat, because, havin' seen 'is face for five consecutive nights, I didn't anticipate any change there more than a condenser in hell, so to speak. The owner emerged later. His face didn't read off at all, so I fell back on his cox, 'oo'd been eight years with him and knew him better than boat signals. Lamson — that was the cox's name — crossed 'is bows once or twice at low speeds an' dropped down to me visibly concerned. 'He's shipped 'is court-martial face,' says Lamson. 'Some one's goin' to be 'ung. I've never seen that look but once before when they chucked the gun-sights overboard in the _Fantastic_.' Throwin' gun-sights overboard, Mr. Hooper, is the equivalent for mutiny in these degenerate days. It's done to attract the notice of the authorities an' the _Western Mornin' News_ — generally by a stoker. Naturally, word went round the lower deck an' we had a private over'aul of our little consciences. But, barrin' a shirt which a second- class stoker said 'ad walked into 'is bag from the marines flat by itself, nothin' vital transpired. The owner went about flyin' the signal for 'attend public execution,' so to say, but there was no corpse at the yardarm. 'E lunched on the beach an' 'e returned with 'is regulation harbour-routine face about 3 P. M. Thus Lamson lost prestige for raising false alarms. The only person 'oo might 'ave connected the epicycloidal gears correctly was one Pyecroft, when he was told that Mr. Vickery would go up country that same evening to take over certain naval ammunition left after the war in Bloemfontein Fort. No details was ordered to accompany Master Vickery. He was told off first person singular — as a unit — by himself."

The marine whistled penetratingly.

" That's what I thought," said Pyecroft. " I went ashore with him in the cutter an' 'e asked me to walk through the station. He was clickin' audibly, but otherwise seemed happy-ish.

" 'You might like to know,' he says, stoppin' just opposite the Admiral's front gate, 'that Phyllis's Circus will be performin' at Worcester to-morrow night. So I shall see 'er yet once again. You've been very patient with me,' he says."

" 'Look here, Vickery,' I said, 'this thing's come to be just as much as I can stand. Consume your own smoke. I don't want to know any more.' "

" 'You!' he said. 'What have you got to complain of? — you've only 'ad to watch. I'm _it_,' he says, 'but that's neither here nor there,' he says. 'I've one thing to say before shakin' 'ands. Remember,' 'e says — we were just by the Admiral's garden-gate then — 'remember, that I am _not_ a murderer, because my lawful wife died in childbed six weeks after I came out. That much at least I am clear of,' 'e says."

" 'Then what have you done that signifies?' I said. 'What's the rest of it?' "

" 'The rest,' 'e says, 'is silence,' an' he shook 'ands and went clickin' into Simons Town station."

" Did he stop to see Mrs. Bathurst at Worcester?" I asked.

" It's not known. He reported at Bloemfontein, saw the ammunition into the trucks, and then 'e disappeared. Went out — deserted, if you care to put it so — within eighteen months of his pension, an' if what 'e said about 'is wife was true he was a free man as 'e then stood. How do you read it off?"

" Poor devil!" said Hooper. " To see her that way every night! I wonder what it was."

" I've made my 'ead ache in that direction many a long night."

" But I'll swear Mrs. B. 'ad no 'and in it," said the Sergeant unshaken.

" No. Whatever the wrong or deceit was, he did it, I'm sure o' that. I 'ad to look at 'is face for five consecutive nights. I'm not so fond o' navigatin' about Cape Town with a South-Easter blowin' these days. I can hear those teeth click, so to say."

" Ah, those teeth," said Hooper, and his hand went to his waistcoat pocket once more. " Permanent things false teeth are. You read about 'em in all the murder trials."

" What d'you suppose the captain knew — or did?" I asked.

" I never turned my searchlight that way," Pyecroft answered unblushingly.

We all reflected together, and drummed on empty beer bottles as the picnic-party, sunburned, wet, and sandy, passed our door singing " The Honeysuckle and the Bee."

" Pretty girl under that kapje," said Pyecroft.

" They never circulated his description?" said Pritchard.

" I was askin' you before these gentlemen came," said Hooper to me, " whether you knew Wankies — on the way to the Zambesi — beyond Buluwayo?"

" Would he pass there — tryin' to get to that Lake what's 'is name?" said Pritchard.

Hooper shook his head and went on: " There's a curious bit o' line there, you see. It runs through solid teak forest — a sort o' mahogany really — seventy-two miles without a curve. I've had a train derailed there twenty- three times in forty miles. I was up there a month ago relievin' a sick inspector, you see. He told me to look out for a couple of tramps in the teak."

" Two?" Pyecroft said. " I don't envy that other man if — "

" We get heaps of tramps up there since the war. The inspector told me I'd find 'em at M'Bindwe siding waiting to go North. He'd given 'em some grub and quinine, you see. I went up on a construction train. I looked out for 'em. I saw them miles ahead along the straight, waiting in the teak. One of 'em was standin' up by the dead-end of tke siding an' the other was squattin' down lookin' up at 'im, you see."

" What did you do for 'em?" said Pritchard.

" There wasn't much I could do, except bury 'em. There'd been a bit of a thunderstorm in the teak, you see, and they were both stone dead and as black as charcoal. That's what they really were, you see — charcoal. They fell to bits when we tried to shift 'em. The man who was standin' up had the false teeth. I saw 'em shinin' against the black. Fell to bits he did too, like his mate squatting down an' watchin' him, both of 'em all wet in the rain. Both burned to charcoal, you see. And — that's what made me ask about marks just now — the false-toother was tattooed on the arms and chest — a crown and foul anchor with M.V. above."

" I've seen that," said Pyecroft quickly. " It was so."

" But if he was all charcoal-like?" said Pritchard, shuddering.

“ You know how writing shows up white on a burned letter? Well, it was like that, you see. We buried ’em in the teak① and I kept... But he was a friend of you two gentlemen, you see.”

Mr. Hooper brought his hand away from his waistcoat-pocket — empty.

Pritchard covered his face with his hands for a moment, like a child shutting out an ugliness.

“ And to think of her at Hauraki!” he murmured — “ with ’er ’air-ribbon on my beer. ‘Ada,’ she said to her niece... Oh, my Gawd!”...

“ On a summer afternoon, when the honeysuckle blooms,
And all Nature seems at rest,
Underneath the bower, ’mid the perfume of the flower,
Sat a maiden with the one she loves the best — ”

sang the picnic-party waiting for their train at Glengariff.

“ Well, I don’t know how you feel about it,” said Pyecroft, “ but ‘avin’ seen ’is face for five consecutive nights on end, I’m inclined to finish what’s left of the beer an’ thank Gawd he’s dead!”

Topics for discussion

1. In the story, the titular protagonist Mrs. Bathurst and her lover Mr. Vickery, the two characters that are most talked about, never appear. Why does the write organize the plot in this way?

2. What is the relationship between the epigraph in the preface to the story and the plot in the story?

3. Do you think the abundant mistakes and coincidences in the story result from the fate in life?

---

① teak: large East Indian tree, Tectona grandis, of the verbena family, yielding ahard, durable, resinous, yellowish-brown wood used for shipbuilding, making furniture, etc.

References for further reading

[1] Bauer, Helen Pike. *Rudyard Kipling: A Study of the Short Fiction.* New York: Twayne, 1994.

[2] Carrington, Charles. *Rudyard Kipling: His Life and Work.* London: Macmillan & Co., 1955.

[3] David, C. *Rudyard Kipling: a critical study*. New Delhi: Anmol, 2007.

[4]Gilbert, Elliot L. ed., *Kipling and the Critics*. New York: New York University Press, 1965.

[5] Green, Roger Lancelyn, ed., *Kipling: the Critical Heritage*. London: Routledge and Kegan Paul, 1971.

[6] Ricketts, Harry. *Rudyard Kipling: A Life.* New York: Da Capo Press, 2001.

H. G. Wells (1866 — 1946)

The Door In the Wall

Introduction to the author

Herbert George Wells (September 21, 1866 — August 13, 1946) was an prolific English writer in many genres, best known for his science fiction novels. He was the author of more than forty-four novels and social and historical books. His most notable science fiction works are *The War of the Worlds, The Time Machine, The Invisible Man, and The Island of Doctor Moreau.* Together with Jules Verne and Hugo Gernsback, Wells has been labeled as " The Father of Science Fiction".

From quite early in his writing career, Wells wrote many Utopian novels, such as *A Modern Utopia (1905), In the Days of the Comet* (1906) and *The Shape of Things to Come* (1933). He also depicted the rise of fascist dictators in *The Autocracy of Mr. Parham* (1930) and *The Holy Terror* (1939). Wells also wrote a dystopian novel, *When the Sleeper* Wakes (1899). Due to his works about war games, such as *Floor Games* (1911) and *Little Wars* (1913), Wells is regarded as " the Father of Miniature War Gaming". Besides, Wells also authored nonfiction works. His bestselling *The Outline of History* (1920) contributed a lot to popularizing world history.

Wells was born on September 21, 1866 in Bromley, Kent, the fourth and last child of Joseph Wells and Sarah Neal. His father once worked as a domestic gardener, a shopkeeper and a professional cricketer. His mother once worked as a domestic servant. In 1891, Wells married his cousin Isabel Mary Wells. The couple agreed to separate in 1894 when he fell in love with one of his students, Amy Catherine Robbins, whom he married in 1895. He had two sons with Jane. Wells died on August 13, 1946 at his home at 13 Hanover Terrace, Regent's Park, London, aged 79.

Major works by H. G. Wells

Fiction

The Time Machine, 1895

The Invisible Man, 1897

The Island of Doctor Moreau, 1896

The War of the Worlds, 1897

The First Men in the Moon, 1901

The Shape of Things to Come, 1933

Nonfiction

The Outline of History, 1920

The Science of Life, 1930

In the Days of the Comet, 1906

A Modern Utopia, 1905

The Shape of Things to Come, 1933

The Autocracy of Mr Parham, 1930

The Holy Terror, 1939

Men Like Gods, 1923

The Outline of History, 1920

Appreciation

" Thc Door in the Wall" was first published in 1911. In the story, Lionel Wallace tells his friend Redmond about an experience which deeply influences his life, even affecting his career as a prominent politician. It was the haunting memory of a fair lady and a group of children that filled his heart with insatiable longings. His mother died when Wallace was born, and he was taken care of by nursery governess. His father was a lawyer, who gave him little attention but expected much of him. At the age of five or six, Wallace once wanders into the streets of West Kensington in London, where he notices a green door in a white wall. Out of strong curiosity, Wallace cannot resist the temptation and goes through the door, finding himself in an enchanted garden. Wallace finds that the garden is just like a children's paradise. Wallace meets many other children and they play games together happily. That is very much to the lonely little boy. Then a woman reads a book to him. It is a living book of " realities". It soon turns out that she is telling him a story of his own life, about all the things that had happened to him since ever I was born. When the book reaches the moment in his life at which Wallace finds himself outside the green door, the enchanted world vanishes, and the boy finds himself once again on the dismal West Kensington street in London. Back at home, Wallace tells people about the garden and the door, but nobody believes him. He is even severely punished by his father. Howere, he cannot completely forget the experience and still often dreams of revisiting the garden. He seems to pass the door in the wall several times at different places, but he does not have the chance to enter it. One morning a few months later, Wallace is found dead, having apparently mistaken a door at a dangerous construction site for the elusive door in the wall.

The story is considered to be Wells's finest story by both the readers and critics. It reflects the conflict between science and imagination. The story examines an issue to which Wells returned repeatedly in his writing: the contrast between aesthetics and science and the difficulty of choosing between them. Also, the story describes the human conditions of existence and interpersonal relationships. It uses symbols, metaphors and fantasy to achieve the purpose of its writing.

Selected Reading

The Door In the Wall

One confidential[1] evening, not three months ago, Lionel Wallace told me this story of the Door in the Wall. And at the time I thought that so far as he was concerned it was a true story.

He told it me with such a direct simplicity of conviction that I could not do otherwise than believe in him. But in the morning, in my own flat, I woke to a different atmosphere, and as I lay in bed and recalled the things he had told me, stripped[2] of the glamour of his earnest slow voice, denuded[3] of the focused shaded table light, the shadowy atmosphere that wrapped about him and the pleasant bright things, the dessert and glasses and napery[4] of the dinner we had shared, making them for the time a bright little world quite cut off from every-day realities, I saw it all as frankly incredible. " He was mystifying!" I said, and then: " How well he did it!... It isn't quite the thing I should have expected him, of all people, to do well."

Afterwards, as I sat up in bed and sipped my morning tea, I found myself trying to account for the flavour of reality that perplexed me in his impossible reminiscences,[5] by supposing they did in some way suggest, present, convey — I hardly know which word to use — experiences it was otherwise impossible to tell.

Well, I don't resort to that explanation now. I have got over my intervening doubts. I believe now, as I believed at the moment of telling, that Wallace did to the very best of his ability strip the truth of his secret for me. But whether he himself saw, or only thought he saw, whether he himself was the possessor of an inestimable

---

① confidential : secret, often in a formal, business, or military situation

② strip: to remove, pull or tear the covering or outer layer from something

③ denude: to remove a valuable possession or quality

④ napery: household linen; especially: table linen

⑤ reminiscence: the act of remembering events and experiences from the past privilege, or the victim of a fantastic dream, I cannot pretend to guess. Even the facts of his death, which ended my doubts forever, throw no light on that. That much the reader must judge for himself.

I forget now what chance comment or criticism of mine moved so reticent a man to confide in me. He was, I think, defending himself against an imputation of slackness and unreliability I had made in relation to a great public movement in which he had disappointed me. But he plunged suddenly. " I have" he said, " a preoccupation — "

" I know," he went on, after a pause that he devoted to the study of his cigar ash, " I have been negligent.[①] The fact is — it isn't a case of ghosts or apparitions — but — it's an odd thing to tell of, Redmond — I am haunted. I am haunted by something — that rather takes the light out of things, that fills me with longings..."

He paused, checked by that English shyness that so often overcomes us when we would speak of moving or grave or beautiful things. " You were at Saint Athelstan's all through," he said, and for a moment that seemed to me quite irrelevant. " Well" — and he paused. Then very haltingly[②] at first, but afterwards more easily, he began to tell of the thing that was hidden in his life, the haunting memory of a beauty and a happiness that filled his heart with insatiable[③] longings that made all the interests and spectacle of worldly life seem dull and tedious and vain to him.

Now that I have the clue to it, the thing seems written visibly in his face. I have a photograph in which that look of detachment has been caught and intensified. It reminds me of what a woman once said of him — a woman who had loved him greatly.

" Suddenly," she said, " the interest goes out of him. He forgets you. He doesn't

① negligent: not being careful or giving enough attention to people or things that are your responsibility

② haltingly: stopping often while you are saying or doing something, especially because you are nervous

③ insatiable: (especially of a desire or need) too great to be satisfied care a rap for you — under his very nose..."

Yet the interest was not always out of him, and when he was holding his attention to a thing Wallace could contrive[①] to be an extremely successful man. His career, indeed, is set with successes. He left me behind him long ago; he soared up over my head, and cut a figure in the world that I couldn't cut — anyhow.

He was still a year short of forty, and they say now that he would have been in office and very probably in the new Cabinet if he had lived. At school he always beat me without effort — as it were by nature. We were at school together at Saint Athelstan's College in West Kensington for almost all our school time. He came into the school as my co-equal, but he left far above me, in a blaze of scholarships and brilliant performance. Yet I think I made a fair average running. And it was at school I heard first of the Door in the Wall — that I was to hear of a second time only a month before his death.

To him at least the Door in the Wall was a real door leading through a real wall to immortal realities. Of that I am now quite assured.

And it came into his life early, when he was a little fellow between five and six. I remember how, as he sat making his confession to me with a slow gravity,[②] he reasoned and reckoned the date of it. " There was," he said, " a crimson Virginia creeper[③] in it — all one bright uniform crimson in a clear amber sunshine against a white wall. That came into the impression somehow, though I don't clearly remember how, and there were horse-chestnut[④] leaves upon the clean pavement outside the green door. They were blotched[⑤] yellow and green, you know, not brown nor dirty,

---

① contrive: to arrange a situation or event, or arrange for something to happen, using clever planning

② gravity: the force which attracts objects towards one another, especially the force that makes things fall to the ground; seriousness

③ Virginia creeper: a vine often grown on walls, the leaves of which become dark red in autumn

④ horse–chestnut: (the poisonous shiny brown nut from) a large tree with pink or white flowers

⑤ blotch: to mark with blotches, that is, large, irregular spots or blots; blot, spot, or blur so that they must have been new fallen. I take it that means October. I look out for horse-chestnut leaves every year, and I ought to know.

" If I'm right in that, I was about five years and four months old."

He was, he said, rather a precocious little boy — he learned to talk at an abnormally early age, and he was so sane and " old-fashioned," as people say, that he was permitted an amount of initiative that most children scarcely attain by seven or eight. His mother died when he was born, and he was under the less vigilant and authoritative care of a nursery governess. His father was a stern, preoccupied lawyer, who gave him little attention, and expected great things of him. For all his brightness he found life a little grey and dull I think. And one day he wandered.

He could not recall the particular neglect that enabled him to get away, nor the course he took among the West Kensington roads.

All that had faded among the incurable blurs of memory. But the white wall and the green door stood out quite distinctly.

As his memory of that remote childish experience ran, he did at the very first sight of that door experience a peculiar emotion, an attraction, a desire to get to the door and open it and walk in.

And at the same time he had the clearest conviction that either it was unwise or it was wrong of him — he could not tell which — to yield to this attraction. He insisted upon it as a curious thing that he knew from the very beginning — unless memory has played him the queerest trick — that the door was unfastened, and that he could go in as he chose.

I seem to see the figure of that little boy, drawn and repelled. And it was very clear in his mind, too, though why it should be so was never explained, that his father would be very angry if he went through that door.

Wallace described all these moments of hesitation to me with the utmost particularity. He went right past the door, and then, with his hands in his pockets, and making an infantile attempt to whistle, strolled right along beyond the end of the wall. There he recalls a number of mean, dirty shops, and particularly that of a plumber and decorator, with a dusty disorder of earthenware pipes, sheet lead ball taps, pattern books of wall paper, and tins of enamel. He stood pretending to examine these things, and coveting, passionately desiring the green door.

Then, he said, he had a gust of emotion. He made a run for it, lest hesitation should grip him again, he went plump with outstretched hand through the green door and let it slam behind him. And so, in a trice, he came into the garden that has haunted all his life.

It was very difficult for Wallace to give me his full sense of that garden into which he came.

There was something in the very air of it that exhilarated, that gave one a sense of lightness and good happening and well being; there was something in the sight of it that made all its colour clean and perfect and subtly luminous.① In the instant of coming into it one was exquisitely② glad — as only in rare moments and when one is young and joyful one can be glad in this world.

And everything was beautiful there...

Wallace mused before he went on telling me. " You see," he said, with the doubtful inflection of a man who pauses at incredible things, " there were two great panthers there...Yes, spotted panthers. And I was not afraid. There was a long wide path with marble-edged flower borders on either side, and these two huge velvety beasts were playing there with a ball. One looked up and came towards me, a little curious as it seemed. It came right up to me, rubbed its soft round ear very gently against the small hand I held out and purred. It was, I tell you, an enchanted garden. I know. And the size? Oh! it stretched far and wide, this way and that. I believe there were hills far away. Heaven knows where West Kensington had suddenly got to. And somehow it was just like coming home.

---

① luminous: producing or reflecting bright light (especially in the dark)

② exquisitely: very beautifully; delicately

“You know, in the very moment the door swung to behind me, I forgot the road with its fallen chestnut leaves, its cabs and tradesmen's carts, I forgot the sort of gravitational pull back to the discipline and obedience of home, I forgot all hesitations and fear, forgot discretion①, forgot all the intimate realities of this life. I became in a moment a very glad and wonder-happy little boy — in another world. It was a world with a different quality, a warmer, more penetrating and mellower light, with a faint clear gladness in its air, and wisps of sun-touched cloud in the blueness of its sky. And before me ran this long wide path, invitingly, with weedless beds on either side, rich with untended flowers, and these two great panthers. I put my little hands fearlessly on their soft fur, and caressed their round ears and the sensitive corners under their ears, and played with them, and it was as though they welcomed me home. There was a keen sense of home-coming in my mind, and when presently a tall, fair girl appeared in the pathway and came to meet me, smiling, and said ‘Well?’ to me, and lifted me, and kissed me, and put me down, and led me by the hand, there was no amazement, but only an impression of delightful rightness, of being reminded of happy things that had in some strange way been overlooked. There were broad steps, I remember, that came into view between spikes of delphinium, and up these we went to a great avenue between very old and shady dark trees. All down this avenue, you know, between the red chapped stems, were marble seats of honour and statuary, and very tame and friendly white doves ...

“And along this avenue my girl-friend led me, looking down — I recall the pleasant lines, the finely-modelled chin of her sweet kind face — asking me questions in a soft, agreeable voice, and telling me things, pleasant things I know, though what they were I was never able to recall... And presently a little Capuchin monkey, very clean, with a fur of ruddy brown and kindly hazel eyes, came down a tree to us and ran beside me, looking up at me and grinning, and presently leapt to my shoulder. So

① discretion: the ability to behave without causing embarrassment or attracting too much attention, especially by keeping information secret we went on our way in great happiness..."

He paused.

" Go on," I said.

" I remember little things. We passed an old man musing among laurels, I remember, and a place gay with paroquets[①], and came through a broad shaded colonnade[②] to a spacious cool palace, full of pleasant fountains, full of beautiful things, full of the quality and promise of heart's desire. And there were many things and many people, some that still seem to stand out clearly and some that are a little vague, but all these people were beautiful and kind. In some way — I don't know how — it was conveyed to me that they all were kind to me, glad to have me there, and filling me with gladness by their gestures, by the touch of their hands, by the welcome and love in their eyes. Yes — "

He mused for awhile. " Playmates I found there. That was very much to me, because I was a lonely little boy. They played delightful games in a grass-covered court where there was a sun-dial set about with flowers. And as one played one loved..."

" But — it's odd — there's a gap in my memory. I don't remember the games we played. I never remembered. Afterwards, as a child, I spent long hours trying, even with tears, to recall the form of that happiness. I wanted to play it all over again — in my nursery — by myself. No! All I remember is the happiness and two dear playfellows who were most with me... Then presently came a sombre dark woman, with a grave, pale face and dreamy eyes, a sombre woman wearing a soft long robe of pale purple, who carried a book and beckoned[③] and took me aside with her into a gallery above a hall — though my playmates were loth to have me go, and ceased

① paroquet: any of numerous small, slender parrots, usually having a long, pointed, graduated tail, often kept as pets and noted for the ability to mimic speech: several species are endangered

② colonnade: a row of columns separated from each other by an equal distance

③ beckon: to move your hand or head in a way that tells someone to come nearer their game and stood watching as I was carried away. 'Come back to us!' they cried. 'Come back to us soon!' I looked up at her face, but she heeded them not at all. Her face was very gentle and grave. She took me to a seat in the gallery, and I stood beside her, ready to look at her book as she opened it upon her knee. The pages fell open. She pointed, and I looked, marvelling, for in the living pages of that book I saw myself; it was a story about myself, and in it were all the things that had happened to me since ever I was born…."

" It was wonderful to me, because the pages of that book were not pictures, you understand, but realities."

Wallace paused gravely — looked at me doubtfully.

" Go on," I said. " I understand."

" They were realities — yes, they must have been; people moved and things came and went in them; my dear mother, whom I had near forgotten; then my father, stern and upright, the servants, the nursery, all the familiar things of home. Then the front door and the busy streets, with traffic to and fro: I looked and marvelled, and looked half doubtfully again into the woman's face and turned the pages over, skipping this and that, to see more of this book, and more, and so at last I came to myself hovering and hesitating outside the green door in the long white wall, and felt again the conflict and the fear."

" 'And next?' I cried, and would have turned on, but the cool hand of the grave woman delayed me."

" 'Next?' I insisted, and struggled gently with her hand, pulling up her fingers with all my childish strength, and as she yielded and the page came over she bent down upon me like a shadow and kissed my brow.

" But the page did not show the enchanted garden, nor the panthers, nor the girl who had led me by the hand, nor the playfellows who had been so loth[①] to let me

① loth: unwilling; reluctant; disinclined; averse

go. It showed a long grey street in West Kensington, on that chill hour of afternoon before the lamps are lit, and I was there, a wretched little figure, weeping aloud, for all that I could do to restrain myself, and I was weeping because I could not return to my dear play-fellows who had called after me, 'Come back to us! Come back to us soon!' I was there. This was no page in a book, but harsh reality; that enchanted place and the restraining hand of the grave mother at whose knee I stood had gone — whither① have they gone?"

He halted again, and remained for a time, staring into the fire.

" Oh! the wretchedness of that return!" he murmured.

" Well?" I said after a minute or so.

" Poor little wretch I was — brought back to this grey world again! As I realised the fulness of what had happened to me, I gave way to quite ungovernable grief. And the shame and humiliation of that public weeping and my disgraceful homecoming remain with me still. I see again the benevolent-looking old gentleman in gold spectacles who stopped and spoke to me — prodding me first with his umbrella. 'Poor little chap,' said he; 'and are you lost then?' — and me a London boy of five and more! And he must needs bring in a kindly young policeman and make a crowd of me, and so march me home. Sobbing, conspicuous② and frightened, I came from the enchanted garden to the steps of my father's house."

" That is as well as I can remember my vision of that garden — the garden that haunts me still. Of course, I can convey nothing of that indescribable quality of translucent③ unreality, that difference from the common things of experience that hung about it all; but that--that is what happened. If it was a dream, I am sure it was a day-time and altogether extraordinary dream...H'm! — naturally there followed a

① whither : to what place? where?

② conspicuous: easily seen or noticed; readily visible or observable:

③ translucent: If an object or a substance is translucent, it is almost transparent, allowing some lig ht through it in an attractive way terrible questioning, by my aunt, my father, the nurse, the governess — everyone ..."

" I tried to tell them, and my father gave me my first thrashing for telling lies. When afterwards I tried to tell my aunt, she punished me again for my wicked persistence. Then, as I said, everyone was forbidden to listen to me, to hear a word about it. Even my fairy tale books were taken away from me for a time — because I was 'too imaginative.' Eh? Yes, they did that! My father belonged to the old school... And my story was driven back upon myself. I whispered it to my pillow — my pillow that was often damp and salt to my whispering lips with childish tears. And I added always to my official and less fervent prayers this one heartfelt request: 'Please God I may dream of the garden. Oh! take me back to my garden! Take me back to my garden! ' I dreamt often of the garden. I may have added to it, I may have changed it; I do not know... All this you understand is an attempt to reconstruct from fragmentary memories a very early experience. Between that and the other consecutive① memories of my boyhood there is a gulf. A time came when it seemed impossible I should ever speak of that wonder glimpse again."

I asked an obvious question.

" No," he said. " I don't remember that I ever attempted to find my way back to the garden in those early years. This seems odd to me now, but I think that very probably a closer watch was kept on my movements after this misadventure to prevent my going astray. No, it wasn't until you knew me that I tried for the garden again. And I believe there was a period — incredible as it seems now — when I forgot the garden altogether — when I was about eight or nine it may have been. Do you remember me as a kid at Saint Athelstan's?"

" Rather!"

" I didn't show any signs did I in those days of having a secret dream?"

He looked up with a sudden smile.

① consecutive: following one after the other in a series: following each other without interruption

" Did you ever play North-West Passage with me?.... No, of course you didn't come my way!"

" It was the sort of game," he went on, " that every imaginative child plays all day. The idea was the discovery of a North-West Passage to school. The way to school was plain enough; the game consisted in finding some way that wasn't plain, starting off ten minutes early in some almost hopeless direction, and working one's way round through unaccustomed streets to my goal. And one day I got entangled among some rather low-class streets on the other side of Campden Hill, and I began to think that for once the game would be against me and that I should get to school late. I tried rather desperately a street that seemed a cul de sac①, and found a passage at the end. I hurried through that with renewed hope. 'I shall do it yet, I said, and passed a row of frowsy little shops that were inexplicably familiar to me, and behold! there was my long white wall and the green door that led to the enchanted garden!"

" The thing whacked② upon me suddenly. Then, after all, that garden, that wonderful garden, wasn't a dream!" ...

He paused.

" I suppose my second experience with the green door marks the world of difference there is between the busy life of a schoolboy and the infinite leisure of a child. Anyhow, this second time I didn't for a moment think of going in straight away. You see... For one thing my mind was full of the idea of getting to school in time — set on not breaking my record for punctuality. I must surely have felt SOME little desire at least to try the door — yes, I must have felt that... But I seem to remember the attraction of the door mainly as another obstacle to my overmastering determination to get to school. I was immediately interested by this discovery I had made, of course — I went on with my mind full of it — but I went on. It didn't check me. I ran past tugging out my watch, found I had ten minutes still to spare, and then

① cul de sac: a street that is designed to connect to another street only at one end

② whack: to hit someone or something noisily

I was going downhill into familiar surroundings. I got to school, breathless, it is true, and wet with perspiration, but in time. I can remember hanging up my coat and hat... Went right by it and left it behind me. Odd, eh?"

He looked at me thoughtfully. " Of course, I didn't know then that it wouldn't always be there. School boys have limited imaginations. I suppose I thought it was an awfully jolly thing to have it there, to know my way back to it, but there was the school tugging at me. I expect I was a good deal distraught and inattentive that morning, recalling what I could of the beautiful strange people I should presently see again. Oddly enough I had no doubt in my mind that they would be glad to see me... Yes, I must have thought of the garden that morning just as a jolly sort of place to which one might resort in the interludes of a strenuous scholastic career."

" I didn't go that day at all. The next day was a half holiday, and that may have weighed with me. Perhaps, too, my state of inattention brought down impositions upon me and docked the margin of time necessary for the detour. I don't know. What I do know is that in the meantime the enchanted garden was so much upon my mind that I could not keep it to myself."

" I told — What was his name? — a ferrety-looking youngster we used to call Squiff."

" Young Hopkins," said I.

" Hopkins it was. I did not like telling him, I had a feeling that in some way it was against the rules to tell him, but I did. He was walking part of the way home with me; he was talkative, and if we had not talked about the enchanted garden we should have talked of something else, and it was intolerable to me to think about any other subject. So I blabbed.① "

" Well, he told my secret. The next day in the play interval I found myself surrounded by half a dozen bigger boys, half teasing and wholly curious to hear more

---

① blab: to talk carelessly or too much, often telling others something you should keep secret of the enchanted garden. There was that big Fawcett — you remember him? — and Carnaby and Morley Reynolds. You weren't there by any chance? No, I think I should have remembered if you were..."

" A boy is a creature of odd feelings. I was, I really believe, in spite of my secret self-disgust, a little flattered to have the attention of these big fellows. I remember particularly a moment of pleasure caused by the praise of Crawshaw — you remember Crawshaw major, the son of Crawshaw the composer? — who said it was the best lie he had ever heard. But at the same time there was a really painful undertow of shame at telling what I felt was indeed a sacred secret. That beast Fawcett made a joke about the girl in green — ."

Wallace's voice sank with the keen memory of that shame. " I pretended not to hear," he said. " Well, then Carnaby suddenly called me a young liar and disputed with me when I said the thing was true. I said I knew where to find the green door, could lead them all there in ten minutes. Carnaby became outrageously① virtuous,② and said I'd have to — and bear out my words or suffer."

Did you ever have Carnaby twist your arm? Then perhaps you'll understand how it went with me. I swore my story was true. There was nobody in the school then to save a chap from Carnaby though Crawshaw put in a word or so. Carnaby had got his game. I grew excited and red-eared, and a little frightened, I behaved altogether like a silly little chap, and the outcome of it all was that instead of starting alone for my enchanted garden, I led the way presently — cheeks flushed, ears hot, eyes smarting, and my soul one burning misery and shame — for a party of six mocking, curious and threatening school-fellows.

" We never found the white wall and the green door..."

" You mean? — "

---

① outrageous: describes something or someone that is shocking because they are unusual or strange

② virtuous: describes a person who thinks himself or herself morally better than other people

" I mean I couldn't find it. I would have found it if I could.

" And afterwards when I could go alone I couldn't find it. I never found it. I seem now to have been always looking for it through my school-boy days, but I've never come upon it again."

" Did the fellows — make it disagreeable?"

" Beastly... Carnaby held a council over me for wanton lying. I remember how I sneaked home and upstairs to hide the marks of my blubbering. But when I cried myself to sleep at last it wasn't for Carnaby, but for the garden, for the beautiful afternoon I had hoped for, for the sweet friendly women and the waiting playfellows and the game I had hoped to learn again, that beautiful forgotten game..."

" I believed firmly that if I had not told — ...I had bad times after that — crying at night and woolgathering by day. For two terms I slackened and had bad reports. Do you remember? Of course you would! It was YOU — your beating me in mathematics that brought me back to the grind again."

For a time my friend stared silently into the red heart of the fire. Then he said: " I never saw it again until I was seventeen."

" It leapt upon me for the third time — as I was driving to Paddington on my way to Oxford and a scholarship. I had just one momentary glimpse. I was leaning over the apron of my hansom① smoking a cigarette, and no doubt thinking myself no end of a man of the world, and suddenly there was the door, the wall, the dear sense of unforgettable and still attainable things.

" We clattered by — I too taken by surprise to stop my cab until we were well past and round a corner. Then I had a queer moment, a double and divergent movement of my will: I tapped the little door in the roof of the cab, and brought my arm down to pull out my watch. 'Yes, sir!' said the cabman, smartly. 'Er — well — it's nothing,' I cried. 'My mistake! We haven't much time! Go on!' and he went on..."

---

① a two-wheeled carriage pulled by a horse, used like a taxi in the past

" I got my scholarship. And the night after I was told of that I sat over my fire in my little upper room, my study, in my father's house, with his praise — his rare praise — and his sound counsels ringing in my ears, and I smoked my favourite pipe — the formidable bulldog of adolescence — and thought of that door in the long white wall. 'If I had stopped,' I thought, 'I should have missed my scholarship, I should have missed Oxford — muddled[①] all the fine career before me! I begin to see things better!' I fell musing deeply, but I did not doubt then this career of mine was a thing that merited sacrifice."

" Those dear friends and that clear atmosphere seemed very sweet to me, very fine, but remote. My grip was fixing now upon the world. I saw another door opening — the door of my career."

He stared again into the fire. Its red lights picked out a stubborn strength in his face for just one flickering moment, and then it vanished again.

" Well", he said and sighed, " I have served that career. I have done — much work, much hard work. But I have dreamt of the enchanted garden a thousand dreams, and seen its door, or at least glimpsed its door, four times since then. Yes — four times. For a while this world was so bright and interesting, seemed so full of meaning and opportunity that the half-effaced charm of the garden was by comparison gentle and remote. Who wants to pat panthers on the way to dinner with pretty women and distinguished men? I came down to London from Oxford, a man of bold promise that I have done something to redeem. Something--and yet there have been disappointments..."

" Twice I have been in love — I will not dwell on that — but once, as I went to someone who, I know, doubted whether I dared to come, I took a short cut at a venture through an unfrequented road near Earl's Court, and so happened on a white wall and a familiar green door. 'Odd!' said I to myself, 'but I thought this place

---

① muddle: to mix up (something) in a confused way

was on Campden Hill. It's the place I never could find somehow — like counting Stonehenge — the place of that queer day dream of mine.' And I went by it intent upon my purpose. It had no appeal to me that afternoon."

"I had just a moment's impulse to try the door, three steps aside were needed at the most--though I was sure enough in my heart that it would open to me — and then I thought that doing so might delay me on the way to that appointment in which I thought my honour was involved. Afterwards I was sorry for my punctuality — I might at least have peeped in I thought, and waved a hand to those panthers, but I knew enough by this time not to seek again belatedly① that which is not found by seeking. Yes, that time made me very sorry..."

"Years of hard work after that and never a sight of the door. It's only recently it has come back to me. With it there has come a sense as though some thin tarnish had spread itself over my world. I began to think of it as a sorrowful and bitter thing that I should never see that door again. Perhaps I was suffering a little from overwork — perhaps it was what I've heard spoken of as the feeling of forty. I don't know. But certainly the keen brightness that makes effort easy has gone out of things recently, and that just at a time with all these new political developments — when I ought to be working. Odd, isn't it? But I do begin to find life toilsome, its rewards, as I come near them, cheap. I began a little while ago to want the garden quite badly. Yes — and I've seen it three times."

"The garden?"

"No — the door! And I haven't gone in!"

He leaned over the table to me, with an enormous sorrow in his voice as he spoke. "Thrice I have had my chance — thrice! If ever that door offers itself to me again, I swore, I will go in out of this dust and heat, out of this dry glitter of vanity, out of these toilsome② futilities. I will go and never return. This time I will stay... I

---

① belated: happening or coming very late or too late

② toilsome: marked by or full of toil or fatigue

swore it and when the time came — I didn't go."

" Three times in one year have I passed that door and failed to enter. Three times in the last year."

" The first time was on the night of the snatch division on the Tenants' Redemption Bill, on which the Government was saved by a majority of three. You remember? No one on our side — perhaps very few on the opposite side — expected the end that night. Then the debate collapsed like eggshells. I and Hotchkiss were dining with his cousin at Brentford, we were both unpaired, and we were called up by telephone, and set off at once in his cousin's motor. We got in barely in time, and on the way we passed my wall and door — livid in the moonlight, blotched with hot yellow as the glare of our lamps lit it, but unmistakable. 'My God!' cried I. 'What?' said Hotchkiss. 'Nothing!' I answered, and the moment passed."

" 'I've made a great sacrifice," I told the whip as I got in. " They all have," he said," and hurried by.

" I do not see how I could have done otherwise then. And the next occasion was as I rushed to my father's bedside to bid that stern old man farewell. Then, too, the claims of life were imperative. But the third time was different; it happened a week ago. It fills me with hot remorse to recall it. I was with Gurker and Ralphs — it's no secret now you know that I've had my talk with Gurker. We had been dining at Frobisher's, and the talk had become intimate between us. The question of my place in the reconstructed ministry lay always just over the boundary of the discussion. Yes — yes. That's all settled. It needn't be talked about yet, but there's no reason to keep a secret from you...Yes — thanks! thanks! But let me tell you my story."

" Then, on that night things were very much in the air. My position was a very delicate one. I was keenly anxious to get some definite word from Gurker, but was hampered by Ralphs' presence. I was using the best power of my brain to keep that light and careless talk not too obviously directed to the point that concerns me. I had to. Ralphs' behaviour since has more than justified my caution... Ralphs, I knew, would leave us beyond the Kensington High Street, and then I could surprise Gurker by a sudden frankness. One has sometimes to resort to these little devices... And then it was that in the margin of my field of vision I became aware once more of the white wall, the green door before us down the road."

"We passed it talking. I passed it. I can still see the shadow of Gurker's marked profile, his opera hat tilted forward over his prominent nose, the many folds of his neck wrap going before my shadow and Ralphs' as we sauntered① past."

"I passed within twenty inches of the door. 'If I say good-night to them, and go in,' I asked myself, 'what will happen?' " And I was all a-tingle for that word with Gurker.

"I could not answer that question in the tangle of my other problems. 'They will think me mad,' I thought. 'And suppose I vanish now! — Amazing disappearance of a prominent politician!' That weighed with me. A thousand inconceivably petty worldlinesses weighed with me in that crisis."

Then he turned on me with a sorrowful smile, and, speaking slowly; "Here I am!" he said.

"Here I am!" he repeated, "and my chance has gone from me. Three times in one year the door has been offered me — the door that goes into peace, into delight, into a beauty beyond dreaming, a kindness no man on earth can know. And I have rejected it, Redmond, and it has gone — "

"How do you know?"

"I know. I know. I am left now to work it out, to stick to the tasks that held me so strongly when my moments came. You say, I have success — this vulgar, tawdry, irksome, envied thing. I have it." He had a walnut in his big hand. "If that was my success," he said, and crushed it, and held it out for me to see.

"Let me tell you something, Redmond. This loss is destroying me. For two

① saunter: to walk in a slow and relaxed way, often in no particular direction months, for ten weeks nearly now, I have done no work at all, except the most necessary and urgent duties. My soul is full of inappeasable regrets. At nights — when it is less likely I shall be recognised — I go out. I wander. Yes. I wonder what people would think of that if they knew. A Cabinet Minister, the responsible head of that most vital of all departments, wandering alone — grieving — sometimes near audibly lamenting — for a door, for a garden!"

I can see now his rather pallid[1] face, and the unfamiliar sombre fire that had come into his eyes. I see him very vividly to-night. I sit recalling his words, his tones, and last evening's Westminster Gazette still lies on my sofa, containing the notice of his death. At lunch to-day the club was busy with him and the strange riddle of his fate.

They found his body very early yesterday morning in a deep excavation near East Kensington Station. It is one of two shafts that have been made in connection with an extension of the railway southward. It is protected from the intrusion of the public by a hoarding upon the high road, in which a small doorway has been cut for the convenience of some of the workmen who live in that direction. The doorway was left unfastened through a misunderstanding between two gangers, and through it he made his way…

My mind is darkened with questions and riddles.

It would seem he walked all the way from the House that night — he has frequently walked home during the past Session — and so it is I figure his dark form coming along the late and empty streets, wrapped up, intent. And then did the pale electric lights near the station cheat the rough planking[2] into a semblance of white? Did that fatal unfastened door awaken some memory?

Was there, after all, ever any green door in the wall at all?

I do not know. I have told his story as he told it to me.

---

① pallid: pale; faint or deficient in color; wan

② planking : heavy boards that are used to build something

There are times when I believe that Wallace was no more than the victim of the coincidence between a rare but not unprecedented type of hallucination① and a careless trap, but that indeed is not my profoundest belief. You may think me superstitious if you will, and foolish; but, indeed, I am more than half convinced that he had in truth, an abnormal gift, and a sense, something — I know not what — that in the guise of wall and door offered him an outlet, a secret and peculiar passage of escape into another and altogether more beautiful world. At any rate, you will say, it betrayed him in the end. But did it betray him? There you touch the inmost mystery of these dreamers, these men of vision and the imagination.

We see our world fair and common, the hoarding and the pit. By our daylight standard he walked out of security into darkness, danger and death. But did he see like that?

Topics for discussion

1. Whose point of view is the story told from? Is he a reliable narrator?
2. What is a leaf symbolic of in the story?
3. What leads to Wallace's death eventually?

References for further reading

[1] Batchelor, John. *H. G. Wells*. Cambridge: Cambridge University Press, 1985.

[2] Brome, Vincent. *H. G. Wells: A Biography*. London, New York, and Toronto: Longmans, Green, 1951.

[3] Gosling, John. *Waging the War of the Worlds*. Jefferson, North Carolina: McFarland, 2009.

---

① hallucination: something (such as an image, a sound, or a smell) that seems real but does not really exist and that is usually caused by mental illness or the effect of a drug

[4] Huntington, John. *Critical essays on H. G. Wells*. G. K. Hall, 1991.

[5] Wells, Geoffrey H. *The Works of H. G. Wells*. London: Routledge, 1925.

[6] Shippey, Tom. ed. *Fictional Space: Essays on Contemporary Science Fiction.* Oxford: Blackwell, 1991.

[7] Gunn, James E. *Inside Science Fiction: Essays on Fantastic Literature*. San Bernardino, CA: Borgo, 1992.

John Galsworthy (1867 — 1933)

The Japanese Quince

Introduction to the author

John Galsworthy (August 14, 1867 — January 31, 1933) was a prolific English novelist, playwright and short story writer. His notable works include *The Forsyte Saga* and its sequels, *A Modern Comedy and End of the Chapter*. Galsworthy received numerous awards. Among them, Galsworthy founded PEN, the important international writers' society, and was elected as the first president of the PEN International literary club in 1921. After turning down a knighthood, Galsworthy was appointed to the Order of Merit in 1929. He won the Nobel Prize in Literature in 1932.

John Galsworthy was born to John and Blanche Bailey Galsworthy on August 14, 1867 in Surrey, England. His family was wealthy and well established. The family had a large estate in Kingston upon Thames. On this estate, there are standing three schools: Marymount International School, Rokeby Preparatory School, and Holy Cross Preparatory School. Galsworthy attended Harrow and New College, Oxford, training as a barrister, and was called to the bar in 1890, but he never took up the practice. Instead, he chose to travel abroad to look after the family's shipping business. Then, during his overseas travels, Galsworthy met Joseph Conrad and the two future novelists became close friends.

In 1895, Galsworthy began an affair with Ada Nemesis Pearson Cooper, the wife of his cousin Major Arthur Galsworthy. After her divorce ten years later, they married on September 23, 1905 and stayed together until his death in 1933. In 1932, He was too ill to attend the Nobel awards ceremony, and died six weeks later of a stroke.

Major works by John Galsworthy

Short story collection

From the Four Winds, 1897

Novels

The Man of Property, 1906

In Chancery, 1920

To Let, 1921

The White Monkey, 1924

A Modern Comedy, 1929

The Silver Spoon, 1926

Swan Song, 1928

End of the Chapter,1934

Flowering Wilderness, 1932

Maid in Waiting,1932

Over the River,1933

Plays

Strife, 1909

The Skin Game,1920

The Silver Box, 1906

Appreciation

" The Japanese Quince" was first published in 1910. The story recounts an episode from the life of Mr. Nelson, whose attention is temporarily distracted by the sights, sounds, and smells of an early spring morning and briefly lifted out of his highly regimented, well-ordered life by the beauty of the natural world. The plot of story appears to be quite simple and straightforward, but it is certainly deceptively so. On a beautiful spring morning. Mr. Nilson opens his dressing room window, only to experience a peculiar sweetish sensation in the back of his throat. When he went downstairs into his dining room, Mr. Nilson again experiences that peculiar sensation as he takes his morning paper in his hand. Hoping to rid himself of this uncomfortable feeling, Mr. Nelson determines to take a walk in the nearby gardens before breakfast. With his newspaper firmly in hand behind him, Mr. Nilson finds that even after two laps around the park, the unsettling sensation is still there. Then his attention was diverted to a flowering tree by some smells and the sounds of a blackbird. Then he notices that his neighbor Mr. Tandram is also admiring the tree. They detects from a nearby label that the tree is a Japanese Quince.

Galsworthy once stated that "The Japanese Quince" was his attempt to " produce in the reader the sort of uneasy feeling that now and then we run up against ourselves." The story presents the hollow life and the primary pathos of a person who is a member of the higher social class. This story has been highly acclaimed for its profound understanding of human nature and for its glimpse into a world that reveals its shortcomings while suggesting the possibilities for its redemption. The language of the story vividly evokes all five senses by presenting vivid images in the nature. despite the natural beauty, the omniscient narrator tells a story about such conditions of modern people as alienation and emptiness. Galsworthy is a conventional writer, having inherited the fine traditions of the great Victorian novelists of the critical realism with satire and humor in his writing.

Selected Reading

The Japanese Quince①

As Mr. Nilson, well known in the City, opened the window of his dressing-room on Campden Hill, he experienced a peculiar sweetish sensation in the back of his throat, and a feeling of emptiness just under his fifth rib. Hooking the window back, he noticed that a little tree in the Square Gardens had come out in blossom, and that the thermometer stood at sixty② . " Perfect morning," he thought; " spring at last!"

Resuming some meditations on the price of Tintos③ , he took up an ivory-backed hand-glass and scrutinised④ his face. His firm, well-coloured cheeks, with their neat brown moustaches, and his round, well-opened, clear grey eyes, wore a reassuring appearance of good health. Putting on his black frock coat, he went downstairs.

In the dining-room his morning paper was laid out on the sideboard. Mr. Nilson had scarcely taken it in his hand when he again became aware of that queer feeling. Somewhat concerned, he went to the French window and descended the scrolled iron steps into the fresh air. A cuckoo clock struck eight.

" Half an hour to breakfast," he thought; " I'll take a turn in the Gardens."

He had them to himself, and proceeded to pace the circular path with his morning paper clasped behind him. He had scarcely made two revolutions⑤ , however, when it was borne in on him that, instead of going away in the fresh air, the feeling had increased. He drew several deep breaths, having heard deep breathing recommended by his wife's doctor; but they augmented rather than diminished the

---

① Japanese Quince: ornamental shrubs of the rose family with usually scarlet, pink, or white flowers.

② Here it refers to 60° F, which is 15.6°C.

③ Tintos: a kind of wine

④ scrutinise: to examine something very carefully in order to discover information

⑤ revolution: the action of moving around something in a path that is similar to a circle sensation — as if some sweetish liquor in course within him, together with a faint aching just above his heart. Running over what he had eaten the night before, he could recollect no unusual dish, and it occurred to him that it might possibly be some smell affecting him. But he could detect nothing except a faint sweet lemony scent, rather agreeable than otherwise, which evidently emanated① from the bushes budding in the sunshine. He was on the point of resuming his promenade②, when a blackbird close by burst into song, and, looking up, Mr. Nilson saw at a distance of perhaps five yards a little tree, in the heart of whose branches the bird was perched. He stood staring curiously at this tree, recognising it for that which he had noticed from his window. It was covered with young blossoms, pink and white, and little bright green leaves both round and spiky; and on all this blossom and these leaves the sunlight glistened. Mr. Nilson smiled; the little tree was so alive and pretty! And instead of passing on, he stayed there smiling at the tree.

" Morning like this!" he thought; " and here I am the only person in the Square who has the — to come out and — !" But he had no sooner conceived this thought than he saw quite near him a man with his hands behind him, who was also staring up and smiling at the little tree. Rather taken aback, Mr. Nilson ceased to smile, and looked furtively at the stranger. It was his next-door neighbour, Mr. Tandram, well known in the City, who had occupied the adjoining house for some five years. Mr. Nilson perceived at once the awkwardness of his position, for, being married, they had not yet had occasion to speak to one another. Doubtful as to his proper conduct, he decided at last to murmur: " Fine morning!" and was passing on, when Mr. Tandram answered: " Beautiful, for the time of year!" Detecting a slight nervousness in his neighbour's voice, Mr. Nilson was emboldened③ to regard him openly. He was of about Mr. Nilson's own height, with firm well-coloured cheeks, neat brown

① emanate: come out from a source

② promenade: a walk taken in a public place for pleasure

③ embolden: to instill with boldness or courage

moustaches, and round, well-opened, clear grey eyes; and he was wearing a black frock coat. Mr. Nilson noticed that he had his morning paper clasped behind him as he looked up at the little tree. And, visited somehow by the feeling that he had been caught out, he said abruptly:

" Er — can you give me the name of that tree?"

Mr. Tandram answered:

" I was about to ask you that," and stepped towards it. Mr. Nilson also approached the tree.

" Sure to have its name on, I should think," he said.

Mr. Tandram was the first to see the little label, close to where the blackbird had been sitting. He read it out.

" Japanese quince!"

" Ah!" said Mr. Nilson, " thought so. Early flowerers."

" Very," assented Mr. Tandram, and added: " Quite a feelin' in the air to-day."

Mr. Nilson nodded.

" It was a blackbird singin'," he said.

" Blackbirds," answered Mr. Tandram, " I prefer them to thrushes myself; more body in the note." And he looked at Mr. Nilson in an almost friendly way.

" Quite," murmured Mr. Nilson. " These exotics, they don't bear fruit. Pretty blossom!" and he again glanced up at the blossom, thinking: " Nice fellow, this, I rather like him."

Mr. Tandram also gazed at the blossom. And the little tree as if appreciating their attention, quivered and glowed. From a distance the blackbird gave a loud, clear call. Mr. Nilson dropped his eyes. It struck him suddenly that Mr. Tandram looked a little foolish; and, as if he had seen himself, he said: " I must be going in. Good morning!"

A shade passed over Mr. Tandram's face, as if he, too, had suddenly noticed something about Mr. Nilson.

" Good morning," he replied, and clasping their journals to their backs they separated.

Mr. Nilson retraced his steps toward his garden window, walking slowly so as to avoid arriving at the same time as his neighbour. Having seen Mr. Tandram mount his scrolled iron steps, he ascended his own in turn. On the top step he paused.

With the slanting① spring sunlight darting and quivering into it, the Japanese quince seemed more living than a tree. The blackbird had returned to it, and was chanting out his heart.

Mr. Nilson sighed; again he felt that queer sensation, that choky feeling in his throat.

The sound of a cough or sigh attracted his attention. There, in the shadow of his French window, stood Mr. Tandram, also looking forth across the Gardens at the little quince tree.

Unaccountably upset, Mr. Nilson turned abruptly into the house, and opened his morning paper.

Topics for discussion

1. When Mr. Nilson finally murmurs a greeting to his neighbor, he detests " a slight nervousness in his neighbor's voice." why?

2. Upon encountering the quince tree, Mr. Nilson's first instinct is to find out exactly what species it is, rather than simply enjoy the flowers. How is this related to the queer sensation that he feels in his throat?

3. What is beneath the surface of the theme of beauty in the story?

References for further reading

[1] Smit, J. Henry. *The Short Stories of John Galsworthy*, Haskell House, 1996.

① slanting: sloping in one direction

[2] Bradbury, Malcolm and James McFarlane, eds. *Modernism: 1890-1930*, Penguin, 1991.

[3] Ginden, James. *John Galsworthy's Life and Art.* University of Michigan Press, 1979.

Virginia Woolf (1882 — 1941)

Kew Gardens

Introduction to the author

Virginia Woolf (January 25, 1882 — March 28, 1941), a British modernist author, is seen as a major twentieth century novelist, a major innovator in the English language and one of the foremost modernists of the twentieth century. Together with her modernist contemporaries like James Joyce and Joseph Conrad, Woolf is considered as one of the most outstanding leaders of stream of consciousness writers. Woolf was a significant figure in London literary society and a central figure in the influential Bloomsbury Group of intellectuals. Her most famous novels include *Mrs Dalloway, To the Lighthouse and Orlando*. Woolf's nonfiction writings, such as *A Room of One's Own* (1929) and *Three Guineas*, powerfully advocate for women's rights.

Virginia Woolf was born Adeline Virginia Stephen, on January 15, 1882, to Sir Leslie Stephen and Julia Stephen in London. Her father was a notable historian, author, critic and mountaineer, a founding editor of the *Dictionary of National Biography*. Woolf was educated by her parents in their literate and well-connected household. Her parents had each been married previously and the household contained the 7 children of three marriages. In 1895, when Woolf was 13, her mother suddenly died, which led to the first of Woolf's several nervous breakdowns. The death of her father in 1904, along with the sexual abuse by her half-brothers, provoked her most alarming collapse and she was briefly institutionalized. In spite of this, she still managed to maintain her literary productivity throughout her life. Later, her family moved to a house in Bloomsbury. Woolf came to know Lytton Strachey, Clive Bell, Rupert Brooke, Saxon Sydney-Turner, Duncan Grant, Leonard Woolf, John Maynard Keynes, David Garnett, and Roger Fry, who together formed the nucleus of the intellectual circle of writers and artists known as the Bloomsbury Group.

Woolf married writer Leonard Woolf on August 10, 1912. The couple shared a close bond and they two also collaborated professionally. In 1917, they co-founded the Hogarth Press, which subsequently published Virginia's novels and the works by T.S. Eliot, Laurens van der Post, and others. In 1922, she met the writer and gardener Vita Sackville-West, wife of Harold Nicolson. They developed a homosexual relationship. The effect of Vita on Virginia is all contained in Orlando, which is referred to as the longest and most charming love letter in literature.

The cruelty of the Second World War, the destruction of her London home during the Blitz as well as the cool reception of her biography of her late friend Roger Fry worsened her condition until she was unable to work. On March 28, 1941, Woolf walked into the River Ouse near her home, the pockets of her overcoat filled with stones. She drowned herself. Her husband buried her cremated remains under an elm in the garden of Monk's House, their home in Rodmell, Sussex.

Major works by Virginia Woolf

Novels

The Voyage Out, 1915

Night and Day, 1919

Jacob's Room, 1922

Mrs Dalloway, 1925

To the Lighthouse, 1927

Orlando, 1928

The Waves, 1931

The Years, 1937

Between the Acts,1941

Short story collections

Kew Gardens, 1919

Monday or Tuesday, 1921

A Haunted House and Other Short Stories, 1944

Biographies

Orlando: A Biography, 1928

Flush: A Biography, 1933

Roger Fry: A Biography, 1940

Non-fiction books

Modern Fiction, 1919

The Common Reader, 1925

A Room of One's Own, 1929

The London Scene, 1931

The Common Reader: Second Series, 1932

Three Guineas, 1938

The Death of the Moth and Other Essays, 1942

The Moment and Other Essays, 1947

The Captain's Death Bed And Other Essays, 1950

Granite and Rainbow, 1958

Books and Portraits, 1978

Women And Writing, 1979

Appreciation

" Kew Gardens" was published in 1919. The story happens on a mild, breezy, summer day in July in Kew Gardens with numerous stalks of colorful flowers and petals unfurled to meet the sunlight. People walk down the garden paths, zigzagging like butterflies. The narrator is paying his attention to the conversations of the passing people. The first group is a husband and wife who are walking just ahead of their children. The second group walking by the flower bed are both men, one elder and the other younger. The elder one talks almost incessantly about the spirits of the dead without getting any real response. Two elderly women of the lower middle class curiously follow the strange old man. As these two women walk away, the snail begins to traverse the leaf in his path by crawling under it. As he moves under the leaf, a fourth pair of feet come by the oval flower bed. This time they are both young, a young man and a young woman.

Each human character in the story seems lost in his or her own reminiscences. Despite the fact that they are all walking with someone in Kew Gardens, each of them has their own way of thinking deeply. The story ends with a final reflection on the garden. One couple after another passed the flower-bed, walking aimlessly. At first their bodies have substance and colour, but later both substance and colour dissolved in the green-blue atmosphere.

In " Kew Gardens", an omniscient third person narrator sets the scene and is able to dig into each character's private thoughts. The garden is situated in a vast and overwhelming world of the machinery and system of industrial production. Kew Gardens is the central image in the story.

Every character in " Kew Gardens" seems lost in his or her own reminiscences and isolated world. Human conditions of the time are presented in the context, a world of isolation, loneliness, aimlessness and transience.

Selected Reading

Kew Gardens

From the oval-shaped flower-bed there rose perhaps a hundred stalks spreading into heart-shaped or tongue-shaped leaves half way up and unfurling[①] at the tip red or blue or yellow petals marked with spots of colour raised upon the surface; and from the red, blue or yellow gloom of the throat emerged a straight bar, rough with gold dust and slightly clubbed at the end. The petals were voluminous enough to be stirred by the summer breeze, and when they moved, the red, blue and yellow lights passed one over the other, staining an inch of the brown earth beneath with a spot of the most intricate colour. The light fell either upon the smooth, grey back of a pebble, or, the shell of a snail with its brown, circular veins, or falling into a raindrop, it expanded with such intensity of red, blue and yellow the thin walls of water that one expected them to burst and disappear. Instead, the drop was left in a second silver grey once more, and the light now settled upon the flesh of a leaf, revealing the branching thread of fibre beneath the surface, and again it moved on and spread its illumination[②] in the vast green spaces beneath the dome of the heart-shaped and tongue-shaped leaves. Then the breeze stirred rather more briskly overhead and the colour was flashed into the air above, into the eyes of the men and women who walk in Kew Gardens in July.

The figures of these men and women straggled past the flower-bed with a curiously irregular movement not unlike that of the white and blue butterflies who crossed the turf in zig-zag flights from bed to bed. The man was about six inches in front of the woman, strolling carelessly, while she bore on with greater purpose,

---

① unfurl: If a flag, sail or banner unfurls, it becomes open from a rolled position, and if you unfurl a flag, etc. you make it do this

② illumination: the lighting that a place has

only turning her head now and then to see that the children were not too far behind. The man kept this distance in front of the woman purposely, though perhaps unconsciously, for he wished to go on with his thoughts.

" Fifteen years ago I came here with Lily," he thought. " We sat somewhere over there by a lake and I begged her to marry me all through the hot afternoon. How the dragonfly kept circling round us: how clearly I see the dragonfly and her shoe with the square silver buckle at the toe. All the time I spoke I saw her shoe and when it moved impatiently I knew without looking up what she was going to say: the whole of her seemed to be in her shoe. And my love, my desire, were in the dragonfly; for some reason I thought that if it settled there, on that leaf, the broad one with the red flower in the middle of it, if the dragonfly settled on the leaf she would say 'Yes' at once. But the dragonfly went round and round: it never settled anywhere — of course not, happily not, or I shouldn't be walking here with Eleanor and the children — Tell me, Eleanor. D'you ever think of the past?"

" Why do you ask, Simon?"

" Because I've been thinking of the past. I've been thinking of Lily, the woman I might have married... Well, why are you silent? Do you mind my thinking of the past?"

" Why should I mind, Simon? Doesn't one always think of the past, in a garden with men and women lying under the trees? Aren't they one's past, all that remains of it, those men and women, those ghosts lying under the trees,... one's happiness, one's reality?"

" For me, a square silver shoe buckle and a dragonfly — "

" For me, a kiss. Imagine six little girls sitting before their easels[①] twenty years ago, down by the side of a lake, painting the water-lilies, the first red water-lilies I'd ever seen. And suddenly a kiss, there on the back of my neck. And my hand

① easel: a wooden frame, usually with legs, that holds a picture, especially one which an artist is painting or drawing shook all the afternoon so that I couldn't paint. I took out my watch and marked the hour when I would allow myself to think of the kiss for five minutes only — it was so precious — the kiss of an old grey-haired woman with a wart① on her nose, the mother of all my kisses all my life. Come, Caroline, come, Hubert."

They walked on the past the flower-bed, now walking four abreast, and soon diminished in size among the trees and looked half transparent as the sunlight and shade swam over their backs in large trembling irregular patches.

In the oval flower bed the snail, whose shell had been stained red, blue, and yellow for the space of two minutes or so, now appeared to be moving very slightly in its shell, and next began to labour over the crumbs of loose earth which broke away and rolled down as it passed over them. It appeared to have a definite goal in front of it, differing in this respect from the singular high stepping angular green insect who attempted to cross in front of it, and waited for a second with its antenna② trembling as if in deliberation, and then stepped off as rapidly and strangely in the opposite direction. Brown cliffs with deep green lakes in the hollows, flat, blade-like trees that waved from root to tip, round boulders of grey stone, vast crumpled surfaces of a thin crackling texture — all these objects lay across the snail's progress between one stalk and another to his goal. Before he had decided whether to circumvent the arched tent of a dead leaf or to breast it there came past the bed the feet of other human beings.

This time they were both men. The younger of the two wore an expression of perhaps unnatural calm; he raised his eyes and fixed them very steadily in front of him while his companion spoke, and directly his companion had done speaking he looked on the ground again and sometimes opened his lips only after a long pause and sometimes did not open them at all. The elder man had a curiously uneven and shaky method of walking, jerking his hand forward and throwing up his head

① wart: a small hard lump (= raised area) which grows on the skin, often on the face and hands

② antenna: either of the two long, thin parts attached to the head of an insect that it uses to know what is around it abruptly, rather in the manner of an impatient carriage horse tired of waiting outside a house; but in the man these gestures were irresolute and pointless. He talked almost incessantly; he smiled to himself and again began to talk, as if the smile had been an answer. He was talking about spirits — the spirits of the dead, who, according to him, were even now telling him all sorts of odd things about their experiences in Heaven.

" Heaven was known to the ancients as Thessaly, William, and now, with this war, the spirit matter is rolling between the hills like thunder." He paused, seemed to listen, smiled, jerked① his head and continued: —

" You have a small electric battery and a piece of rubber to insulate the wire — isolate? — insulate? — well, we'll skip the details, no good going into details that wouldn't be understood — and in short the little machine stands in any convenient position by the head of the bed, we will say, on a neat mahogany stand. All arrangements being properly fixed by workmen under my direction, the widow applies her ear and summons the spirit by sign as agreed. Women! Widows! Women in black — "

Here he seemed to have caught sight of a woman's dress in the distance, which in the shade looked a purple black. He took off his hat, placed his hand upon his heart, and hurried towards her muttering and gesticulating② feverishly. But William caught him by the sleeve and touched a flower with the tip of his walking-stick in order to divert the old man's attention. After looking at it for a moment in some confusion the old man bent his ear to it and seemed to answer a voice speaking from it, for he began talking about the forests of Uruguay which he had visited hundreds of years ago in company with the most beautiful young woman in Europe. He could be heard murmuring about forests of Uruguay blanketed with the wax petals of tropical roses, nightingales, sea beaches, mermaids, and women drowned at sea, as

① jerk: to make a short sudden movement, or to cause someone or something to do this

② gesticulate: to make movements with your hands or arms, to express something or to emphasize what you are saying he suffered himself to be moved on by William, upon whose face the look of stoical patience grew slowly deeper and deeper.

Following his steps so closely as to be slightly puzzled by his gestures came two elderly women of the lower middle class, one stout and ponderous[①], the other rosy cheeked and nimble. Like most people of their station they were frankly fascinated by any signs of eccentricity betokening a disordered brain, especially in the well-to-do; but they were too far off to be certain whether the gestures were merely eccentric or genuinely mad. After they had scrutinised the old man's back in silence for a moment and given each other a queer, sly look, they went on energetically piecing together their very complicated dialogue:

" Nell, Bert, Lot, Cess, Phil, Pa, he says, I says, she says, I says, I says, I says — "

" My Bert, Sis, Bill, Grandad, the old man, sugar,

Sugar, flour, kippers, greens,

Sugar, sugar, sugar."

The ponderous woman looked through the pattern of falling words at the flowers standing cool, firm, and upright in the earth, with a curious expression. She saw them as a sleeper waking from a heavy sleep sees a brass candlestick reflecting the light in an unfamiliar way, and closes his eyes and opens them, and seeing the brass candlestick again, finally starts broad awake and stares at the candlestick with all his powers. So the heavy woman came to a standstill opposite the oval-shaped flower bed, and ceased even to pretend to listen to what the other woman was saying. She stood there letting the words fall over her, swaying the top part of her body slowly backwards and forwards, looking at the flowers. Then she suggested that they should find a seat and have their tea.

The snail had now considered every possible method of reaching his goal

① ponderous: slow and awkward because of being very heavy or large without going round the dead leaf or climbing over it. Let alone the effort needed for climbing a leaf, he was doubtful whether the thin texture which vibrated with such an alarming crackle when touched even by the tip of his horns would bear his weight; and this determined him finally to creep beneath it, for there was a point where the leaf curved high enough from the ground to admit him. He had just inserted his head in the opening and was taking stock of the high brown roof and was getting used to the cool brown light when two other people came past outside on the turf. This time they were both young, a young man and a young woman. They were both in the prime of youth, or even in that season which precedes the prime of youth, the season before the smooth pink folds of the flower have burst their gummy case, when the wings of the butterfly, though fully grown, are motionless in the sun.

" Lucky it isn't Friday," he observed.

" Why? D'you believe in luck?"

" They make you pay sixpence on Friday."

" What's sixpence anyway? Isn't it worth sixpence?"

" What's 'it' — what do you mean by 'it'?"

" O, anything — I mean — you know what I mean."

Long pauses came between each of these remarks; they were uttered in toneless and monotonous voices. The couple stood still on the edge of the flower bed, and together pressed the end of her parasol deep down into the soft earth. The action and the fact that his hand rested on the top of hers expressed their feelings in a strange way, as these short insignificant words also expressed something, words with short wings for their heavy body of meaning, inadequate to carry them far and thus alighting awkwardly upon the very common objects that surrounded them, and were to their inexperienced touch so massive; but who knows (so they thought as they pressed the parasol into the earth) what precipices aren't concealed in them, or what slopes of ice don't shine in the sun on the other side? Who knows? Who has ever seen this before? Even when she wondered what sort of tea they gave you at Kew, he felt that something loomed up behind her words, and stood vast and solid behind them; and the mist very slowly rose and uncovered — O, Heavens, what were those shapes? — little white tables, and waitresses who looked first at her and then at him; and there was a bill that he would pay with a real two shilling piece, and it was real, all real, he assured himself, fingering the coin in his pocket, real to everyone except to him and to her; even to him it began to seem real; and then — but it was too exciting to stand and think any longer, and he pulled the parasol out of the earth with a jerk and was impatient to find the place where one had tea with other people, like other people.

"Come along, Trissie; it's time we had our tea."

"Wherever does one have one's tea?" she asked with the oddest thrill of excitement in her voice, looking vaguely round and letting herself be drawn on down the grass path, trailing her parasol①, turning her head this way and that way, forgetting her tea, wishing to go down there and then down there, remembering orchids and cranes among wild flowers, a Chinese pagoda and a crimson crested bird; but he bore her on.

Thus one couple after another with much the same irregular and aimless movement passed the flower-bed and were enveloped in layer after layer of green blue vapour, in which at first their bodies had substance and a dash of colour, but later both substance and colour dissolved in the green-blue atmosphere. How hot it was! So hot that even the thrush chose to hop, like a mechanical bird, in the shadow of the flowers, with long pauses between one movement and the next; instead of rambling vaguely the white butterflies danced one above another, making with their white shifting flakes the outline of a shattered marble column above the tallest flowers; the glass roofs of the palm house shone as if a whole market full of shiny green umbrellas had opened in the sun; and in the drone of the aeroplane the voice of the summer

① parasol: a type of sunshade (= round frame covered in cloth on a stick) carried especially by women in the past, to give protection from the sun sky murmured its fierce soul. Yellow and black, pink and snow white, shapes of all these colours, men, women, and children were spotted for a second upon the horizon, and then, seeing the breadth of yellow that lay upon the grass, they wavered① and sought shade beneath the trees, dissolving like drops of water in the yellow and green atmosphere, staining it faintly with red and blue. It seemed as if all gross and heavy bodies had sunk down in the heat motionless and lay huddled upon the ground, but their voices went wavering from them as if they were flames lolling② from the thick waxen bodies of candles. Voices. Yes, voices. Wordless voices, breaking the silence suddenly with such depth of contentment, such passion of desire, or, in the voices of children, such freshness of surprise; breaking the silence? But there was no silence; all the time the motor omnibuses were turning their wheels and changing their gear; like a vast nest of Chinese boxes all of wrought steel turning ceaselessly one within another the city murmured; on the top of which the voices cried aloud and the petals of myriads of flowers flashed their colours into the air.

Topics for discussion

1. How is the image of garden used ironically in the story?

2. Do you think the very language itself that human beings use to connect to other human beings is a wall that prevents communications in the story?

3. How does each couple that passes through the garden represent ideas regarding what men and women are supposed to do in society?

References for further reading

[1] Briggs, Julia. *Virginia Woolf: An Inner Life*. New York: Mariner Books,

① waver: to lose strength, determination or purpose, especially temporarily

② loll: to lie, sit or hang down in a relaxed informal or uncontrolled way

2006.

[2] Goldman, Jane. *The Feminist Aesthetics of Virginia Woolf.* Cambridge University Press, 2001.

[3] Gordon, Lyndall. *Virginia Woolf: A Writer's Life*. New York: Norton, 1984.

[4] Bell, Quentin. *Virginia Woolf: A Biography*. New York, Harcourt Brace Jovanovich, 1972.

[5] Dalgarno, Emily. *Virginia Woolf and the Visible World*. Cambridge University Press, 2007.

[6] Simons, Ilana. *A Life of One's Own: A Guide to Better Living through the Work and Wisdom of Virginia Woolf.* New York: Penguin Press, 2007.

James Joyce (1882 — 1941)

Araby

Introduction to the author

James Joyce (1882 — 1941) was an Irish novelist, noted for his experimental use of language in such works as *Ulysses* (1922) and *Finnegans Wake* (1939). Joyce is one of the most famous writers of the Modernist period of literature. Characters who are spiritually lost, an extensive use of interior monologue, a complex network of symbolic parallels drawn from the mythology, history, and literature character Joyce's works, creating a unique language of invented words, puns, and allusions.

James Joyce was born to John Stanislaus Joyce and Mary Jane Murray in Dublin, on February 2, 1882, the oldest son of ten children. Joyce's father tried various kinds of professions, including politics and tax collecting, but he failed. Being a drinker, he wasted a lot of money. Joyce's mother was an accomplished pianist and she held a firm belief in the Roman Catholic Church. Despite their poverty, the family struggled to maintain a solid middle-class facade. At the age of six, Joyce was sent to Clongowes Wood College at Clane, a Jesuit catholic boarding school. Then he studied at Belvedere College in Dublin (1893 — 1897), where he began to show his talent as a writer. In 1898, he entered the University College, Dublin and he began to rebel against his Catholic upbringing. After graduation in 1902, Joyce went to Paris and worked as a journalist, teacher and held a variety of other jobs.

After graduation, Joyce met Nora Barnacle. They did not get married until 1931, after 27 years of living together due to Joyce's objection to the institution of marriage. They left Dublin in 1904 after Joyce's mother died and lived in Continental Europe all the rest of their life. they stayed in several countries, first in Pola, in the former Yugoslavia, then Trieste, Italy, and then Zurich, Switzerland. During WWI, they moved to Paris. It was after the publication of *Ulysses* in 1922 that Joyce reached a financial stability enabling him to work as a full-time writer. In March 1923, Joyce started in Paris his second major work, *Finnegans Wake*. He suffered at the same time chronic eye troubles caused by glaucoma and underwent several eye operations. After the fall of France in WWII, Joyce returned to Zürich, where he died on January 13, 1941, aged 58.

Major works by James Joyce

Novel

A Portrait of the Artist as a Young Man, 1916 *Ulysses*, 1922

Finnegans Wake, 1939

Short-story collection

Dubliners, 1914

poems

Chamber Music, 1907 *Pomes Penyeach*, 1927

Collected Poems, 1936

play

Exiles, 1918

Appreciation

" Araby" was published in 1914, one of the fifteen short stories in Joyce's short story collection, *Dubliners*. The story is set on North Richmond street in Dublin. the unnamed narrator is a part of the group of boys who often play together in the street. The boy secretly falls in love with Mangan's sister, a girl who captivates his imagination. Although he rarely speaks to her, he thinks only of her. At last, the girl speaks to him, asking if he will attend a fair called Araby. When he learns that the girl cannot go to the fair herself because of a retreat that week in her convent, the boy promises to go there and bring her a gift from the fair. when the boy arrives, Araby is closing down. While walking around, he overhears a conversation, which makes him realize that he has been confusing things. He has romanticized the fair which is actually a commercial place to buy things and maybe he has taken too seriously about his promise.

In the story, the boy's complicated inner world during his frustrated quest for beauty is vividly described from the first person's point of view. Many symbolisms are used in this story, such as Mangan's sister, for whom the boy has tender feelings, the journey to the bazaar, the young lady at the door of a stall. The boy's disillusionment about Araby comes along with his disillusionment about the idealized vision of Mangan's sister and of love. The boy's simple and pure love can be revealed through his action, his self-narration and his mentality. Joyce is well-known for the creation of moments of epiphany. The unnamed boy narrator is a good example.

Selected Reading

Araby

North Richmond Street being blind, was a quiet street except at the hour when the Christian Brothers' School set the boys free. An uninhabited house of two storeys stood at the blind end, detached from its neighbours in a square ground. The other houses of the street, conscious of decent lives within them, gazed at one another with brown imperturbable① faces.

The former tenant of our house, a priest, had died in the back drawing-room. Air, musty from having been long enclosed, hung in all the rooms, and the waste room behind the kitchen was littered with old useless papers. Among these I found a few paper-covered books, the pages of which were curled and damp: *The Abbot*, by Walter Scott, *The Devout Communnicant* and *The Memoirs of Vidocq*. I liked the last best because its leaves were yellow. The wild garden behind the house contained a central apple-tree and a few straggling bushes under one of which I found the late tenant's rusty bicycle-pump. He had been a very charitable priest; in his will he had left all his money to institutions and the furniture of his house to his sister.

When the short days of winter came dusk fell before we had well eaten our dinners. When we met in the street the houses had grown sombre. The space of sky above us was the colour of ever-changing violet and towards it the lamps of the street lifted their feeble lanterns. The cold air stung us and we played till our bodies glowed. Our shouts echoed in the silent street. The career of our play brought us through the dark muddy lanes behind the houses where we ran the gauntlet of the rough tribes from the cottages, to the back doors of the dark dripping gardens where odours arose from the ashpits, to the dark odorous stables where a coachman smoothed and combed the horse or shook music from the buckled harness. When we returned to the street light from the kitchen windows had filled the areas. If my uncle was seen turning the corner we hid in the shadow until we had seen him safely housed. Or if Mangan's sister came out on the doorstep to call her brother in to his tea we watched her from our shadow peer up and down the street. We waited to see whether she

---

① imperturbable: calm and relaxed

would remain or go in and, if she remained, we left our shadow and walked up to Mangan's steps resignedly. She was waiting for us, her figure defined by the light from the half-opened door. Her brother always teased her before he obeyed and I stood by the railings looking at her. Her dress swung as she moved her body and the soft rope of her hair tossed from side to side.

Every morning I lay on the floor in the front parlour watching her door. The blind was pulled down to within an inch of the sash so that I could not be seen. When she came out on the doorstep my heart leaped. I ran to the hall, seized my books and followed her. I kept her brown figure always in my eye and, when we came near the point at which our ways diverged, I quickened my pace and passed her. This happened morning after morning. I had never spoken to her, except for a few casual words, and yet her name was like a summons to all my foolish blood.

Her image accompanied me even in places the most hostile to romance. On Saturday evenings when my aunt went marketing I had to go to carry some of the parcels. We walked through the flaring streets, jostled① by drunken men and bargaining women, amid the curses of labourers, the shrill litanies of shop-boys who stood on guard by the barrels of pigs' cheeks, the nasal chanting of street-singers, who sang a come-all-you about O'Donovan Rossa, or a ballad about the troubles in our native land. These noises converged in a single sensation of life for me: I imagined that I bore my chalice safely through a throng of foes. Her name sprang to my lips at moments in strange prayers and praises which I myself did not understand. My eyes were often full of tears (I could not tell why) and at times a flood from my heart seemed to pour itself out into my bosom. I thought little of the future. I did not know whether I would ever speak to her or not or, if I spoke to her, how I could tell her of my confused adoration. But my body was like a harp and her words and gestures were like fingers running upon the wires.

---

① jostled: crowded

One evening I went into the back drawing-room in which the priest had died. It was a dark rainy evening and there was no sound in the house. Through one of the broken panes I heard the rain impinge① upon the earth, the fine incessant② needles of water playing in the sodden beds. Some distant lamp or lighted window gleamed below me. I was thankful that I could see so little. All my senses seemed to desire to veil themselves and, feeling that I was about to slip from them, I pressed the palms of my hands together until they trembled, murmuring: " O love! O love!" many times.

At last she spoke to me. When she addressed the first words to me I was so confused that I did not know what to answer. She asked me was I going to Araby. I forgot whether I answered yes or no. It would be a splendid bazaar③ , she said she would love to go.

" And why can't you?" I asked.

While she spoke she turned a silver bracelet round and round her wrist. She could not go, she said, because there would be a retreat that week in her convent. Her brother and two other boys were fighting for their caps and I was alone at the railings. She held one of the spikes, bowing her head towards me. The light from the lamp opposite our door caught the white curve of her neck, lit up her hair that rested there and, falling, lit up the hand upon the railing. It fell over one side of her dress and caught the white border of a petticoat, just visible as she stood at ease.

" It's well for you," she said.

" If I go," I said, " I will bring you something."

What innumerable follies laid waste my waking and sleeping thoughts after that evening! I wished to annihilate④ the tedious intervening days. I chafed against the work of school. At night in my bedroom and by day in the classroom her image

① impinge: to have an effect on something, often by limiting it in some way

② incessant: never stopping, especially in an annoying or unpleasant way

③ bazaar: an area of small shops and people selling things, especially in the Middle East and South Asia

④ annihilate: to destroy something completely so that nothing is left came between me and the page I strove to read. The syllables of the word Araby were called to me through the silence in which my soul luxuriated and cast an Eastern enchantment over me. I asked for leave to go to the bazaar on Saturday night. My aunt was surprised and hoped it was not some Freemason affair. I answered few questions in class. I watched my master's face pass from amiability to sternness; he hoped I was not beginning to idle. I could not call my wandering thoughts together. I had hardly any patience with the serious work of life which, now that it stood between me and my desire, seemed to me child's play, ugly monotonous child's play.

On Saturday morning I reminded my uncle that I wished to go to the bazaar in the evening. He was fussing at the hallstand, looking for the hat-brush, and answered me curtly:

" Yes, boy, I know."

As he was in the hall I could not go into the front parlour and lie at the window. I left the house in bad humour and walked slowly towards the school. The air was pitilessly raw and already my heart misgave me.

When I came home to dinner my uncle had not yet been home. Still it was early. I sat staring at the clock for some time and when its ticking began to irritate me, I left the room. I mounted the staircase and gained the upper part of the house. The high cold empty gloomy rooms liberated me and I went from room to room singing. From the front window I saw my companions playing below in the street. Their cries reached me weakened and indistinct and, leaning my forehead against the cool glass, I looked over at the dark house where she lived. I may have stood there for an hour, seeing nothing but the brown-clad figure cast by my imagination, touched discreetly by the lamplight at the curved neck, at the hand upon the railings and at the border below the dress.

When I came downstairs again I found Mrs. Mercer sitting at the fire. She was an old garrulous woman, a pawnbroker's widow, who collected used stamps for some pious purpose. I had to endure the gossip of the tea-table. The meal was prolonged beyond an hour and still my uncle did not come. Mrs. Mercer stood up to go: she was sorry she couldn't wait any longer, but it was after eight o'clock and she did not like to be out late as the night air was bad for her. When she had gone I began to walk up and down the room, clenching my fists. My aunt said:

" I'm afraid you may put off your bazaar for this night of Our Lord."

At nine o'clock I heard my uncle's latchkey in the halldoor. I heard him talking to himself and heard the hallstand rocking when it had received the weight of his overcoat. I could interpret these signs. When he was midway through his dinner I asked him to give me the money to go to the bazaar. He had forgotten.

" The people are in bed and after their first sleep now," he said.

I did not smile. My aunt said to him energetically:

" Can't you give him the money and let him go? You've kept him late enough as it is."

My uncle said he was very sorry he had forgotten. He said he believed in the old saying: " All work and no play makes Jack a dull boy." He asked me where I was going and, when I had told him a second time he asked me did I know The Arab's Farewell to his Steed. When I left the kitchen he was about to recite the opening lines of the piece to my aunt.

I held a florin tightly in my hand as I strode down Buckingham Street towards the station. The sight of the streets thronged with buyers and glaring with gas recalled to me the purpose of my journey. I took my seat in a third-class carriage of a deserted train. After an intolerable delay the train moved out of the station slowly. It crept onward among ruinous house and over the twinkling river. At Westland Row Station a crowd of people pressed to the carriage doors; but the porters moved them back, saying that it was a special train for the bazaar. I remained alone in the bare carriage. In a few minutes the train drew up beside an improvised wooden platform. I passed out on to the road and saw by the lighted dial of a clock that it was ten minutes to ten. In front of me was a large building which displayed the magical name.

I could not find any sixpenny entrance and, fearing that the bazaar would be closed, I passed in quickly through a turnstile① , handing a shilling to a weary-looking man. I found myself in a big hall girdled② at half its height by a gallery. Nearly all the stalls were closed and the greater part of the hall was in darkness. I recognised a silence like that which pervades a church after a service. I walked into the centre of the bazaar timidly. A few people were gathered about the stalls which were still open. Before a curtain, over which the words Cafe Chantant were written in coloured lamps, two men were counting money on a salver. I listened to the fall of the coins.

Remembering with difficulty why I had come I went over to one of the stalls and examined porcelain vases and flowered tea-sets. At the door of the stall a young lady was talking and laughing with two young gentlemen. I remarked their English accents and listened vaguely to their conversation.

" O, I never said such a thing!"

" O, but you did!"

" O, but I didn't!"

" Didn't she say that?"

" Yes. I heard her."

" O, there's a... fib!"

Observing me the young lady came over and asked me did I wish to buy anything. The tone of her voice was not encouraging; she seemed to have spoken to me out of a sense of duty. I looked humbly at the great jars that stood like eastern guards at either side of the dark entrance to the stall and murmured:

" No, thank you."

The young lady changed the position of one of the vases and went back to the

---

① turnstile: a device that controls the way into or out of a building, room, or area of land, especially one that you have to pay to enter

② girdled: surrounded

two young men. They began to talk of the same subject. Once or twice the young lady glanced at me over her shoulder.

I lingered before her stall, though I knew my stay was useless, to make my interest in her wares seem the more real. Then I turned away slowly and walked down the middle of the bazaar. I allowed the two pennies to fall against the sixpence in my pocket. I heard a voice call from one end of the gallery that the light was out. The upper part of the hall was now completely dark.

Gazing up into the darkness I saw myself as a creature driven and derided by vanity; and my eyes burned with anguish and anger.

Topics for discussion

1. Why does the author describe the back drawing-room in the house?

2. What does Araby symbolize for the young boy? Do you think that he changed a lot in the end?

3. Discuss author's use of images and symbol

4. Make some comment on epiphany used by the author?

References for further reading

[1] Bulson, Eric. *The Cambridge Introduction to James Joyce*. Cambridge and New York: Cambridge University Press, 2006.

[2] Costello, Peter. *James Joyce: the years of growth, 1892–1915*. New York: Pantheon Books, a division of Random House, 1992.

[3] Deming, Robert H. *James Joyce: The Critical Heritage*. Abingdon, Oxon: Routledge, 1997.

[4] McCourt, John, ed. *James Joyce in Context*. Cambridge and New York: Cambridge University Press, 2009.

D. H. Lawrence (1885 — 1930)

The Rocking Horse Winner

Introduction to the author

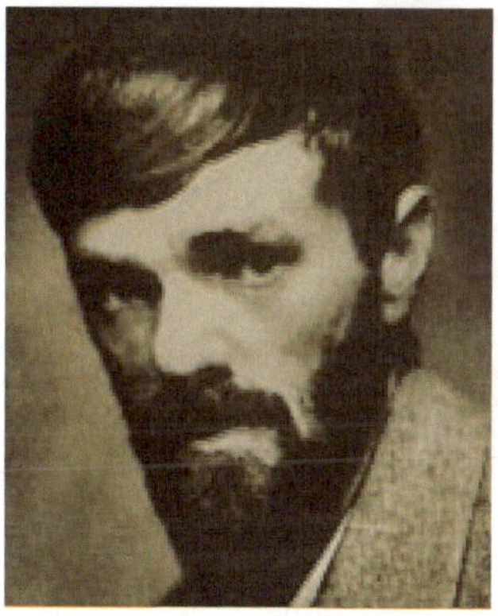

David Herbert Lawrence (September 11, 1885 — March 2, 1930) was an English novelist, poet, playwright, essayist, literary critic and painter. His collected works make a profound reflection and meditation on the dehumanization of modernity and industrialization. Lawrence is a representative of modernism, objecting to the literary conventions of the nineteenth-century morality, taste and tradition. Much of Lawrence's fiction are placed within the " great tradition" of the English novel. Lawrence is now agreed by many as a visionary thinker and significant representative of modernism in English literature.

Lawrence was born on September 11, 1885, the fourth child of Lydia and Arthur John Lawrence. His father was a barely literate miner and his mother was a former pupil teacher. Lawrence had an extremely close relationship with his mother. Lawrence grew up in the coal mining town of Eastwood, Nottinghamshire. His working-class background and the tensions between his parents provided the raw material for a number of his early works. Lawrence attended Beauvale Board School.

Then he worked for three months as a junior clerk at Haywood's surgical appliances factory. In the years 1902 to 1906 Lawrence served as a pupil teacher at the British School, Eastwood. He went on to become a full-time student and received a teaching certificate from University College, Nottingham, in 1908. During these early years he was working on his first poems, some short stories, and a draft of a novel, *Laetitia*, that was eventually to become *The White Peacock*. At the end of 1907 he won a short story competition in the Nottingham Guardian, the first time that he had gained any wider recognition for his literary talents.

At the age of 27, Lawrence eloped with Ernest Weekley, the wife of one of his college professors. They got married in 1914 and had three young children. In a self-exile, Lawrence visited Australia, Italy, Ceylon (now Sri Lanka), the United States, Mexico and the South of France. On March 2, 1930, Lawrence died in Vence, France, aged 44. After Lawrence's death, Frieda married Angelo Ravagli, who brought Lawrence's ashes to be interred in a small chapel set amid the mountains of New Mexico, U.S.A.

Major works by D. H. Lawrence

Novels

The White Peacock, 1911

The Trespasser, 1912

Sons and Lovers, 1913

The Rainbow, 1915

Women in Love, 1920

The Lost Girl,1920

Aaron's Rod, 1922

Kangaroo, 1923

The Boy in the Bush, 1924

The Plumed Serpent, 1926

Lady Chatterley's Lover (1928)

Short stories collections

The Prussian Officer and Other Stories, 1914 *England, My England and Other*

Stories, 1922

The Horse Dealer's Daughter, 1922

The Fox, The Captain's Doll, The Ladybird, 1923

St Mawr and other stories, 1925

The Woman who Rode Away and other stories, 1928

The Rocking-Horse Winner, 1926

Love Among the Haystacks and other stories, 1930

Poetry collections

Love Poems and others, 1913

Look! We have come through!, 1917

New Poems, 1918

Bay: a book of poems, 1919

Tortoises, 1921

Birds, Beasts and Flowers, 1923

The Collected Poems of D H Lawrence, 1928

Pansies, 1929

Nettles, 1930

Last Poems, 1932

Fire and other poems, 1940

The White Horse, 1964

Plays

The Daughter-in-Law, 1912

The Widowing of Mrs Holroyd, 1914

Touch and Go, 1920

David, 1926

The Fight for Barbara, 1933

A Collier's Friday Night, 1934

The Married Man, 1940

The Merry-Go-Round, 1941

Appreciation

" The Rocking-Horse Winner" was first published in July 1926, in *Harper's Bazaar*. The story is of a boy's gift for picking the winners in horse races. the boy lives in a family which is constantly short of money. His mother is a young middle-class commercial artist who is obsessed with the material success. Anxiety about money permeates the household. Her children, a son Paul and his two sisters, are clearly aware of the mother's desire for money, the son in particular. Paul believes that he is luck and he can pick the winners in horse races.

Paul proves magically talented at dividing the winners of the horse races. He places bets using his pocket money and saved a considerable amount of money. His uncle Oscar and the gardener Bassett both place large bets on the horses Paul names. Paul reveals to Oscar that he wants to give the money to his mother. Paul arranges through Oscar to give a thousand pounds to his mother as an anonymous gift each year for five years. But when the mother gets the present, instead of being happy, she is indifferent. Desperate to please his mother, the boy agrees to let his mother to have the whole five thousand pound at once, but the gift only lets her spend more. Disappointed, Paul tries harder than ever to be " lucky". As the Derby approaches, Paul is determined to learn the winner. Concerned about his health, his mother rushes home from a party and discovers his secret. He has been spending hours riding his rocking horse, sometimes all night long, until he gets into a clairvoyant state where he can be sure of the winner's name. Paul remains seriously ill through the day of the Derby. Informed by Oscar, Bassett places Paul's bet on Malabar, which earned him over 80,000 pounds. Although the boy has sacrificed his life for his mother and his family, it seems that his mother still does not truly love him.

Although Lawrence is best remembered for his novels such as *Sons and Lovers*, *Women in Love*, *Lady Chatterley's Lover and The Rainbow*, many critics agree that his short stories, including " The Rocking Horse Winner", are better than his novels. Obviously, " The Rocking Horse Winner" severely attacks the conspicuous consumption, greedy materialism and indifference in parenting. It contains the typical themes in Lawrence's works, including the relationships between the sexes, the dehumanization brought by industry and human desires for wealth and the exploration of the human psyche.

Selected Reading

The Rocking-Horse Winner

There was a woman who was beautiful, who started with all the advantages, yet she had no luck. She married for love, and the love turned to dust. She had bonny children, yet she felt they had been thrust upon her, and she could not love them. They looked at her coldly, as if they were finding fault with her. And hurriedly she felt she must cover up some fault in herself. Yet what it was that she must cover up she never knew. Nevertheless, when her children were present, she always felt the center of her heart go hard. This troubled her, and in her manner she was all the more gentle and anxious for her children, as if she loved them very much. Only she herself knew that at the center of her heart was a hard little place that could not feel love, no, not for anybody. Everybody else said of her: " She is such a good mother. She adores her children." Only she herself, and her children themselves, knew it was not so. They read it in each other's eyes.

There were a boy and two little girls. They lived in a pleasant house, with a garden, and they had discreet servants, and felt themselves superior to anyone in the neighborhood.

Although they lived in style, they felt always an anxiety in the house. There was never enough money. The mother had a small income, and the father had a small income, but not nearly enough for the social position which they had to keep up. The father went in to town to some office. But though he had good prospects, these prospects never materialized. There was always the grinding sense of the shortage of money, though the style was always kept up.

At last the mother said: " I will see if I can't make something." But she did not know where to begin. She racked her brains, and tried this thing and the other, but could not find anything successful. The failure made deep lines come into her face.

Her children were growing up, they would have to go to school. There must be more money, there must be more money. The father, who was always very handsome and expensive in his tastes, seemed as if he never would be able to do anything worth doing. And the mother, who had a great belief in herself, did not succeed any better, and her tastes were just as expensive.

And so the house came to be haunted by the unspoken phrase: There must be more money! There must be more money! The children could hear it all the time, though nobody said it aloud. They heard it at Christmas, when the expensive and splendid toys filled the nursery. Behind the shining modern rocking-horse, behind the smart doll's house, a voice would start whispering: " There must be more money! There must be more money!" And the children would stop playing, to listen for a moment. They would look into each other's eyes, to see if they had all heard. And each one saw in the eyes of the other two that they too had heard. " There must be more money! There must be more money!"

It came whispering from the springs of the still-swaying rocking-horse, and even the horse, bending his wooden, champing head, heard it. The big doll, sitting so pink and smirking in her new pram, could hear it quite plainly, and seemed to be smirking all the more self-consciously because of it. The foolish puppy, too, that took the place of the teddy-bear, he was looking so extraordinarily foolish for no other reason but that he heard the secret whisper all over the house: " There must be more money!"

Yet nobody ever said it aloud. The whisper was everywhere, and therefore no one spoke it. Just as no one ever says: " We are breathing!" in spite of the fact that breath is coming and going all the time.

" Mother," said the boy Paul one day, " why don't we keep a car of our own? Why do we always use uncle's, or else a taxi?"

" Because we're the poor members of the family," said the mother.

" But why are we, mother?"

" Well — I suppose," she said slowly and bitterly, " it's because your father has no luck."

The boy was silent for some time.

" Is luck money, mother?" he asked rather timidly.

" No, Paul. Not quite. It's what causes you to have money."

" Oh!" said Paul vaguely. " I thought when Uncle Oscar said filthy lucker, it meant money."

" Filthy lucre does mean money," said the mother. " But it's lucre, not luck."

" Oh!" said Paul vaguely. " Then what is luck, mother?"

" It's what causes you to have money. If you're lucky you have money. That's why it's better to be born lucky than rich. If you're rich, you may lose your money. But if you're lucky, you will always get more money."

" Oh! Will you? And is father not lucky?"

" Very unlucky, I should say," she said bitterly.

The boy watched her with unsure eyes.

" Why?" he asked.

" I don't know. Nobody ever know why one person is lucky and another unlucky."

" Don't they? Nobody at all? Does nobody know?"

" Perhaps God. But He never tells."

" He ought to, then. And aren't you lucky either, mother?"

" I can't be, if I married an unlucky husband."

" But by yourself, aren't you?"

" I used to think I was, before I married. Now I think I am very unlucky indeed."

" Why?"

" Well — never mind! Perhaps I'm not really," she said.

The child looked at her, to see if she meant it. But he saw, by the lines of her mouth, that she was only trying to hide something from him.

"Well, anyhow," he said stoutly[①], "I'm a lucky person."

"Why?" said his mother, with a sudden laugh.

He stared at her. He didn't even know why he had said it.

"God told me," he asserted, brazening it out[②].

"I hope He did, dear!" she said, again with a laugh, but rather bitter.

"He did, mother!"

"Excellent!" said the mother, using one of her husband's exclamations.

The boy saw she did not believe him; or, rather, that she paid no attention to his assertion. This angered him somewhat, and made him want to compel her attention.

He went off by himself, vaguely, in a childish way, seeking for the clue to "luck." Absorbed, taking no heed of other people, he went about with a sort of stealth, seeking inwardly for luck. He wanted luck, he wanted it, he wanted it. When the two girls were playing dolls in the nursery, he would sit on his big rocking-horse, charging madly into space, with a frenzy that made the little girls peer at him uneasily. Wildly the horse careered the waving dark hair of the boy tossed, his eyes had a strange glare in them. The little girls dared not speak to him.

When he had ridden to the end of his made little journey, he climbed down and stood in front of his rocking-horse, staring fixedly into its lowered face. Its red mouth was slightly open, its big eye was wide and glassy-bright.

"Now!" he would silently command the snorting steed. "Now, take me to where there is luck! Now take me!"

And he would slash the horse on the neck with the little whip he had asked Uncle Oscar for. He knew the horse could take him to where there was luck, if only he forced it. So he would mount again, and start on his furious ride, hoping at last to get there. He knew he could get there.

"You'll break your horse, Paul!" said the nurse.

---

① stoutly: in a firm and determined way

② brazening it out: continue doing something without considering others

" He's always riding like that! I wish he'd leave off !" said his elder sister Joan.

But he only glared down on them in silence. Nurse gave him up. She could make nothing of him. Anyhow he was growing beyond her.

One day his mother and his Uncle Oscar came in when he was on one of his furious rides. He did not speak to them.

" Hallo, you young jockey① ! Riding a winner?" said his uncle. " Aren't you growing too big for a rocking-horse? You're not a very little boy any longer, you know," said his mother.

But Paul only gave a blue glare from his big, rather close-set eyes. He would speak to nobody when he was in full tilt. His mother watched him with an anxious expression on her face.

At last he suddenly stopped forcing his horse into the mechanical gallop, and slid down.

" Well, I got there!" he announced fiercely, his blue eyes still flaring, and his sturdy long legs straddling apart.

" Where did you get to?" asked his mother.

" Where I wanted to go," he flared back at her.

" That's right, son!" said Uncle Oscar. " Don't you stop till you get there. What's the horse's name?"

" He doesn't have a name," said the boy.

" Gets on without all right?" asked the uncle.

" Well, he has different names. He was called Sansovino last week."

" Sansovino, eh? Won the Ascot. How did you know his name?"

" He always talks about horse-races with Bassett," said Joan.

The uncle was delighted to find that his small nephew was posted with all the racing news. Bassett, the young gardener, who had been wounded in the left foot in

---

① jockey: a person whose job is riding horses in races

the war and had got his present job through Oscar Cresswell whose batman he had been was a perfect blade of the " turf". He lived in the racing events, and the small boy lived with him.

Oscar Cresswell got it all from Bassett.

" Master Paul comes and asks me, so I can't do more than tell him, sir," said Bassett, his face terribly serious, as if he were speaking of religious matters.

" And does he ever put anything on a horse he fancies?"

" Well — I don't want to give him away — he's a young sport, a fine sport, sir. Would you mind asking him himself? He sort of takes a pleasure in it, and perhaps he'd feel I was giving him away, sir, if you don't mind."

Bassett was serious as a church.

The uncle went back to his nephew and took him off for a ride in the car.

" Say, Paul, old man, do you ever put anything on a horse?" the uncle asked.

The boy watched the handsome man closely.

" Why, do you think I oughtn't to?" he parried.

" Not a bit of it. I thought perhaps you might give me a tip for the Lincoln."

The car sped on into the country, going down to Uncle Oscar's place in Hampshire.

" Honor bright?" said the nephew.

" Honor bright, son!" said the uncle.

" Well, then, Daffodil."

" Daffodil! I doubt it, sonny. What about Mirza?"

" I only know the winner," said the boy. " That's Daffodil."

" Daffodil, eh?"

There was a pause. Daffodil was an obscure horse comparatively.

" Uncle!"

" Yes, son?"

" You won't let it go any further, will you? I promised Bassett."

" Bassett be damned, old man! What's he got to do with it?"

" We're partners. We've been partners from the first. Uncle, he lent me my first five shillings, which I lost, I promised him, honor bright, it was only between me and him; only you gave me that ten-shilling note I started winning with, so I thought you were lucky. You won't let it go any further, will you?"

The boy gazed at his uncle from those big, hot, blue eyes, set rather close together. The uncle stirred and laughed uneasily.

" Right you are, son! I'll keep your tip private. Daffodil, eh? How much are you putting on him?"

" All except twenty pounds," said the boy. " I keep that in reserve."

The uncle thought it a good joke.

" You keep twenty pounds in reserve, do you, you young romancer? What are you betting, then?"

" I'm betting three hundred," said the boy gravely. " But it's between you and me, Uncle Oscar! Honor bright?"

The uncle burst into a roar of laughter.

" It's between you and me all right, you young Nat Gould," he said, laughing. " But where's your three hundred?"

" Bassett keeps it for me. We're partners."

" You are, are you! And what is Bassett putting on Daffodil?"

" He won't go quite as high as I do, I expect. Perhaps he'll go a hundred and fifty."

" What, pennies?" laughed the uncle.

" Pounds," said the child, with a surprised look at his uncle. " Bassett keeps a bigger reserve than I do."

Between wonder and amusement Uncle Oscar was silent. He pursued the matter no further, but he determined to take his nephew with him to the Lincoln races.

" Now, son," he said, " I'm putting twenty on Mirza, and I'll put five for you on any horse you fancy. What's your pick?"

" Daffodil, uncle."

" No, not the fiver on Daffodil!"

" I should if it was my own fiver," said the child.

" Good! Good! Right you are! A fiver for me and a fiver for you on Daffodil."

The child had never been to a race-meeting before, and his eyes were blue fire. He pursed his mouth tight, and watched. A Frenchman just in front had put his money on Lancelot. Wild with excitement, he flayed his arms up and down, yelling, " Lancelot! Lancelot!" in his French accent.

Daffodil came in first, Lancelot second, Mirza third. The child flushed and with eyes blazing, was curiously serene. His uncle brought him four five-pound notes, four to one.

" What am I to do with these?" he cried, waving them before the boy's eyes.

" I suppose we'll talk to Bassett," said the boy. " I expect I have fifteen hundred now; and twenty in reserve; and this twenty."

His uncle studied him for some moments.

" Look here, son!" he said. " You're not serious about Bassett and that fifteen hundred, are you?"

" Yes, I am. But it's between you and me, uncle. Honor bright!"

" Honor bright all bright, son! But I must talk to Bassett."

" If you'd like to be a partner, uncle, with Bassett and me, we could all be partners. Only, you'd have to promise, honor bright, uncle, not to let it go beyond us three. Bassett and I are lucky, and you must be lucky, because it was your ten shillings I started winning with..."

Uncle Oscar took both Bassett and Paul into Richmond Park for an afternoon, and there they talked.

" It's like this, you see, sir," Bassett said. " Master Paul would get me talking about racing events, spinning yearns, you know, sir. And he was always keen on knowing if I'd made or if I'd lost. It's about a year since, now, that I put five shillings on Blush of Dawn for him — and we lost. Then the luck turned, with that ten shillings he had from you, that we put on Singhalese. And since that time, it's been pretty steady, all things considering. What do you say, Master Paul?"

" We're all right when we're sure," said Paul. " It's when we're not quite sure that we go down.

" Oh, but we're careful then," said Bassett.

" But when are you sure?" smiled Uncle Oscar.

" It's Master Paul, sir," said Bassett, in a secret, religious voice. " It's as if he had it from heaven. Like daffodil, now, for the Lincoln. That was as sure as eggs."

Did you put anything on Daffodil?" asked Oscar Cresswell.

" Yes, sir. I made my bid."

" And my nephew?"

Bassett was obstinately silent, looking at Paul.

" I made twelve hundred, didn't I, Bassett? I told uncle I was putting three hundred on Daffodil."

" That's right," said Bassett, nodding.

" But where's the money?" asked the uncle.

" I keep it safe locked up, sir. Master Paul he can have it any minute he likes to ask for it."

" What, fifteen hundred pounds?"

" And twenty! And forty, that is, with the twenty he made on the course."

" It's amazing!" said the uncle.

" If Master Paul offers you to be partners, sir, I would if I were you; if you'll excuse me," said Bassett.

Oscar Cresswell thought about it.

" I'll see the money," he said.

They drove home again, and sure enough, Bassett came round to the garden-house with fifteen hundred pounds in notes. The twenty pounds reserve was left with Joe Glee in the Turf Commission deposit.

" You see, it's all right, uncle, when I'm sure! Then we go strong, for all we're worth. Don't we, Bassett?"

" We do that, Master Paul."

" And when are you sure?" said the uncle, laughing.

" Oh, well, sometimes I'm absolutely sure, like about Daffodil," said the boy; " and sometimes I have an idea; and sometimes I haven't even an idea, have I, Bassett? Then we're careful, because we mostly go down."

" You do, do you! And when you're sure, like about Daffodil, what makes you sure, sonny?"

" Oh, well, I don't know," said the boy uneasily. " I'm sure, you know, uncle; that's all."

" It's as if he had it from heaven, sir," Bassett reiterated①.

" I should say so!" said the uncle.

But he became a partner. And when he Leger was coming on Paul was " sure" about Lively Spark, which was a quite inconsiderable horse. The boy insisted on putting a thousand on the horse, Bassett went for five hundred, and Oscar Cresswell two hundred. Lively Spark came in first, and the betting had been ten to one against him. Paul had made ten thousand.

" You see," he said, " I was absolutely sure of him."

Even Oscar Cresswell had cleared two thousand.

" Look here, son," he said, " this sort of thing makes me nervous."

" It needn't, uncle! Perhaps I shan't be sure again for a long time."

" But what are you going to do with your money?" asked the uncle.

" Of course," said the boy, " I started it for mother. She said she had no luck,

① reiterate: to say something again, once or several times

because father is unlucky, so I thought if I was lucky, it might stop whispering."

" What might stop whispering?"

" Our house. I hate our house for whispering."

" What does it whisper?"

" Why — why" — the boy fidgeted — "why, I don't know. But it's always short of money, you know, uncle."

I know it, son, I know it."

" You know people send mother writs, don't you, uncle?"

" I'm afraid I do," said the uncle.

" And then the house whispers, like people laughing at you behind your back. It's awful, that is! I thought if I was lucky … "

" You might stop it," added the uncle.

The boy watched him with big blue eyes, that had an uncanny cold fire in them, and he said never a word.

" Well, then!" said the uncle. " What are we doing?"

" I shouldn't like mother to know I was lucky," said the boy.

" Why not, son?"

" She'd stop me."

" I don't think she would."

" Oh!" — and the boy writhed in and odd way — " I don't want her to know, uncle."

" All right, son! We'll manage it without her knowing."

They managed it very easily. Paul, at the other's suggestion, handed over five thousand pounds to his uncle, who deposited it with the family lawyer, who was then to inform Paul's mother that a relative had put five thousand pounds into his hands, which sum was to be paid out a thousand pounds at a time, on the mother's birthday, for the next five years.

" So she'll have a birthday present of a thousand pounds for five successive years," said Uncle Oscar. " I hope it won't make it all the harder for her later."

Paul's mother had her birthday in November. The house had been " whispering" worse than ever lately, and, even in spite of his luck, Paul could not bear up against it. He was very anxious to see the effect of the birthday letter, telling his mother about the thousand pounds.

When there was no visitors, Paul now took his meals with his parents, as he was beyond the nursery control. His mother went into town nearly every day. She had discovered that she had an odd knack of sketching furs and dress materials, so she worked secretly in the studio of a friend who was the chief " artist" for the leading drapers. She drew the figures of ladies in furs and ladies in silk and sequins① for the newspaper advertisements. This young woman artist earned several thousand pounds a year, but Paul's mother only made several hundreds, and she was again dissatisfied. She so wanted to be first in something, and she did not succeed, even in making sketches for drapery② advertisements.

She was down to breakfast on the morning of her birthday. Paul watched her face as she read her letters. He knew the lawyer's letter. As his mother read it, her face hardened and became more expressionless. Then a cold, determined look came on her mouth. She hid the letter under the pile of others, and said not a word about it.

" Didn't you have anything nice in the post for your birthday, mother?" said Paul.

" Quite moderately nice," she said, her voice cold and absent.

She went away to town without saying more.

But in the afternoon Uncle Oscar appeared. He said Paul's mother had had a long interview with the lawyer, asking if the whole five thousand could not be advanced at once, as she was in debt.

---

① sequins: a small, shiny metal or plastic disc sewn onto clothes for decoration

② drapery: cloth hanging or arranged in folds; general words for textiles UK (US dry goods) old-fashioned cloth, pins, thread, etc. used for sewing Knitting and sewing

" What do you think, uncle?" said the boy.

" I leave it to you, son."

" Oh, let her have it, then! We can get some more with the other," said the boy.

" A bird in the hand is worth two in the bush, laddie!" said Uncle Oscar.

" But I'm sure to know for the Grand National; or the Lincolnshire; or else the Derby. I'm sure to know for one of them," said Paul.

So Uncle Oscar signed the agreement, and Paul's mother touched the whole five thousand. Then something very curious happened. The voices in the house suddenly went mad, like a chorus of frogs on a spring evening. There were certain new furnishings, and Paul had a tutor. He was really going to Eton, his father's school, in the following autumn. There were flowers in the winter, and a blossoming of the luxury Paul's mother had been used to. And yet the voices in the house, behind the sprays of mimosa and almond blossom, and from under the piles of iridescent cushions, simply trilled and screamed in a sort of ecstasy: " There must be more money! Oh-h-h; there must be more money. Oh, now, now-w! Now-w-w — there must be more money! — more than ever! More than ever!"

It frightened Paul terribly. He studied away at his Latin and Greek with his tutors. But his intense hours were spent with Bassett. The Grand National had bone by: he had not " known", and had lost a hundred pounds. Summer was at hand. He was in agony for the Lincoln. But even for the Lincoln he didn't " know", and he lost fifty pounds. He became wild-eyed and strange, as if something were going to explode in him.

" Let it alone, son! Don't you bother about it!" urged Uncle Oscar. But it was as if the boy couldn't really hear what his uncle was saying.

" I've got to know for the Derby! I've got to know for the Derby!" the child reiterated, his big blue eyes blazing with a sort of madness.

His mother noticed how overwrought he was.

" You'd better go to the seaside. Wouldn't you like to go now to the seaside, instead of waiting? I think you'd better," she said, looking down at him anxiously, her heart curiously heavy about him.

But the child lifted his uncanny blue eyes.

"I couldn't possibly go before the derby, mother!" he said. "I couldn't possibly!"

"Why not?" she said, her voice becoming heavy when she was opposed. "Why not? You can still go from the seaside to see the Derby with your Uncle Oscar, if that's what you wish. No need for you to wait here. Besides, I think you care too much about these races. It's a bad sign. My family has been a gambling family, and you won't know till you grow up how much damage it has done. But it has done damage. I shall have to send Bassett away, and ask Uncle Oscar not to talk racing to you, unless you promise to be reasonable about it; go away to the seaside and forget it. You're all nerves!"

"I'll do what you like, mother, so long as you don't send me away till after the Derby," the boy said.

"Send you away from where? Just from this house?"

"Yes," he said, gazing at her.

"Why, you curious child, what makes you care about this house so much, suddenly? I never knew you loved it."

He gazed at her without speaking. He had a secret within a secret, something he had not divulged, even to Bassett or to his Uncle Oscar.

But his mother, after standing undecided and a little bit sullen for some moments, said:

"Very well, then! Don't go to the seaside till after the Derby, if you don't wish it. But promise me you won't let your nerves to go pieces. Promise you won't think so much about horse-racing and events, as you call them!"

"Oh, no," said the boy casually. "I won't think much about them, mother. You needn't worry. I wouldn't worry, mother, if I were you."

" If you were me and I were you," said his mother, " I wonder what we should do!"

" But you know you needn't worry, mother, don't you?" the boy repeated.

" I should be awfully glad to know it," she said wearily.

" Oh, well, you can, you know. I mean, you ought to know you needn't worry," he insisted.

" Ought I? Then I'll see about it," she said.

Paul's secret of secrets was his wooden horse, that which had no name. Since he was emancipated from a nurse and a nursery-governess, he had had his rocking-horse[①] removed to his own bedroom at the top of the house.

" Surely, you're too big for a rocking-horse!" his mother had remonstrated.

" Well, you see, mother, till I can have a real horse, I like to have some sort of animal about," had been his quaint answer.

" Do you feel he keeps you company?" she laughed.

" Oh, yes! He's very good, he always keeps me company, when I'm there," said Paul.

So the horse, rather shabby, stood in an arrested prance in the boy's bedroom.

The Derby was drawing near, and the boy grew more and more tense. He hardly heard what was spoken to him, he was very frail, and his eyes were really uncanny. His mother had sudden strange seizures of uneasiness about him. Sometimes, for half-an-hour, she would feel a sudden anxiety about him that was almost anguish. She wanted to rush to him at once, and know he was safe.

Two nights before the Derby, she was at a big party in town, when one of her rushes of anxiety about her boy, her first-born, gripped her heart till she could hardly speak. She fought with the feeling,might and main, for she believed in common sense. But it was too strong. She had to leave the dance and go downstairs to

① rocking–horse: a toy horse that a child sits on and goes backward and forward telephone to the country. The children's nursery-governess was terribly surprised and startled at being rung up in the night.

"Are all the children all right, Miss Wilmot?"

"Oh, yes, they are quite all right."

"Master Paul? Is he all right?"

"He went to bed as right as a trivet[①]. Shall I run up and look at him?"

"No," said Paul's mother reluctantly. "No! Don't trouble. It's all right. Don't sit up. We shall be home fairly soon." She did not want her son's privacy intruded upon.

"Very good," said the governess.

It was about one o'clock when Paul's mother and father drove up to their house. All was still. Paul's mother went to her room and slipped off her white fur cloak. She had told her maid not to wait up for her. she heard her husband downstairs, mixing a whisky-and-soda.

And then, because of the strange anxiety at her heart, she stole upstairs to her son's room. Noiselessly she went along the upper corridor. Was there a faint noise? What was it?

She stood, with arrested muscles, outside his door, listening. There was a strange, heavy, and yet not loud noise. Her heart stood still. It was a soundless noise, yet rushing and powerful. Something huge, in violent, hushed motion. What was it? What in God's name was it? She ought to know. She felt that she knew the noise. She knew what it was.

Yet she could not place it. She couldn't say what it was. And on and on it went, like a madness.

Softly, frozen with anxiety and fear, she turned the door-handle.

The room was dark. Yet in the space near the window, she heard and saw something plunging to and fro. She gazed in fear and amazement.

---

① as right as a trivet: stably

Then suddenly she switched on the light, and saw her son, in his green pajamas, madly surging on the rocking-horse. The blaze of light suddenly lit him up, as he urged the wooden horse, and lit her up, as she stood, blonde, in her dress of pale green and crystal, in the doorway.

" Paul!" she cried. " Whatever are you doing?"

" It's Malabar!" he screamed, in a powerful, strange voice. " It's Malabar!"

His eyes blazed at her for one strange and senseless second, as he ceased urging his wooden horse. Then he fell with a crash to the ground, and she, all her tormented motherhood flooding upon her, rushed to gather him up.

But he was unconscious, and unconscious he remained, with some brain-fever. He talked and tossed, and his mother sat stonily by his side.

" Malabar! It's Malabar! Bassett, Bassett, I know! It's Malabar!"

So the child cried, trying to get up and urge the rocking-horse that gave him his inspiration.

" What does he mean by Malabar?" asked the heart-frozen mother.

" I don't know," said the father stonily.

" What does he mean by Malabar?" she asked her brother Oscar.

" It's one of the horses running for the Derby," was the answer.

And, in spite of herself, Oscar Cresswell spoke to Bassett, and himself put a thousand on Malabar: at fourteen to one.

The third day of the illness was critical: they were waiting for a change. The boy, with his rather long, curly hair, was tossing ceaselessly on the pillow. He neither slept nor regained consciousness, and his eyes were like blue stones. His mother sat, feeling her heart had gone, turned actually into a stone.

In the evening, Oscar Cresswell did not come, but Bassett sent a message, saying could he come up for one moment, just one moment? Paul's mother was very angry at the intrusion, but on second thought she agreed. The boy was the same. Perhaps Bassett might bring him to consciousness.

The gardener, a shortish fellow with a little brown moustache, and sharp little brown eyes, tiptoed into the room touched his imaginary cap to Paul's mother, and stole to the bedside, staring with glittering, smallish eyes, at the tossing, dying child.

" Master Paul!" he whispered. " Master Paul! Malabar came in first all right,a clean win. I did as you told me. You've made over seventy thousand pounds, you have; you've got over eight thousand. Malabar came in all right, Master Paul."

" Malabar! Malabar! Did I say Malabar, mother? Did I say Malabar? Do you think I'm lucky, mother? I knew Malabar, didn't I? Over eighty thousand pounds! I call that lucky, don't you, mother? Over eighty thousand pounds! I knew, didn't I know I knew? Malabar came in all right. If I ride my horse till I'm sure, then I tell you, Bassett, you can go as high as you like. Did you go for all you were worth, Bassett?"

" I went a thousand on it, Master Paul."

" I never told you, mother, that if I can ride my horse, and get there, then I'm absolutely sure — oh, absolutely! Mother, did I ever tell you? I am lucky!"

" No, you never did," said the mother.

But the boy died in the night.

And even as he lay dead, his mother heard her brother's voice saying to her: " My God, Hester, you're eighty-odd thousand to the good, and a poor devil of a son to the bad. But, poor devil, poor devil, he's best gone out of a life where he rides his rocking-horse to find a winner."

Topics for discussion

1. How does " The Rocking-Horse Winner" portray the desire for material wealth?

2. What were women's career options during the 1920s? How might this reality figure into the mother's lack of love for children?

3. What do you think Lawrence was trying to say about the role of men in the raising of their sons?

4. Make some comment on how does " The Rocking-Horse Winner" exhibit the attributes of a myth through its style and symbolism?

References for further reading

[1] Bell, Michael, *D. H. Lawrence: Language and Being*, Cambridge: Cambridge University Press, 1992.

[2] Black, Michael. *D. H. Lawrence: The Early Philosophical Works: A Commentary*, London and Basingstoke: Macmillan, 1991.

[3] Keith Brown, ed. *Rethinking Lawrence*, Milton Keynes: Open University Press, 1990.

[4] Fernihough, Anne. ed. *The Cambridge Companion to D H Lawrence*, Cambridge, Cambridge University Press, 2001.

[5] Montgomery, Robert E. *The Visionary D. H. Lawrence: Beyond Philosophy and Art*, Cambridge: Cambridge University Press, 1994.

Katherine Mansfield (1888 — 1923)

The Garden Party

Introduction to the author

Katherine Mansfield (October 14, 1888 — January 9, 1923) was a New Zealand-born English master of the short story, a prominent modernist writer of short story. Katherine Mansfield has an international reputation as a writer of short stories, poetry, letters, journals and reviews. Mansfield has much influence on the development of the short story as a genre. She developed a distinctive prose style with many overtones of poetry. Her delicate stories feature psychological conflicts, the subtlety of observation and the bitterness of marital and family relationships in her middle-class world and her own feelings of loneliness, illness, jealousy, and alienation. Her short stories are also notable for their use of stream of consciousness. Like the Russian writer Anton Chekhov, Mansfield depicted trivial events and subtle changes in human behavior.

Katherine Mansfield, originally named Kathleen Mansfield Beauchamp, was born in Wellington, New Zealand, on October 14, 1888. Katherine Mansfield was born to a socially prominent middle-class colonial family. Her father, Harold Beauchamp, was a banker and her mother, Annie Burnell Dyer, was of genteel origins. In 1903, the family sailed to England and she attended Queen's College in London until 1906. After finishing her schooling, Mansfield returned to New Zealand, and began to write short stories. French Symbolists and Oscar Wilde influenced her deeply. In 1907, at the age of 19, Mansfield returned to the U. K, where she befriended modernist writers such as D.H. Lawrence and Virginia Woolf.

A brief affair left her pregnant and she hastily entered into a marriage with George Bowden, whom she knew only three weeks and who was not the father of her child. In 1911, Mansfield met John Middleton Murry. In 1918, Mansfield and Bowden got divorced eventually and she married Murry in the same year. Although she lived together with Murry on and off for many years, Mansfield had several other affairs. She had two lesbian relationships and continued to have male lovers. In 1917, Mansfield was diagnosed with extrapulmonary tuberculosis. She died on January 9, 1923 and was buried in Avon, aged 34.

Mansfield was a prolific writer in her final years. Much of her work remained unpublished at her death. Murry edited and published her unpublished work, including two additional volumes of short stories, The Dove's Nest in 1923 and Something Childish in 1924.

Major works by Katherine Mansfield

Short stories collections

In a German Pension, 1911

Bliss: and Other Stories, 1920

The Garden Party and Other Stories, 1922

The Doves' Nest: and Other Stories, 1923

The Montana Stories, 1923

Something Childish, 1924

Novel

The Aloe, 1930

Poem

Poems, 1923

Others

The Journal of Katherine Mansfield, 1927, 1954

The Letters of Katherine Mansfield (2 vols.), 1928–29

Novels and Novelists, 1930

The Short Stories of Katherine Mansfield, 1937

Short stories

"The Tiredness of Rosabel", 1908

"The Woman at the Store", 1912

"Millie", 1913

"The Little Governess", 1915

"A Dill Pickle", 1917

"Prelude", 1918

"An Indiscreet Journey", 1920

"Sun and Moon", 1920

"The Wind Blows", 1920

"The Voyage", 1921

"Life of Ma Parker", 1921

"The Little Girl", 1912

"The Stranger", 1921

"At The Bay", 1922

"The Garden Party", 1922

"A Cup of Tea", 1922

"The Doll's House", 1922

"A Married Man's Story", 1923

Appreciation

"The Garden Party" was first published in the short story collection entitled The *Garden Party: and Other Stories*. Its luxurious setting has a clear connection to

Mansfield's own childhood home in Wellington, New Zealand. The Sheridan family is preparing to host an afternoon garden party. Laura, an idealistic and sensitive young girl, is surrounded by her more conventional family. everyone is busy preparing when news comes that their working-class neighbor Mr. Scott has died. The working class family lives in the cottage down the hill from the Sheridan house. Laura believes that the party should be canceled. The rest of the story is structured around the family members' reactions to Laura's suggestion and the death of the working class man. The family's general hostility toward their poor neighbors is revealed. The party is a success and Mrs. Sheridan suggests that Laura deliver some leftovers to the Scotts' house. At first, Laura does not think it appropriate to do so, but she is convinced by her mother. Laura is shown into the poor neighbors' house by Mrs. Scott's sister, then sees the widow and her late husband's corpse. She is struck by the peacefulness and beauty by the dead young man. when Laura runs out and encounters her brother Laurie, she tries to explain what has happened, but she finds the momentary sight of the transcendent unexplainable.

Widely anthologized, the story is considered to be Mansfield's best short story, a classic example of the short story form. The story deals with many themes that are typical of Mansfield's works, including class consciousness, class conflict, illusion versus reality, sensitivity and insensitivity, death and life, innocence and experience. The text is written in the modernist mode, without a set structure, and with many shifts in the narrative.

Selected Reading

The Garden Party

AND AFTER all the weather was ideal. They could not have had a more perfect day for a garden-party if they had ordered it. Windless, warm, the sky without a cloud. Only the blue was veiled with a haze of light gold, as it is sometimes in early summer. The gardener had been up since dawn, mowing the lawns and sweeping them, until the grass and the dark flat rosettes where the daisy plants had been seemed to shine. As for the roses, you could not help feeling they understood that roses are the only flowers that impress people at garden-parties; the only flowers that everybody is certain of knowing. Hundreds, yes, literally hundreds, had come out in a single night; the green bushes bowed down as though they had been visited by archangels.

Breakfast was not yet over before the men came to put up the marquee①.

" Where do you want the marquee put, mother?"

" My dear child, it's no use asking me. I'm determined to leave everything to you children this year. Forget I am your mother. Treat me as an honoured guest."

But Meg could not possibly go and supervise the men. She had washed her hair before breakfast, and she sat drinking her coffee in a green turban, with a dark wet curl stamped on each cheek. Jose, the butterfly, always came down in a silk petticoat② and a kimono③ jacket.

" You'll have to go, Laura; you're the artistic one."

Away Laura flew, still holding her piece of bread-and-butter. It's so delicious to have an excuse for eating out of doors, and besides, she loved having to arrange things; she always felt she could do it so much better than anybody else.

Four men in their shirt-sleeves stood grouped together on the garden path. They carried staves covered with rolls of canvas, and they had big tool-bags slung on their backs. They looked impressive. Laura wished now that she had not got the bread-and-butter, but there was nowhere to put it, and she couldn't possibly throw it away.

---

① marquee: a large tent used for eating and drinking in at events held mainly outside that involve a lot of people

② petticoat: skirt

③ kimono: a long, loose piece of outer clothing with very wide sleeves

She blushed and tried to look severe and even a little bit short-sighted as she came up to them.

" Good morning," she said, copying her mother's voice. But that sounded so fearfully affected that she was ashamed, and stammered like a little girl, " Oh — er — have you come — is it about the marquee?"

" That's right, miss," said the tallest of the men, a lanky①, freckled fellow, and he shifted his tool-bag, knocked back his straw hat and smiled down at her.

" That's about it."

His smile was so easy, so friendly that Laura recovered. What nice eyes he had, small, but such a dark blue! And now she looked at the others, they were smiling too. " Cheer up, we won't bite," their smile seemed to say. How very nice workmen were! And what a beautiful morning! She mustn't mention the morning; she must be business-like. The marquee.

" Well, what about the lily-lawn? Would that do?"

And she pointed to the lily-lawn with the hand that didn't hold the bread-and-butter. They turned, they stared in the direction. A little fat chap thrust out his under-lip, and the tall fellow frowned.

" I don't fancy it," said he. " Not conspicuous enough. You see, with a thing like a marquee," and he turned to Laura in his easy way, " you want to put it somewhere where it'll give you a bang slap in the eye, if you follow me."

Laura's upbringing made her wonder for a moment whether it was quite respectful of a workman to talk to her of bangs slap in the eye. But she did quite follow him.

" A corner of the tennis-court," she suggested. " But the band's going to be in one corner."

" H'm, going to have a band, are you?" said another of the workmen. He was

---

① lanky: tall and thin and often moving awkwardly as a result pale. He had a haggard① look as his dark eyes scanned the tennis-court. What was he thinking?

" Only a very small band," said Laura gently. Perhaps he wouldn't mind so much if the band was quite small. But the tall fellow interrupted.

" Look here, miss, that's the place. Against those trees. Over there. That'll do fine."

Against the karakas. Then the karaka-trees would be hidden. And they were so lovely, with their broad, gleaming leaves, and their clusters of yellow fruit. They were like trees you imagined growing on a desert island, proud, solitary, lifting their leaves and fruits to the sun in a kind of silent splendour. Must they be hidden by a marquee?

They must. Already the men had shouldered their staves and were making for the place. Only the tall fellow was left. He bent down, pinched a sprig of lavender②, put his thumb and forefinger to his nose and snuffed up the smell. When Laura saw that gesture she forgot all about the karakas in her wonder at him caring for things like that — caring for the smell of lavender. How many men that she knew would have done such a thing? Oh, how extraordinarily nice workmen were, she thought. Why couldn't she have workmen for her friends rather than the silly boys she danced with and who came to Sunday night supper? She would get on much better with men like these.

It's all the fault, she decided, as the tall fellow drew something on the back of an envelope, something that was to be looped up or left to hang, of these absurd class distinctions. Well, for her part, she didn't feel them. Not a bit, not an atom... And now there came the chock-chock of wooden hammers. Some one whistled, some one sang out, " Are you right there, matey?" " Matey!" The friendliness of it, the-the-Just to

① haggard: (of a person) having dark areas around the eyes and lines on the face, esp. from being tired or from suffering

② lavender: a plant that has grey-green leaves like needles and small, pale purple flowers ; the dried flowers and stems of the plant that are used in soap, etc. because of their strong, pleasant smell prove how happy she was, just to show the tall fellow how at home she felt, and how she despised stupid conventions, Laura took a big bite of her bread-and-butter as she stared at the little drawing. She felt just like a work-girl.

" Laura, Laura, where are you? Telephone, Laura!" a voice cried from the house.

" Coming!" Away she skimmed, over the lawn, up the path, up the steps, across the veranda,① and into the porch. In the hall her father and Laurie were brushing their hats ready to go to the office.

" I say, Laura," said Laurie very fast, " you might just give a squiz at my coat before this afternoon. See if it wants pressing."

" I will," said she. Suddenly she couldn't stop herself. She ran at Laurie and gave him a small, quick squeeze. " Oh, I do love parties, don't you?" gasped Laura.

" Ra-ther," said Laurie's warm, boyish voice, and he squeezed his sister too, and gave her a gentle push. " Dash off to the telephone, old girl."

The telephone. " Yes, yes; oh yes. Kitty? Good morning, dear. Come to lunch? Do, dear. Delighted of course. It will only be a very scratch meal — just the sandwich crusts and broken meringue-shells and what's left over. Yes, isn't it a perfect morning? Your white? Oh, I certainly should. One moment — hold the line. Mother's calling." And Laura sat back. " What, mother? Can't hear."

Mrs. Sheridan's voice floated down the stairs. " Tell her to wear that sweet hat she had on last Sunday."

" Mother says you're to wear that sweet hat you had on last Sunday. Good. One o'clock. Bye-bye."

Laura put back the receiver, flung her arms over her head, took a deep breath, stretched and let them fall. " Huh," she sighed, and the moment after the sigh she sat up quickly. She was still, listening. All the doors in the house seemed to be open. The house was alive with soft, quick steps and running voices. The green baize door that

① veranda: a raised, open area, often covered, attached to the front or side of a house led to the kitchen regions swung open and shut with a muffled thud. And now there came a long, chuckling absurd sound. It was the heavy piano being moved on its stiff castors. But the air! If you stopped to notice, was the air always like this? Little faint winds were playing chase, in at the tops of the windows, out at the doors. And there were two tiny spots of sun, one on the inkpot, one on a silver photograph frame, playing too. Darling little spots. Especially the one on the inkpot lid. It was quite warm. A warm little silver star. She could have kissed it.

The front door bell pealed, and there sounded the rustle of Sadie's print skirt on the stairs. A man's voice murmured; Sadie answered, careless, " I'm sure I don't know. Wait. I'll ask Mrs Sheridan."

" What is it, Sadie?" Laura came into the hall.

" It's the florist, Miss Laura."

It was, indeed. There, just inside the door, stood a wide, shallow tray full of pots of pink lilies. No other kind. Nothing but lilies — canna① lilies, big pink flowers, wide open, radiant, almost frighteningly alive on bright crimson stems.

" O-oh, Sadie!" said Laura, and the sound was like a little moan. She crouched down as if to warm herself at that blaze of lilies; she felt they were in her fingers, on her lips, growing in her breast.

" It's some mistake," she said faintly. " Nobody ever ordered so many. Sadie, go and find mother."

But at that moment Mrs. Sheridan joined them.

" It's quite right," she said calmly. " Yes, I ordered them. Aren't they lovely?" She pressed Laura's arm. " I was passing the shop yesterday, and I saw them in the window. And I suddenly thought for once in my life I shall have enough canna lilies. The garden-party will be a good excuse."

" But I thought you said you didn't mean to interfere," said Laura. Sadie had

---

① canna: a kind of plant

gone. The florist's man was still outside at his van. She put her arm round her mother's neck and gently, very gently, she bit her mother's ear.

" My darling child, you wouldn't like a logical mother, would you? Don't do that. Here's the man."

He carried more lilies still, another whole tray.

" Bank them up, just inside the door, on both sides of the porch, please," said Mrs. Sheridan. " Don't you agree, Laura?"

" Oh, I do, mother."

In the drawing-room Meg, Jose and good little Hans had at last succeeded in moving the piano.

" Now, if we put this chesterfield against the wall and move everything out of the room except the chairs, don't you think?"

" Quite."

" Hans, move these tables into the smoking-room, and bring a sweeper to take these marks off the carpet and — one moment, Hans — ." Jose loved giving orders to the servants, and they loved obeying her. She always made them feel they were taking part in some drama. " Tell mother and Miss Laura to come here at once."

" Very good, Miss Jose."

She turned to Meg. " I want to hear what the piano sounds like, just in case I'm asked to sing this afternoon. Let's try over 'This life is Weary.' "

Pom! Ta-ta-ta Tee-ta! The piano burst out so passionately that Jose's face changed. She clasped her hands. She looked mournfully and enigmatically at her mother and Laura as they came in.

This Life is Wee-ary,
A Tear — a Sigh.
A Love that Chan-ges,
This Life is Wee-ary,
A Tear — a Sigh.

A Love that Chan-ges,

And then... Good-bye!

But at the word " Good-bye," and although the piano sounded more desperate than ever, her face broke into a brilliant, dreadfully unsympathetic smile.

" Aren't I in good voice, mummy?" she beamed.

This Life is Wee-ary,

Hope comes to Die.

A Dream — a Wa-kening.

But now Sadie interrupted them. " What is it, Sadie?"

" If you please, m'm, cook says have you got the flags for the sandwiches?"

" The flags for the sandwiches, Sadie?" echoed Mrs. Sheridan dreamily. And the children knew by her face that she hadn't got them. " Let me see." And she said to Sadie firmly, " Tell cook I'll let her have them in ten minutes."

Sadie went.

" Now, Laura," said her mother quickly, " come with me into the smoking-room. I've got the names somewhere on the back of an envelope. You'll have to write them out for me. Meg, go upstairs this minute and take that wet thing off your head. Jose, run and finish dressing this instant. Do you hear me, children, or shall I have to tell your father when he comes home to-night? And — and, Jose, pacify cook if you do go into the kitchen, will you? I'm terrified of her this morning."

The envelope was found at last behind the dining-room clock, though how it had got there Mrs. Sheridan could not imagine.

" One of you children must have stolen it out of my bag, because I remember vividly — cream cheese and lemon-curd① . Have you done that?"

" Yes."

" Egg and — " Mrs. Sheridan held the envelope away from her. " It looks like

① lemon-curd: a thick, sweet substance made from lemons, sugar, eggs, and butter that you can spread on bread or cakes mice. It can't be mice, can it?"

" Olive, pet," said Laura, looking over her shoulder.

" Yes, of course, olive. What a horrible combination it sounds. Egg and olive."

They were finished at last, and Laura took them off to the kitchen. She found Jose there pacifying the cook, who did not look at all terrifying.

" I have never seen such exquisite sandwiches," said Jose's rapturous voice. " How many kinds did you say there were, cook? Fifteen?"

" Fifteen, Miss Jose."

" Well, cook, I congratulate you."

Cook swept up crusts with the long sandwich knife, and smiled broadly.

" Godber's has come," announced Sadie, issuing out of the pantry. She had seen the man pass the window.

That meant the cream puffs① had come. Godber's were famous for their cream puffs. Nobody ever thought of making them at home.

" Bring them in and put them on the table, my girl," ordered cook.

Sadie brought them in and went back to the door. Of course Laura and Jose were far too grown-up to really care about such things. All the same, they couldn't help agreeing that the puffs looked very attractive. Very. Cook began arranging them, shaking off the extra icing sugar.

" Don't they carry one back to all one's parties?" said Laura.

" I suppose they do," said practical Jose, who never liked to be carried back. " They look beautifully light and feathery, I must say."

" Have one each, my dears," said cook in her comfortable voice. " Yer ma won't know."

Oh, impossible. Fancy cream puffs so soon after breakfast. The very idea made one shudder. All the same, two minutes later Jose and Laura were licking their fingers

① cream puff: a womanish man, cowardice

with that absorbed inward look that only comes from whipped cream.

" Let's go into the garden, out by the back way," suggested Laura. " I want to see how the men are getting on with the marquee. They're such awfully nice men."

But the back door was blocked by cook, Sadie, Godber's man and Hans.

Something had happened.

" Tuk-tuk-tuk," clucked cook like an agitated① hen. Sadie had her hand clapped to her cheek as though she had toothache. Hans's face was screwed up in the effort to understand. Only Godber's man seemed to be enjoying himself; it was his story.

" What's the matter? What's happened?"

" There's been a horrible accident," said Cook. " A man killed."

" A man killed! Where? How? When?"

But Godber's man wasn't going to have his story snatched from under his very nose.

" Know those little cottages just below here, miss?" Know them? Of course, she knew them. " Well, there's a young chap living there, name of Scott, a carter. His horse shied at a traction-engine, corner of Hawke Street this morning, and he was thrown out on the back of his head. Killed."

" Dead!" Laura stared at Godber's man.

" Dead when they picked him up," said Godber's man with relish② . " They were taking the body home as I come up here." And he said to the cook, " He's left a wife and five little ones."

" Jose, come here." Laura caught hold of her sister's sleeve and dragged her through the kitchen to the other side of the green baize door. There she paused and leaned against it. " Jose!" she said, horrified, " however are we going to stop everything?"

" Stop everything, Laura!" cried Jose in astonishment. " What do you mean?"

---

① agitated: making others feel worried or angry

② with relish: with strong interest

" Stop the garden-party, of course." Why did Jose pretend?

But Jose was still more amazed. " Stop the garden-party? My dear Laura, don't be so absurd. Of course we can't do anything of the kind. Nobody expects us to. Don't be so extravagant."

" But we can't possibly have a garden-party with a man dead just outside the front gate."

That really was extravagant, for the little cottages were in a lane to themselves at the very bottom of a steep rise that led up to the house. A broad road ran between. True, they were far too near. They were the greatest possible eyesore, and they had no right to be in that neighbourhood at all. They were little mean dwellings painted a chocolate brown. In the garden patches there was nothing but cabbage stalks, sick hens and tomato cans. The very smoke coming out of their chimneys was poverty-stricken. Little rags and shreds of smoke, so unlike the great silvery plumes that uncurled from the Sheridans' chimneys. Washerwomen lived in the lane and sweeps and a cobbler, and a man whose house-front was studded all over with minute bird-cages. Children swarmed. When the Sheridans were little they were forbidden to set foot there because of the revolting language and of what they might catch. But since they were grown up, Laura and Laurie on their prowls sometimes walked through. It was disgusting and sordid. They came out with a shudder. But still one must go everywhere; one must see everything. So through they went.

" And just think of what the band would sound like to that poor woman," said Laura.

" Oh, Laura!" Jose began to be seriously annoyed. " If you're going to stop a band playing every time some one has an accident, you'll lead a very strenuous life. I'm every bit as sorry about it as you. I feel just as sympathetic." Her eyes hardened. She looked at her sister just as she used to when they were little and fighting together. " You won't bring a drunken workman back to life by being sentimental," she said softly.

" Drunk! Who said he was drunk?" Laura turned furiously on Jose. She said, just as they had used to say on those occasions, " I'm going straight up to tell mother."

" Do, dear," cooed Jose.

" Mother, can I come into your room?" Laura turned the big glass door-knob.

" Of course, child. Why, what's the matter? What's given you such a colour?" And Mrs. Sheridan turned round from her dressing-table. She was trying on a new hat.

" Mother, a man's been killed," began Laura.

" Not in the garden?" interrupted her mother.

" No, no!"

" Oh, what a fright you gave me!" Mrs. Sheridan sighed with relief, and took off the big hat and held it on her knees.

" But listen, mother," said Laura. Breathless, half-choking, she told the dreadful story. " Of course, we can't have our party, can we?" she pleaded. " The band and everybody arriving. They'd hear us, mother; they're nearly neighbours!"

To Laura's astonishment her mother behaved just like Jose; it was harder to bear because she seemed amused. She refused to take Laura seriously.

" But, my dear child, use your common sense. It's only by accident we've heard of it. If some one had died there normally — and I can't understand how they keep alive in those poky little holes — we should still be having our party, shouldn't we?"

Laura had to say " yes" to that, but she felt it was all wrong. She sat down on her mother's sofa and pinched the cushion frill.

" Mother, isn't it terribly heartless of us?" she asked.

" Darling!" Mrs. Sheridan got up and came over to her, carrying the hat. Before Laura could stop her she had popped it on. " My child!" said her mother, " the hat is yours. It's made for you. It's much too young for me. I have never seen you look such a picture. Look at yourself!" And she held up her hand-mirror.

" But, mother," Laura began again. She couldn't look at herself; she turned aside.

This time Mrs. Sheridan lost patience just as Jose had done.

" You are being very absurd, Laura," she said coldly. " People like that don't expect sacrifices from us. And it's not very sympathetic to spoil everybody's enjoyment as you're doing now."

" I don't understand," said Laura, and she walked quickly out of the room into her own bedroom. There, quite by chance, the first thing she saw was this charming girl in the mirror, in her black hat trimmed with gold daisies, and a long black velvet ribbon. Never had she imagined she could look like that. Is mother right? she thought. And now she hoped her mother was right. Am I being extravagant? Perhaps it was extravagant. Just for a moment she had another glimpse of that poor woman and those little children, and the body being carried into the house. But it all seemed blurred, unreal, like a picture in the newspaper. I'll remember it again after the party's over, she decided. And somehow that seemed quite the best plan...

Lunch was over by half-past one. By half-past two they were all ready for the fray. The green-coated band had arrived and was established in a corner of thc tennis-court.

" My dear!" trilled Kitty Maitland, " aren't they too like frogs for words? You ought to have arranged them round the pond with the conductor in the middle on a leaf."

Laurie arrived and hailed them on his way to dress. At the sight of him Laura remembered the accident again. She wanted to tell him. If Laurie agreed with the others, then it was bound to be all right. And she followed him into the hall.

" Laurie!"

" Hallo!" He was half-way upstairs, but when he turned round and saw Laura he suddenly puffed out his cheeks and goggled his eyes at her. " My word, Laura! You do look stunning," said Laurie. " What an absolutely topping hat!"

Laura said faintly " Is it?" and smiled up at Laurie, and didn't tell him after all.

Soon after that people began coming in streams. The band struck up; the hired waiters ran from the house to the marquee. Wherever you looked there were couples strolling, bending to the flowers, greeting, moving on over the lawn. They were like bright birds that had alighted in the Sheridans' garden for this one afternoon, on their way to — where? Ah, what happiness it is to be with people who all are happy, to press hands, press cheeks, smile into eyes.

" Darling Laura, how well you look!"

" What a becoming hat, child!"

" Laura, you look quite Spanish. I've never seen you look so striking."

And Laura, glowing, answered softly, " Have you had tea? Won't you have an ice? The passion-fruit ices really are rather special." She ran to her father and begged him. " Daddy darling, can't the band have something to drink?"

And the perfect afternoon slowly ripened, slowly faded, slowly its petals closed.

" Never a more delightful garden-party..." " The greatest success..." " Quite the most... "

Laura helped her mother with the good-byes. They stood side by side in the porch till it was all over.

" All over, all over, thank heaven," said Mrs. Sheridan. " Round up the others, Laura. Let's go and have some fresh coffee. I'm exhausted. Yes, it's been very successful. But oh, these parties, these parties! Why will you children insist on giving parties!" And they all of them sat down in the deserted marquee.

" Have a sandwich, daddy dear. I wrote the flag."

" Thanks." Mr. Sheridan took a bite and the sandwich was gone. He took another. " I suppose you didn't hear of a beastly accident that happened to-day?" he said.

" My dear," said Mrs. Sheridan, holding up her hand, " we did. It nearly ruined the party. Laura insisted we should put it off."

" Oh, mother!" Laura didn't want to be teased about it.

" It was a horrible affair all the same," said Mr. Sheridan. " The chap[①] was married too. Lived just below in the lane, and leaves a wife and half a dozen kiddies, so they say."

An awkward little silence fell. Mrs. Sheridan fidgeted[②] with her cup. Really, it was very tactless of father...

Suddenly she looked up. There on the table were all those sandwiches, cakes, puffs, all uneaten, all going to be wasted. She had one of her brilliant ideas.

" I know," she said. " Let's make up a basket. Let's send that poor creature some of this perfectly good food. At any rate, it will be the greatest treat for the children. Don't you agree? And she's sure to have neighbours calling in and so on. What a point to have it all ready prepared. Laura!" She jumped up. " Get me the big basket out of the stairs cupboard."

" But, mother, do you really think it's a good idea?" said Laura.

Again, how curious, she seemed to be different from them all. To take scraps from their party. Would the poor woman really like that?

" Of course! What's the matter with you to-day? An hour or two ago you were insisting on us being sympathetic, and now — "

Oh well! Laura ran for the basket. It was filled, it was heaped by her mother.

" Take it yourself, darling," said she. " Run down just as you are. No, wait, take the arum lilies too. People of that class are so impressed by arum lilies."

" The stems will ruin her lace frock," said practical Jose.

So they would. Just in time. " Only the basket, then. And, Laura!" — her mother followed her out of the marquee — " don't on any account — "

" What mother?"

No, better not put such ideas into the child's head! " Nothing! Run along."

It was just growing dusky as Laura shut their garden gates. A big dog ran by like

---

① chap: (also chappie, chappy) UK informal old-fashioned, man or fellow

② fidget: to make continuous small movements

a shadow. The road gleamed white, and down below in the hollow the little cottages were in deep shade. How quiet it seemed after the afternoon. Here she was going down the hill to somewhere where a man lay dead, and she couldn't realize it. Why couldn't she? She stopped a minute. And it seemed to her that kisses, voices, tinkling spoons, laughter, the smell of crushed grass were somehow inside her. She had no room for anything else. How strange! She looked up at the pale sky, and all she thought was, " Yes, it was the most successful party."

Now the broad road was crossed. The lane began, smoky and dark. Women in shawls① and men's tweed caps hurried by. Men hung over the palings; the children played in the doorways. A low hum came from the mean little cottages. In some of them there was a flicker of light, and a shadow, crab-like, moved across the window. Laura bent her head and hurried on. She wished now she had put on a coat. How her frock shone! And the big hat with the velvet streamer② — if only it was another hat! Were the people looking at her? They must be. It was a mistake to have come; she knew all along it was a mistake. Should she go back even now?

No, too late. This was the house. It must be. A dark knot of people stood outside. Beside the gate an old, old woman with a crutch sat in a chair, watching. She had her feet on a newspaper. The voices stopped as Laura drew near. The group parted. It was as though she was expected, as though they had known she was coming here.

Laura was terribly nervous. Tossing the velvet ribbon over her shoulder, she said to a woman standing by, " Is this Mrs. Scott's house?" and the woman, smiling queerly, said, " It is, my lass."

Oh, to be away from this! She actually said, " Help me, God," as she walked up the tiny path and knocked. To be away from those staring eyes, or to be covered up in anything, one of those women's shawls even. I'll just leave the basket and go, she

---

① shawl: a large piece of cloth worn especially by women or girls over their shoulders and/or head Coats, jackets and cloaks

② streamer: a long, narrow strip of brightly coloured paper that is used as a decoration decided. I shan't even wait for it to be emptied.

Then the door opened. A little woman in black showed in the gloom.

Laura said, " Are you Mrs. Scott?" But to her horror the woman answered, " Walk in please, miss," and she was shut in the passage.

" No," said Laura, " I don't want to come in. I only want to leave this basket. Mother sent — "

The little woman in the gloomy passage seemed not to have heard her. " Step this way, please, miss," she said in an oily voice, and Laura followed her.

She found herself in a wretched little low kitchen, lighted by a smoky lamp. There was a woman sitting before the fire.

" Em," said the little creature who had let her in. " Em! It's a young lady." She turned to Laura. She said meaningly, " I'm 'er sister, miss. You'll excuse 'er, won't you?"

" Oh, but of course!" said Laura. " Please, please don't disturb her. I — I only want to leave — "

But at that moment the woman at the fire turned round. Her face, puffed up[①] , red, with swollen eyes and swollen lips, looked terrible. She seemed as though she couldn't understand why Laura was there. What did it mean? Why was this stranger standing in the kitchen with a basket? What was it all about? And the poor face puckered up[②] again.

" All right, my dear," said the other. " I'll thank the young lady."

And again she began, " You'll excuse her, miss, I'm sure," and her face, swollen too, tried an oily smile.

Laura only wanted to get out, to get away. She was back in the passage. The door opened. She walked straight through into the bedroom, where the dead man was lying.

" You'd like a look at 'im, wouldn't you?" said Em's sister, and she brushed past

① puffed up: bigger

② puckered up: to press together and form small folds in something such as cloth or skin

Laura over to the bed. " Don't be afraid, my lass," — and now her voice sounded fond and sly, and fondly she drew down the sheet — " 'e looks a picture. There's nothing to show. Come along, my dear."

Laura came.

There lay a young man, fast asleep — sleeping so soundly, so deeply, that he was far, far away from them both. Oh, so remote, so peaceful. He was dreaming. Never wake him up again. His head was sunk in the pillow, his eyes were closed; they were blind under the closed eyelids. He was given up to his dream. What did garden-parties and baskets and lace frocks matter to him? He was far from all those things. He was wonderful, beautiful. While they were laughing and while the band was playing, this marvel had come to the lane. Happy... happy... All is well, said that sleeping face. This is just as it should be. I am content.

But all the same you had to cry, and she couldn't go out of the room without saying something to him. Laura gave a loud childish sob.

" Forgive my hat," she said.

And this time she didn't wait for Em's sister. She found her way out of the door, down the path, past all those dark people. At the corner of the lane she met Laurie.

He stepped out of the shadow. " Is that you, Laura?"

" Yes."

" Mother was getting anxious. Was it all right?"

" Yes, quite. Oh, Laurie!" She took his arm, she pressed up against him.

" I say, you're not crying, are you?" asked her brother.

Laura shook her head. She was.

Laurie put his arm round her shoulder. " Don't cry," he said in his warm, loving voice. " Was it awful?"

" No," sobbed Laura. " It was simply marvellous. But Laurie — " She stopped, she looked at her brother. " Isn't life," she stammered, " isn't life — " But what life was she couldn't explain. No matter. He quite understood.

" Isn't it, darling?" said Laurie.

Topics for discussion

1. In which way does Katherine Mansfield use contrasts between social classes to illustrate how the classes define each other?

2. Explain the importance of irony in " The Garden Party"

3. What do you think of the conflict between characters in " The Garden Party"?

References for further reading

[1] Jones, Kathleen. *Katherine Mansfield: the story teller*, Edinburgh: Edinburgh University Press, 2001.

[2] Fulbrook, Kate. " Late Fiction" in *Katherine Mansfield*, Harvester Press, 1986.

PART TWO AMERICAN SHORT STORIES

Washington Irving (1783 — 1859)

Rip Van Winkle

Introduction to the author

Washington Irving (April 3, 1783 — November 28, 1859) was an American author, essayist, biographer and historian of the early 19th century. Irving acted as the U.S. ambassador to Spain. He began writing a series of observational letters to the Morning Chronicle in 1802 under the pseudonym Jonathan Oldstyle. In 1815, he was internationally famous with the publication of *The Sketch Book of Geoffrey Crayon, Gent. in 1819 — 1820*. Irving became one of the first American writers to earn acclaim in Europe. He continued to publish regularly throughout his life, and he died at age 76, in Tarrytown, New York. He influenced many American writers including Nathaniel Hawthorne, Herman Melville, Henry Wadsworth Longfellow, and Edgar Allan Poe. He maintained laws should protect American writers from copyright infringement.

Washington Irving's parents were William Irving, Sr., originally of Quholm, Shapinsay, Orkney, and Sarah (née Sanders), Scottish-English immigrants.

Washington Irving's most siblings died in infancy. Irving began writing letters to the New York Morning Chronicle and created the literary magazine Salmagundi in January 1807. He criticized New York culture and politics. His first major book is *A History of New-York from the Beginning of the World to the End of the Dutch Dynasty, by Diedrich Knickerbocker* (1809). Irving also wrote biographies of naval heroes. Irving had military experience and understood the harm of disastrous war. Irving pursued his writing career in England and he was often regarded as an anomaly of literature. *A History of the Life and Voyages of Christopher Columbus* was published in 1828 and his writings on Columbus are romantic history. The first book written and published by Irving in the United States is *A History of New York in 1809*.Critics thought Irving had turned his back on his American heritage in favor of English aristocracy. Actually, he affected many American writers like Edgar Allan Poe. Irving made great contribution in promoting American literature, especially in perfecting American short stories. His short stories were written in vernacular rather than moral or didactic way, and he placed his stories firmly in the United States for the first time. Irving was regarded by William Makepeace Thackeray as a banner in literary circle throughout the 19th and 20th centuries. Meanwhile, Irving's contribution was beyond literature field. He popularized the nickname " Gotham" for New York City, revived the Christmas holiday, and introduced flat-Earth myth to the New World.

Major works by Washington Irving

Short stories/Essays/ Biography/History

A History of New York,1809

*The Sketch Book of Geoffrey Crayon, Gent.*1819 — 1820

Bracebridge Hall,1822

Tales of a Traveller,1824

The Life and Voyages of Christopher Columbus,1828

The Chronicles of the Conquest of Granada,1829

Voyages and Discoveries of the Companions of Columbus,1831

Tales of the Alhambra,1832

The Life of Oliver Goldsmith,1840 (revised 1849)

Mahomet and His Successors,1850

The Life of George Washington (5 volumes),1855 — 1859

Appreciation

The story of " Rip Van Winkle" happens in the years before and after the American Revolutionary War. Rip Van Winkle is a colonial British-American villager of Dutch ancestry. He lives in a village at the foot of New York's Catskill Mountains and is loved by the children in town because he tells stories and gives toys to them. However, he appreciates peaceful and isolated life in the wilderness. Above all, he makes great effort to avoid hard work and his nagging wife. His farm often is in mess and confusion. Rip Van Winkle is a henpecked man. He could not tolerate his nagging wife. One winter day, to escape his wife, Van Winkle is tired of wife's nagging and he leaves his home with his faithful dog, Wolf, wandering around the mountains. Later he meets a man wearing antiquated Dutch clothing and carrying a keg. He asks Van Winkle for help. They continue their trip to a hollow and Rip discovers the hollow is where thunderous noises come. Many men playing nine-pins silently are ornately dressed, and have long bearded. They know Rip Van Winkle's name. Rip drinks some of their moonshine and soon falls asleep. Rip does not know how long he sleeps and when he wakes he is astonished to find that everything changed: his rotting and rusty musket, his foot-long beard. Even his dog is missing.

After Rip Van Winkle returns to his village, no one recognizes him. He could not find his wife and his old friends. He learns that his wife and some of his close friends have died, others have left the town. Rip does not know that the American

Revolution has taken place. He is shocked that George Washington's portrait replaces King George's portrait in the inn. He is also confused to find another man called Rip Van Winkle. It is his son that now has grown up.

Rip Van Winkle gradually understands the confusions. Rip has been away from the village for at least twenty years. It is rumored that the men he met in the mountains are the ghosts of Hendrick (Henry) Hudson's crew. They once explored the Hudson River but disappeared many years ago. Luckily, Rip was recognized by an old woman in the town at last. The oldest resident of the village confirms Rip's identity and prove the truth of Rip's strange tale.

Rip's grown daughter takes him in. He again comes back to previous life style, idle, easygoing and free. The Dutch settlers remember Rip's strange tale and spread it. Other hen-pecked men wish they could have gone to a hollow, sleeping through the hardships of American Revolution, like Rip. " Rip Van Winkle" was one of the first stories Irving proposed for his new book, *The Sketch Book of Geoffrey Crayon, Gent*.

Selected Reading

Rip Van Winkle

A POSTHUMOUS WRITING OF DIEDRICH KNICKERBOCKER.

By Woden[①] , God of Saxons,
From whence comes Wensday, that is Wodensday,
Truth is a thing that ever I will keep
Unto thylke day in which I creep into

① Woden: the Anglo-Saxon name for Odin, the king of the gods. The word " Wednesday" is based on his name.

My sepulcher[1] —
Cartwright[2]

The following Tale was found among the papers of the late Diedrich Knickerbocker, an old gentleman of New York, who was very curious in the Dutch history of the province, and the manners of the descendants from its primitive settlers. His historical researches, however, did not lie so much among books as among men; for the former are lamentably[3] scanty on his favorite topics; whereas he found the old burghers, and still more their wives, rich in that legendary lore, so invaluable to true history. Whenever, therefore, he happened upon a genuine Dutch family, snugly shut up in its low-roofed farmhouse, under a spreading sycamore[4], he looked upon it as a little clasped volume of black-letter[5], and studied it with the zeal of a book-worm.

The result of all these researches was a history of the province during the reign of the Dutch governors, which he published some years since. There have been various opinions as to the literary character of his work, and, to tell the truth, it is not a whit better than it should be. Its chief merit is its scrupulous accuracy, which indeed was a little questioned on its first appearance, but has since been completely established; and it is now admitted into all historical collections, as a book of unquestionable authority.

The old gentleman died shortly after the publication of his work, and now that he is dead and gone, it cannot do much harm to his memory to say that his time might have been better employed in weightier labors. He, however, was apt to ride

---

① sepulcher: a small room or building in which the bodies of dead people were put

② William Cartwright (1611–1643), English playwright The quotation is from The Ordinary (1651)

③ lamentably: very unsatisfactorily or disappointingly

④ sycamore: a North American tree with broad leaves, or the wood of this tree

⑤ volume of black-letter: a heavy-faced type, now called Gothic and Old English his hobby his own way; and though it did now and then kick up the dust a little in the eyes of his neighbors, and grieve the spirit of some friends, for whom he felt the truest deference and affection; yet his errors and follies are remembered " more in sorrow than in anger," ① and it begins to be suspected, that he never intended to injure or offend. But however his memory may be appreciated by critics, it is still held dear by many folks, whose good opinion is well worth having; particularly by certain biscuit-bakers, who have gone so far as to imprint his likeness on their new-year cakes; and have thus given him a chance for immortality, almost equal to the being stamped on a Waterloo Medal, or a Queen Anne's Farthing② .

Whoever has made a voyage up the Hudson must remember the Kaatskill③ mountains. They are a dismembered branch of the great Appalachian family, and are seen away to the west of the river, swelling up to a noble height, and lording it over the surrounding country. Every change of season, every change of weather, indeed, every hour of the day, produces some change in the magical hues and shapes of these mountains, and they are regarded by all the good wives, far and near, as perfect barometers. When the weather is fair and settled, they are clothed in blue and purple, and print their bold outlines on the clear evening sky, but, sometimes, when the rest of the landscape is cloudless, they will gather a hood of gray vapors about their summits, which, in the last rays of the setting sun, will glow and light up like a crown of glory.

At the foot of these fairy mountains, the voyager may have described the light smoke curling up from a village, whose shingle-roofs gleam among the trees, just where the blue tints of the upland melt away into the fresh green of the nearer landscape. It is a little village of great antiquity, having been founded by some of

① Hamlet, Act I, Scene II, Line 232

② The Waterloo Medal commemorated the British victory over Napoleon in 1815. Farthing (small coins) minted in the reign of England's Queen Anne (1702–1714) bore her image

③ the Kaatskill mountains is southeastern New York

the Dutch colonists, in the early times of the province, just about the beginning of the government of the good Peter Stuyvesant① , (may he rest in peace!) and there were some of the houses of the original settlers standing within a few years, built of small yellow bricks brought from Holland, having latticed windows and gable fronts, surmounted with weather-cocks.

In that same village, and in one of these very houses (which, to tell the precise truth, was sadly time-worn and weather-beaten), there lived many years since, while the country was yet a province of Great Britain, a simple good-natured fellow of the name of Rip Van Winkle. He was a descendant of the Van Winkles who figured so gallantly in the chivalrous② days of Peter Stuyvesant, and accompanied him to the siege of Fort Christina③ . He inherited, however, but little of the martial character of his ancestors. I have observed that he was a simple good-natured man; he was, moreover, a kind neighbor, and an obedient hen-pecked husband. Indeed, to the latter circumstance might be owing that meekness of spirit which gained him such universal popularity; for those men are most apt to be obsequious④ and conciliating⑤ abroad, who are under the discipline of shrews at home. Their tempers, doubtless, are rendered pliant and malleable in the fiery furnace of domestic tribulation; and a curtain lecture is worth all the sermons in the world for teaching the virtues of patience and long-suffering. A termagant⑥ wife may, therefore, in some respects, be considered a tolerable blessing; and if so, Rip Van Winkle was thrice blessed.

---

① Peter Stuyvesant (1612–1672), known as Petrus, served as the last Dutch Director–General of the colony of New Netherland from 1647 until it was ceded provisionally to the English in 1664, after which it was renamed New York. He was a major figure in the early history of New York City.

② chivalrous: politely and respectfully

③ In 1655, Dutch forces under Peter Stuyvesant defeated the colonists of New Sweden at Fort Christina, near present–day Wilmington, Delaware.

④ obsequious：too eager to praise or obey someone

⑤ conciliate：end a disagreement or someone's anger by acting in a friendly way or slightly changing your opinions, or to satisfy someone who disagrees with you by acting in this way

⑥ termagant: a woman who argues noisily to get or achieve what she wants

Certain it is, that he was a great favorite among all the good wives of the village, who, as usual, with the amiable sex, took his part in all family squabbles; and never failed, whenever they talked those matters over in their evening gossipings, to lay all the blame on Dame Van Winkle. The children of the village, too, would shout with joy whenever he approached. He assisted at their sports, made their playthings, taught them to fly kites and shoot marbles, and told them long stories of ghosts, witches, and Indians. Whenever he went dodging about the village, he was surrounded by a troop of them, hanging on his skirts, clambering on his back, and playing a thousand tricks on him with impunity① ; and not a dog would bark at him throughout the neighborhood.

The great error in Rip's composition was an insuperable aversion to all kinds of profitable labor. It could not be from the want of assiduity or perseverance; for he would sit on a wet rock, with a rod as long and heavy as a Tartar's lance, and fish all day without a murmur, even though he should not be encouraged by a single nibble. He would carry a fowling-piece on his shoulder for hours together, trudging through woods and swamps, and up hill and down dale, to shoot a few squirrels or wild pigeons. He would never refuse to assist a neighbor even in the roughest toil, and was a foremost man at all country frolics for husking Indian corn, or building stone-fences; the women of the village, too, used to employ him to run their errands, and to do such little odd jobs as their less obliging husbands would not do for them. In a word Rip was ready to attend to anybody's business but his own; but as to doing family duty, and keeping his farm in order, he found it impossible.

In fact, he declared it was of no use to work on his farm; it was the most pestilent little piece of ground in the whole country; everything about it went wrong, and would go wrong, in spite of him. His fences were continually falling to pieces; his cow would either go astray, or get among the cabbages; weeds were sure to grow

---

① impunity: freedom from punishment or from the unpleasant results of something that has been done quicker in his fields than anywhere else; the rain always made a point of setting in just as he had some out-door work to do; so that though his patrimonial[①] estate had dwindled away under his management, acre by acre, until there was little more left than a mere patch of Indian corn and potatoes, yet it was the worst conditioned farm in the neighborhood.

His children, too, were as ragged and wild as if they belonged to nobody. His son Rip, an urchin begotten in his own likeness, promised to inherit the habits, with the old clothes of his father. He was generally seen trooping like a colt at his mother's heels, equipped in a pair of his father's cast-off galligaskins, which he had much ado to[②] hold up with one hand, as a fine lady does her train in bad weather.

Rip Van Winkle, however, was one of those happy mortals, of foolish, well-oiled dispositions, who take the world easy, eat white bread or brown, whichever can be got with least thought or trouble, and would rather starve on a penny than work for a pound. If left to himself, he would have whistled life away in perfect contentment; but his wife kept continually dinning in his ears about his idleness, his carelessness, and the ruin he was bringing on his family. Morning, noon, and night, her tongue was incessantly going, and everything he said or did was sure to produce a torrent of household eloquence. Rip had but one way of replying to all lectures of the kind, and that, by frequent use, had grown into a habit. He shrugged his shoulders, shook his head, cast up his eyes, but said nothing. This, however, always provoked a fresh volley from his wife; so that he was fain to draw off his forces, and take to the outside of the house — the only side which, in truth, belongs to a hen-pecked husband.

Rip's sole domestic adherent[③] was his dog Wolf, who was as much hen-pecked as his master; for Dame Van Winkle regarded them as companions in idleness, and even looked upon Wolf with an evil eye, as the cause of his master's going so

---

① patrimony: property that someone gets from their father or grandfather after his death

② have much ado to: make great effort to

③ adherent: someone who strongly supports an idea, plan, person, etc often astray. True it is, in all points of spirit befitting an honorable dog, he was as courageous an animal as ever scoured the woods — but what courage can withstand the ever-during and all-besetting terrors of a woman's tongue? The moment Wolf entered the house his crest fell, his tail drooped to the ground, or curled between his legs, he sneaked about with a gallows air, casting many a sidelong glance at Dame Van Winkle, and at the least flourish of a broom-stick or ladle, he would fly to the door with yelping precipitation.

Times grew worse and worse with Rip Van Winkle as years of matrimony① rolled on; a tart temper never mellows with age, and a sharp tongue is the only edged tool that grows keener with constant use. For a long while he used to console himself, when driven from home, by frequenting a kind of perpetual club of the sages, philosophers, and other idle personages of the village; which held its sessions on a bench before a small inn, designated by a rubicund portrait of His Majesty George the Third. Here they used to sit in the shade through a long lazy summer's day, talking listlessly over village gossip, or telling endless sleepy stories about nothing. But it would have been worth any statesman's money to have heard the profound discussions that sometimes took place, when by chance an old newspaper fell into their hands from some passing traveller. How solemnly they would listen to the contents, as drawled out by Derrick Van Bummel, the schoolmaster, a dapper learned little man, who was not to be daunted by the most gigantic word in the dictionary; and how sagely they would deliberate upon public events some months after they had taken place.

The opinions of this junto were completely controlled by Nicholas Vedder, a patriarch of the village, and landlord of the inn, at the door of which he took his seat from morning till night, just moving sufficiently to avoid the sun and keep in the shade of a large tree; so that the neighbors could tell the hour by his movements as

---

① matrimony: the state of being married

accurately as by a sundial[①]. It is true he was rarely heard to speak, but smoked his pipe incessantly. His adherents, however (for every great man has his adherents), perfectly understood him, and knew how to gather his opinions. When anything that was read or related displeased him, he was observed to smoke his pipe vehemently[②], and to send forth short, frequent and angry puffs; but when pleased, he would inhale the smoke slowly and tranquilly, and emit it in light and placid clouds; and sometimes, taking the pipe from his mouth, and letting the fragrant vapor curl about his nose, would gravely nod his head in token of perfect approbation[③].

From even this stronghold the unlucky Rip was at length routed by his termagant wife, who would suddenly break in upon the tranquility of the assemblage and call the members all to naught; nor was that august personage, Nicholas Vedder himself, sacred from the daring tongue of this terrible virago[④], who charged him outright with encouraging her husband in habits of idleness.

Poor Rip was at last reduced almost to despair; and his only alternative, to escape from the labor of the farm and clamor of his wife, was to take gun in hand and stroll away into the woods. Here he would sometimes seat himself at the foot of a tree, and share the contents of his wallet with Wolf, with whom he sympathized as a fellow-sufferer in persecution. " Poor Wolf," he would say, " thy mistress leads thee a dog's life of it; but never mind, my lad, whilst I live thou shalt never want a friend to stand by thee!" Wolf would wag his tail, look wistfuly in his master's face, and if dogs can feel pity I verily believe he reciprocated[⑤] the sentiment with all his heart.

In a long ramble of the kind on a fine autumnal day, Rip had unconsciously scrambled to one of the highest parts of the Kaatskill mountains. He was after his

---

① sundial: a device that uses the light of the sun to show the time of day

② vehemently: in a strong and emotional way

③ approbation: approval or agreement, often given by an official group

④ a virago: violent, unpleasant woman who shouts a lot

⑤ reciprocate: formal to share the same feelings as someone else, or to behave in the same way as someone else favorite sport of squirrel shooting, and the still solitudes had echoed and re-echoed with the reports of his gun. Panting and fatigued, he threw himself, late in the afternoon, on a green knoll, covered with mountain herbage, that crowned the brow of a precipice. From an opening between the trees he could overlook all the lower country for many a mile of rich woodland. He saw at a distance the lordly Hudson, far, far below him, moving on its silent but majestic course, with the reflection of a purple cloud, or the sail of a lagging bark, here and there sleeping on its glassy bosom, and at last losing itself in the blue highlands.

On the other side he looked down into a deep mountain glen, wild, lonely, and shagged, the bottom filled with fragments from the impending cliffs, and scarcely lighted by the reflected rays of the setting sun. For some time Rip lay musing on this scene; evening was gradually advancing; the mountains began to throw their long blue shadows over the valleys; he saw that it would be dark long before he could reach the village, and he heaved a heavy sigh when he thought of encountering the terrors of Dame Van Winkle.

As he was about to descend, he heard a voice from a distance, hallooing, " Rip Van Winkle! Rip Van Winkle!" He looked round, but could see nothing but a crow winging its solitary flight across the mountain. He thought his fancy must have deceived him, and turned again to descend, when he heard the same cry ring through the still evening air: " Rip Van Winkle! Rip Van Winkle!" — at the same time Wolf bristled up his back, and giving a low growl, skulked to his master's side, looking fearfully down into the glen. Rip now felt a vague apprehension stealing over him; he looked anxiously in the same direction, and perceived a strange figure slowly toiling up the rocks, and bending under the weight of something he carried on his back. He was surprised to see any human being in this lonely and unfrequented place, but supposing it to be some one of the neighborhood in need of his assistance, he hastened down to yield it.

On nearer approach he was still more surprised at the singularity① of the stranger's appearance. He was a short square-built old fellow, with thick bushy hair, and a grizzled beard. His dress was of the antique Dutch fashion — a cloth jerkin② strapped round the waist — several pair of breeches, the outer one of ample volume, decorated with rows of buttons down the sides, and bunches at the knees. He bore on his shoulder a stout keg, that seemed full of liquor, and made signs for Rip to approach and assist him with the load. Though rather shy and distrustful of this new acquaintance, Rip complied with his usual alacrity; and mutually relieving one another, they clambered up a narrow gully, apparently the dry bed of a mountain torrent. As they ascended, Rip every now and then heard long rolling peals, like distant thunder, that seemed to issue out of a deep ravine, or rather cleft, between lofty rocks, toward which their rugged path conducted. He paused for an instant, but supposing it to be the muttering of one of those transient thunder-showers which often take place in mountain heights, he proceeded. Passing through the ravine, they came to a hollow, like a small amphitheatre, surrounded by perpendicular precipices③ , over the brinks of which impending trees shot their branches, so that you only caught glimpses of the azure sky and the bright evening cloud. During the whole time Rip and his companion had labored on in silence; for though the former marvelled greatly what could be the object of carrying a keg of liquor up this wild mountain, yet there was something strange and incomprehensible about the unknown, that inspired awe and checked familiarity.

On entering the amphitheatre, new objects of wonder presented themselves. On a level spot in the centre was a company of odd-looking personages playing at nine-pins. They were dressed in a quaint outlandish fashion; some wore short doublets④ ,

① singularity: the quality of being strange

② a cloth jerkin: tight, hip–length, armless jacket

③ precipice: a very steep side of a cliff or a mountain

④ doublets: close–fitting, waist–length jacket

others jerkins, with long knives in their belts, and most of them had enormous breeches, of similar style with that of the guide's. Their visages, too, were peculiar: one had a large beard, broad face, and small piggish eyes: the face of another seemed to consist entirely of nose, and was surmounted by a white sugar-loaf hat set off with a little red cock's tail. They all had beards, of various shapes and colors. There was one who seemed to be the commander. He was a stout old gentleman, with a weather-beaten countenance; he wore a laced doublet, broad belt and hanger, high-crowned hat and feather, red stockings, and high-heeled shoes, with roses in them. The whole group reminded Rip of the figures in an old Flemish① painting, in the parlor of Dominie Van Shaick, the village parson, and which had been brought over from Holland at the time of the settlement.

What seemed particularly odd to Rip was, that though these folks were evidently amusing themselves, yet they maintained the gravest faces, the most mysterious silence, and were, withal, the most melancholy party of pleasure he had ever witnessed. Nothing interrupted the stillness of the scene but the noise of the balls, which, whenever they were rolled, echoed along the mountains like rumbling peals of thunder.

As Rip and his companion approached them, they suddenly desisted from their play, and stared at him with such fixed statue-like gaze, and such strange, uncouth, lack-lustre countenances, that his heart turned within him, and his knees smote together. His companion now emptied the contents of the keg into large flagons, and made signs to him to wait upon the company. He obeyed with fear and trembling; they quaffed the liquor in profound silence, and then returned to their game.

By degrees Rip's awe and apprehension subsided. He even ventured, when no eye was fixed upon him, to taste the beverage, which he found had much of the flavor of excellent Hollands② . He was naturally a thirsty soul, and was soon tempted to

① Flemish: the people of northern Belgium

② Hollands: a strong, colorless alcoholic beverage made by Hollanders; Dutch gin repeat the draught. One taste provoked another; and he reiterated his visits to the flagon so often that at length his senses were overpowered, his eyes swam in his head, his head gradually declined, and he fell into a deep sleep.

On waking, he found himself on the green knoll whence he had first seen the old man of the glen. He rubbed his eyes — it was a bright sunny morning. The birds were hopping and twittering among the bushes, and the eagle was wheeling aloft, and breasting the pure mountain breeze. " Surely," thought Rip, " I have not slept here all night." He recalled the occurrences before he fell asleep. The strange man with a keg of liquor — the mountain ravine — the wild retreat among the rocks — the woe-begone party at ninepins — the flagon — " Oh! that flagon! that wicked flagon!" thought Rip — " what excuse shall I make to Dame Van Winkle!"

He looked round for his gun, but in place of the clean well-oiled fowling-piece, he found an old firelock lying by him, the barrel incrusted with rust, the lock falling off, and the stock worm-eaten. He now suspected that the grave roysterers of the mountain had put a trick upon him, and having dosed him with liquor, had robbed him of his gun. Wolf, too, had disappeared, but he might have strayed away after a squirrel or partridge. He whistled after him and shouted his name, but all in vain; the echoes repeated his whistle and shout, but no dog was to be seen.

He determined to revisit the scene of the last evening's gambol, and if he met with any of the party, to demand his dog and gun. As he rose to walk, he found himself stiff in the joints, and wanting in his usual activity. " These mountain beds do not agree with me," thought Rip; " and if this frolic should lay me up with a fit of the rheumatism, I shall have a blessed time with Dame Van Winkle." With some difficulty he got down into the glen: he found the gully up which he and his companion had ascended the preceding evening; but to his astonishment a mountain stream was now foaming down it, leaping from rock to rock, and filling the glen with babbling murmurs. He, however, made shift to scramble up its sides, working his toilsome way through thickets of birch, sassafras, and witch-hazel, and sometimes tripped up or entangled by the wild grapevines that twisted their coils or tendrils from tree to tree, and spread a kind of network in his path.

At length he reached to where the ravine① had opened through the cliffs to the amphitheatre; but no traces of such opening remained. The rocks presented a high impenetrable wall over which the torrent came tumbling in a sheet of feathery foam, and fell into a broad deep basin, black from the shadows of the surrounding forest. Here, then, poor Rip was brought to a stand. He again called and whistled after his dog; he was only answered by the cawing of a flock of idle crows, sporting high in air about a dry tree that overhung a sunny precipice; and who, secure in their elevation, seemed to look down and scoff at the poor man's perplexities. What was to be done? the morning was passing away, and Rip felt famished for want of his breakfast. He grieved to give up his dog and gun; he dreaded to meet his wife; but it would not do to starve among the mountains. He shook his head, shouldered the rusty firelock, and, with a heart full of trouble and anxiety, turned his steps homeward.

As he approached the village he met a number of people, but none whom he knew, which somewhat surprised him, for he had thought himself acquainted with every one in the country round. Their dress, too, was of a different fashion from that to which he was accustomed. They all stared at him with equal marks of surprise, and whenever they cast their eyes upon him, invariably stroked their chins. The constant recurrence of this gesture induced Rip, involuntarily, to do the same, when to his astonishment, he found his beard had grown a foot long!

He had now entered the skirts of the village. A troop of strange children ran at his heels, hooting after him, and pointing at his gray beard. The dogs, too, not one of which he recognized for an old acquaintance, barked at him as he passed. The very village was altered; it was larger and more populous. There were rows of houses which he had never seen before, and those which had been his familiar haunts had

① ravine: a deep narrow valley with steep sides valleys

disappeared. Strange names were over the doors — strange faces at the windows — every thing was strange. His mind now misgave him; he began to doubt whether both he and the world around him were not bewitched. Surely this was his native village, which he had left but the day before. There stood the Kaatskill mountains — there ran the silver Hudson at a distance – there was every hill and dale precisely as it had always been — Rip was sorely perplexed – " That flagon last night," thought he, " has addled my poor head sadly!"

It was with some difficulty that he found the way to his own house, which he approached with silent awe, expecting every moment to hear the shrill voice of Dame Van Winkle. He found the house gone to decay — the roof fallen in, the windows shattered, and the doors off the hinges. A half-starved dog that looked like Wolf was skulking about it. Rip called him by name, but the cur snarled, showed his teeth, and passed on. This was an unkind cut indeed — " My very dog," sighed poor Rip, " has forgotten me!"

He entered the house, which, to tell the truth, Dame Van Winkle had always kept in neat order. It was empty, forlorn① , and apparently abandoned. This desolateness overcame all his connubial fears — he called loudly for his wife and children — the lonely chambers rang for a moment with his voice, and then all again was silence.

He now hurried forth, and hastened to his old resort, the village inn — but it too was gone. A large rickety wooden building stood in its place, with great gaping windows, some of them broken and mended with old hats and petticoats, and over the door was painted, " the Union Hotel, by Jonathan Doolittle." Instead of the great tree that used to shelter the quiet little Dutch inn of yore② , there now was reared a tall naked pole, with something on the top that looked like a red night-cap③ , and from

① forlorn: alone and unhappy; left alone and not cared for

② of yore: of a long time ago

③ a red night-cap: the Liberty Pole and Liberty Cap, used as symbols of liberty in the American and French Revolution it was fluttering a flag, on which was a singular assemblage of stars and stripes — all this was strange and incomprehensible. He recognized on the sign, however, the ruby face of King George, under which he had smoked so many a peaceful pipe; but even this was singularly metamorphosed. The red coat was changed for one of blue and buff① , a sword was held in the hand instead of a sceptre, the head was decorated with a cocked hat, and underneath was painted in large characters, GENERAL WASHINGTON.

There was, as usual, a crowd of folk about the door, but none that Rip recollected. The very character of the people seemed changed. There was a busy, bustling, disputatious tone about it, instead of the accustomed phlegm and drowsy tranquility. He looked in vain for the sage Nicholas Vedder, with his broad face, double chin, and fair long pipe, uttering clouds of tobacco-smoke instead of idle speeches; or Van Bummel, the schoolmaster, doling forth the contents of an ancient newspaper. In place of these, a lean, bilious-looking fellow, with his pockets full of handbills, was haranguing vehemently about rights of citizens — elections — members of congress   liberty   Bunker's Hill   heroes of seventy six   and other words, which were a perfect Babylonish jargon② to the bewildered Van Winkle.

The appearance of Rip, with his long grizzled beard, his rusty fowling-piece③ , his uncouth dress, and an army of women and children at his heels, soon attracted the attention of the tavern politicians. They crowded round him, eyeing him from head to foot with great curiosity. The orator bustled up to him, and, drawing him partly aside, inquired " on which side he voted?" Rip stared in vacant stupidity. Another short but busy little fellow pulled him by the arm, and, rising on tiptoe, inquired in his ear, " Whether he was Federal or Democrat④ ?" Rip was equally at a loss to comprehend

---

① blue and buff: colors of the uniforms of the Revolutionary Army

② Gibberish. Referring to the " confusion of tongues" and the Tower of Babel in Genesis 11:1–9

③ fowling–piece: gun for killing birds, a shotgun

④ A Federalist (conservative) or Democratic–Republican (liberal) in his politics the question; when a knowing, self-important old gentleman, in a sharp cocked hat, made his way through the crowd, putting them to the right and left with his elbows as he passed, and planting himself before Van Winkle, with one arm akimbo, the other resting on his cane, his keen eyes and sharp hat penetrating, as it were, into his very soul, demanded in an austere tone, " what brought him to the election with a gun on his shoulder, and a mob at his heels, and whether he meant to breed a riot in the village?" — " Alas! gentlemen," cried Rip, somewhat dismayed, " I am a poor quiet man, a native of the place, and a loyal subject of the king, God bless him!"

Here a general shout burst from the by-standers — " A tory! a tory! a spy! a refugee! hustle him! away with him!" It was with great difficulty that the self-important man in the cocked hat restored order; and, having assumed a tenfold austerity of brow, demanded again of the unknown culprit① , what he came there for, and whom he was seeking? The poor man humbly assured him that he meant no harm, but merely came there in search of some of his neighbors, who used to keep about the tavern.

" Well — who are they? — name them."

Rip bethought himself a moment, and inquired, " Where's Nicholas Vedder?"

There was a silence for a little while, when an old man replied, in a thin piping voice, " Nicholas Vedder! why, he is dead and gone these eighteen years! There was a wooden tombstone in the church-yard that used to tell all about him, but that's rotten and gone too."

" Where's Brom Dutcher?"

" Oh, he went off to the army in the beginning of the war; some say he was killed at the storming of Stony Point② — others say he was drowned in a squall at

① culprit: someone who has committed a crime or done something wrong

② Stony Point: on the west bank of the Hudson River, below West Point. It was captured by General Anthony Wayne in the American Revolution the foot of Antony's Nose.[①] I don't know — he never came back again."

" Where's Van Bummel, the schoolmaster?"

" He went off to the wars too, was a great militia general, and is now in congress."

Rip's heart died away at hearing of these sad changes in his home and friends, and finding himself thus alone in the world. Every answer puzzled him too, by treating of such enormous lapses of time, and of matters which he could not understand: war — congress — Stony Point! — he had no courage to ask after any more friends, but cried out in despair, " Does nobody here know Rip Van Winkle?"

" Oh, Rip Van Winkle!" exclaimed two or three, " Oh, to be sure! that's Rip Van Winkle yonder, leaning against the tree."

Rip looked, and beheld a precise counterpart of himself, as he went up the mountain: apparently as lazy, and certainly as ragged. The poor fellow was now completely confounded. He doubted his own identity, and whether he was himself or another man. In the midst of his bewilderment, the man in the cocked hat demanded who he was, and what was his name?

" God knows," exclaimed he, at his wit's end; " I'm not myself — I'm somebody else — that's me yonder — no — that's somebody else got into my shoes — I was myself last night, but I fell asleep on the mountain, and they've changed my gun, and every thing's changed, and I'm changed, and I can't tell what's my name, or who I am!"

The by-standers began now to look at each other, nod, wink significantly, and tap their fingers against their foreheads. There was a whisper also, about securing the gun, and keeping the old fellow from doing mischief, at the very suggestion of which the self-important man in the cocked hat retired with some precipitation. At this critical moment a fresh comely woman pressed through the throng to get a peep

---

① Antony's Nose: a mountain near West Point, on the Hudson River at the gray-bearded man. She had a chubby[①] child in her arms, which, frightened at his looks, began to cry. " Hush[②] , Rip," cried she, " hush, you little fool; the old man won't hurt you." The name of the child, the air of the mother, the tone of her voice, all awakened a train of recollections in his mind. " What is your name, my good woman?" asked he.

" Judith Gardenier."

" And your father's name?"

" Ah, poor man, Rip Van Winkle was his name, but it's twenty years since he went away from home with his gun, and never has been heard of since — his dog came home without him; but whether he shot himself, or was carried away by the Indians, nobody can tell. I was then but a little girl."

Rip had but one question more to ask; but he put it with a faltering[③] voice:

" Where's your mother?"

" Oh, she too had died but a short time since; she broke a blood-vessel in a fit of passion at a New-England peddler."

There was a drop of comfort, at least, in this intelligence. The honest man could contain himself no longer. He caught his daughter and her child in his arms. " I am your father!" cried he – " Young Rip Van Winkle once — old Rip Van Winkle now! — Does nobody know poor Rip Van Winkle?"

All stood amazed, until an old woman, tottering out from among the crowd, put her hand to her brow, and peering under it in his face for a moment, exclaimed, " Sure enough! it is Rip Van Winkle — it is himself! Welcome home again, old neighbor — Why, where have you been these twenty long years?"

Rip's story was soon told, for the whole twenty years had been to him but as one night. The neighbors stared when they heard it; some were seen to wink at each other,

---

① chubby: rounded in a pleasant and attractive way

② hush: be quiet, keep silent

③ faltering: hesitating, uncertain

and put their tongues in their cheeks: and the self-important man in the cocked hat, who, when the alarm was over, had returned to the field, screwed down the corners of his mouth, and shook his head — upon which there was a general shaking of the head throughout the assemblage.

It was determined, however, to take the opinion of old Peter Vanderdonk, who was seen slowly advancing up the road. He was a descendant of the historian of that name①, who wrote one of the earliest accounts of the province. Peter was the most ancient inhabitant of the village, and well versed in all the wonderful events and traditions of the neighborhood. He recollected Rip at once, and corroborated his story in the most satisfactory manner. He assured the company that it was a fact, handed down from his ancestor the historian, that the Kaatskill mountains had always been haunted by strange beings. That it was affirmed that the great Hendrick Hudson, the first discoverer of the river and country, kept a kind of vigil there every twenty years, with his crew of the Half-moon; being permitted in this way to revisit the scenes of his enterprise, and keep a guardian eye upon the river, and the great city called by his name②. That his father had once seen them in their old Dutch dresses playing at nine-pins in a hollow of the mountain; and that he himself had heard, one summer afternoon, the sound of their balls, like distant peals of thunder.

To make a long story short, the company broke up, and returned to the more important concerns of the election. Rip's daughter took him home to live with her; she had a snug, well-furnished house, and a stout cheery farmer for a husband, whom Rip recollected for one of the urchins③ that used to climb upon his back. As to Rip's son and heir, who was the ditto④ of himself, seen leaning against the tree, he was employed to work on the farm; but evinced an hereditary disposition to attend to

① Adriaen Van der Donck (1620?–1635), author of a description of New Netherland published at Amsterdam in 1655

② The city of Hudson, on the Hudson River

③ urchin: a small child, especially one who behaves badly and is dirty or untidily dressed

④ ditto: similar and the same; describing people with the same qualities anything else but his business.

Rip now resumed his old walks and habits; he soon found many of his former cronies, though all rather the worse for the wear and tear of time; and preferred making friends among the rising generation, with whom he soon grew into great favor.

Having nothing to do at home, and being arrived at that happy age when a man can be idle with impunity, he took his place once more on the bench at the inn door, and was reverenced as one of the patriarchs of the village, and a chronicle of the old times " before the war." It was some time before he could get into the regular track of gossip, or could be made to comprehend the strange events that had taken place during his torpor. How that there had been a revolutionary war — that the country had thrown off the yoke of old England — and that, instead of being a subject of his Majesty George the Third, he was now a free citizen of the United States. Rip, in fact, was no politician; the changes of states and empires made but little impression on him; but there was one species of despotism under which he had long groaned, and that was — petticoat government. Happily that was at an end; he had got his neck out of the yoke of matrimony, and could go in and out whenever he pleased, without dreading the tyranny of Dame Van Winkle. Whenever her name was mentioned, however, he shook his head, shrugged his shoulders, and cast up his eyes; which might pass either for an expression of resignation to his fate, or joy at his deliverance.

He used to tell his story to every stranger that arrived at Mr. Doolittle's hotel. He was observed, at first, to vary on some points every time he told it, which was, doubtless, owing to his having so recently awaked. It at last settled down precisely to the tale I have related, and not a man, woman, or child in the neighborhood, but knew it by heart. Some always pretended to doubt the reality of it, and insisted that Rip had been out of his head, and that this was one point on which he always remained flighty. The old Dutch inhabitants, however, almost universally gave it full credit. Even to this day they never hear a thunderstorm of a summer afternoon about the

Kaatskill, but they say Hendrick Hudson and his crew are at their game of nine-pins; and it is a common wish of all hen-pecked husbands in the neighborhood, when life hangs heavy on their hands, that they might have a quieting draught out of Rip Van Winkle's flagon.

NOTE — The foregoing Tale, one would suspect, had been suggested to Mr. Knickerbocker by a little German superstition about the Emperor Frederick der Rothbart, and the Kypphauser mountain① : the subjoined note, however, which he had appended to the tale, shows that it is an absolute fact, narrated with his usual fidelity:

" The story of Rip Van Winkle may seem incredible to many, but nevertheless I give it my full belief, for I know the vicinity of our old Dutch settlements to have been very subject to marvellous events and appearances. Indeed, I have heard many stranger stories than this, in the villages along the Hudson; all of which were too well authenticated to admit of a doubt. I have even talked with Rip Van Winkle myself who, when last I saw him, was a very venerable old man, and so perfectly rational and consistent on every other point, that I think no conscientious② person could refuse to take this into the bargain; nay, I have seen a certificate on the subject taken before a country justice and signed with a cross, in the justice's own handwriting. The story, therefore, is beyond the possibility of doubt."

D. K.

Topics for discussion

1. How do you appreciate the conflicts between past and present, old and new,

① Frederick I (1123–1190), Holy Roman emperor(1152–1190). Legend holds that he sleeps in a cavern in the Kypphauser mountain in Germany, waiting until his country's need shall bring him forth

② conscientious: feeling a moral responsibility to do your work carefully and to be fair to others leisure and work, innocence and experience in Rip Van Winkle?

2. Why did Rip leave his home? What kind of women does his wife represent?

3. What are the distinguished features in Washington Irving's Rip Van Winkle?

4. Please make some comment on Washington Irving's contribution to American literature.

References for further reading

[1] Brodwin, Stanley. ed. *The Old and New World romanticism of Washington Irving*, New York : Greenwood Press, 1986.

[2] Myers, Andrew B. *The worlds of Washington Irving, 1783-1859* Tarrytown, New York: Sleepy Hollow Restorations, 1974.

[3] Springer, Haskell S. *Washington Irving's " Sketch book": a critical edition*, Ann Arbor, Mich. : UMI, 1969.

[4] Warner, Charles Dudley. *Washington Irving, Boston : Houghton Mifflin Co.*, 1909.

[5] Williams, Stanley Thomas. *The life of Washington Irving*, Oxford: Oxford University Press, 1935.

Edgar Allen Poe (1809 — 1849)

The Masque of the Red Death

Introduction to the author

Edgar Allan Poe (January 19, 1809 — October 7, 1849) was an American author, poet, editor, and literary critic. He is well-known for his mysterious tales and short story. He invents the detective fiction genre, promotes the emergence of science fiction genre. He led in a financially difficult life, depending on writing alone to make a living. Edgar Poe was born in Boston, Massachusetts, the second child of English-born actress Elizabeth Arnold Hopkins Poe and actor David Poe, Jr. Poe was orphaned at any early age, as his father abandoned him and his mother died of tuberculosis when he was still a very young child, he was then adopted by John Allan and Francis Allan, but Mrs. Allan, Poe's beloved foster mother, died of tuberculosis in 1829. Although John never legally adopted him, Poe added the Allan surname to his own. Poe attended the University of Virginia studying ancient and modern languages but gave up on the university after a year. Poe spent his early adult life in and out of the army, engaging in an ongoing struggle over money with his foster father, and developing the notorious habits of alcoholism and debt. Poe traveled to Boston in April 1827, sustaining himself with odd jobs as a clerk and newspaper writer. In 1827, he joined in the Army and began his publishing career. His collection of poems *Tamerlane and Other Poems* (1827) came out, but did not aroused attention. Poe published his second book *Al Aaraaf* in 1829. Poe was admitted as a cadet at West Point in 1930 and left there one year later. He left for New York in February 1831, and released a third volume of poems, simply titled *Poems*.

In 1836, Poe married his 13-year-old cousin, Virginia Clemm. However, she died eleven years later, and Poe wrote many works for his wife. He published several poems, book reviews, critiques, and stories in the paper. *The Narrative of Arthur Gordon Pym of Nantucket* was published in 1838. Poe worked as an assistant editor in Burton's Gentleman's Magazine and Graham's Magazine. Finally, he started his own journal *The Penn.* In 1845, his poem " The Raven" appeared in the *Evening Mirror*. " The Raven," launched him into instant national, and eventually, international, success. Poe spent the last few years of his life in this small cottage in the Bronx, New York. On October 3, 1849, Poe was found unconscious on a street in Baltimore, he died three days later and now is buried in Baltimore, Maryland.

Poe's works' themes deal with questions of death, are linked to the dark romanticism genre and included elements of popular pseudosciences. In addition, Poe also wrote satires, humor tales, and hoaxes, and reinvented science fiction. During his lifetime, Poe was mostly recognized as a literary critic. Henry Wadsworth Longfellow was his favorite criticism target. Poe was also known as a writer of fiction and became one of the first American authors of the 19th century to become more popular in Europe than in the United States. Poe's work was also extremely influential on French and Russian literature.

Major works by Edgar Allen Poe

Tales

"The Black Cat"

"A Descent into the Maelström"

"The Fall of the House of Usher"

"Hop-Frog"

"Ligeia"

"Morella"

"The Oval Portrait"

"The Premature Burial"

"The Tell-Tale Heart"

"The Cask of Amontillado"

"The Facts in the Case of M. Valdemar"

"The Gold-Bug"

"The Imp of the Perverse"

"The Masque of the Red Death"

"The Murders in the Rue Morgue"

"The Pit and the Pendulum"

"The Purloined Letter"

Poetry

"Al Aaraaf"

"The Bells"

"The Conqueror Worm"

"Eldorado"

"The Haunted Palace"

"Lenore"

"The Raven"

"Annabel Lee"

"The City in the Sea"

"A Dream Within a Dream"

"Eulalie"

"To Helen"

"Tamerlane"

"Ulalume"

Other works

Politian, 1835

The Narrative of Arthur Gordon Pym of Nantucket,1838

"The Balloon-Hoax", 1844

"The Philosophy of Composition", 1846

Eureka: A Prose Poem, 1848

"The Poetic Principle", 1848

"The Light-House", 1849

Appreciation

The title of the story's original publication was " mask" and changed to " masque". In this macabre tale, the Red Death is a deadly pestilence which appeared in the country. In order to protect them from suffering and disease spreading throughout the rest of their country, a Prince Prospero seals himself and a thousand of his friends into the abbey of a castle. The people in the abbey tried to distract themselves from the suffering and death by the Red Death. They were lost in a lavish costume ball. A costumed guest enters and claims the lives of everyone present.

The story explored themes of man's fear of death, sin, madness, and the end of the world. It is prime example of Poe's Gothic horror fiction. Some images of blood and death, elements of the supernatural occurred in the tale. In " The Masque of the Red Death," powerful imagery and an illusive narrative voice are tightly woven into a macabre tale of horror with insight into the human condition. The story presented man's fear of his own mortality. People made great effort to escape the clutches of the Red Death. Poe told people that no one, not even the powerful and wealthy, can escape death. " The Masque of the Red Death" can also be interpreted as the interior monologue of a madman. It is considered an allegorical tale because it is symbol of how humans respond to the knowledge of their own mortality.

At the most literal level, this story is told in the " third person," but the narrator of the story may be the Red Death itself. Personification is used in the story. The Red Death, Time, Beauty, Darkness, and Decay all are personified. The tale is considered one of the early masters of Gothic horror fiction since it is characterized by elements of the supernatural, gruesome scenes of horror, dark settings, and a preoccupation with death and madness.

Selected Reading

The Masque of the Red Death

The " Red Death" had long devastated the country. No pestilence had ever been so fatal, or so hideous. Blood was its Avatar① and its seal — the redness and the horror of blood. There were sharp pains, and sudden dizziness, and then profuse bleeding at the pores, with dissolution. The scarlet stains upon the body and especially upon the face of the victim, were the pest ban which shut him out from the aid and from the sympathy of his fellow-men. And the whole seizure, progress and termination of the disease, were the incidents of half an hour.

But the Prince Prospero② was happy and dauntless and sagacious. When his dominions were half depopulated, he summoned to his presence a thousand hale and light-hearted friends from among the knights and dames of his court, and with these retired to the deep seclusion of one of his castellated abbeys. This was an extensive and magnificent structure, the creation of the prince's own eccentric yet august taste. A strong and lofty wall girdled it in. This wall had gates of iron. The courtiers, having entered, brought furnaces and massy hammers and welded the bolts. They resolved to leave means neither of ingress or egress to the sudden impulses of despair or of frenzy from within. The abbey was amply provisioned. With such precautions the courtiers might bid defiance to③ contagion. The external world could take care of itself. In the meantime it was folly to grieve, or to think. The prince had provided all

---

① Avatar: an image that represents something

② Prospero: Prospero a fictional character and the protagonist of William Shakespeare's play The Tempest. He is the rightful Duke of Milan, who (with his young daughter, Miranda) was put to sea on " a rotten carcass of a butt boat" to die by his usurping brother, Antonio, twelve years before the play begins.

③ bid defiance to: refuse to obey someone or something

the appliances of pleasure. There were buffoons, there were improvisatori[1] , there were ballet-dancers, there were musicians, there was Beauty, there was wine. All these and security were within. Without was the " Red Death."

It was toward the close of the fifth or sixth month of his seclusion, and while the pestilence raged most furiously abroad, that the Prince Prospero entertained his thousand friends at a masked ball of the most unusual magnificence.

It was a voluptuous[2] scene, that masquerade. But first let me tell of the rooms in which it was held. There were seven – an imperial suite. In many palaces, however, such suites form a long and straight vista, while the folding doors slide back nearly to the walls on either hand, so that the view of the whole extent is scarcely impeded. Here the case was very different; as might have been expected from the duke's love of the bizarre. The apartments were so irregularly disposed that the vision embraced but little more than one at a time. There was a sharp turn at every twenty or thirty yards, and at each turn a novel effect. To the right and left, in the middle of each wall, a tall and narrow Gothic window looked out upon a closed corridor which pursued the windings of the suite. These windows were of stained glass whose color varied in accordance with the prevailing hue of the decorations of the chamber into which it opened. That at the eastern extremity was hung, for example, in blue — and vividly blue were its windows. The second chamber was purple in its ornaments and tapestries, and here the panes were purple. The third was green throughout, and so were the casements. The fourth was furnished and lighted with orange — the fifth with white — the sixth with violet. The seventh apartment was closely shrouded in black velvet tapestries that hung all over the ceiling and down the walls, falling in heavy folds upon a carpet of the same material and hue. But in this chamber only, the color of the windows failed to correspond with the decorations. The panes here were scarlet — a deep blood color. Now in no one of the seven apartments was there any

---

① improvisatori: impromptu, musical composition

② voluptuous: luxurious and easy

lamp or candelabrum, amid the profusion of golden ornaments that lay scattered to and fro or depended from the roof. There was no light of any kind emanating from lamp or candle within the suite of chambers. But in the corridors that followed the suite, there stood, opposite to each window, a heavy tripod, bearing a brazier of fire that protected its rays through the tinted glass and so glaringly illumined the room. And thus were produced a multitude of gaudy and fantastic appearances. But in the western or black chamber the effect of the fire-light that streamed upon the dark hangings through the blood-tinted panes, was ghastly in the extreme, and produced so wild a look upon the countenances of those who entered, that there were few of the company bold enough to set foot within its precincts at all.

It was in this apartment, also, that there stood against the western wall, a gigantic clock of ebony. Its pendulum swung to and fro with a dull, heavy, monotonous clang; and when the minute-hand made the circuit of the face, and the hour was to be stricken, there came from the brazen lungs of the clock a sound which was clear and loud and deep and exceedingly musical, but of so peculiar a note and emphasis that, at each lapse of an hour, the musicians of the orchestra were constrained to pause, momentarily, in their performance, to hearken to the sound; and thus the waltzers perforce ceased their evolutions; and there was a brief disconcert of the whole gay company; and, while the chimes of the clock yet rang, it was observed that the giddiest grew pale, and the more aged and sedate passed their hands over their brows as if in confused reverie or meditation. But when the echoes had fully ceased, a light laughter at once pervaded the assembly; the musicians looked at each other and smiled as if at their own nervousness and folly, and made whispering vows, each to the other, that the next chiming of the clock should produce in them no similar emotion; and then, after the lapse of sixty minutes, (which embrace three thousand and six hundred seconds of the Time that flies,) there came yet another chiming of the clock, and then were the same disconcert and tremulousness① and meditation as before.

But, in spite of these things, it was a gay and magnificent revel. The tastes of the duke were peculiar. He had a fine eye for colors and effects. He disregarded the decora of mere fashion. His plans were bold and fiery, and his conceptions glowed with barbaric lustre. There are some who would have thought him mad. His followers felt that he was not. It was necessary to hear and see and touch him to be sure that he was not.

He had directed, in great part, the moveable embellishments② of the seven chambers, upon occasion of this great fete; and it was his own guiding taste which had given character to the masqueraders. Be sure they were grotesque. There were much glare and glitter and piquancy and phantasm — much of what has been since seen in " Hernani." There were arabesque③ figures with unsuited limbs and appointments. There were delirious fancies such as the madman fashions. There was much of the beautiful, much of the wanton, much of the bizarre, something of the terrible, and not a little of that which might have excited disgust. To and fro in the seven chambers there stalked, in fact, a multitude of dreams. And these — the dreams — writhed in and about, taking hue from the rooms, and causing the wild music of the orchestra to seem as the echo of their steps. And, anon, there strikes the ebony clock which stands in the hall of the velvet. And then, for a moment, all is still, and all is silent save the voice of the clock. The dreams are stiff-frozen as they stand. But the echoes of the chime die away — they have endured but an instant — and a light, half-subdued laughter floats after them as they depart. And now again the music swells, and the dreams live, and writhe to and fro more merrily than ever, taking hue

① tremulous: shaking, swinging and vibrating

② embellishment: to make something more beautiful or interesting by adding something to it

③ arabesque: a position in ballet in which the dancer stands on one leg with the other leg held out straight behind from the many-tinted windows through which stream the rays from the tripods. But to the chamber which lies most westwardly of the seven, there are now none of the maskers who venture; for the night is waning away; and there flows a ruddier light through the blood-colored panes; and the blackness of the sable drapery appals; and to him whose foot falls upon the sable carpet, there comes from the near clock of ebony a muffled peal more solemnly emphatic than any which reaches their ears who indulge in the more remote gaieties of the other apartments.

But these other apartments were densely crowded, and in them beat feverishly the heart of life. And the revel went whirlingly on, until at length there commenced the sounding of midnight upon the clock. And then the music ceased, as I have told; and the evolutions of the waltzers were quieted; and there was an uneasy cessation of all things as before. But now there were twelve strokes to be sounded by the bell of the clock; and thus it happened, perhaps, that more of thought crept, with more of time, into the meditations of the thoughtful among those who revelled. And thus, too, it happened, perhaps, that before the last echoes of the last chime had utterly sunk into silence, there were many individuals in the crowd who had found leisure to become aware of the presence of a masked figure which had arrested the attention of no single individual before. And the rumor of this new presence having spread itself whisperingly around, there arose at length from the whole company a buzz, or murmur, expressive of disapprobation and surprise — then, finally, of terror, of horror, and of disgust.

In an assembly of phantasms① such as I have painted, it may well be supposed that no ordinary appearance could have excited such sensation. In truth the masquerade license of the night was nearly unlimited; but the figure in question had

① phantasm: something that is seen or imagined but is not real; unreal things and unreality out-Heroded Herod[①], and gone beyond the bounds of even the prince's indefinite decorum. There are chords in the hearts of the most reckless which cannot be touched without emotion. Even with the utterly lost, to whom life and death are equally jests, there are matters of which no jest can be made. The whole company, indeed, seemed now deeply to feel that in the costume and bearing of the stranger neither wit nor propriety existed. The figure was tall and gaunt, and shrouded from head to foot in the habiliments of the grave. The mask which concealed the visage was made so nearly to resemble the countenance of a stiffened corpse that the closest scrutiny must have had difficulty in detecting the cheat. And yet all this might have been endured, if not approved, by the mad revellers around. But the mummer had gone so far as to assume the type of the Red Death. His vesture was dabbled in blood — and his broad brow, with all the features of the face, was besprinkled with the scarlet horror.

When the eyes of Prince Prospero fell upon this spectral image (which with a slow and solemn movement, as if more fully to sustain its role, stalked to and fro among the waltzers) he was seen to be convulsed, in the first moment with a strong shudder either of terror or distaste; but, in the next, his brow reddened with rage.

"Who dares?" he demanded hoarsely of the courtiers who stood near him — "who dares insult us with this blasphemous[②] mockery? Seize him and unmask him — that we may know whom we have to hang at sunrise, from the battlements!"

It was in the eastern or blue chamber in which stood the Prince Prospero as he uttered these words. They rang throughout the seven rooms loudly and clearly — for the prince was a bold and robust man, and the music had become hushed at the waving of his hand.

It was in the blue room where stood the prince, with a group of pale courtiers

---

① Herod: also known as Herod the Great and Herod I, was a Roman client king of Judea. He has been described as a madman who murdered his own family and a great many rabbis, "the evil genius of the Judean nation", "prepared to commit any crime in order to gratify his unbounded ambition" and "the greatest builder in Jewish history".

② blasphemous: (of speech or writing) showing lack of respect to God or to a religion by his side. At first, as he spoke, there was a slight rushing movement of this group in the direction of the intruder, who at the moment was also near at hand, and now, with deliberate and stately step, made closer approach to the speaker. But from a certain nameless awe with which the mad assumptions of the mummer had inspired the whole party, there were found none who put forth hand to seize him; so that, unimpeded, he passed within a yard of the prince's person; and, while the vast assembly, as if with one impulse, shrank from the centres of the rooms to the walls, he made his way uninterruptedly, but with the same solemn and measured step which had distinguished him from the first, through the blue chamber to the purple — through the purple to the green — through the green to the orange — through this again to the white — and even thence to the violet, ere① a decided movement had been made to arrest him. It was then, however, that the Prince Prospero, maddening with rage and the shame of his own momentary cowardice, rushed hurriedly through the six chambers, while none followed him on account of a deadly terror that had seized upon all. He bore aloft a drawn dagger, and had approached, in rapid impetuosity② , to within three or four feet of the retreating figure, when the latter, having attained the extremity of the velvet apartment, turned suddenly and confronted his pursuer. There was a sharp cry — and the dagger dropped gleaming upon the sable carpet, upon which, instantly afterwards, fell prostrate in death the Prince Prospero. Then, summoning the wild courage of despair, a throng of the revellers at once threw themselves into the black apartment, and, seizing the mummer, whose tall figure stood erect and motionless within the shadow of the ebony clock, gasped in unutterable horror at finding the grave-cerements and corpse-like mask which they handled with so violent a rudeness, untenanted by any tangible form.

And now was acknowledged the presence of the Red Death. He had come like a thief in the night. And one by one dropped the revellers in the blood-bedewed halls

---

① ere: (literary or old use) before

② impetuosity: action is said or done suddenly, without considering the likely results of their revel, and died each in the despairing posture of his fall. And the life of the ebony clock went out with that of the last of the gay. And the flames of the tripods expired. And Darkness and Decay and the Red Death held illimitable dominion over all.

Topics for discussion

1. How did Poe use the allusions to *The Tempest* and *the Bible* in *The Masque of the Red Death* ?

2. How do you understand allegory of time and the seven rooms in Prince Prospero's imperial suite?

3. Some critics thinks that the Red Death figure is regarded as an allegory of life itself, how do you understand the statement?

4. What are the main themes of *The Masque of the Red Death*?

References for further reading

[1] Deas, Michael. *The Portraits and Daguerreotypes of Edgar Allan Poe*. Charlottesville: University Press of Virginia, 1989.

[2] Hayes, Kevin J. ed. The Cambridge companion to Edgar Allan Poe. Shanghai : Shanghai Foreign Language Education Press, 2004.

[3] Hutchisson, James M. ed. *Edgar Allan Poe: beyond gothicis*. Newark: University of Delaware Press, 2011.

[4] Kopley, Richard. *Edgar Allan Poe and the Dupin mysteries*. New York: Palgrave Macmillan, 2008.

[5] Tschachler, Heinz. *The monetary imagination of Edgar Allan Poe: banking, currency, and politics in the writings*. Jefferson, North Carolina: McFarland & Company, Inc., Publishers, 2013.

Nathaniel Hawthorne (1804 — 1864)

The Minister's Black Veil

Introduction to the author

Nathaniel Hawthorne (July 4, 1804 — May 19, 1864) was an American novelist and short story writer. He was born in 1804 in Salem, Massachusetts to Nathaniel Hathorne and the former Elizabeth Clarke Manning. He graduated from Bowdoin College. Hawthorne published his first work *Fanshawe* in 1828. His Twice-Told Tales is a collection of short stories published in various periodicals. His published works include novels, short stories, and a biography of his friend Franklin Pierce. Hawthorne's writings deal with moral allegories with a Puritan inspiration. His themes often center on the inherent evil and sin of humanity, and his works often have moral messages and deep psychological complexity and are of Dark Romanticism.

Hawthorne's forebears are notorious and his great-great-great-grandfather, William Hathorne, was magistrate and judge, infamous for his harsh sentencing. Hawthorne's great-great-grandfather, John Hathorne, as a judge, oversaw the Salem witch trials. Hawthorne's father, Nathaniel Hathorne, Sr., died in 1808 of yellow fever in Suriname, and Nathaniel Hawthorne and his family moved in Salem. Hawthorne had close relationship with some reputed figures including president Franklin Pierce, poet Henry Wadsworth Longfellow, congressman Jonathan Cilley, and naval reformer Horatio Bridge. In 1836 Hawthorne served as the editor of a magazine. He contributed short stories, including " Young Goodman Brown" and " The Minister's Black Veil", to various magazines and annuals. Hawthorne married Sophia Peabody in 1842 and moved to The Old Manse in Concord, Massachusetts, where he met Ralph Waldo Emerson. In 1850 Hawthorne became friends with Herman Melville.

In The Berkshires, Hawthorne began his productive period, and his works include *The House of the Seven Gables* (1851) and *The Blithedale Romance* (1852), a collection of short stories *A Wonder-Book for Girls and Boys*. In 1852, the Hawthornes returned to Concord, where he neighbored Emerson and Henry David Thoreau and began to write *The Life of Franklin Pierce*. In 1860, *The Marble Faun* was published. At the outset of the American Civil War, Hawthorne met Abraham Lincoln and other notable figures, which was described in his essay " Chiefly About War Matters" in 1862. Hawthorne died on a tour of the White Mountains in Plymouth, New Hampshire in 1864. Hawthorne was buried on what is now known as " Authors' Ridge" in Sleepy Hollow Cemetery, Concord, Massachusetts.

Hawthorne's works belong to romanticism. His tales suggest that guilt, sin, and evil are inherent natural qualities of humanity. His works are historical romances loaded with symbolism. The ancestral sin, guilt and retribution are common themes of his works. His later writings reflect his negative view of the Transcendentalism movement. In his early years he wrote a short story *Twice-Told Tales*. His four major romances were written between 1850 and 1860: *The Scarlet Letter* (1850), *The House of the Seven Gables* (1851), *The Blithedale Romance* (1852) and *The Marble Faun* (1860). Critics praised not only Hawthorne's sentimentality and moral purity but also his works' dark psychological complexity.

Major works by Edgar Allen Poe

Novels

Fanshawe (published anonymously, 1828)

The Scarlet Letter, 1850

The House of the Seven Gables, 1851

The Blithedale Romance, 1852

The Marble Faun: Or, The Romance of Monte Beni, 1860

The Dolliver Romance, 1863 (unfinished)

Septimus Felton; or, the Elixir of Life, 1872

Short story collections

Twice-Told Tales, 1837

Grandfather's Chair, 1840

Mosses from an Old Manse, 1846

The Snow-Image, and Other Twice-Told Tales, 1852

A Wonder-Book for Girls and Boys, 1852

Tanglewood Tales, 1853

The Dolliver Romance and Other Pieces, 1876

The Great Stone Face and Other Tales of the White Mountains, 1889

A Wonder-Book for Young and Old, 1851

Appreciation

As the story opens, the sexton responsible for maintaining the church is ringing the bell. He stops abruptly ringing the bell when he is startled by the Reverend Mr. Hooper. Mr. Hooper wears a black semi-transparent veil that covers his whole face but his mouth and chin. Mr. Hooper's irrational behavior bewilders the townspeople and they talk about the veil and its significance. Mr. Hooper delivers a sermon on secret sin, which seems to penetrate everyone's soul. After the sermon, Mr. Hopper officiates a funeral for a young lady of the town who has died. Mr. Hooper's veil falls away when he leans forward to utter to the deceased. Some mourners believe that Hooper and the deceased were walking hand in hand. Later Mr. Hooper attends a wedding wearing his black veil and his arriving damages the joyous atmosphere of the wedding. The black veil even becomes a hot topic among the people including the schoolchildren. They are eager to know the meaning and purpose of the veil, but no one inquires Mr. Hooper directly about it, except for his fiancée Elizabeth. Elizabeth asks him to take off the veil but fails, she gives up and leaves him eventually.

Despite the discomfort with the reactions of his parishioners, Mr. Hooper intends to keep wearing the veil. In meanwhile, the veil makes Mr. Hooper a more efficient minister. Many 0feel that they too are behind the black veil with him. Dying sinners call out for him alone. The Reverend Mr. Hooper lives a lonely life. On his own deathbed Elizabeth and the Reverend ask him once again to remove the veil, but he refuses. He tells people around him that they all wear black veils. Father Hooper is in his coffin with the black still firmly on his face.

Hawthorne deplores a psychological exploration of the themes of sin, repentance, and morality in *The Minister's Black Veil*. Hawthorne uses people's reaction as a critique of the Puritan image of original sin, using the veil as a representation not of " secret sin" but the inherent sinful nature of all people. Nathaniel Hawthorne uses a didactic tone to reveal sin and underlying guilt. The veil is symbolic and ironic. Hawthorne uses ambiguity in different perspectives including setting, lighting and effects, and an unreliable narrator.

Selected Reading

The Minister's Black Veil

A Parable[①]

The sexton[②] stood in the porch of Milford[③] meeting-house, pulling busily at the bell-rope. The old people of the village came stooping along the street. Children, with bright faces, tripped merrily beside their parents, or mimicked a graver gait, in the conscious dignity of their Sunday clothes. Spruce bachelors looked sidelong at the pretty maidens, and fancied that the Sabbath sunshine made them prettier than on week days. When the throng had mostly streamed into the porch, the sexton began to toll the bell, keeping his eye on the Reverend Mr. Hooper's door. The first glimpse of the clergyman's figure was the signal for the bell to cease its summons.

" But what has good Parson Hooper got upon his face?" cried the sexton in astonishment.

All within hearing immediately turned about, and beheld the semblance of Mr. Hooper, pacing slowly his meditative way towards the meetinghouse. With one accord[④] they started, expressing more wonder than if some strange minister were coming to dust the cushions of Mr. Hooper's pulpit.

" Are you sure it is our parson?" inquired Goodman Gray of the sexton.

" Of a certainty it is good Mr. Hooper," replied the sexton. " He was to have

---

① A Parable: " another clergyman in New England, Mr. Joseph Moody of York, Maine, who died about eight years since, made himself remarkable by the same eccentricity that is here related of the Reverend Mr. Hooper. In this case, however, the symbol had a different import. In early life he had accidentally killed a beloved friend; and from that day till the hour of his own death, he hid his face from men." — Hawthone's note

② sexton: a person whose job is to take care of a church building and its graveyard, and sometimes to ring the church bells

③ Milford: a town southwest of Boston

④ with one accord: acting, being or existing together; in complete agreement exchanged pulpits with Parson Shute, of Westbury; but Parson Shute sent to excuse himself yesterday, being to preach a funeral sermon."

The cause of so much amazement may appear sufficiently slight. Mr. Hooper, a gentlemanly person, of about thirty, though still a bachelor, was dressed with due clerical neatness, as if a careful wife had starched his band[①], and brushed the weekly dust from his Sunday's garb. There was but one thing remarkable in his appearance. Swathed about his forehead, and hanging down over his face, so low as to be shaken by his breath, Mr. Hooper had on a black veil. On a nearer view it seemed to consist of two folds of crape, which entirely concealed his features, except the mouth and chin, but probably did not intercept his sight, further than to give a darkened aspect to all living and inanimate things. With this gloomy shade before him, good Mr. Hooper walked onward, at a slow and quiet pace, stooping somewhat, and looking on the ground, as is customary with abstracted men, yet nodding kindly to those of his parishioners who still waited on the meeting-house steps. But so wonder-struck were they that his greeting hardly met with a return.

" I can't really feel as if good Mr. Hooper's face was behind that piece of crape," said the sexton.

" I don't like it," muttered an old woman, as she hobbled into the meeting-house. " He has changed himself into something awful, only by hiding his face."

" Our parson has gone mad!" cried Goodman Gray, following him across the threshold.

A rumor of some unaccountable phenomenon had preceded Mr. Hooper into the meeting-house, and set all the congregation astir. Few could refrain from twisting their heads towards the door; many stood upright, and turned directly about; while several little boys clambered upon the seats, and came down again with a terrible racket. There was a general bustle, a rustling of the women's gowns and shuffling

① band: clerical collar

of the men's feet, greatly at variance with[①] that hushed repose which should attend the entrance of the minister. But Mr. Hooper appeared not to notice the perturbation of his people. He entered with an almost noiseless step, bent his head mildly to the pews on each side, and bowed as he passed his oldest parishioner, a white-haired great grandsire, who occupied an arm-chair in the centre of the aisle. It was strange to observe how slowly this venerable man became conscious of something singular in the appearance of his pastor. He seemed not fully to partake of the prevailing wonder, till Mr. Hooper had ascended the stairs, and showed himself in the pulpit, face to face with his congregation, except for the black veil. That mysterious emblem was never once withdrawn. It shook with his measured breath, as he gave out the psalm; it threw its obscurity between him and the holy page, as he read the Scriptures; and while he prayed, the veil lay heavily on his uplifted countenance. Did he seek to hide it from the dread Being whom he was addressing?

Such was the effect of this simple piece of crape, that more than one woman of delicate nerves was forced to leave the meeting-house. Yet perhaps the pale-faced congregation was almost as fearful a sight to the minister, as his black veil to them.

Mr. Hooper had the reputation of a good preacher, but not an energetic one: he strove to win his people heavenward by mild, persuasive influences, rather than to drive them thither[②] by the thunders of the Word. The sermon which he now delivered was marked by the same characteristics of style and manner as the general series of his pulpit oratory. But there was something, either in the sentiment of the discourse itself, or in the imagination of the auditors, which made it greatly the most powerful effort that they had ever heard from their pastor's lips. It was tinged, rather more darkly than usual, with the gentle gloom of Mr. Hooper's temperament. The subject had reference to secret sin, and those sad mysteries which we hide from

---

① at variance with: to be in disagreement with someone or something, or to be different from them or it

② thither: to that place, in that direction

our nearest and dearest, and would fain conceal from our own consciousness, even forgetting that the Omniscient① can detect them. A subtle power was breathed into his words. Each member of the congregation, the most innocent girl, and the man of hardened breast, felt as if the preacher had crept upon them, behind his awful veil, and discovered their hoarded iniquity of deed or thought. Many spread their clasped hands on their bosoms. There was nothing terrible in what Mr. Hooper said, at least, no violence; and yet, with every tremor of his melancholy voice, the hearers quaked. An unsought pathos came hand in hand with awe. So sensible were the audience of some unwonted attribute in their minister, that they longed for a breath of wind to blow aside the veil, almost believing that a stranger's visage would be discovered, though the form, gesture, and voice were those of Mr. Hooper.

At the close of the services, the people hurried out with indecorous confusion, eager to communicate their pent-up② amazement, and conscious of lighter spirits the moment they lost sight of the black veil. Some gathered in little circles, huddled closely together, with their mouths all whispering in the centre; some went homeward alone, wrapt in silent meditation; some talked loudly, and profaned the Sabbath day with ostentatious③ laughter. A few shook their sagacious heads, intimating that they could penetrate the mystery; while one or two affirmed that there was no mystery at all, but only that Mr. Hooper's eyes were so weakened by the midnight lamp, as to require a shade. After a brief interval, forth came good Mr. Hooper also, in the rear of his flock. Turning his veiled face from one group to another, he paid due reverence to the hoary heads, saluted the middle aged with kind dignity as their friend and spiritual guide, greeted the young with mingled authority and love, and laid his hands on the little children's heads to bless them. Such was always his custom on the Sabbath day. Strange and bewildered looks repaid him for his courtesy. None, as on

---

① Omniscient: having or seeming to have unlimited knowledge

② pent-up: (feelings are)not allowed to be expressed or released

③ ostentatious: intended to attract admiration or notice

former occasions, aspired to the honor of walking by their pastor's side. Old Squire Saunders, doubtless by an accidental lapse of memory, neglected to invite Mr. Hooper to his table, where the good clergyman had been wont to bless the food, almost every Sunday since his settlement. He returned, therefore, to the parsonage, and, at the moment of closing the door, was observed to look back upon the people, all of whom had their eyes fixed upon the minister. A sad smile gleamed faintly from beneath the black veil, and flickered about his mouth, glimmering as he disappeared.

" How strange," said a lady, " that a simple black veil, such as any woman might wear on her bonnet, should become such a terrible thing on Mr. Hooper's face!"

" Something must surely be amiss with Mr. Hooper's intellects," observed her husband, the physician of the village. " But the strangest part of the affair is the effect of this vagary①, even on a sober-minded man like myself. The black veil, though it covers only our pastor's face, throws its influence over his whole person, and makes him ghostlike from head to foot. Do you not feel it so?"

" Truly do I," replied the lady; " and I would not be alone with him for the world. I wonder he is not afraid to be alone with himself!"

" Men sometimes are so," said her husband.

The afternoon service was attended with similar circumstances. At its conclusion, the bell tolled for the funeral of a young lady. The relatives and friends were assembled in the house, and the more distant acquaintances stood about the door, speaking of the good qualities of the deceased, when their talk was interrupted by the appearance of Mr. Hooper, still covered with his black veil. It was now an appropriate emblem. The clergyman stepped into the room where the corpse was laid, and bent over the coffin, to take a last farewell of his deceased parishioner. As he stooped, the veil hung straight down from his forehead, so that, if her eyelids had not been closed forever, the dead maiden might have seen his face. Could Mr.

---

① vagary: strange behavior, unusual activity

Hooper be fearful of her glance, that he so hastily caught back the black veil? A person who watched the interview between the dead and living, scrupled not to affirm, that, at the instant when the clergyman's features were disclosed, the corpse had slightly shuddered, rustling the shroud and muslin cap, though the countenance retained the composure of death. A superstitious old woman was the only witness of this prodigy. From the coffin Mr. Hooper passed into the chamber of the mourners, and thence to the head of the staircase, to make the funeral prayer. It was a tender and heart-dissolving prayer, full of sorrow, yet so imbued with① celestial hopes, that the music of a heavenly harp, swept by the fingers of the dead, seemed faintly to be heard among the saddest accents of the minister. The people trembled, though they but darkly understood him when he prayed that they, and himself, and all of mortal race, might be ready, as he trusted this young maiden had been, for the dreadful hour that should snatch the veil from their faces. The bearers went heavily forth, and the mourners followed, saddening all the street, with the dead before them, and Mr. Hooper in his black veil behind.

" Why do you look back?" said one in the procession to his partner.

" I had a fancy," replied she, " that the minister and the maiden's spirit were walking hand in hand."

" And so had I, at the same moment," said the other.

That night, the handsomest couple in Milford village were to be joined in wedlock. Though reckoned a melancholy man, Mr. Hooper had a placid cheerfulness for such occasions, which often excited a sympathetic smile where livelier merriment would have been thrown away. There was no quality of his disposition which made him more beloved than this. The company at the wedding awaited his arrival with impatience, trusting that the strange awe, which had gathered over him throughout the day, would now be dispelled. But such was not the result. When Mr. Hooper

---

① imbued with: to fill something or someone with a particular feeling, quality, or idea came, the first thing that their eyes rested on was the same horrible black veil, which had added deeper gloom to the funeral, and could portend nothing but evil to the wedding. Such was its immediate effect on the guests that a cloud seemed to have rolled duskily from beneath the black crape, and dimmed the light of the candles. The bridal pair stood up before the minister. But the bride's cold fingers quivered in the tremulous hand of the bridegroom, and her deathlike paleness caused a whisper that the maiden who had been buried a few hours before was come from her grave to be married. If ever another wedding were so dismal, it was that famous one where they tolled the wedding knell. After performing the ceremony, Mr. Hooper raised a glass of wine to his lips, wishing happiness to the newmarried couple in a strain of mild pleasantry that ought to have brightened the features of the guests, like a cheerful gleam from the hearth. At that instant, catching a glimpse of his figure in the looking-glass, the black veil involved his own spirit in the horror with which it overwhelmed all others. His frame shuddered, his lips grew white, he spilt the untasted wine upon the carpet, and rushed forth into the darkness. For the Earth, too, had on her Black Veil.

The next day, the whole village of Milford talked of little else than Parson Hooper's black veil. That, and the mystery concealed behind it, supplied a topic for discussion between acquaintances meeting in the street, and good women gossiping at their open windows. It was the first item of news that the tavern-keeper told to his guests. The children babbled① of it on their way to school. One imitative little imp② covered his face with an old black handkerchief, thereby so affrighting his playmates that the panic seized himself, and he well-nigh lost his wits by his own waggery③.

It was remarkable that all of the busybodies and impertinent people in the parish,

---

① babble: to speak quickly, in a confused, excited, or foolish way

② imp: small evil spirit; often humorous a child that behaves badly, but in a way that is funny rather than serious

③ waggery: mischievous joke

not one ventured to put the plain question to Mr. Hooper, wherefore he did this thing. Hitherto, whenever there appeared the slightest call for such interference, he had never lacked advisers, nor shown himself averse to be guided by their judgment. If he erred at all, it was by so painful a degree of self-distrust, that even the mildest censure would lead him to consider an indifferent action as a crime. Yet, though so well acquainted with this amiable weakness, no individual among his parishioners chose to make the black veil a subject of friendly remonstrance. There was a feeling of dread, neither plainly confessed nor carefully concealed, which caused each to shift the responsibility upon another, till at length it was found expedient to send a deputation of the church, in order to deal with Mr. Hooper about the mystery, before it should grow into a scandal. Never did an embassy so ill discharge its duties. The minister received then with friendly courtesy, but became silent, after they were seated, leaving to his visitors the whole burden of introducing their important business. The topic, it might be supposed, was obvious enough. There was the black veil swathed round Mr. Hooper's forehead, and concealing every feature above his placid mouth, on which, at times, they could perceive the glimmering of a melancholy smile. But that piece of crape, to their imagination, seemed to hang down before his heart, the symbol of a fearful secret between him and them. Were the veil but cast aside, they might speak freely of it, but not till then. Thus they sat a considerable time, speechless, confused, and shrinking uneasily from Mr. Hooper's eye, which they felt to be fixed upon them with an invisible glance. Finally, the deputies returned abashed to their constituents, pronouncing the matter too weighty to be handled, except by a council of the churches, if, indeed, it might not require a general synod.①

But there was one person in the village unappalled by the awe with which the black veil had impressed all beside herself. When the deputies returned without an explanation, or even venturing to demand one, she, with the calm energy of her

① synod: an assembly of church officials

character, determined to chase away the strange cloud that appeared to be settling round Mr. Hooper, every moment more darkly than before. As his plighted① wife, it should be her privilege to know what the black veil concealed. At the minister's first visit, therefore, she entered upon the subject with a direct simplicity, which made the task easier both for him and her. After he had seated himself, she fixed her eyes steadfastly upon the veil, but could discern nothing of the dreadful gloom that had so overawed the multitude: it was but a double fold of crape, hanging down from his forehead to his mouth, and slightly stirring with his breath.

" No," said she aloud, and smiling, " there is nothing terrible in this piece of crape, except that it hides a face which I am always glad to look upon. Come, good sir, let the sun shine from behind the cloud. First lay aside your black veil: then tell me why you put it on."

Mr. Hooper's smile glimmered faintly.

" There is an hour to come," said he, " when all of us shall cast aside our veils. Take it not amiss, beloved friend, if I wear this piece of crape till then."

" Your words are a mystery, too," returned the young lady. " Take away the veil from them, at least."

" Elizabeth, I will," said he, " so far as my vow may suffer me. Know, then, this veil is a type and a symbol, and I am bound to wear it ever, both in light and darkness, in solitude and before the gaze of multitudes, and as with strangers, so with my familiar friends. No mortal eye will see it withdrawn. This dismal shade must separate me from the world: even you, Elizabeth, can never come behind it!"

" What grievous affliction② hath③ befallen you," she earnestly inquired, " that you should thus darken your eyes forever?"

" If it be a sign of mourning," replied Mr. Hooper, " I, perhaps, like most other

① plighted: intended, promised

② affliction : something that makes you suffer

③ hath: has

mortals, have sorrows dark enough to be typified by a black veil."

"But what if the world will not believe that it is the type of an innocent sorrow?" urged Elizabeth. "Beloved and respected as you are, there may be whispers that you hide your face under the consciousness of secret sin. For the sake of your holy office, do away this scandal!"

The color rose into her cheeks as she intimated the nature of the rumors that were already abroad in the village. But Mr. Hooper's mildness did not forsake him. He even smiled again — that same sad smile, which always appeared like a faint glimmering of light, proceeding from the obscurity beneath the veil.

"If I hide my face for sorrow, there is cause enough," he merely replied; "and if I cover it for secret sin, what mortal might not do the same?"

And with this gentle, but unconquerable obstinacy① did he resist all her entreaties. At length Elizabeth sat silent. For a few moments she appeared lost in thought, considering, probably, what new methods might be tried to withdraw her lover from so dark a fantasy, which, if it had no other meaning, was perhaps a symptom of mental disease. Though of a firmer character than his own, the tears rolled down her cheeks. But, in an instant, as it were, a new feeling took the place of sorrow: her eyes were fixed insensibly on the black veil, when, like a sudden twilight in the air, its terrors fell around her. She arose, and stood trembling before him.

"And do you feel it then, at last?" said he mournfully.

She made no reply, but covered her eyes with her hand, and turned to leave the room. He rushed forward and caught her arm.

"Have patience with me, Elizabeth!" cried he, passionately. "Do not desert me, though this veil must be between us here on earth. Be mine, and hereafter there shall be no veil over my face, no darkness between our souls! It is but a mortal veil — it is not for eternity! O! you know not how lonely I am, and how frightened, to be alone

① obstinacy: strength of will and determination

behind my black veil. Do not leave me in this miserable obscurity forever!"

" Lift the veil but once, and look me in the face," said she.

" Never! It cannot be!" replied Mr. Hooper.

" Then farewell!" said Elizabeth.

She withdrew her arm from his grasp, and slowly departed, pausing at the door, to give one long shuddering gaze, that seemed almost to penetrate the mystery of the black veil. But, even amid his grief, Mr. Hooper smiled to think that only a material emblem had separated him from happiness, though the horrors, which it shadowed forth, must be drawn darkly between the fondest of lovers.

From that time no attempts were made to remove Mr. Hooper's black veil, or, by a direct appeal, to discover the secret which it was supposed to hide. By persons who claimed a superiority to popular prejudice, it was reckoned merely an eccentric whim, such as often mingles with the sober actions of men otherwise rational, and tinges them all with its own semblance of insanity. But with the multitude, good Mr. Hooper was irreparably a bugbear.① He could not walk the street with any peace of mind, so conscious was he that the gentle and timid would turn aside to avoid him, and that others would make it a point of hardihood to throw themselves in his way. The impertinence of the latter class compelled him to give up his customary walk at sunset to the burial ground; for when he leaned pensively over the gate, there would always be faces behind the gravestones, peeping at his black veil. A fable went the rounds that the stare of the dead people drove him thence. It grieved him, to the very depth of his kind heart, to observe how the children fled from his approach, breaking up their merriest sports, while his melancholy figure was yet afar off. Their instinctive dread caused him to feel more strongly than aught else, that a preternatural② horror was interwoven with the threads of the black crape. In truth, his own antipathy to the veil was known to be so great, that he never willingly passed

① bugbear: an object to fear and dread

② preternatural: more than is usual or natural

before a mirror, nor stooped to drink at a still fountain, lest, in its peaceful bosom, he should be affrighted① by himself. This was what gave plausibility to the whispers, that Mr. Hooper's conscience tortured him for some great crime too horrible to be entirely concealed, or otherwise than so obscurely intimated. Thus, from beneath the black veil, there rolled a cloud into the sunshine, an ambiguity of sin or sorrow, which enveloped the poor minister, so that love or sympathy could never reach him. It was said that ghost and fiend consorted② with him there. With self-shudderings and outward terrors, he walked continually in its shadow, groping darkly within his own soul, or gazing through a medium that saddened the whole world. Even the lawless wind, it was believed, respected his dreadful secret, and never blew aside the veil. But still good Mr. Hooper sadly smiled at the pale visages of the worldly throng as he passed by.

Among all its bad influences, the black veil had the one desirable effect, of making its wearer a very efficient clergyman. By the aid of his mysterious emblem — for there was no other apparent cause — he became a man of awful power over souls that were in agony for sin. His converts always regarded him with a dread peculiar to themselves, affirming, though but figuratively, that, before he brought them to celestial light, they had been with him behind the black veil. Its gloom, indeed, enabled him to sympathize with all dark affections. Dying sinners cried aloud for Mr. Hooper, and would not yield their breath till he appeared; though ever, as he stooped to whisper consolation, they shuddered at the veiled face so near their own. Such were the terrors of the black veil, even when Death had bared his visage! Strangers came long distances to attend service at his church, with the mere idle purpose of gazing at his figure, because it was forbidden them to behold his face. But many were made to quake ere they departed! Once, during Governor Belcher's

---

① affrighted: frightened

② consort: to spend time in the company of particular people administration,[1] Mr. Hooper was appointed to preach the election sermon.[2] Covered with his black veil, he stood before the chief magistrate, the council, and the representatives, and wrought so deep an impression, that the legislative measures of that year were characterized by all the gloom and piety of our earliest ancestral sway.

In this manner Mr. Hooper spent a long life, irreproachable in outward act, yet shrouded in dismal suspicions; kind and loving, though unloved, and dimly feared; a man apart from men, shunned in their health and joy, but ever summoned to their aid in mortal anguish. As years wore on, shedding their snows above his sable[3] veil, he acquired a name throughout the New England churches, and they called him Father Hooper. Nearly all his parishioners, who were of mature age when he was settled, had been borne away by many a funeral: he had one congregation in the church, and a more crowded one in the churchyard; and having wrought so late into the evening, and done his work so well, it was now good Father Hooper's turn to rest.

Several persons were visible by the shaded candlelight, in the death chamber of the old clergyman. Natural connections he had none. But there was the decorously grave, though unmoved physician, seeking only to mitigate[4] the last pangs of the patient whom he could not save. There were the deacons, and other eminently pious members of his church. There, also, was the Reverend Mr. Clark, of Westbury, a young and zealous divine, who had ridden in haste to pray by the bedside of the expiring minister. There was the nurse, no hired handmaiden of death, but one whose calm affection had endured thus long in secrecy, in solitude, amid the chill of age, and would not perish, even at the dying hour. Who, but Elizabeth! And there lay the

---

① Governor Belcher: Jonathan Belcher (1682–1757), royal Governor of Massachusetts (1730–1741)

② A special sermon delivered during the installation of the Colony's newly elected government officials. To be chosen to preach the sermon was a high distinction.

③ sable: black

④ mitigate: to make something less harmful, unpleasant, or bad hoary[①] head of good Father Hooper upon the death pillow, with the black veil still swathed about his brow, and reaching down over his face, so that each more difficult gasp of his faint breath caused it to stir. All through life that piece of crape had hung between him and the world: it had separated him from cheerful brotherhood and woman's love, and kept him in that saddest of all prisons, his own heart; and still it lay upon his face, as if to deepen the gloom of his darksome chamber, and shade him from the sunshine of eternity.

For some time previous, his mind had been confused, wavering doubtfully between the past and the present, and hovering forward, as it were, at intervals, into the indistinctness of the world to come. There had been feverish turns, which tossed him from side to side, and wore away what little strength he had. But in his most convulsive struggles, and in the wildest vagaries of his intellect, when no other thought retained its sober influence, he still showed an awful solicitude lest the black veil should slip aside. Even if his bewildered soul could have forgotten, there was a faithful woman at this pillow, who, with averted eyes, would have covered that aged face, which she had last beheld in the comeliness of manhood. At length the death-stricken old man lay quietly in the torpor of mental and bodily exhaustion, with an imperceptible pulse, and breath that grew fainter and fainter, except when a long, deep, and irregular inspiration seemed to prelude the flight of his spirit.

The minister of Westbury approached the bedside.

" Venerable Father Hooper," said he, " the moment of your release is at hand. Are you ready for the lifting of the veil that shuts in time from eternity?"

Father Hooper at first replied merely by a feeble motion of his head; then, apprehensive, perhaps, that his meaning might be doubted, he exerted himself to speak.

" Yea," said he, in faint accents, " my soul hath a patient weariness until that veil

---

① hoary: literary (of a person) very old and with white or grey hair be lifted."

" And is it fitting," resumed the Reverend Mr. Clark, " that a man so given to prayer, of such a blameless example, holy in deed and thought, so far as mortal judgment may pronounce; is it fitting that a father in the church should leave a shadow on his memory, that may seem to blacken a life so pure? I pray you, my venerable brother, let not this thing be! Suffer us to be gladdened by your triumphant aspect as you go to your reward. Before the veil of eternity be lifted, let me cast aside this black veil from your face!"

And thus speaking, the Reverend Mr. Clark bent forward to reveal the mystery of so many years. But, exerting a sudden energy, that made all the beholders stand aghast,① Father Hooper snatched both his hands from beneath the bedclothes, and pressed them strongly on the black veil, resolute to struggle, if the minister of Westbury would contend with a dying man.

" Never!" cried the veiled clergyman. " On earth, never!"

" Dark old man!" exclaimed the affrighted minister, " with what horrible crime upon your soul are you now passing to the judgment?"

Father Hooper's breath heaved; it rattled in his throat; but, with a mighty effort, grasping forward with his hands, he caught hold of life, and held it back till he should speak. He even raised himself in bed; and there he sat, shivering with the arms of death around him, while the black veil hung down, awful, at that last moment, in the gathered terrors of a lifetime. And yet the faint, sad smile, so often there, now seemed to glimmer from its obscurity, and linger on Father Hooper's lips.

" Why do you tremble at me alone?" cried he, turning his veiled face round the circle of pale spectators. " Tremble also at each other! Have men avoided me, and women shown no pity, and children screamed and fled, only for my black veil? What, but the mystery which it obscurely typifies, has made this piece of crape so awful?

① aghast: suddenly filled with strong feelings of shock and worry

When the friend shows his inmost heart to his friend; the lover to his best beloved; when man does not vainly shrink from the eye of his Creator, loathsomely treasuring up the secret of his sin; then deem me a monster, for the symbol beneath which I have lived, and die! I look around me, and, lo!① on every visage a Black Veil!"

While his auditors shrank from one another, in mutual affright, Father Hooper fell back upon his pillow, a veiled corpse, with a faint smile lingering on the lips. Still veiled, they laid him in his coffin, and a veiled corpse they bore him to the grave. The grass of many years has sprung up and withered on that grave, the burial stone is moss-grown, and good Mr. Hooper's face is dust; but awful is still the thought that it mouldered beneath the Black Veil!

Topics for discussion

1. Some critics think the veil is a " symbol of symbols", what do you think of the statement?

2. How do you understand the Reverend Mr. Hooper's alienation from the rest of humankind?

3. Please make some comment on Hawthorne's psychological themes in *The Minister's Black Veil*

4. Have you realized the darkness of the soul that Hawthorne connects with Calvinism in *The Minister's Black Veil*? Please make some comment on it.

References for further reading

[1] Coale, Samuel. *The entanglements of Nathaniel Hawthorne: haunted minds and ambiguous approaches*, Rochester, N.Y. : Camden House, 2011.

---

① lo: exclamation(old use); used to tell people to pay attention and look at something interesting

[2] Grews, Frederick. *The Sins of the Fathers: Hawthorne's Psychological Themes*, Oxford: Oxford University Press. 1966.

[3] Semrau, Janusz. *New essays on the short stories of Nathaniel Hawthorne*, Frankfurt am Main ; Berlin : Peter Lang, 2012.

[4] Turner, Arlin. *Nathaniel Hawthorne: A Biography*, Oxford: Oxford University Press. 1980.

Mark Twain (1835 — 1910)

The Celebrated Jumping Frog of Calaveras Count

Introduction to the author

Samuel Langhorne Clemens (November 30, 1835 — April 21, 1910), better known by his pen name Mark Twain, was an American author and humorist. " Mark Twain" was a reference to his riverboat days; it was a term that the men who worked on the boats used to indicate the depth of the water.

Samuel Langhorne Clemens was born in Florida, Missouri. He was the son of Jane and John Marshall Clemens. He was the sixth of seven children, but only three of his siblings survived childhood. He spent much of his childhood in Hannibal, Missouri, a town located on the Mississippi River. He never finished school and became an apprentice to a printer at the age of 12. Later he began working as a typesetter and contributor of articles for his brother Orion's newspaper *The Hannibal Journal*. In the 1850s, he worked as a boat pilot and later briefly served in the Confederate Army during the Civil War. During this time he submitted his first journalism pieces, using the pseudonym Thomas Jefferson Snodgrass. He then traveled west and found work as a miner and a reporter. Twain's " The Private

History of a Campaign That Failed" told his experience as Confederate volunteer. His travel literature *Roughing It* was about his experiences in the American West and " The Celebrated Jumping Frog of Calaveras County" was based on his experiences in Angels Camp, California. *The Innocents Abroad* was a collection of travel letters of Europe and the Middle East.

In 1870, Twain and Olivia Langdon were married, and through his wife Twain met Harriet Beecher Stowe, Frederick Douglass and William Dean Howells. During the years of 1874 — 1891 at Quarry Farm, Twain wrote many of his classic novels, including *The Adventures of Tom Sawyer* (1876), *The Prince and the Pauper* (1881), *Life on the Mississippi* (1883), *Adventures of Huckleberry Finn* (1885) and *A Connecticut Yankee in King Arthur's Court* (1889). *A Tramp Abroad* was about his second tour of Europe. *The Adventures of Tom Sawyer* and *Huckleberry Finn* described his youth in Hannibal. *The Prince and the Pauper* and *Pudd'nhead Wilson* contained the tale of two boys born on the same day who switch positions in life. *A Connecticut Yankee* showed the absurdities of political and social norms. *The Mysterious Stranger* depicted various visits of Satan to the Earth. In his life, Twain earned a substantial amount of money from his writings and lectures, but he lost a great deal through investments. With the help of Henry Huttleston Rogers he eventually overcame his financial troubles. His daughters' death made him in gloom once. Twain died of a heart attack on April 21, 1910, in Redding, Connecticut.

Twain began his career writing light, humorous verse, but developed into a chronicler of the vanities, hypocrisies and murderous acts of mankind. At mid-career, he combined rich humor, sturdy narrative and social criticism. Twain's views became more radical as he grew older. Before 1899, Twain was an ardent imperialist. He was strongly in favor of American interests. After 1899, he was critical of imperialism in different countries. In meanwhile, Twain was an firm supporter of the abolition of slavery and emancipation of slaves, and a strong supporter of women's rights and an active campaigner for women's suffrage. Twain was a master at rendering colloquial speech and helped to create and popularize a distinctive American literature built on American themes and language.

Major works by Mark Twain

Novels

The Gilded Age: A Tale of Today, 1873

The Adventures of Tom Sawyer, 1876

The Prince and the Pauper, 1881

Adventures of Huckleberry Finn, 1884

A Connecticut Yankee in King Arthur's Court, 1889

The American Claimant, 1892

Pudd'nhead Wilson, 1894

Tom Sawyer Abroad, 1894

Personal Recollections of Joan of Arc, 1896

Tom Sawyer, Detective, 1896

A Double Barrelled Detective Story, 1902

A Horse's Tale, 1907

The Mysterious Stranger, 1916(posthumous)

Short stories

" Advice to Little Girls" 1865

" The Celebrated Jumping Frog of Calaveras County" 1867

" Some Learned Fables for Good Old Boys and Girls" 1875

" A Literary Nightmare" 1876

" A Murder, a Mystery, and a Marriage" 1876

" The Stolen White Elephant" 1882

" Luck", 1891

" Those Extraordinary Twins" 1892

" The War Prayer" 1905

Short story collections

Mark Twain's (Burlesque) Autobiography and First Romance, 1871

Sketches New and Old, 1875

A True Story and the Recent Carnival of Crime, 1877

Mark Twain's Library of Humor, 1888

Essay collections

How to Tell a Story and other Essays, 1897

Letters from the Earth, 1962

The Bible According to Mark Twain, 1996

Appreciation

" The Celebrated Jumping Frog of Calaveras County" was first published in the November 18, 1865, edition of *The New York Saturday Press*. The story has also been published as " Jim Smiley and His Jumping Frog" (its original title) and " The Notorious Jumping Frog of Calaveras County". The story is set in a gold-mining camp in Calaveras County, California. It helped establish Mark Twain's reputation as a humorist.

In the story, the narrator retells a story about the gambler Jim Smiley. The story is from Simon Wheeler, a bartender at the Angels Hotel in Angels Camp, California. The narrator asks the fat, bald-headed man named Simon Wheeler about Leonidas. The talkative man relates to Mark Twain that he doesn't know a Leonidas Smiley, but he knows a Jim Smiley. He told the narrator that Jim Smiley was a gambler named and he often used amazing animals in his schemes. He loved to make bets; he would bet on nearly anything. Wheeler relates some of Smiley's more famous gambling escapades, one of which concerns a pet frog. Jim caught a frog and named it Dan'l Webster and the frog was trained to jump over more ground than any other. Jim says his frog can outjump any other frog in Calaveras County. In order to make a bet with a stranger over the frog, Jim gives the box in which his frog stays to the stranger to hold while Jim hunts for another frog for the stranger. But the stranger pours lead shot into the mouth of Jim's frog while Jim is not here. Therefore, Dan'l is so heavy that it is beaten by the stranger's frog. When Dan'l coughs up handfuls of shot, Jim gets the truth. The stranger is long gone, however, and Jim never catches him. The narrator realizes that Jim Smiley has nothing to do with Leonidas W. Smiley, and prepares to leave. Simon catches the narrator at the door, and starts telling him another story about Jim's one-eyed cow. The narrator excuses himself and leaves.

Mark Twain focus on existing cultural differences between western and eastern regions of the United States, the clash between settled, eastern portion of the United States and the still-developing West. The story asserted that Americans could be resourceful, innovative, as well as shortsighted, narrow-minded.

Selected Reading

The Celebrated Jumping Frog of Calaveras County

In compliance with the request of a friend of mine, who wrote me from the East, I called on good-natured, garrulous① old Simon Wheeler, and inquired after my friend's friend, Leonidas W. Smiley, as requested to do, and I hereunto append the result. I have a lurking② suspicion that Leonidas W. Smiley is a myth; that my friend never knew such a personage; and that he only conjectured③ that, if I asked old Wheeler about him, it would remind him of his infamous Jim Smiley, and he would go to work and bore me nearly to death with some infernal reminiscence of him as

① garrulous: habitually

② lurking: existing unseen

③ conjectured: guessed

long and tedious as it should be useless to me. If that was the design, it certainly succeeded.

I found Simon Wheeler dozing comfortably by the bar-room stove of the old, dilapidated tavern in the ancient mining camp of Angel's,① and I noticed that he was fat and bald-headed, and had an expression of winning gentleness and simplicity upon his tranquil countenance. He roused up and gave me good-day. I told him a friend of minc had commissioned me to make some inquiries about a cherished companion of his boyhood named Leonidas W. Smile — Rev. Leonidas W. Smiley a young minister of the Gospel, who he had heard was at one time a resident of Angel's Camp. I added that, if Mr. Wheeler could tell me any thing about this Rev. Leonidas W. Smiley, I would feel under many obligations to him.

Simon Wheeler backed me into a corner and blockaded me there with his chair, and then sat me down and reeled off the monotonous narrative which follows this paragraph. He never smiled, he never frowned, he never changed his voice from the gentle-flowing key to which he tuned the initial sentence, he never betrayed the slightest suspicion of enthusiasm; but all through the interminable narrative there ran a vein of impressive earnestness and sincerity, which showed me plainly that, so far from his imagining that there was anything ridiculous or funny about his story, he regarded it as a really important matter, and admired its two heroes as men of transcendent genius in finesse. To me, the spectacle of a man drifting serenely along through such a queer yarn without ever smiling, was exquisitely absurd. As I said before, I asked him to tell me what he knew of Rev. Leonidas W. Smiley, and he replied as follows. I let him go on in his own way, and never interrupted him once:

" Rev. Leonidas W. H'm, Reverend Le — Well. There was a feller here once by the name of Jim Smiley, in the winter of '49 — or may be it was the spring of '50 I don't recollect exactly, somehow, though what makes me think it was one or the

① Angel's Camp, a mining settlement in Calaveras County, California other is because I remember the big flume[①] wasn't finished when he first came to the camp; but any way, he was the curiousest man about always betting on anything that turned up you ever see, if he could get anybody to bet on the other side; and if he couldn't, he'd change sides. Any way that suited the other man would suit him — any way just so's he got a bet, he was satisfied. But still he was lucky, uncommon lucky; he most always come out winner. He was always ready and laying for a chance; there couldn't be no solit'ry thing mentioned but that feller'd offer to bet on it[②], and take any side you please, as I was just telling you. If there was a horse-race, you'd find him flush[③], or you'd find him busted[④] at the end of it; if there was a dog-fight, he'd bet on it; if there was a cat-fight, he'd bet on it; if there was a chicken-fight, he'd bet on it; why, if there was two birds setting on a fence, he would bet you which one would fly first; or if there was a camp-meeting, he would be there reg'lar, to bet on Parson Walker, which he judged to be the best exhorter about here, and so he was, too, and a good man. If he even seen a straddle-bug[⑤] start to go anywheres, he would bet you how long it would take him to get wherever he was going to, and if you took him up, he would foller that straddle-bug to Mexico but what he would find out where he was bound for and how long he was on the road. Lots of the boys here has seen that Smiley, and can tell you about him. Why, it never made no difference to him — he would bet on any thing — the dangdest feller. Parson Walker's wife laid very sick once, for a good while, and it seemed as if they warn's going to save her; but one morning he come in, and Smiley asked how she was, and he said she was

---

① big flume: an inclined waterway, usually made of wood, through which water is carried for use in hydraulic mining

② there couldn't be no solit'ry thing mentioned but that feller'd offer to bet on it: that fellow would offer a bet on anything mentioned

③ flush: having plenty of money

④ busted: broke, penniless

⑤ straddle–bug: a beetle with long legs, a tumble–bug

considerable better — thank the Lord for his inf'nit'[1] — mercy and coming on so smart that, with the blessing of Providence, she'd get well yet; and Smiley, before he thought, says, " Well, I'll risk two- and-a-half that she don't, anyway."

Thish-yer[2] Smiley had a mare — the boys called her the fifteen-minute nag, but that was only in fun, you know, because, of course, she was faster — than that and he used to win money on that horse, for all she was so slow and always had the asthma, or the distemper, or the consumption, or something of that kind. They used to give her two or three hundred yards start, and then pass her under way; but always at the fag-end of the race she'd get excited and desperate-like, and come cavorting and straddling up, and scattering her legs around limber, sometimes in the air, and sometimes out to one side amongst the fences, and kicking up m-o-r-e dust, and raising m-o-r-e racket with her coughing and sneezing and blowing her nose — and always fetch up at the stand just about a neck ahead, as near as you could cipher it down[3] .

And he had a little small bull pup, that to look at him you'd think he warn't[4] worth a cent, but to set around and look ornery[5] , and lay for a chance to steal something. But as soon as money was up on him, he was a different dog; his underjaw'd begin to stick out like the fo'castle[6] of a steamboat, and his teeth would uncover, and shine savage like the furnaces. And a dog might tackle him, and bully-rag him, and bite him, and throw him over his shoulder two or three times, and Andrew Jackson — which was the name of the pup Andrew Jackson would never let on[7] but what he was satisfied, and hadn't expected nothing else — and the bets

---

① inf'nit': infinite

② Thish–yer: This

③ cipher it down: calculate it

④ warn't: wasn't

⑤ ornery: bad–tempered

⑥ fo'castle: forecastle

⑦ let on: reveal

being doubled and doubled on the other side all the time, till the money was all up; and then all of a sudden he would grab that other dog jes[①] t by the j'int[②] of his hind leg and freeze on it — not chew, you understand, but only jest grip and hang on till they thronged up the sponge, if it was a year. Smiley always come out winner on that pup, till he harnessed a dog once that didn't have no hind legs, because they'd been sawed off by a circular saw, and when the thing had gone along far enough, and the money was all up, and he come to make a snatch for his pet bolt, he saw in a minute how he'd been imposed on, and how the other dog had him in the door, so to speak, and he 'peered[③] sur-prised, and then he looked sorter[④] discouraged-like, and didn't try no more to win the fight, and so he got shucked out bad. He give Smiley a look, as much as to say his heart was broke, and it was his fault, for putting up a dog that hadn't no hind legs for him to take bolt of, which was his main dependence in a fight, and then he limped off a piece and laid down and died. It was a good pup, was that Andrew Jackson, and would have made a name for hisself if he'd lived, for the stuff was in him, and he had genius — I know it, because he hadn't had no opportunities to speak of, and it don't stand to reason that a dog could make such a fight as he could under them circumstances, if he hadn't no talent. It always makes me feel sorry when I think of that last fight of hisn[⑤] , and the way it turned out.

Well, thish-yer Smiley had rat tarriers[⑥] , and chicken cocks, and tomcats, and all of them kind of things, till you couldn't rest, and you couldn't fetch nothing for him to bet on but he'd match you. He ketched[⑦] a frog one day, and took him home, and

---

① jest: just

② j'int: joint

③ 'peered: appeared

④ sorter: sort of

⑤ hisn: his

⑥ rat tarriers: (rat terriers) dogs used for catching rats

⑦ ketched: caught

said he cal'lated① to educate him; and so he never done nothing for three months but set in his back yard and learn that frog to jump. And you bet you he did learn him, too. He'd give him a little punch behind, and the next minute you'd see that frog whirling in the air like a doughnut — see him turn one summerset② , or may be a couple, if he got a good start, and come down flat-footed and all right, like a cat. He got him up so in the matter of catching flies, and kept him in practice so constant, that he'd nail a fly every time as fur as③ he could see him. Smiley said all a frog wanted was education, and he could do 'most④ any thing — and I believe him. Why, I've seen him set Dan'l Webster down here on this floor — Dan'l Webster was the name of the frog and sing out, " Flies, Dan'l, flies!" and quicker'n⑤ you could wink, he'd spring straight up, and snake a fly off'n⑥ the counter there, and flop down on the floor again as solid as a gob of mud, and fall to⑦ scratching the side of his head with his hind foot as indifferent as if he hadn't no idea he'd been doin' any more'n any frog might do. You never see a frog so modest and straightforward as he was, for all he was so gifted. And when it come to fair and square jumping on a dead level, he could get over more ground at one straddle than any animal of his breed you ever see. Jumping on a dead level was his strong suit, you understand; and when it come to that, Smiley would ante up money on him as long as he had a red⑧ . Smiley was monstrous proud of his frog, and well he might be, for fellers that had traveled and been everywheres, all said he laid over⑨ any frog that ever they see.

Well, Smiley kept the beast in a little lattice box, and he used to fetch him down

① cal'lated: calculate
② summerset: somersault
③ as fur as: as far as
④ 'most : almost
⑤ quicker'n: quicker than
⑥ off'n: off on
⑦ fall to: begin
⑧ A " red cent," a copper penny
⑨ laid over: defeated

town sometimes and lay for a bet. One day a feller — a stranger in the camp, he was — come across him with his box, and says:

" What might it be that you've got in the box?"

And Smiley says, sorter indifferent like, " It might be a parrot, or it might be a canary, may be, but it an't — it's only just a frog."

And the feller took it, and looked at it careful, and turned it round this way and that, and says, " H'm so 'tis. Well, what's he good for?"

" Well," Smiley says, easy and careless, " He's good enough for one thing, I should judge he can outjump any frog in Calaveras county."

The feller took the box again, and took another long, particular look, and give it back to Smiley, and says, very deliberate, " Well, I don't see no p'ints① about that frog that's any better'n any other frog."

" May be you don't," Smiley says. " May be you understand frogs, and may be you don't understand 'em; may be you've had experience, and may be you an't only a amature, as it were. Anyways, I've got my opinion, and I'll risk forty dollars that he can outjump any frog in Calaveras county."

And the feller studied a minute, and then says, kinder sad like, " Well, I'm only a stranger here, and I an't got no frog; but if I had a frog, I'd bet you."

And then Smiley says, " That's all right — that's all right — if you'll hold my box a minute, I'll go and get you a frog." And so the feller took the box, and put up his forty dollars along with Smiley's, and set down to wait.

So he set there a good while thinking and thinking to hisself, and then he got the frog out and prized② his mouth open and took a tea-spoon and filled him full of quail shot — filled him pretty near up to his chin — and set him on the floor. Smiley he went to the swamp and slopped around in the mud for a long time, and finally he ketched a frog, and fetched him in, and give him to this feller, and says:

---

① p'ints: points

② prize: pry

" Now, if you're ready, set him alongside of Dan'l, with his fore- paws just even with Dan'l, and I'll give the word." Then he says, " One two three jump!" and him and the feller touched up the frogs from behind, and the new frog hopped off, but Dan'l give a heave, and hysted① up his shoulders so like a Frenchman, but it wan's no use — he couldn't budge; he was planted as solid as an anvil, and he couldn't no more stir than if he was anchored out. Smiley was a good deal surprised, and he was disgusted too, but he didn't have no idea what the matter was, of course.

The feller took the money and started away; and when he was going out at the door, he sorter jerked his thumb over his shoulders this way at Dan'l, and says again, very deliberate, " Well, I don't see no p'ints about that frog that's any better'n any other frog."

Smiley he stood scratching his head and looking down at Dan'l a long time, and at last he says, " I do wonder what in the nation② that frog throw'd off for — I wonder if there an't something the matter with him he 'pears to look mighty baggy, somehow." And he ketched Dan'l by the nap of the neck, and lifted him up and says, " Why, blame my cats, if he don't weigh five pound!" and turned him upside down, and he belched out③ a double handful of shot. And then he see how it was, and he was the maddest man he set the frog down and took out after that feller, but he never ketchd him. And —

[Here Simon Wheeler heard his name called from the front yard, and got up to see what was wanted.] And turning to me as he moved away, he said: " Just set where you are, stranger, and rest easy I an't going to be gone a second."

But, by your leave④ , I did not think that a continuation of the history of the enterprising vagabond Jim Smiley would be likely to afford me much information

① hysted: hoisted
② Euphemism for " damnation"
③ belch out: send forth violently
④ by your leave: a request for permission

concerning the Rev. Leonidas W. Smiley, and so I started away.

At the door I met the sociable Wheeler returning, and he button- holed me and recommenced:

" Well, thish-yer Smiley had a yeller one-eyed cow that didn't have no tail, only jest a short stump like a bannanner, and — "

" Oh! hang Smiley and his afflicted cow!" I muttered, good-naturedly, and bidding the old gentleman good-day, I departed.

Topics for discussion

1. Compare Twain's use of satire with that of Jonathan Swift in his " A Modest Proposal". What and who do these stories satirize?

2. Compare this tale to Twain's other travel sketches or humorous writings. Discuss their similarity and differences.

3. Discuss the significance of the character names in " The Celebrated Jumping Frog of Calaveras County".

4. Why do the critics think the story is a satiric piece of literature, rather than simply a clever tale?

References for further reading

[1] Coulombe, Joseph L. *Mark Twain and the American West*, Columbia: University of Missouri Press, 2003.

[2] Fenger, Gerald J. *The perspectives of satire in Mark Twain's short stories*, Ann Arbor, Mich: UMI, 1974.

[3] Messent, Peter ed. *A companion to Mark Twain*, Malden, MA: Blackwell Pub, 2005.

[4] Smith, Harriet Elinor ed. *Autobiography of Mark Twain*, Berkeley: University

of California Press, 2010-2013.

[5] Wilson, James D. *A reader's guide to the short stories of Mark Twain*, Boston, Mass: G.K. Hall, 1987.

Kate Chopin (1850 — 1904)

The Story of an Hour

Introduction to the author

Kate Chopin, born Katherine O'Flaherty (February 8, 1850 — August 22, 1904), was an American author of short stories and novels. She is an advocate of the feminist authors of the 20th century. Her short stories were published in such magazines as *Atlantic Monthly, Vogue, The Century Magazine*, and *The Youth's Companion*. Her major works were two short story collections, *Bayou Folk* (1894) and *A Night in Acadie* (1897). Her important short stories included " Desiree's Baby" " The Story of an Hour" (1894), and " The Storm"(1898). Chopin also wrote two novels: *At Fault* (1890) and *The Awakening*(1899). Many of her works are set in Natchitoches in north central Louisiana. Chopin was born in St. Louis, Missouri. Her father, Thomas O'Flaherty, emigrated from Galway, Ireland. Her mother, Eliza Faris, was a member of the French community in St. Louis. She has four siblings but all of them died early. She was thus the only child to live past the age of twenty-five. She liked reading fairy tales, poetry, and religious allegories, and novels. In 1870, she married Oscar Chopin and settled in

New Orleans. Later the family moved to Cloutierville in south Natchitoches Parish. Oscar Chopin died in 1882 and Chopin sold her Louisiana business, moved back to St. Louis. Chopin's mother died later. The loss of her husband and her mother made Chopin depressed. *The Awakening*, published in 1899, is regarded as an early feminist work. Chopin, deeply discouraged by the criticism, turned to short story writing. In 1900, she wrote " The Gentleman from New Orleans". While visiting the St. Louis World's Fair on August 20, 1904, Chopin suffered a brain hemorrhage and died two days later, at the age of 54. She was interred in Calvary Cemetery in St. Louis.

Kate Chopin's various experiences in life permitted her to analyze late 19th-century American society. As a result of her childhood upbringing by women with ancestry descending from both Irish and French family and life in the Cajun and Creole part of the nation, after she joined her husband in Louisiana, many of her stories and sketches were about her life in Louisiana and incorporated her less than typical portrayals of women as their own individuals with wants and needs. She had an ability to perceive life and put it down on paper creatively. She invested substantial concentration and emphasis on women's lives and their continual struggles to create an identity of their own within the Southern society of the late nineteenth century.

Kate Chopin took women extremely seriously and she showed her sympathies with the individual in the context of his and her personal life and society. Through her stories, Kate Chopin wrote her autobiography and documented the abolitionist movements and the emergence of feminism.

Major works by Kate Chopin

" Bayou Folk"

" A Night in Acadie"

" At the Cadian Ball", 1892

" Desiree's Baby", 1893

" The Story of an Hour", 1894

" The Storm", 1898

" A Pair of Silk Stockings"

" The Locket"

" Athenaise"

" A Respectable Woman"

" The Kiss"

" Beauty of the Baby"

" Fedora"

" Madame Célestin's Divorce"

The Awakening, 1899

" Lilacs"

" The Unexpected"

" Beyond the Bayou"

" A No-Account Creole"

" Regret"

At Fault, 1890

Appreciation

Chopin's " The Story of an Hour" is the story of an hour in life of Mrs. Louise Mallard. Her wrinkles show the " repression" and " strength" in her life. Mrs. Mallard has " heart trouble." Having heard that Mr. Mallard died of a railroad disaster, Mrs. Mallard's sister Josephine and her husband's friend Richards worried about Mrs. Mallard and come to her. The news surprised Mrs. Mallard, and she locked herself in her bedroom. She learned that some fundamental changes appear in her life. A strange idea comes into her mind, and it seems that she is joyful that her husband is dead. However, she makes her effort to suppress the thought. She found that she would be " Free! Body and soul free!" She will decide anything on her own will. But it is impossible for her to do as she will when her husband is alive. Later, Mrs. Mallard leaves her room and rejoins her sister who has been outside the door worrying. She feels joyful as if she were " a goddess of Victory". When she steps downstairs, someone come into the house and it is Mr. Mallard. He was on the spot when the accident happened. Mrs. Mallard does not feel happy but astonished. She died abruptly and her doctors explain that her " joy" kills her.

Mrs. Mallard's response to the news that her husband has been killed and her demise upon his appearance, illustrates Chopin's view about women's roles in marriage and feminine identity. The story is an expression of the inequities of marriage. If the world does not change, women have no hope to be independent, to survive in the society. In " The Story of an Hour", Chopin uses irony and ambiguity to exemplify its theme.

Selected Reading

The Story of an hour

Knowing that Mrs. Mallard was afflicted with① a heart trouble, great care was taken to break to her as gently as possible the news of her husband's death.

It was her sister Josephine who told her, in broken sentences, veiled hints that revealed in half concealing. Her husband's friend Richards was there, too, near her. It was he who had been in the newspaper office when intelligence of the railroad disaster was received, with Brently Mallard's name leading the list of " killed." He had only taken the time to assure himself of its truth by a second telegram, and had hastened to forestall any less careful, less tender friend in bearing the sad message.

She did not hear the story as many women have heard the same, with a paralyzed inability to accept its significance. She wept at once, with sudden, wild abandonment, in her sister's arms. When the storm of grief had spent itself she went away to her room alone. She would have no one follow her.

There stood, facing the open window, a comfortable, roomy armchair. Into this she sank, pressed down by a physical exhaustion that haunted her body and seemed to reach into her soul.

She could see in the open square before her house the tops of trees that were all aquiver with the new spring life. The delicious breath of rain was in the air. In the street below a peddler was crying his wares. The notes of a distant song which

① be afflicted with: suffer from

someone was singing reached her faintly, and countless sparrows were twittering[①] in the eaves.

There were patches of blue sky showing here and there through the clouds that had met and piled above the other in the west facing her window.

She sat with her head thrown back upon the cushion of the chair, quite motionless, except when a sob came up into her throat and shook her, as a child who has cried itself to sleep continues to sob in its dreams.

She was young, with a fair, calm face, whose lines bespoke repression and even a certain strength. But now there was a dull stare in her eyes, whose gaze was fixed away off yonder on one of those patches of blue sky. It was not a glance of reflection, but rather indicated a suspension of intelligent thought.

There was something coming to her and she was waiting for it, fearfully. What was it? She did not know; it was too subtle and elusive to name. But she felt it, creeping out of the sky, reaching toward her through the sounds, the scents, the color that filled the air.

Now her bosom rose and fell tumultuously[②]. She was beginning to recognize this thing that was approaching to possess her, and she was striving to beat it back with her will — as powerless as her two white slender hands would have been.

When she abandoned herself a little whispered word escaped her slightly parted lips. She said it over and over under her breath: " Free, free, free!" The vacant stare and the look of terror that had followed it went from her eyes. They stayed keen and bright. Her pulses beat fast, and the coursing blood warmed and relaxed every inch of her body.

She did not stop to ask if it were or were not a monstrous joy that held her. A clear and exalted perception enabled her to dismiss the suggestion as trivial.

She knew that she would weep again when she saw the kind, tender hands folded

---

① twitter: (of a bird) to make a series of short, high sounds

② tumultuous: very loud, or full of confusion, change, or uncertainty in death; the face that had never looked save with love upon her, fixed and gray and dead. But she saw beyond that bitter moment a long procession of years to come that would belong to her absolutely. And she opened and spread her arms out to them in welcome.

There would be no one to live for her during those coming years; she would live for herself. There would be no powerful will bending her in that blind persistence with which men and women believe they have a right to impose a private will upon a fellow-creature. A kind intention or a cruel intention made the act seem no less a crime as she looked upon it in that brief moment of illumination.

And yet she had loved him — sometimes. Often she had not. What did it matter! What could love, the unsolved mystery, count for in face of this possession of self-assertion, which she suddenly recognized as the strongest impulse of her being!

" Free! Body and soul free!" she kept whispering.

Josephine was kneeling before the closed door — with her lips to the keyhole, imploring for admission. " Louise, open the door! I beg; open the door — you will make yourself ill. What are you doing, Louise? For heaven's sake open the door."

" Go away. I am not making myself ill." No; she was drinking in a very elixir① of life through that open window.

Her fancy was running riot along those days ahead of her. Spring days, and summer days, and all sorts of days that would be her own. She breathed a quick prayer that life might be long. It was only yesterday she had thought with a shudder that life might be long.

She arose at length and opened the door to her sister's importunities. There was a feverish triumph in her eyes, and she carried herself unwittingly like a goddess of Victory. She clasped her sister's waist, and together they descended the stairs. Richards stood waiting for them at the bottom.

---

① elixir: a substance, usually a liquid, with a magical power to cure, improve, or preserve something

Someone was opening the front door with a latchkey. It was Brently Mallard who entered, a little travel-stained, composedly carrying his gripsack and umbrella. He had been far from the scene of accident, and did not even know there had been one. He stood amazed at Josephine's piercing cry; at Richards' quick motion to screen him from the view of his wife.

But Richards was too late.

When the doctors came they said she had died of heart disease of joy that kills.

Topics for discussion

1. How you do think of the doctor's explanation about Mrs. Mallard's death at the end of the story?

2. How do you understand Mrs. Mallard as a sympathetic character or as a cruel and selfish character?

3. Discuss the symbolism in the " The Story of an hour"

4. How do you think the role of women in marriage in " The Story of an hour"?

References for further reading

[1] Beer, Janet ed. *The Cambridge companion to Kate Chopin*, New York: Cambridge University Press, 2008.

[2] Martin, Richard Arthur. *The fictive world of Kate Chopin*, Ann Arbor, Mich.: UMI, 1972.

[3] Skaggs, Peggy Dechert. *A woman's place: the search for identity in Kate Chopin's female characters*, Ann Arbor, Mich.: UMI, 1973.

[4] Toth, Emily. *Unveiling Kate Chopin*, Jackson: University Press of Mississippi, 1999.

Charlotte Perkins Gilman (1860 — 1935)

Yellow Wallpaper

Introduction to the author

Charlotte Perkins Gilman (July 3, 1860 — August 17, 1935) was an outstanding American feminist, sociologist, novelist, writer of short stories and poetry. " The Yellow Wallpaper" is her semi-autobiographical short story which she wrote after a severe bout of postpartum psychosis. Gilman was born on July 3, 1860 in Hartford, Connecticut to Mary Perkins (formerly Mary Fitch Westcott) and Frederic Beecher Perkins. Her father directed Gilman's early education, stressing study in the science and history. Perkins left his wife and children, which made the family in poverty. This brought Gilman into frequent contact her aunts on her father's side of the family, namely Isabella Beecher Hooker, an ardent suffragist, Harriet Beecher Stowe, an abolitionist and author of *Uncle Tom's Cabin* and Catharine Beecher, an advocate of " domestic feminism".

Gilman's childhood was full of isolation and loneliness, but she had strong interest in reading, she often visited the public library. Her father's love for literature also influenced her, offering many books for her to read. Gilman spent her youth in

Providence, Rhode Island. She attended seven different public schools. Her teachers felt deeply impressed by her natural intelligence and breadth of knowledge. Later she enrolled in classes at the Rhode Island School of Design, and became subsequently an artist of trade cards. In 1884, she married the artist Charles Walter Stetson. Their only child, Katharine Beecher Stetson, was born the following year. Charlotte Perkins Gilman suffered a very serious bout of post-partum depression in the months after Katharine's birth. In 1894, Charlotte legally divorced her husband, and moved with her daughter to Pasadena, California. She became an active feminist and reformist. Houghton Gilman, her first cousin, married her and they lived in New York City happily until Houghton's sudden death from a cerebral hemorrhage in 1934. In January 1932, Gilman was diagnosed with incurable breast cancer. An advocate of euthanasia for the terminally ill, Gilman committed suicide on August 17, 1935 by taking an overdose of chloroform.

Gilman's first book was *Art Gems for the Home and Fireside* (1888). Her first volume of poetry was *In This Our World* (1893). She delivered lectures on women's issues, ethics, labor, human rights, and social reform, which became themes in her fiction. In 1894 — 1895 Gilman served as editor of the magazine *The Impress*. Her book *Women and Economics* was published in 1900, which brought Gilman fame in international circle. *The Home: Its Work and Influence* emphasized that women are oppressed in their home and their environment needs to be modified.

Major works by Charlotte Perkins Gilman

Poetry

In This Our World,1893

Suffrage Songs and Verses, 1911

The Later Poetry of Charlotte Perkins Gilman, 1996

Novels and novellas

What Diantha Did,1909 — 1910

The Crux, 1911

Moving the Mountain, 1911

Mag-Marjorie,1912

Benigna Machiavelli, 1914

Herland, 1915

With Her in Ourland,1916

Non-fiction

Gems of Art for the Home and Fireside, 1888

Concerning Children, 1900

The Home: Its Work and Influence, 1903

Human Work, 1904

Social Ethics, 1914

Our Changing Morality, 1930

Appreciation

" The Yellow Wallpaper" was Gilman's most famous piece. The story is based on Gilman's own experiences with postpartum depression. It is about a woman suffering from mental illness. In order to treat the illness, the unnamed protagonist was closeted in a room by her husband. She is advised to isolate herself from any physical activities and intellectual stimulation. She is not allowed to read, write or even see her new baby. She is kept in a former nursery decorated with yellow wallpaper and has a total bed rest. Finally she becomes obsessed in the room's revolting yellow wallpaper until, at the end of the story, she goes insane. " The Yellow Wallpaper" was essentially a response to the doctor. He had tried to cure his wife of her depression through a " rest cure".

Gilman wrote this story to change people's minds about the role of women in society. " The Yellow Wallpaper" examines the role of women in nineteenth-century American society, including the relationship between husbands and wives, and the repression of female individuality and sexuality. Women's subordinative status does harm to their mental, emotional, and even physical wellbeing. They are lack of mental stimulation and the freedom and unable to escape confinement from outside. John's treatment of his wife represents the powerlessness and repression of women during the late nineteenth-century women. The women directly confront the sexual politics of the male-female, husband-wife relationship..

Selected Reading

The Yellow Wall-paper①

It is very seldom that mere ordinary people like John and myself secure ancestral halls for the summer.

A colonial mansion, a hereditary estate, I would say a haunted house, and reach the height of romantic felicity② — but that would be asking too much of fate!

Still I will proudly declare that there is something queer about it.

Else, why should it be let so cheaply? And why have stood so long untenanted?

John laughs at me, of course, but one expects that in marriage.

John is practical in the extreme. He has no patience with faith, an intense horror of superstition, and he scoffs openly at any talk of things not to be felt and seen and put down in figures.

John is a physician, and *perhaps* — (I would not say it to a living soul, of course, but this is dead paper and a great relief to my mind —) *perhaps* that is one reason I do not get well faster.

You see, he does not believe I am sick!

And what can one do?

---

① The variant spellings of " wall–paper" in the first, 1892, printing of the story are preserved here. Some typographical errors and misspellings have been silently corrected

② felicity: happiness, luck, or a condition that produces positive results

If a physician of high standing, and one's own husband, assures friends and relatives that there is really nothing the matter with one but temporary nervous depression — a slight hysterical tendency — what is one to do?

My brother is also a physician, and also of high standing, and he says the same thing.

So I take phosphates or phosphites① — whichever it is, and tonics, and journeys, and air, and exercise, and am absolutely forbidden to " work" until I am well again.

Personally, I disagree with their ideas.

Personally, I believe that congenial work, with excitement and change, would do me good.

But what is one to do?

I did write for a while in spite of them; but it does exhaust me a good deal — having to be so sly about it, or else meet with heavy opposition.

I sometimes fancy that my condition if I had less opposition and more society and stimulus — but John says the very worst thing I can do is to think about my condition, and I confess it always makes me feel bad.

So I will let it alone and talk about the house.

The most beautiful place! It is quite alone, standing well back from the road, quite three miles from the village. It makes me think of English places that you read about, for there are hedges and walls and gates that lock, and lots of separate little houses for the gardeners and people.

There is a delicious garden! I never saw such a garden — large and shady, full of box-bordered② paths, and lined with long grape-covered arbors with seats under them.

There were greenhouses, too, but they are all broken now.

There was some legal trouble, I believe, something about the heirs and co-heirs;

① phosphates or phosphites: carbonated water and acid phosphate, flavored with a fruit syrup

② box-bordered: with borders of box, an evergreen shrub

anyhow, the place has been empty for years.

That spoils my ghostliness, I am afraid, but I don't care — there is something strange about the house — I can feel it.

I even said so to John one moonlight evening, but he said what I felt was a draught, and shut the window.

I get unreasonably angry with John sometimes. I am sure I never used to be so sensitive. I think it is due to this nervous condition.

But John says if I feel so, I shall neglect proper self-control; so I take pains to control myself — before him, at least, and that makes me very tired.

I don't like our room a bit. I wanted one downstairs that opened on the piazza and had roses all over the window, and such pretty old-fashioned chintz① hangings! but John would not hear of it.

He said there was only one window and not room for two beds, and no near room for him if he took another.

He is very careful and loving, and hardly lets me stir without special direction.

I have a schedule prescription for each hour in the day; he takes all care from me, and so I feel basely ungrateful not to value it more.

He said we came here solely on my account, that I was to have perfect rest and all the air I could get. " Your exercise depends on your strength, my dear," said he, " and your food somewhat on your appetite; but air you can absorb all the time." So we took the nursery at the top of the house.

It is a big, airy room, the whole floor nearly, with windows that look all ways, and air and sunshine galore. It was nursery first and then playroom and gymnasium, I should judge; for the windows are barred for little children, and there are rings and things in the walls.

The paint and paper look as if a boys' school had used it. It is stripped off — the

---

① chintz: cotton cloth, usually with patterns of flowers, that has a slightly shiny appearance Textiles made from natural fibres paper — in great patches all around the head of my bed, about as far as I can reach, and in a great place on the other side of the room low down. I never saw a worse paper in my life.

One of those sprawling flamboyant patterns committing every artistic sin.

It is dull enough to confuse the eye in following, pronounced enough to constantly irritate and provoke study, and when you follow the lame uncertain curves for a little distance they suddenly commit suicide — plunge off at outrageous angles, destroy themselves in unheard of contradictions.

The color is repellent, almost revolting; a smouldering unclean yellow, strangely faded by the slow-turning sunlight.

It is a dull yet lurid orange in some places, a sickly sulphur① tint in others.

No wonder the children hated it! I should hate it myself if I had to live in this room long.

There comes John, and I must put this away, — he hates to have me write a word.

※※※

We have been here two weeks, and I haven't felt like writing before, since that first day.

I am sitting by the window now, up in this atrocious② nursery, and there is nothing to hinder my writing as much as I please, save lack of strength.

John is away all day, and even some nights when his cases are serious.

I am glad my case is not serious!

But these nervous troubles are dreadfully depressing.

John does not know how much I really suffer. He knows there is no reason to suffer, and that satisfies him.

---

① sulphur: a pale yellow chemical element that exists in various physical forms

② atrocious: of very bad quality

Of course it is only nervousness. It does weigh on me so not to do my duty in any way!

I meant to be such a help to John, such a real rest and comfort, and here I am a comparative burden already!

Nobody would believe what an effort it is to do what little I am able, — to dress and entertain, and other things.

It is fortunate Mary is so good with the baby. Such a dear baby!

And yet I cannot be with him, it makes me so nervous.

I suppose John never was nervous in his life. He laughs at me so about this wall-paper!

At first he meant to repaper the room, but afterwards he said that I was letting it get the better of me, and that nothing was worse for a nervous patient than to give way to such fancies.

He said that after the wall-paper was changed it would be the heavy bedstead, and then the barred windows, and then that gate at the head of the stairs, and so on.

" You know the place is doing you good," he said, " and really, dear, I don't care to renovate the house just for a three months' rental."

" Then do let us go downstairs," I said, " there are such pretty rooms there."

Then he took me in his arms and called me a blessed little goose, and said he would go down to the cellar, if I wished, and have it whitewashed into the bargain.

But he is right enough about the beds and windows and things.

It is an airy and comfortable room as any one need wish, and, of course, I would not be so silly as to make him uncomfortable just for a whim.

I'm really getting quite fond of the big room, all but that horrid paper.

Out of one window I can see the garden, those mysterious deep-shaded arbors, the riotous old-fashioned flowers, and bushes and gnarly trees.

Out of another I get a lovely view of the bay and a little private wharf belonging to the estate. There is a beautiful shaded lane that runs down there from the house. I always fancy I see people walking in these numerous paths and arbors, but John has cautioned me not to give way to fancy in the least. He says that with my imaginative power and habit of story-making, a nervous weakness like mine is sure to lead to all manner of excited fancies, and that I ought to use my will and good sense to check the tendency. So I try.

I think sometimes that if I were only well enough to write a little it would relieve the press of ideas and rest me. But I find I get pretty tired when I try.

It is so discouraging not to have any advice and companionship about my work. When I get really well, John says we will ask Cousin Henry and Julia down for a long visit; but he says he would as soon put fireworks in my pillow-case as to let me have those stimulating people about now.

I wish I could get well faster.

But I must not think about that. This paper looks to me as if it knew what a vicious influence it had!

There is a recurrent spot where the pattern lolls[1] like a broken neck and two bulbous[2] eyes stare at you upside down.

I get positively angry with the impertinence[3] of it and the everlastingness. Up and down and sideways they crawl, and those absurd, unblinking eyes are everywhere. There is one place where two breadths didn't match, and the eyes go all up and down the line, one a little higher than the other.

I never saw so much expression in an inanimate thing before, and we all know how much expression they have! I used to lie awake as a child and get more entertainment and terror out of blank walls and plain furniture than most children could find in a toy store.

---

① loll: to lie, sit, or hang down in a relaxed, informal, or uncontrolled way

② bulbous: round

③ impertinence: rude and not showing respect, especially towards someone older or in a higher position than you

I remember what a kindly wink the knobs of our big, old bureau used to have, and there was one chair that always seemed like a strong friend.

I used to feel that if any of the other things looked too fierce I could always hop into that chair and be safe.

The furniture in this room is no worse than inharmonious, however, for we had to bring it all from downstairs. I suppose when this was used as a playroom they had to take the nursery things out, and no wonder! I never saw such ravages as the children have made here.

The wall-paper, as I said before, is torn off in spots, and it sticketh closer than a brother① — they must have had perseverance as well as hatred.

Then the floor is scratched and gouged and splintered, the plaster itself is dug out here and there, and this great heavy bed which is all we found in the room, looks as if it had been through the wars.

But I don't mind it a bit — only the paper.

There comes John's sister. Such a dear girl as she is, and so careful of me! I must not let her find me writing.

She is a perfect and enthusiastic housekeeper, and hopes for no better profession. I verily believe she thinks it is the writing which made me sick!

But I can write when she is out, and see her a long way off from these windows.

There is one that commands the road, a lovely shaded winding road, and one that just looks off over the country. A lovely country, too, full of great elms and velvet meadows.

This wall-paper has a kind of sub-pattern in a different shade, a particularly irritating one, for you can only see it in certain lights, and not clearly then.

But in the places where it isn't faded and where the sun is just so — I can see a strange, provoking, formless sort of figure, that seems to skulk about behind that silly

① "There is a friend that sticketh closer than a brother" (Proverbs 18:24)

and conspicuous front design.

There's sister on the stairs!

※※※

Well, the Fourth of July is over! The people are gone and I am tired out. John thought it might do me good to see a little company, so we just had mother and Nellie and the children down for a week.

Of course I didn't do a thing. Jennie sees to everything now.

But it tired me all the same.

John says if I don't pick up faster he shall send me to Weir Mitchell① in the fall.

But I don't want to go there at all. I had a friend who was in his hands once, and she says he is just like John and my brother, only more so!

Besides, it is such an undertaking to go so far.

I don't feel as if it was worth while to turn my hand over for anything, and I'm getting dreadfully fretful and querulous.②

I cry at nothing, and cry most of the time.

Of course I don't mind when John is here, or anybody else, but when I am alone.

And I am alone a good deal just now. John is kept in town very often by serious cases, and Jennie is good and lets me alone when I want her to.

So I walk a little in the garden or down that lovely lane, sit on the porch under the roses, and lie down up here a good deal.

I'm getting really fond of the room in spite of the wall-paper. Perhaps because of the wall-paper.

It dwells in my mind so!

I lie here on this great immovable bed, — it is nailed down, I believe — and

① Silas Weir Mitchell: (1829–1914), American physician known for his "rest–cure" treatment of "nervous disorders."

② querulous: often complaining, especially in a weak high voice follow that pattern about by the hour. It is as good as gymnastics, I assure you. I start, we'll say, at the bottom, down in the corner over there where it has not been touched, and I determine for the thousandth time that I will follow that pointless pattern to some sort of a conclusion.

I know a little of the principle of design, and I know this thing was not arranged on any laws of radiation, or alternation, or repetition, or symmetry, or anything else that I ever heard of.

It is repeated, of course, by the breadths, but not otherwise.

Looked at in one way each breadth stands alone, the bloated curves and flourishes — a kind of "debased Romanesque"① with *delirium tremens*② — go waddling up and down in isolated columns of fatuity.

But, on the other hand, they connect diagonally, and the sprawling outlines run off in great slanting waves of optic horror, like a lot of wallowing seaweeds in full chase.

The whole thing goes horizontally, too, at least it seems so, and I exhaust myself in trying to distinguish the order of its going in that direction.

They have used a horizontal breadth for a frieze, and that adds wonderfully to the confusion.

There is one end of the room where it is almost intact, and there, when the crosslights fade and the low sun shines directly upon it, I can almost fancy radiation after all, — the interminable grotesques seem to form around a common centre and rush off in headlong plunges of equal distraction.

It makes me tired to follow it. I will take a nap I guess.

---

① debased Romanesque: ornate style of architecture marked by curves and rounded arches

② delirium tremens: a violent mental disturbance accompanied by hallucinations, caused by alcoholism

※※※

I don't know why I should write this.

I don't want to.

I don't feel able.

And I know John would think it absurd. But I must say what I feel and think in some way — it is such a relief!

But the effort is getting to be greater than the relief.

Half the time now I am awfully lazy, and lie down ever so much.

John says I mustn't lose my strength, and has me take cod liver oil and lots of tonics and things, to say nothing of ale and wine and rare meat.

Dear John! He loves me very dearly, and hates to have me sick. I tried to have a real earnest reasonable talk with him the other day, and tell him how I wish he would let me go and make a visit to Cousin Henry and Julia.

But he said I wasn't able to go, nor able to stand it after I got there; and I did not make out a very good case for myself, for I was crying before I had finished.

It is getting to be a great effort for me to think straight. Just this nervous weakness I suppose.

And dear John gathered me up in his arms, and just carried me upstairs and laid me on the bed, and sat by me and read to me till it tired my head.

He said I was his darling and his comfort and all he had, and that I must take care of myself for his sake, and keep well.

He says no one but myself can help me out of it, that I must use my will and self-control and not let any silly fancies run away with me.

There's one comfort, the baby is well and happy, and does not have to occupy this nursery with the horrid wall-paper.

If we had not used it, that blessed child would have! What a fortunate escape! Why, I wouldn't have a child of mine, an impressionable little thing, live in such a room for worlds.

I never thought of it before, but it is lucky that John kept me here after all, I can stand it so much easier than a baby, you see.

Of course I never mention it to them any more — I am too wise, — but I keep watch of it all the same.

There are things in that paper that nobody knows but me, or ever will.

Behind that outside pattern the dim shapes get clearer every day.

It is always the same shape, only very numerous.

And it is like a woman stooping down and creeping about behind that pattern. I don't like it a bit. I wonder — I begin to think — I wish John would take me away from here!

※※※

It is so hard to talk with John about my case, because he is so wise, and because he loves me so.

But I tried it last night.

It was moonlight. The moon shines in all around just as the sun does.

I hate to see it sometimes, it creeps so slowly, and always comes in by one window or another.

John was asleep and I hated to waken him, so I kept still and watched the moonlight on that undulating① wall-paper till I felt creepy.

The faint figure behind seemed to shake the pattern, just as if she wanted to get out.

I got up softly and went to feel and see if the paper did move, and when I came back John was awake.

" What is it, little girl?" he said. " Don't go walking about like that — you'll get cold."

---

① undulating: twisting and curving, moving gently up and down

I thought it was a good time to talk, so I told him that I really was not gaining here, and that I wished he would take me away.

" Why darling!" said he, " our lease will be up in three weeks, and I can't see how to leave before.

" The repairs are not done at home, and I cannot possibly leave town just now. Of course if you were in any danger, I could and would, but you really are better, dear, whether you can see it or not. I am a doctor, dear, and I know. You are gaining flesh and color, your appetite is better, I feel really much easier about you."

" I don't weigh a bit more," said I, " nor as much; and my appetite may be better in the evening when you are here, but it is worse in the morning when you are away!"

" Bless her little heart!" said he with a big hug, " she shall be as sick as she pleases! But now let's improve the shining hours① by going to sleep, and talk about it in the morning!"

" And you won't go away?" I asked gloomily.

" Why, how can I, dear? It is only three weeks more and then we will take a nice little trip of a few days while Jennie is getting the house ready. Really dear you are better!"

" Better in body perhaps — " I began, and stopped short, for he sat up straight and looked at me with such a stern, reproachful look that I could not say another word.

" My darling," said he, " I beg of you, for my sake and for our child's sake, as well as for your own, that you will never for one instant let that idea enter your mind! There is nothing so dangerous, so fascinating, to a temperament like yours. It is a

① An adaptation of " Song XX" from The Divine Songs of Isaac Watts (1674-1784), English hymnist:

How doeth the little busy bee
Improve each shining hour,
And gather honey all the day
From every opening flower.

false and foolish fancy. Can you not trust me as a physician when I tell you so?"

So of course I said no more on that score, and we went to sleep before long. He thought I was asleep first, but I wasn't, and lay there for hours trying to decide whether that front pattern and the back pattern really did move together or separately.

※※※

On a pattern like this, by daylight, there is a lack of sequence, a defiance of law, that is a constant irritant to a normal mind.

The color is hideous enough, and unreliable enough, and infuriating enough, but the pattern is torturing.

You think you have mastered it, but just as you get well underway in following, it turns a back-somersault and there you are. It slaps you in the face, knocks you down, and tramples upon you. It is like a bad dream.

The outside pattern is a florid arabesque,① reminding one of a fungus.② If you can imagine a toadstool in joints, an interminable string of toadstools, budding and sprouting in endless convolutions③ — why, that is something like it.

That is, sometimes!

There is one marked peculiarity about this paper, a thing nobody seems to notice but myself, and that is that it changes as the light changes.

When the sun shoots in through the east window — I always watch for that first long, straight ray — it changes so quickly that I never can quite believe it.

That is why I watch it always.

By moonlight — the moon shines in all night when there is a moon — I wouldn't know it was the same paper.

---

① arabesque: a position in ballet in which the dancer stands on one leg with the other leg held out straight behind

② fungus: Mushrooms

③ convolutions: bending, twisting and curving

At night in any kind of light, in twilight, candle light, lamplight, and worst of all by moonlight, it becomes bars! The outside pattern I mean, and the woman behind it is as plain as can be.

I didn't realize for a long time what the thing was that showed behind, that dim sub-pattern, but now I am quite sure it is a woman.

By daylight she is subdued, quiet. I fancy it is the pattern that keeps her so still. It is so puzzling. It keeps me quiet by the hour.

I lie down ever so much now. John says it is good for me, and to sleep all I can.

Indeed he started the habit by making me lie down for an hour after each meal.

It is a very bad habit I am convinced, for you see I don't sleep.

And that cultivates deceit, for I don't tell them I'm awake — O no!

The fact is I am getting a little afraid of John.

He seems very queer sometimes, and even Jennie has an inexplicable look.

It strikes me occasionally, just as a scientific hypothesis, — that perhaps it is the paper!

I have watched John when he did not know I was looking, and come into the room suddenly on the most innocent excuses, and I've caught him several times looking at the paper! And Jennie too. I caught Jennie with her hand on it once.

She didn't know I was in the room, and when I asked her in a quiet, a very quiet voice, with the most restrained manner possible, what she was doing with the paper — she turned around as if she had been caught stealing, and looked quite angry — asked me why I should frighten her so!

Then she said that the paper stained everything it touched, that she had found yellow smooches① on all my clothes and John's, and she wished we would be more careful!

Did not that sound innocent? But I know she was studying that pattern, and I am

---

① smooches: smudges, smears

determined that nobody shall find it out but myself!

※※※

Life is very much more exciting now than it used to be. You see I have something more to expect, to look forward to, to watch. I really do eat better, and am more quiet than I was.

John is so pleased to see me improve! He laughed a little the other day, and said I seemed to be flourishing in spite of my wall-paper.

I turned it off with a laugh. I had no intention of telling him it was because of the wallpaper — he would make fun of me. He might even want to take me away.

I don't want to leave now until I have found it out. There is a week more, and I think that will be enough.

※※※

I'm feeling ever so much better! I don't sleep much at night, for it is so interesting to watch developments; but I sleep a good deal in the daytime.

In the daytime it is tiresome and perplexing.

There are always new shoots on the fungus, and new shades of yellow all over it. I cannot keep count of them, though I have tried conscientiously.

It is the strangest yellow, that wallpaper! It makes me think of all the yellow things I ever saw — not beautiful ones like buttercups, but old foul, bad yellow things.

But there is something else about that paper — the smell! I noticed it the moment we came into the room, but with so much air and sun it was not bad. Now we have had a week of fog and rain, and whether the windows are open or not, the smell is here.

It creeps all over the house.

I find it hovering in the dining-room, skulking in the parlor, hiding in the hall, lying in wait for me on the stairs.

It gets into my hair.

Even when I go to ride, if I turn my head suddenly and surprise it — there is that smell!

Such a peculiar odor, too! I have spent hours in trying to analyze it, to find what it smelled like.

It is not bad–at first, and very gentle, but quite the subtlest, most enduring odor I ever met.

In this damp weather it is awful, I wake up in the night and find it hanging over me.

It used to disturb me at first. I thought seriously of burning the house — to reach the smell.

But now I am used to it. The only thing I can think of that it is like is the color of the paper! A yellow smell.

There is a very funny mark on this wall, low down, near the mopboard. A streak that runs round the room. It goes behind every piece of furniture, except the bed, a long, straight, even smooch, as if it had been rubbed over and over.

I wonder how it was done and who did it, and what they did it for. Round and round and round — round and round and round — it makes me dizzy!

※※※

I really have discovered something at last.

Through watching so much at night, when it changes so, I have finally found out.

The front pattern does move — and no wonder! The woman behind shakes it!

Sometimes I think there are a great many women behind, and sometimes only one, and she crawls around fast, and her crawling shakes it all over.

Then in the very bright spots she keeps still, and in the very shady spots she just takes hold of the bars and shakes them hard.

And she is all the time trying to climb through. But nobody could climb through that pattern — it strangles so; I think that is why it has so many heads.

They get through, and then the pattern strangles them off and turns them upside down, and makes their eyes white!

If those heads were covered or taken off it would not be half so bad.

※※※

I think that woman gets out in the daytime!

And I'll tell you why — privately — I've seen her!

I can see her out of every one of my windows!

It is the same woman, I know, for she is always creeping, and most women do not creep by daylight.

I see her in that long shaded lane, creeping up and down. I see her in those dark grape arbors, ① creeping all around the garden.

I see her on that long road under the trees, creeping along, and when a carriage comes she hides under the blackberry vines.

I don't blame her a bit. It must be very humiliating to be caught creeping by daylight!

I always lock the door when I creep by daylight. I can't do it at night, for I know John would suspect something at once.

And John is so queer now, that I don't want to irritate him. I wish he would take another room! Besides, I don't want anybody to get that woman out at night but myself.

I often wonder if I could see her out of all the windows at once.

But, turn as fast as I can, I can only see out of one at a time.

---

① arbor: a sheltered place in a garden formed by trees and bushes that are grown to partly surround it

And though I always see her, she may be able to creep faster than I can turn!

I have watched her sometimes away off in the open country, creeping as fast as a cloud shadow in a high wind.

※※※

If only that top pattern could be gotten off from the under one! I mean to try it, little by little.

I have found out another funny thing, but I shan't tell it this time! It does not do to trust people too much.

There are only two more days to get this paper off, and I believe John is beginning to notice. I don't like the look in his eyes.

And I heard him ask Jennie a lot of professional questions about me. She had a very good report to give.

She said I slept a good deal in the daytime.

John knows I don't sleep very well at night, for all I'm so quiet!

He asked me all sorts of questions, too, and pretended to be very loving and kind.

As if I couldn't see through him!

Still, I don't wonder he acts so, sleeping under this paper for three months.

It only interests me, but I feel sure John and Jennie are secretly affected by it.

※※※

Hurrah![①] This is the last day, but it is enough. John is to stay in town over night, and won't be out until this evening.

Jennie wanted to sleep with me — the sly thing! but I told her I should undoubtedly rest better for a night all alone.

---

① Hurrah: exclamation (also hoorah), used to express excitement, pleasure, or approval

That was clever, for really I wasn't alone a bit! As soon as it was moonlight and that poor thing began to crawl and shake the pattern, I got up and ran to help her.

I pulled and she shook, I shook and she pulled, and before morning we had peeled off yards of that paper.

A strip about as high as my head and half around the room.

And then when the sun came and that awful pattern began to laugh at me, I declared I would finish it to-day!

We go away to-morrow, and they are moving all my furniture down again to leave things as they were before.

Jennie looked at the wall in amazement, but I told her merrily that I did it out of pure spite at the vicious thing.

She laughed and said she wouldn't mind doing it herself, but I must not get tired.

How she betrayed herself that time!

But I am here, and no person touches this paper but me — not alive!

She tried to get me out of the room — it was too patent! But I said it was so quiet and empty and clean now that I believed I would lie down again and sleep all I could; and not to wake me even for dinner — I would call when I woke.

So now she is gone, and the servants are gone, and the things are gone, and there is nothing left but that great bedstead nailed down, with the canvas mattress we found on it.

We shall sleep downstairs to-night, and take the boat home to-morrow.

I quite enjoy the room, now it is bare again.

How those children did tear about here!

This bedstead is fairly gnawed!

But I must get to work.

I have locked the door and thrown the key down into the front path.

I don't want to go out, and I don't want to have anybody come in, till John comes. I want to astonish him.

I've got a rope up here that even Jennie did not find. If that woman does get out, and tries to get away, I can tie her!

But I forgot I could not reach far without anything to stand on!

This bed will not move!

I tried to lift and push it until I was lame, and then I got so angry I bit off a little piece at one corner--but it hurt my teeth.

Then I peeled off all the paper I could reach standing on the floor. It sticks horribly and the pattern just enjoys it! All those strangled heads and bulbous eyes and waddling fungus growths just shriek with derision![①]

I am getting angry enough to do something desperate. To jump out of the window would be admirable exercise, but the bars are too strong even to try.

Besides I wouldn't do it. Of course not. I know well enough that a step like that is improper and might be misconstrued.

I don't like to look out of the windows even — there are so many of those creeping women, and they creep so fast.

I wonder if they all come out of that wall-paper as I did?

But I am securely fastened now by my well-hidden rope — you don't get me out in the road there!

I suppose I shall have to get back behind the pattern when it comes night, and that is hard!

It is so pleasant to be out in this great room and creep around as I please!

I don't want to go outside. I won't, even if Jennie asks me to.

For outside you have to creep on the ground, and everything is green instead of yellow.

But here I can creep smoothly on the floor, and my shoulder just fits in that long smooch around the wall, so I cannot lose my way.

① derision: the situation in which someone or something is laughed at and considered stupid or of no value

Why there's John at the door!

It is no use, young man, you can't open it!

How he does call and pound!

Now he's crying for an axe.

It would be a shame to break down that beautiful door!

" John dear!" said I in the gentlest voice, " the key is down by the front steps, under a plantain leaf!"

That silenced him for a few moments.

Then he said — very quietly indeed, " Open the door, my darling!"

" I can't," said I. " The key is down by the front door under a plantain leaf!"

And then I said it again, several times, very gently and slowly, and said it so often that he had to go and see, and he got it of course, and came in. He stopped short by the door.

" What is the matter?" he cried. " For God's sake, what are you doing!"

I kept on creeping just the same, but I looked at him over my shoulder.

" I've got out at last," said I, " in spite of you and Jane. And I've pulled off most of the paper, so you can't put me back!"

Now why should that man have fainted? But he did, and right across my path by the wall, so that I had to creep over him every time!

Topics for discussion

1. Do you think " The Yellow Wallpaper" is a story of female confinement and escape? If so, why?

2. Make some comment on the unnamed protagonist under the background of the American women role in the nineteenth century.

3. What role does John feel a woman should play in society? How might a contemporary feminist view John? What the attitudes toward acceptable roles for

women today?

4. Discuss the symbolism in " The Yellow Wallpaper".

References for further reading

[1] Allen, Judith A. *The feminism of Charlotte Perkins Gilman: sexualities, histories, progressivism* Chicago : University of Chicago Press, 2009.

[2] Beer, Janet. *Kate Chopin, Edith Wharton, and Charlotte Perkins Gilman: studies in short fiction*, New York: St. Martin's Press, 1997.

[3] Karpinski, Joanne B. *An introduction to Critical Essays on Charlotte Perkins Gilman*, G. K. Hall & Co. 1992.

[4] Lane, Ann J. *To Herland and Beyond*, Penguin, 1991.

[5] Patricia Lengermann, G. ed. *Charlotte Perkins Gilman*, Farnham, Surrey: Ashgate Publishing Limited, 2013.

Edith Wharton (1862 — 1937)

Roman Fever

Introduction to the author

Edith Wharton (January 24, 1862 — August 11, 1937) was an American novelist and short story writer, who won a Pulitzer Prize. Wharton was born to George Frederic Jones and Lucretia Stevens Rhinelander in New York City. Wharton once stayed in Europe with her fiance for several years but their engagement broke off. Instead Edith married the banker Edward Wharton. Wharton wrote stories to popular magazines firstly. Her first collection of stories, *The Greater biclination* made her a recognized professional writer. She had close relationship with Henry James, and James became her mentor. In the fourteen years since 1900, Wharton completed almost 50 short stories and some of her finest novels, including *The House of Mirth and Ethan Frome*. From 1911, Wharton resided in France permanently. In 1913, she divorced her husband. Wharton traveled extensively throughout Europe in her later years. Wharton continued to write until her death. In 1934, Wharton published her memoirs, *A Backward Glance*. Her novel, *The Buccaneers*, a finest piece of work, was published after her death.

In addition to novels, Wharton wrote at least 85 short stories and some design books. Her novel *The Age of Innocence* (1920) won the 1921 Pulitzer Prize for literature. Wharton became the first woman to win the award. In 1934, Wharton's autobiography *A Backward Glance* was published. Wharton subtly uses dramatic irony in her novels. She also became one of its most astute critics of the society she lived. In addition to her novels, Wharton's short ghost stories aroused attention among critics.

Major works by Edith Wharton

Novels

The Touchstone, 1900
The Valley of Decision, 1902
Sanctuary, 1903
The House of Mirth, 1905
Madame de Treymes, 1907
The Fruit of the Tree, 1907
Ethan Frome, 1911
The Reef, 1912
The Custom of the Country, 1913
Bunner Sisters, 1916
Summer, 1917
The Marne, 1918
The Age of Innocence, 1920 (Pulitzer Prize winner)
The Glimpses of the Moon, 1922
A Son at the Front, 1923
The Mother's Recompense, 1925
Twilight Sleep, 1927
The Children, 1928
Hudson River Bracketed, 1929
The Gods Arrive, 1932
The Buccaneers, 1938

Poetry

Verses, 1878
Artemis to Actaeon and Other Verse, 1909

Twelve Poems, 1926

Short story collections

The Greater Inclination, 1899

Souls Belated, 1899

Crucial Instances, 1901

The Descent of Man and Other Stories, 1903

The Hermit and the Wild Woman and Other Stories, 1908

Tales of Men and Ghosts, 1910

Xingu and Other Stories, 1916

Old New York, 1924

Here and Beyond, 1926

Certain People, 1930

Human Nature, 1933

The World Over, 1936

Ghosts, 1937

Roman Fever and Other Stories, 1964

Non-fiction

The Decoration of Houses, 1897

Italian Villas and Their Gardens, 1904

Italian Backgrounds, 1905

A Motor-Flight Through France, 1908 (travel)

France, from Dunkerque to Belfort, 1915 (war)

French Ways and Their Meaning, 1919

In Morocco, 1920 (travel)

The Writing of Fiction, 1925 (essays on writing)

A Backward Glance, 1934 (autobiography)

Appreciation

" Roman Fever" was first published in Liberty magazine in 1934, and it was included in Wharton's final collection of short stories, *The World Over*, in 1936. " Roman Fever" is artistic, complex, and reflective of Wharton's moral landscape.

Mrs. Slade and Mrs. Ansley, two middle-aged American ladies, are lifelong friends, and they enjoyed themselves in Rome with their respective daughters — Jenny Slade and Barbara Ansley. The two middle-aged women remembered old times when revisiting Rome. Mrs. Slade reminds Mrs. Ansley of the serious illness in Rome many years ago. In order to hurt her friend, Mrs. Slade uncovered some secret between them. They show a deep-felt animosity to each other in their dialogue. Mrs. Slade is not only envious of Mrs. Ansley's lively daughter but jealous of her past love for Mrs. Slade's husband. The final sentence of the story reveals that Mrs. Slade has a valid reason for her feelings of competition with Mrs. Ansley though she only learns of it after years of ill-feeling.

Obviously, Mrs. Slade and Mrs. Ansley have been rivals throughout their long friendship. The rivalry between these women runs very deep. The story is told from a third-person, omniscient point of view. This means that readers see and hear what the characters see and hear. The story is divided into two sections — the background and history of Mrs. Slade and Mrs. Ansley and rivalry between the two women. Wharton makes use of a number of symbols and images to reinforce the emotions of the story.

Selected Reading

Roman Fever

I

From the table at which they had been lunching two American ladies of ripe but well-cared-for middle age moved across the lofty terrace of the Roman restaurant and, leaning on its parapet, looked first at each other, and then down on the outspread glories of the Palatine and the Forum, with the same expression of vague but benevolent approval.

As they leaned there a girlish voice echoed up gaily from the stairs leading to the court below. " Well, come along, then," it cried, not to them but to an invisible companion, " and let's leave the young things to their knitting," and a voice as fresh laughed back: " Oh, look here, Babs, not actually knitting — " " Well, I mean figuratively," rejoined the first. " After all, we haven't left our poor parents much else to do..." At that point the turn of the stairs engulfed the dialogue.

The two ladies looked at each other again, this time with a tinge of smiling embarrassment, and the smaller and paler one shook her head and colored slightly.

" Barbara!" she murmured, sending an unheard rebuke① after the mocking voice in the stairway.

The other lady, who was fuller, and higher in color, with a small determined nose supported by vigorous black eyebrows, gave a good-humored laugh. " That's what our daughters think of us."

Her companion replied by a deprecating② gesture. " Not of us individually. We must remember that. It's just the collective modern idea of Mothers. And you

① rebuke: criticizing someone strongly because you disapprove of what the person has said or done

② deprecating: showing that you think something is of little value or importance see — " Half guiltily she drew from her handsomely mounted black handbag a twist of crimson silk run through by two fine knitting needles. " One never knows," she murmured. " The new system has certainly given us a good deal of time to kill; and sometimes I get tired just looking — even at this." Her gesture was now addressed to the stupendous scene at their feet.

The dark lady laughed again, and they both relapsed upon the view, contemplating it in silence, with a sort of diffused serenity① which might have been borrowed from the spring effulgence of the Roman skies. The luncheon hour was long past, and the two had their end of the vast terrace to themselves. At its opposite extremity a few groups, detained by a lingering look at the outspread city, were gathering up guidebooks and fumbling for tips. The last of them scattered, and the two ladies were alone on the air-washed height.

" Well, I don't see why we shouldn't just stay here," said Mrs. Slade, the lady of the high color and energetic brows. Two derelict② basket chairs stood near, and she pushed them into the angle of the parapet, and settled herself in one, her gaze upon the Palatine. " After all, it's still the most beautiful view in the world."

" It always will be, to me," assented her friend Mrs. Ansley, with so slight a stress on the " me" that Mrs. Slade, though she noticed it, wondered if it were not merely accidental, like the random underlinings of old-fashioned letter writers.

" Grace Ansley was always old-fashioned," she thought; and added aloud, with a retrospective smile: " It's a view we've both been familiar with for a good many years. When we first met here we were younger than our girls are now. You remember!"

" Oh, yes, I remember," murmured Mrs. Ansley, with the same undefinable stress — " There's that head-waiter wondering," she interpolated. She was evidently far less sure than her companion of herself and of her rights in the world.

① serenity: being Calm and relaxed

② derelict: in bad condition

" I'll cure him of wondering," said Mrs. Slade, stretching her hand toward a bag as discreetly opulent-looking as Mrs. Ansley's. Signing to the headwaiter, she explained that she and her friend were old lovers of Rome, and would like to spend the end of the afternoon looking down on the view — that is, if it did not disturb the service! The headwaiter, bowing over her gratuity,① assured her that the ladies were most welcome, and would be still more so if they would condescend to remain for dinner. A full moon night, they would remember....

Mrs. Slade's black brows drew together, as though references to the moon were out of place and even unwelcome. But she smiled away her frown as the headwaiter retreated. " Well, why not! We might do worse. There's no knowing, I suppose, when the girls will be back. Do you even know back from where? I don't!"

Mrs. Ansley again colored slightly. " I think those young Italian aviators we met at the Embassy invited them to fly to Tarquinia for tea. I suppose they'll want to wait and fly back by moonlight."

" Moonlight — moonlight! What a part it still plays. Do you suppose they're as sentimental as we were?"

" I've come to the conclusion that I don't in the least know what they are," said Mrs. Ansley. " And perhaps we didn't know much more about each other."

" No, perhaps we didn't."

Her friend gave her a shy glance. " I never should have supposed you were sentimental, Alida."

" Well, perhaps I wasn't." Mrs. Slade drew her lids together in retrospect; and for a few moments the two ladies, who had been intimate since childhood, reflected how little they knew each other. Each one, of course, had a label ready to attach to the other's name; Mrs. Delphin Slade, for instance, would have told herself, or anyone who asked her, that Mrs. Horace Ansley, twenty-five years ago, had been

① gratuity: an amount of money given as a reward for a service exquisitely lovely — no, you wouldn't believe it, would you! though, of course, still charming, distinguished.... Well, as a girl she had been exquisite; far more beautiful than her daughter, Barbara, though certainly Babs, according to the new standards at any rate, was more effective — had more edge, as they say. Funny where she got it, with those two nullities as parents. Yes; Horace Ansley was — well, just the duplicate of his wife. Museum specimens of old New York. Good-looking, irreproachable,[1] exemplary. Mrs. Slade and Mrs. Ansley had lived opposite each other — actually as well as figuratively — for years. When the drawing-room curtains in No. 20 East Seventy-third Street were renewed, No. 23, across the way, was always aware of it. And of all the movings, buyings, travels, anniversaries, illnesses — the tame chronicle of an estimable pair. Little of it escaped Mrs. Slade. But she had grown bored with it by the time her husband made his big coup in Wall Street, and when they bought in upper Park Avenue had already begun to think: " I'd rather live opposite a speakeasy for a change; at least one might see it raided." The idea of seeing Grace raided was so amusing that (before the move) she launched it at a woman's lunch. It made a hit, and went the rounds — she sometimes wondered if it had crossed the street, and reached Mrs. Ansley. She hoped not, but didn't much mind. Those were the days when respectability was at a discount, and it did the irreproachable no harm to laugh at them a little.

A few years later, and not many months apart, both ladies lost their husbands. There was an appropriate exchange of wreaths and condolences, and a brief renewal of intimacy in the half shadow of their mourning; and now, after another interval, they had run across each other in Rome, at the same hotel, each of them the modest appendage of a salient[2] daughter. The similarity of their lot had again drawn them together, lending itself to mild jokes, and the mutual confession that, if in old days it must have been tiring to " keep up" with daughters, it was now, at times, a little dull

---

① irreproachable: without fault and therefore impossible to criticize

② salient: clearly and concisely

not to.

No doubt, Mrs. Slade reflected, she felt her unemployment more than poor Grace ever would. It was a big drop from being the wife of Delphin Slade to being his widow. She had always regarded herself (with a certain conjugal[①] pride) as his equal in social gifts, as contributing her full share to the making of the exceptional couple they were: but the difference after his death was irremediable. As the wife of the famous corporation lawyer, always with an international case or two on hand, every day brought its exciting and unexpected obligation: the impromptu entertaining of eminent colleagues from abroad, the hurried dashes on legal business to London, Paris or Rome, where the entertaining was so handsomely reciprocated; the amusement of hearing in her wakes: " What, that handsome woman with the good clothes and the eyes is Mrs. Slade — the Slade's wife! Really! Generally the wives of celebrities are such frumps[②] ."

Yes; being the Slade's widow was a dullish business after that. In living up to such a husband all her faculties had been engaged; now she had only her daughter to live up to, for the son who seemed to have inherited his father's gifts had died suddenly in boyhood. She had fought through that agony because her husband was there, to be helped and to help; now, after the father's death, the thought of the boy had become unbearable. There was nothing left but to mother her daughter; and dear Jenny was such a perfect daughter that she needed no excessive mothering. " Now with Babs Ansley I don't know that I should be so quiet," Mrs. Slade sometimes half-enviously reflected; but Jenny, who was younger than her brilliant friend, was that rare accident, an extremely pretty girl who somehow made youth and prettiness seem as safe as their absence. It was all perplexing — and to Mrs. Slade a little boring. She wished that Jenny would fall in love — with the wrong man, even; that she

① conjugal: connected with marriage or the relationship between two married people, especially their sexual relationship

② frump: a woman who wears old-fashioned clothes that do not look attractive might have to be watched, out-maneuvered, rescued. And instead, it was Jenny who watched her mother, kept her out of drafts, made sure that she had taken her tonic...

Mrs. Ansley was much less articulate than her friend, and her mental portrait of Mrs. Slade was slighter, and drawn with fainter touches. " Alida Slade's awfully brilliant; but not as brilliant as she thinks," would have summed it up; though she would have added, for the enlightenment of strangers, that Mrs. Slade had been an extremely dashing girl; much more so than her daughrer, who was pretty, of course, and clever in a way, but had none of her mother's — well, " vividness," someone had once called it. Mrs. Ansley would take up current words like this, and cite them in quotation marks, as unheard-of audacities. No; Jenny was not like her mother. Sometimes Mrs. Ansley thought Alida Slade was disappointed; on the whole she had had a sad life. Full of failures and mistakes; Mrs. Ansley had always been rather sorry for her...

So these two ladies visualized each other, each through the wrong end of her little telescope.

II

For a long time they continued to sit side by side without speaking. It seemed as though, to both, there was a relief in laying down their somewhat futile activities in the presence of the vast Memento Mori which faced them. Mrs. Slade sat quite still, her eyes fixed on the golden slope of the Palace of the Caesars, and after a while Mrs. Ansley ceased to fidget with her bag, and she too sank into meditation. Like many intimate friends, the two ladies had never before had occasion to be silent together, and Mrs. Ansley was slightly embarrassed by what seemed, after so many years, a new stage in their intimacy, and one with which she did not yet know how to deal.

Suddenly the air was full of that deep clangor① of bells which periodically

① clangor: formal the continuous loud noise of something, especially something made of metal, being hit or rung covers Rome with a roof of silver. Mrs. Slade glanced at her wristwatch. " Five o'clock already," she said, as though surprised.

Mrs. Ansley suggested interrogatively: " There's bridge at the Embassy at five." For a long time Mrs. Slade did not answer. She appeared to be lost in contemplation, and Mrs. Ansley thought the remark had escaped her. But after a while she said, as if speaking out of a dream: " Bridge, did you say! Not unless you want to.... But I don't think I will, you know."

" Oh, no," Mrs. Ansley hastened to assure her. " I don't care to at all. It's so lovely here; and so full of old memories, as you say." She settled herself in her chair, and almost furtively drew forth her knitting. Mrs. Slade took sideways note of this activity, but her own beautifully cared-for hands remained motionless on her knee.

" I was just thinking," she said slowly, " what different things Rome stands for to each generation of travelers. To our grandmothers, Roman fever; to our mothers, sentimental dangers — how we used to be guarded! — to our daughters, no more dangers than the middle of Main Street. They don't know it — but how much they're missing!"

The long golden light was beginning to pale, and Mrs. Ansley lifted her knitting a little closer to her eyes. " Yes, how we were guarded"

" I always used to think," Mrs. Slade continued, " that our mothers had a much more difficult job than our grandmothers. When Roman fever stalked the streets it must have been comparatively easy to gather in the girls at the danger hour; but when you and I were young, with such beauty calling us, and the spice of disobedience thrown in, and no worse risk than catching cold during the cool hour after sunset, the mothers used to be put to it to keep us in — didn't they!"

She turned again toward Mrs. Ansley, but the latter had reached a delicate point in her knitting. " One, two, three — slip two; yes, they must have been," she assented, without looking up.

Mrs. Slade's eyes rested on her with a deepened attention. " She can knit — in the face of this! How like her. ..."

Mrs. Slade leaned back, brooding, her eyes ranging from the ruins which faced her to the long green hollow of the Forum, the fading glow of the church fronts beyond it, and the outlying immensity of the Colosseum. Suddenly she thought: " It's all very well to say that our girls have done away with sentiment and moonlight. But if Babs Ansley isn't out to catch that young aviator — the one who's a Marchese — then I don't know anything. And Jenny has no chance beside her. I know that too. I wonder if that's why Grace Ansley likes the two girls to go everywhere together! My poor Jenny as a foil — !" Mrs. Slade gave a hardly audible laugh, and at the sound Mrs. Ansley dropped her knitting.

" Yes — ?"

" I — oh, nothing. I was only thinking how your Babs carries everything before her. That Campolieri boy is one of the best matches in Rome. Don't look so innocent, my dear — you know he is. And I was wondering, ever so respectfully, you understand... wondering how two such exemplary characters as you and Horace had managed to produce anything quite so dynamic." Mrs. Slade laughed again, with a touch of asperity.①

Mrs. Ansley's hands lay inert across her needles. She looked straight out at the great accumulated wreckage of passion and splendor at her feet. But her small profile was almost expressionless. At length she said, " I think you overrate Babs, my dear."

Mrs. Slade's tone grew easier. " No; I don't. I appreciate her. And perhaps envy you. Oh, my girl's perfect; if I were a chronic invalid I'd — well, I think I'd rather be in Jenny's hands. There must be times... but there! I always wanted a brilliant daughter... and never quite understood why I got an angel instead."

Mrs. Ansley echoed her laugh in a faint murmur. " Babs is an angel too."

" Of course — of course! But she's got rainbow wings. Well, they're wandering

① asperity: the quality of being severe in the way that you speak and behave by the sea with their young men; and here we sit... and it all brings back the past a little too acutely[①] ."

Mrs. Ansley had resumed her knitting. One might almost have imagined (if one had known her less well, Mrs. Slade reflected) that, for her also, too many memories rose from the lengthening shadows of those august ruins. But no; she was simply absorbed in her work. What was there for her to worry about! She knew that Babs would almost certainly come back engaged to the extremely eligible Campolieri. " And she'll sell the New York house, and settle down near them in Rome, and never be in their way... she's much too tactful. But she'll have an excellent cook, and just the right people in for bridge and cocktails... and a perfectly peaceful old age among her grandchildren."

Mrs. Slade broke off this prophetic flight with a recoil of self-disgust. There was no one of whom she had less right to think unkindly than of Grace Ansley. Would she never cure herself of envying her! Perhaps she had begun too long ago.

She stood up and leaned against the parapet, filling her troubled eyes with the tranquilizing magic of the hour. But instead of tranquilizing her the sight seemed to increase her exasperation[②] . Her gaze turned toward the Colosseum. Already its golden flank was drowned in purple shadow, and above it the sky curved crystal clear, without light or color. It was the moment when afternoon and evening hang balanced in midheaven.

Mrs. Slade turned back and laid her hand on her friend's arm. The gesture was so abrupt that Mrs. Ansley looked up, startled.

" The sun's set. You're not afraid, my dear?"

" Afraid — ?"

" Of Roman fever or pneumonia! I remember how ill you were that winter. As a girl you had a very delicate throat, hadn't you?"

---

① acutely: completely or extremely

② exasperation: anger and displeasure

" Oh, we're all right up here. Down below, in the Forum, it does get deathly cold, all of a sudden... but not here."

" Ah, of course you know because you had to be so careful." Mrs. Slade turned back to the parapet. She thought: " I must make one more effort not to hate her." Aloud she said: " Whenever I look at the Forum from up here, I remember that story about a great-aunt of yours, wasn't she? A dreadfully wicked great-aunt?"

" Oh, yes; Great-aunt Harriet. The one who was supposed to have sent her young sister out to the Forum after sunset to gather a nightblooming flower for her album. All our great-aunts and grandmothers used to have albums of dried flowers."

Mrs. Slade nodded. " But she really sent her because they were in love with the same man — "

" Well, that was the family tradition. They said Aunt Harriet confessed it years afterward. At any rate, the poor little sister caught the fever and died. Mother used to frighten us with the story when we were children."

" And you frightened me with it, that winter when you and I were here as girls. The winter I was engaged to Delphin."

Mrs. Ansley gave a faint laugh. " Oh, did I! Really frightened you? I don't believe you're easily frightened."

" Not often; but I was then. I was easily frightened because I was too happy. I wonder if you know what that means?"

" I — yes... " Mrs. Ansley faltered.

" Well, I suppose that was why the story of your wicked aunt made such an impression on me. And I thought: 'There's no more Roman fever, but the Forum is deathly cold after sunset — especially after a hot day. And the Colosseum's even colder and damper.' "

" The Colosseum — ?"

" Yes. It wasn't easy to get in, after the gates were locked for the night. Far from easy. Still, in those days it could be managed; it was managed, often. Lovers met there who couldn't meet elsewhere. You knew that?"

"I — I daresay. I don't remember."

"You don't remember? You don't remember going to visit some ruins or other one evening, just after dark, and catching a bad chill! You were supposed to have gone to see the moonrise. People always said that expedition was what caused your illness."

There was a moment's silence; then Mrs. Ansley rejoined: "Did they? It was all so long ago."

"Yes. And you got well again — so it didn't matter. But I suppose it struck your friends — the reason given for your illness. I mean — because everybody knew you were so prudent on account of your throat, and your mother took such care of you... You had been out late sightseeing, hadn't you, that night"

"Perhaps I had. The most prudent girls aren't always prudent. What made you think of it now?"

Mrs. Slade seemed to have no answer ready. But after a moment she broke out: "Because I simply can't bear it any longer — "

Mrs. Ansley lifted her head quickly. Her eyes were wide and very pale. "Can't bear what?"

"Why — your not knowing that I've always known why you went."

"Why I went — ?"

"Yes. You think I'm bluffing,[①] don't you? Well, you went to meet the man I was engaged to — and I can repeat every word of the letter that took you there."

While Mrs. Slade spoke Mrs. Ansley had risen unsteadily to her feet. Her bag, her knitting and gloves, slid in a panic-stricken heap to the ground. She looked at Mrs. Slade as though she were looking at a ghost.

"No, no — don't," she faltered out.

---

① bluffing : Cheating and tricking

" Why not? Listen, if you don't believe me. 'My one darling, things can't go on like this. I must see you alone. Come to the Colosseum immediately after dark tomorrow. There will be somebody to let you in. No one whom you need fear will suspect' — but perhaps you've forgotten what the letter said?"

Mrs. Ansley met the challenge with an unexpected composure① . Steadying herself against the chair she looked at her friend, and replied: " No; I know it by heart too."

" And the signature? 'Only your D.S.' Was that it? I'm right, am I? That was the letter that took you out that evening after dark?"

Mrs. Ansley was still looking at her. It seemed to Mrs. Slade that a slow struggle was going on behind the voluntarily controlled mask of her small quiet face. " I shouldn't have thought she had herself so well in hand," Mrs. Slade reflected, almost resentfully. But at this moment Mrs. Ansley spoke. " I don't know how you knew. I burned that letter at once."

" Yes; you would, naturally — you're so prudent!" The sneer was open now. " And if you burned the letter you're wondering how on earth I know what was in it. That's it, isn't it?"

Mrs. Slade waited, but Mrs. Ansley did not speak.

" Well, my dear, I know what was in that letter because I wrote it!"

" You wrote it?"

" Yes."

The two women stood for a minute staring at each other in the last golden light. Then Mrs. Ansley dropped back into her chair. " Oh," she murmured, and covered her face with her hands.

Mrs. Slade waited nervously for another word or movement. None came, and at length she broke out: " I horrify you."

① composure: the feeling of being calm, confident, and in control

Mrs. Ansley's hands dropped to her knees. The face they uncovered was streaked with tears. " I wasn't thinking of you. I was thinking — it was the only letter I ever had from him!"

" And I wrote it. Yes; I wrote it! But I was the girl he was engaged to. Did you happen to remember that?"

Mrs. Ansley's head drooped again. " I'm not trying to excuse myself... I remembered... "

" And still you went?"

" Still I went."

Mrs. Slade stood looking down on the small bowed figure at her side. The flame of her wrath had already sunk, and she wondered why she had ever thought there would be any satisfaction in inflicting so purposeless a wound on her friend. But she had to justify herself.

" You do understand? I'd found out — and I hated you, hated you. I knew you were in love with Delphin — and I was afraid; afraid of you, of your quiet ways, your sweetness... your... well, I wanted you out of the way, that's all. Just for a few weeks; just till I was sure of him. So in a blind fury I wrote that letter... I don't know why I'm telling you now."

" I suppose," said Mrs. Ansley slowly, " it's because you've always gone on hating me."

" Perhaps. Or because I wanted to get the whole thing off my mind." She paused. " I'm glad you destroyed the letter. Of course I never thought you'd die."

Mrs. Ansley relapsed① into silence, and Mrs. Slade, leaning above her, was conscious of a strange sense of isolation, of being cut off from the warm current of human communion. " You think me a monster!"

" I don't know... It was the only letter I had, and you say he didn't write it"

① relapse: start behaving badly again, after making an improvement

" Ah, how you care for him still!"

" I cared for that memory," said Mrs. Ansley.

Mrs. Slade continued to look down on her. She seemed physically reduced by the blow — as if, when she got up, the wind might scatter her like a puff of dust. Mrs. Slade's jealousy suddenly leaped up again at the sight. All these years the woman had been living on that letter. How she must have loved him, to treasure the mere memory of its ashes! The letter of the man her friend was engaged to. Wasn't it she who was the monster?

" You tried your best to get him away from me, didn't you? But you failed; and I kept him. That's all."

" Yes. That's all."

" I wish now I hadn't told you. I'd no idea you'd feel about it as you do; I thought you'd be amused. It all happened so long ago, as you say; and you must do me the justice to remember that I had no reason to think you'd ever taken it seriously. How could I, when you were married to Horace Ansley two months afterward? As soon as you could get out of bed your mother rushed you off to Florence and married you. People were rather surprised — they wondered at its being done so quickly; but I thought I knew. I had an idea you did it out of pique① — to be able to say you'd got ahead of Delphin and me. Kids have such silly reasons for doing the most serious things. And your marrying so soon convinced me that you'd never really cared."

" Yes. I suppose it would," Mrs. Ansley assented.

The clear heaven overhead was emptied of all its gold. Dusk spread over it, abruptly darkening the Seven Hills. Here and there lights began to twinkle through the foliage at their feet. Steps were coming and going on the deserted terrace — waiters looking out of the doorway at the head of the stairs, then reappearing with trays and napkins and flasks of wine. Tables were moved, chairs straightened. A

---

① out of pique: a feeling of anger, especially caused by damage to your feeling of being proud of yourself feeble string of electric lights flickered out. A stout lady in a dustcoat suddenly appeared, asking in broken Italian if anyone had seen the elastic band which held together her tattered Baedeker. She poked with her stick under the table at which she had lunched, the waiters assisting.

The corner where Mrs. Slade and Mrs. Ansley sat was still shadowy and deserted. For a long time neither of them spoke. At length Mrs. Slade began again: " I suppose I did it as a sort of joke — "

" A joke?"

" Well, girls are ferocious① sometimes, you know. Girls in love especially. And I remember laughing to myself all that evening at the idea that you were waiting around there in the dark, dodging② out of sight, listening for every sound, trying to get in — of course I was upset when I heard you were so ill afterward."

Mrs. Ansley had not moved for a long time. But now she turned slowly toward her companion. " But I didn't wait. He'd arranged everything. He was there. We were let in at once," she said.

Mrs. Slade sprang up from her leaning position. " Delphin there! They let you in! Ah, now you're lying!" she burst out with violence.

Mrs. Ansley's voice grew clearer, and full of surprise. " But of course he was there. Naturally he came — "

" Came? How did he know he'd find you there? You must be raving!"

Mrs. Ansley hesitated, as though reflecting. " But I answered the letter. I told him I'd be there. So he came."

Mrs. Slade flung her hands up to her face. " Oh, God — you answered! I never thought of your answering..."

" It's odd you never thought of it, if you wrote the letter."

" Yes. I was blind with rage."

---

① ferocious: frightening and violent

② dodging: to avoid being hit by something by moving quickly to one side

Mrs. Ansley rose, and drew her fur scarf about her. " It is cold here. We'd better go... I'm sorry for you," she said, as she clasped the fur about her throat.

The unexpected words sent a pang through Mrs. Slade. " Yes; we'd better go." She gathered up her bag and cloak. " I don't know why you should be sorry for me," she muttered.

Mrs. Ansley stood looking away from her toward the dusky mass of the Colosseum. " Well — because I didn't have to wait that night."

Mrs. Slade gave an unquiet laugh. " Yes, I was beaten there. But I oughtn't to begrudge it to you, I suppose. At the end of all these years. After all, I had everything; I had him for twenty-five years. And you had nothing but that one letter that he didn't write."

Mrs. Ansley was again silent. At length she took a step toward the door of the terrace, and turned back, facing her companion.

" I had Barbara," she said, and began to move ahead of Mrs. Slade toward the stairway.

Topics for discussion

1. Although " Roman Fever" was written in the 1930s, it is set in the mid-1920. Which decade does the story more accurately reflect?

2. How would you assess " Roman Fever" in terms of artistic composition and message?

3. Conduct research on the Roman ruins mentioned in the story. What role do you think their history and presence have in the unfolding drama?

4. Read one of Edith Wharton's novels, such as the *The House of Mirth and The Age of Innocence*. How do the characters and the social framework in the novel compare to those in " Roman Fever"?

References for further reading

[1] Bloom, Harold. ed. *Edith Wharton*. New York: Chelsea House, 1986.

[2] Dwight, Eleanor. *Edith Wharton, An Extraordinary Life*. New York: Harry N. Abrams, 1994.

[3] Lewis. R. W. B. *Edith Wharton, A Biography*. New York: Harper & Row, 1975.

[4] McDowell, Margaret B. *Edith Wharton*. Boston: Twayne Publishers, 1991.

[5] Nevius, Black. *Edith Wharton, A Study of Her Fiction*. Berkeley: University of Californian Press, 1953.

Jack London (1876 — 1916)

To Build a Fire

Introduction to the author

John Griffith " Jack" London (January 12, 1876 — November 22, 1916) was an American novelist, journalist, short story writer and social activist. His works reflect American Realism and Naturalism. London was born in San Francisco, California to Flora Wellman and William Chaney. He was the illegitimate son of a father who was a wandering astrologer and a mother who was a spiritualist and medium. He took his surname from his stepfather, John London. The family settled in Oakland, California. London was essentially self-educated. London quit school when he was 14 years ago and took different jobs including a longshoreman, a seaman, or a worker in cannery. After many experiences as a hobo and a sailor, he returned to Oakland and attended Oakland High School. He became of a member of the Socialist Labor Party and studied at University of California, Berkeley, for a short time, but quit school due to lack of money.

London married Elizabeth " Bessie" Maddern in 1900, but divorced later.

London married Charmian Kittredge in 1905. Many of London's stories are based on his visits to Hawaii with his wife. *The Kempton-Wace Letters*, co-authored with Anna Strunsky is an epistolary novel contrasting two philosophies of love — the " Mother Woman" and the " Mate Woman". During his lifetime, London also wrote novels and stories about his political beliefs and his journeys in the South Seas. He published his autobiography. He married twice and had two daughters by his first wife. London's last years were marked by struggles with alcoholism and mental disintegration and he suffered from dysentery, uremia, and late stage alcoholism. He died November 22, 1916 at the age of forty from uremia and an overdose of morphine.

His novel *The Son of the Wolf* brought him fame, which describes the life in the wilds of Alaska and northwestern Canada. *The Call of the Wild and White Fang*, the two novels of man and beast struggling against the tremendous forces of nature, made London well-known internationally. His dystopian novel *The Iron Heel, The People of the Abyss*, and *The War of the Classes* concern the themes of unionization, socialism, and the rights of workers. London absorbed Darwinism that man must adapt to irresistible natural forces to survive. He also borrowed from Nietzsche the idea of the super human beings, from Marx the idea of need for social reform and of the power of economic determinism.

On London's religious views, he was an atheist. He was also a socialist and his viewpoint is reflected in his novel *The Iron Heel*. London joined the Socialist Labor Party in 1896 but he left the Party in 1901 and joined the new Socialist Party of America. His two collections of essays — *The War of the Classes* (1905) and *Revolution, and other Essays* (1906), are about socialism. In " the yellow peril" and " The Unparalleled Invasion", London concerns races, particularly, Asian immigration. His short stories portrayed many characters such as Mexican (" The Mexican"), Asian (" The Chinago"), and Hawaiian (" Koolau the Leper").

Major works by Jack London

Novels

The Son of the Wolf, 1900

The Call of the Wild, 1903

The People of the Abyss, 1903

The Sea Wolf, 1904

The War of the Classes, 1905

White Fang, 1906

Before Adam, 1907

The Iron Heel, 1908

Martin Eden, 1909

Lost Face, 1910

Burning Daylight, 1910

Revolution, and other Essays, 1910

South Sea Tales, 1911

John Barleycorn, 1913

The Abysmal Brute, 1913

Jerry of the Islands, 1917

The Human Drift, 1917

Short stories

" To Build a Firc"

" All Gold Canyon"

" The Law of Life"

" Love of Life"

" To the Man on Trail"

" An Odyssey of the North"

" A Piece of Steak"

" The Mexican"

Appreciation

" To Build a Fire", which is regarded as American classic, is about an unnamed man's disastrous trek across the Yukon Territory near Alaska. The tale is based on London's own travels across the harsh, frozen terrain of Alaska and Canada in 1897 — 1898 during the Klondike gold rush. It portrays the conflict of man and nature.

The story begins on winter morning as an unnamed man leaves the Yukon Trail accompanied by a big wolf dog. The cold weather freezes his mouth shut, so that he has to build a fire to thaw out to eat lunch, but the fire is extinguished by the snow from a tree. His fingers are frozen too numbed to light a match. The fire started by holding his matches with the heels of his hands burn his flesh. In order to keep him alive, he runs toward his destination, hoping that the running can warm his body. But he can lose the sense of his feet and falls down. At last, he dies from hypothermia.

London describes precisely the brutal coldness and unforgiving landscape of the Northland. The protagonist struggles to save himself from freezing to death, but experiencing a series of mishaps, he meets with failure finally. The story concerns such themes as fear, death, and the individual versus nature. In the story, human being becomes subject to the laws of nature and they are controlled by their environment.

Selected Reading

To Build A Fire

He travels fastest who travels alone...but not after the frost has dropped below zero fifty degrees or more.

— Yukon Code.

Day had broken cold and gray, exceedingly cold and gray, when the man turned aside from the main Yukon trail and climbed the high earth-bank, where a dim and little-travelled trail led eastward through the fat spruce timberland. It was a steep bank, and he paused for breath at the top, excusing the act to himself by looking at his watch. It was nine o'clock. There was no sun nor hint of sun, though there was not a cloud in the sky. It was a clear day, and yet there seemed an intangible pall over the face of things, a subtle gloom that made the day dark, and that was due to the absence of sun. This fact did not worry the man. He was used to the lack of sun. It had been days since he had seen the sun, and he knew that a few more days must pass before that cheerful orb, due south, would just peep above the sky-line and dip immediately from view.

The man flung a look back along the way he had come. The Yukon lay a mile wide and hidden under three feet of ice. On top of this ice were as many feet of snow. It was all pure white, rolling in gentle undulations① where the ice-jams of the freeze-up had formed. North and south, as far as his eye could see, it was unbroken white, save for a dark hair-line that curved and twisted from around the spruce-covered island to the south, and that curved and twisted away into the north, where it disappeared behind another spruce-covered island. This dark hair-line was the trail — the main trail — that led south five hundred miles to the Chilcoot Pass② , Dyea③ , and salt water; and that led north seventy miles to Dawson, and still on to the north a thousand miles to Nulato④ , and finally to St. Michael on Bering Sea, a thousand miles and half a thousand more.

But all this — the mysterious, far-reaching hair-line trail, the absence of sun from the sky, the tremendous cold, and the strangeness and weirdness of it all — made no impression on the man. It was not because he was long used to it. He was a newcomer in the land, a *chechaquo*⑤ , and this was his first winter. The trouble with him was that he was without imagination. He was quick and alert in the things of life, but only in the things, and not in the significances. Fifty degrees below zero meant eighty-odd degrees of frost. Such fact impressed him as being cold and

① undulation: bending, twisting and curving state

② Chilkoot Pass: a high mountain pass through the Boundary Ranges of the Coast Mountains in the U.S. state of Alaska and British Columbia, Canada. It is the highest point along the Chilkoot Trail that leads from Dyea, Alaska to Bennett Lake, British Columbia. The Chilkoot Trail was long a route used by the Tlingit for trade.

③ Dyea: a former town in the U.S. state of Alaska. A few people live on individual small homesteads in the valley, however, it is largely abandoned

④ Nulato: a city in Yukon-Koyukuk Census Area, Alaska, United States

⑤ chechaquo: a Chinook jargon word meaning " newcomer"

uncomfortable, and that was all. It did not lead him to meditate upon his frailty as a creature of temperature, and upon man's frailty in general, able only to live within certain narrow limits of heat and cold; and from there on it did not lead him to the conjectural field of immortality and man's place in the universe. Fifty degrees below zero stood for a bite of frost that hurt and that must be guarded against by the use of mittens, ear-flaps, warm moccasins, and thick socks. Fifty degrees below zero was to him just precisely fifty degrees below zero. That there should be anything more to it than that was a thought that never entered his head.

As he turned to go on, he spat speculatively. There was a sharp, explosive crackle that startled him. He spat again. And again, in the air, before it could fall to the snow, the spittle crackled. He knew that at fifty below spittle crackled on the snow, but this spittle had crackled in the air. Undoubtedly it was colder than fifty below — how much colder he did not know. But the temperature did not matter. He was bound for the old claim on the left fork of Henderson Creek, where the boys were already. They had come over across the divide from the Indian Creek country, while he had come the roundabout way to take a look at the possibilities of getting out logs in the spring from the islands in the Yukon. He would be in to camp by six o'clock; a bit after dark, it was true, but the boys would be there, a fire would be going, and a hot supper would be ready. As for lunch, he pressed his hand against the protruding bundle under his jacket. It was also under his shirt, wrapped up in a handkerchief and lying against the naked skin. It was the only way to keep the biscuits from freezing. He smiled agreeably to himself as he thought of those biscuits, each cut open and sopped in bacon grease, and each enclosing a generous slice of fried bacon.

He plunged in among the big spruce trees. The trail was faint. A foot of snow had fallen since the last sled had passed over, and he was glad he was without a sled, travelling light. In fact, he carried nothing but the lunch wrapped in the handkerchief. He was surprised, however, at the cold. It certainly was cold, he concluded, as he rubbed his numb nose and cheek-bones with his mittened hand. He was a warm-whiskered man, but the hair on his face did not protect the high cheek-bones and the eager nose that thrust itself aggressively into the frosty air.

At the man's heels trotted a dog, a big native husky, the proper wolf-dog, gray-coated and without any visible or temperamental difference from its brother, the wild wolf. The animal was depressed by the tremendous cold. It knew that it was no time for travelling. Its instinct told it a truer tale than was told to the man by the man's judgment. In reality, it was not merely colder than fifty below zero; it was colder than sixty below, than seventy below. It was seventy-five below zero. Since the freezing-point is thirty-two above zero, it meant that one hundred and seven degrees of frost obtained. The dog did not know anything about thermometers. Possibly in its brain there was no sharp consciousness of a condition of very cold such as was in the man's brain. But the brute had its instinct. It experienced a vague but menacing apprehension that subdued it and made it slink along at the man's heels, and that made it question eagerly every unwonted① movement of the man as if expecting him to go into camp or to seek shelter somewhere and build a fire. The dog had learned fire, and it wanted fire, or else to burrow under the snow and cuddle its warmth away from the air.

The frozen moisture of its breathing had settled on its fur in a fine powder of frost, and especially were its jowls, muzzle, and eyelashes whitened by its crystalled breath. The man's red beard and mustache were likewise frosted, but more solidly, the deposit taking the form of ice and increasing with every warm, moist breath he exhaled. Also, the man was chewing tobacco, and the muzzle of ice held his lips so rigidly that he was unable to clear his chin when he expelled the juice. The result was that a crystal beard of the color and solidity of amber was increasing its length on his chin. If he fell down it would shatter itself, like glass, into brittle fragments. But he did not mind the appendage. It was the penalty all tobacco-chewers paid in that

① unwonted: unusual; not often experienced or shown

country, and he had been out before in two cold snaps. They had not been so cold as this, he knew, but by the spirit thermometer at Sixty Mile he knew they had been registered at fifty below and at fifty-five.

He held on through the level stretch of woods for several miles, crossed a wide flat of niggerheads, and dropped down a bank to the frozen bed of a small stream. This was Henderson Creek, and he knew he was ten miles from the forks. He looked at his watch. It was ten o'clock. He was making four miles an hour, and he calculated that he would arrive at the forks at half-past twelve. He decided to celebrate that event by eating his lunch there.

The dog dropped in again at his heels, with a tail drooping discouragement, as the man swung along the creek-bed. The furrow of the old sled-trail was plainly visible, but a dozen inches of snow covered the marks of the last runners. In a month no man had come up or down that silent creek. The man held steadily on. He was not much given to thinking, and just then particularly he had nothing to think about save that he would eat lunch at the forks and that at six o'clock he would be in camp with the boys. There was nobody to talk to; and, had there been, speech would have been impossible because of the ice-muzzle on his mouth. So he continued monotonously to chew tobacco and to increase the length of his amber beard.

Once in a while the thought reiterated itself that it was very cold and that he had never experienced such cold. As he walked along he rubbed his cheek-bones and nose with the back of his mittened hand. He did this automatically, now and again changing hands. But rub as he would, the instant he stopped his cheek-bones went numb, and the following instant the end of his nose went numb. He was sure to frost his cheeks; he knew that, and experienced a pang of regret that he had not devised a nose-strap of the sort Bud wore in cold snaps. Such a strap passed across the cheeks, as well, and saved them. But it didn't matter much, after all. What were frosted cheeks? A bit painful, that was all; they were never serious.

Empty as the man's mind was of thoughts, he was keenly observant, and he noticed the changes in the creek, the curves and bends and timber jams, and always he sharply noted where he placed his feet. Once, coming around a bend, he shied abruptly, like a startled horse, curved away from the place where he had been walking, and retreated several paces back along the trail. The creek he knew was frozen clear to the bottom, — no creek could contain water in that arctic winter, — but he knew also that there were springs that bubbled out from the hillsides and ran along under the snow and on top the ice of the creek. He knew that the coldest snaps never froze these springs, and he knew likewise their danger. They were traps. They hid pools of water under the snow that might be three inches deep, or three feet. Sometimes a skin of ice half an inch thick covered them, and in turn was covered by the snow. Sometimes there were alternate layers of water and ice-skin, so that when one broke through he kept on breaking through for a while, sometimes wetting himself to the waist.

That was why he had shied in such panic. He had felt the give under his feet and heard the crackle of a snow-hidden ice-skin. And to get his feet wet in such a temperature meant trouble and danger. At the very least it meant delay, for he would be forced to stop and build a fire, and under its protection to bare his feet while he dried his socks and moccasins① . He stood and studied the creek-bed and its banks, and decided that the flow of water came from the right. He reflected awhile, rubbing his nose and cheeks, then skirted to the left, stepping gingerly② and testing the footing for each step. Once clear of the danger, he took a fresh chew of tobacco and swung along at his four-mile gait. In the course of the next two hours he came upon several similar traps. Usually the snow above the hidden pools had a sunken, candied appearance that advertised the danger. Once again, however, he had a close call; and once, suspecting danger, he compelled the dog to go on in front. The dog did not want to go. It hung back until the man shoved it forward, and then it went quickly across

① moccasin: a light shoe made completely of soft leather and having stitches around the top

② gingerly: carefully or cautiously

the white, unbroken surface. Suddenly it broke through, floundered to one side, and got away to firmer footing. It had wet its forefeet and legs, and almost immediately the water that clung to it turned to ice. It made quick efforts to lick the ice off its legs, then dropped down in the snow and began to bite out the ice that had formed between the toes. This was a matter of instinct. To permit the ice to remain would mean sore feet. It did not know this. It merely obeyed the mysterious prompting that arose from the deep crypts of its being. But the man knew, having achieved a judgment on the subject, and he removed the mitten from his right hand and helped tear out the ice-particles. He did not expose his fingers more than a minute, and was astonished at the swift numbness that smote them. It certainly was cold. He pulled on the mitten hastily, and beat the hand savagely across his chest.

At twelve o'clock the day was at its brightest. Yet the sun was too far south on its winter journey to clear the horizon. The bulge of the earth intervened between it and Henderson Creek, where the man walked under a clear sky at noon and cast no shadow. At half-past twelve, to the minute, he arrived at the forks of the creek. He was pleased at the speed he had made. If he kept it up, he would certainly be with the boys by six. He unbuttoned his jacket and shirt and drew forth his lunch. The action consumed no more than a quarter of a minute, yet in that brief moment the numbness laid hold of the exposed fingers. He did not put the mitten on, but, instead, struck the fingers a dozen sharp smashes against his leg. Then he sat down on a snow-covered log to eat. The sting that followed upon the striking of his fingers against his leg ceased so quickly that he was startled. He had had no chance to take a bite of biscuit. He struck the fingers repeatedly and returned them to the mitten, baring the other hand for the purpose of eating. He tried to take a mouthful, but the ice-muzzle prevented. He had forgotten to build a fire and thaw out. He chuckled at his foolishness, and as he chuckled he noted the numbness creeping into the exposed fingers. Also, he noted that the stinging which had first come to his toes when he sat down was already passing away. He wondered whether the toes were warm or numb.

He moved them inside the moccasins and decided that they were numb.

He pulled the mitten on hurriedly and stood up. He was a bit frightened. He stamped up and down until the stinging returned into the feet. It certainly was cold, was his thought. That man from Sulphur Creek had spoken the truth when telling how cold it sometimes got in the country. And he had laughed at him at the time! That showed one must not be too sure of things. There was no mistake about it, it was cold. He strode up and down, stamping his feet and threshing① his arms, until reassured by the returning warmth. Then he got out matches and proceeded to make a fire. From the undergrowth, where high water of the previous spring had lodged a supply of seasoned twigs, he got his fire-wood. Working carefully from a small beginning, he soon had a roaring fire, over which he thawed the ice from his face and in the protection of which he ate his biscuits. For the moment the cold of space was outwitted. The dog took satisfaction in the fire, stretching out close enough for warmth and far enough away to escape being singed.

When the man had finished, he filled his pipe and took his comfortable time over a smoke. Then he pulled on his mittens, settled the ear-flaps② of his cap firmly about his ears, and took the creek trail up the left fork. The dog was disappointed and yearned back toward the fire. This man did not know cold. Possibly all the generations of his ancestry had been ignorant of cold, of real cold, of cold one hundred and seven degrees below freezing-point. But the dog knew; all its ancestry knew, and it had inherited the knowledge. And it knew that it was not good to walk abroad in such fearful cold. It was the time to lie snug in a hole in the snow and wait for a curtain of cloud to be drawn across the face of outer space whence this cold came. On the other hand, there was no keen intimacy between the dog and the man.

---

① thresh: to remove the seeds of crop plants by hitting them, using either a machine or a hand tool

② ear–flap: one of the two pieces of material or fur on some hats that can be pulled down to cover the ears

The one was the toil-slave of the other, and the only caresses it had ever received were the caresses of the whip-lash and of harsh and menacing throat-sounds that threatened the whip-lash. So the dog made no effort to communicate its apprehension to the man. It was not concerned in the welfare of the man; it was for its own sake that it yearned back toward the fire. But the man whistled, and spoke to it with the sound of whip-lashes, and the dog swung in at the man's heels and followed after.

The man took a chew of tobacco and proceeded to start a new amber beard. Also, his moist breath quickly powdered with white his mustache, eyebrows, and lashes. There did not seem to be so many springs on the left fork of the Henderson, and for half an hour the man saw no signs of any. And then it happened. At a place where there were no signs, where the soft, unbroken snow seemed to advertise solidity beneath, the man broke through. It was not deep. He wet himself halfway to the knees before he floundered out to the firm crust.

He was angry, and cursed his luck aloud. He had hoped to get into camp with the boys at six o'clock, and this would delay him an hour, for he would have to build a fire and dry out his foot-gear. This was imperative at that low temperature — he knew that much; and he turned aside to the bank, which he climbed. On top, tangled in the underbrush about the trunks of several small spruce trees, was a high-water deposit of dry fire-wood — sticks and twigs, principally, but also larger portions of seasoned branches and fine, dry, last-year's grasses. He threw down several large pieces on top of the snow. This served for a foundation and prevented the young flame from drowning itself in the snow it otherwise would melt. The flame he got by touching a match to a small shred of birch-bark that he took from his pocket. This burned even more readily than paper. Placing it on the foundation, he fed the young flame with wisps of dry grass and with the tiniest dry twigs.

He worked slowly and carefully, keenly aware of his danger. Gradually, as the flame grew stronger, he increased the size of the twigs with which he fed it. He squatted in the snow, pulling the twigs out from their entanglement in the brush and feeding directly to the flame. He knew there must be no failure. When it is seventy-five below zero, a man must not fail in his first attempt to build a fire — that is, if his feet are wet. If his feet are dry, and he fails, he can run along the trail for half a mile and restore his circulation. But the circulation of wet and freezing feet cannot be restored by running when it is seventy-five below. No matter how fast he runs, the wet feet will freeze the harder.

All this the man knew. The old-timer on Sulphur Creek had told him about it the previous fall, and now he was appreciating the advice. Already all sensation had gone out of his feet. To build the fire he had been forced to remove his mittens, and the fingers had quickly gone numb. His pace of four miles an hour had kept his heart pumping blood to the surface of his body and to all the extremities. But the instant he stopped, the action of the pump eased down. The cold of space smote the unprotected tip of the planet, and he, being on that unprotected tip, received the full force of the blow. The blood of his body recoiled before it. The blood was alive, like the dog, and like the dog it wanted to hide away and cover itself up from the fearful cold. So long as he walked four miles an hour, he pumped that blood, willy-nilly[①] , to the surface; but now it ebbed away and sank down into the recesses of his body. The extremities were the first to feel its absence. His wet feet froze the faster, and his exposed fingers numbed the faster, though they had not yet begun to freeze. Nose and cheeks were already freezing, while the skin of all his body chilled as it lost its blood.

But he was safe. Toes and nose and cheeks would be only touched by the frost, for the fire was beginning to burn with strength. He was feeding it with twigs the size of his finger. In another minute he would be able to feed it with branches the size of his wrist, and then he could remove his wet foot-gear, and, while it dried, he could keep his naked feet warm by the fire, rubbing them at first, of course, with snow. The fire was a success. He was safe. He remembered the advice of the old-timer on

① willy–nilly: Being or occurring whether desired or not

Sulphur Creek, and smiled. The old-timer had been very serious in laying down the law that no man must travel alone in the Klondike after fifty below. Well, here he was; he had had the accident; he was alone; and he had saved himself. Those old-timers were rather womanish, some of them, he thought. All a man had to do was to keep his head, and he was all right. Any man who was a man could travel alone. But it was surprising, the rapidity with which his cheeks and nose were freezing. And he had not thought his fingers could go lifeless in so short a time. Lifeless they were, for he could scarcely make them move together to grip a twig, and they seemed remote from his body and from him. When he touched a twig, he had to look and see whether or not he had hold of it. The wires were pretty well down between him and his finger-ends.

All of which counted for little. There was the fire, snapping and crackling and promising life with every dancing flame. He started to untie his moccasins. They were coated with ice; the thick German socks were like sheaths of iron halfway to the knees; and the moccasin strings were like rods of steel all twisted and knotted as by some conflagration① . For a moment he tugged with his numb fingers, then, realizing the folly of it, he drew his sheath-knife.

But before he could cut the strings, it happened. It was his own fault or, rather, his mistake. He should not have built the fire under the spruce tree. He should have built it in the open. But it had been easier to pull the twigs from the brush and drop them directly on the fire. Now the tree under which he had done this carried a weight of snow on its boughs. No wind had blown for weeks, and each bough was fully freighted. Each time he had pulled a twig he had communicated a slight agitation② to the tree — an imperceptible agitation, so far as he was concerned, but an agitation sufficient to bring about the disaster. High up in the tree one bough capsized③

① conflagration: a large fire that causes a lot of damage
② agitation: worry and anxiety
③ capsize: turn upside down

its load of snow. This fell on the boughs beneath, capsizing them. This process continued, spreading out and involving the whole tree. It grew like an avalanche, and it descended without warning upon the man and the fire, and the fire was blotted out! Where it had burned was a mantle of fresh and disordered snow.

The man was shocked. It was as though he had just heard his own sentence of death. For a moment he sat and stared at the spot where the fire had been. Then he grew very calm. Perhaps the old-timer on Sulphur Creek was right. If he had only had a trail-mate he would have been in no danger now. The trail-mate could have built the fire. Well, it was up to him to build the fire over again, and this second time there must be no failure. Even if he succeeded, he would most likely lose some toes. His feet must be badly frozen by now, and there would be some time before the second fire was ready.

Such were his thoughts, but he did not sit and think them. He was busy all the time they were passing through his mind. He made a new foundation for a fire, this time in the open, where no treacherous tree could blot it out. Next, he gathered dry grasses and tiny twigs from the high-water flotsam. He could not bring his fingers together to pull them out, but he was able to gather them by the handful. In this way he got many rotten twigs and bits of green moss that were undesirable, but it was the best he could do. He worked methodically, even collecting an armful of the larger branches to be used later when the fire gathered strength. And all the while the dog sat and watched him, a certain yearning wistfulness in its eyes, for it looked upon him as the fire-provider, and the fire was slow in coming.

When all was ready, the man reached in his pocket for a second piece of birch-bark. He knew the bark was there, and, though he could not feel it with his fingers, he could hear its crisp rustling as he fumbled for it. Try as he would, he could not clutch hold of it. And all the time, in his consciousness, was the knowledge that each instant his feet were freezing. This thought tended to put him in a panic, but he fought against it and kept calm. He pulled on his mittens with his teeth, and threshed his arms back and forth, beating his hands with all his might against his sides. He did this sitting down, and he stood up to do it; and all the while the dog sat in the snow, its wolf-brush of a tail curled around warmly over its forefeet, its sharp wolf-ears pricked forward intently as it watched the man. And the man, as he beat and threshed with his arms and hands, felt a great surge of envy as he regarded the creature that was warm and secure in its natural covering.

After a time he was aware of the first faraway signals of sensation in his beaten fingers. The faint tingling grew stronger till it evolved into a stinging ache that was excruciating①, but which the man hailed with satisfaction. He stripped the mitten from his right hand and fetched forth the birch-bark. The exposed fingers were quickly going numb again. Next he brought out his bunch of sulphur matches. But the tremendous cold had already driven the life out of his fingers. In his effort to separate one match from the others, the whole bunch fell in the snow. He tried to pick it out of the snow, but failed. The dead fingers could neither touch nor clutch. He was very careful. He drove the thought of his freezing feet, and nose, and cheeks, out of his mind, devoting his whole soul to the matches. He watched, using the sense of vision in place of that of touch, and when he saw his fingers on each side the bunch, he closed them — that is, he willed to close them, for the wires were down, and the fingers did not obey. He pulled the mitten on the right hand, and beat it fiercely against his knee. Then, with both mittened hands, he scooped the bunch of matches, along with much snow, into his lap. Yet he was no better off.

After some manipulation he managed to get the bunch between the heels of his mittened hands. In this fashion he carried it to his mouth. The ice crackled and snapped when by a violent effort he opened his mouth. He drew the lower jaw in, curled the upper lip out of the way, and scraped the bunch with his upper teeth in order to separate a match. He succeeded in getting one, which he dropped on his

① excruciating: (of pain) extremely strong

lap. He was no better off. He could not pick it up. Then he devised a way. He picked it up in his teeth and scratched it on his leg. Twenty times he scratched before he succeeded in lighting it. As it flamed he held it with his teeth to the birch-bark. But the burning brimstone went up his nostrils and into his lungs, causing him to cough spasmodically. The match fell into the snow and went out.

The old-timer on Sulphur Creek was right, he thought in the moment of controlled despair that ensued: after fifty below, a man should travel with a partner. He beat his hands, but failed in exciting any sensation. Suddenly he bared both hands, removing the mittens with his teeth. He caught the whole bunch between the heels of his hands. His arm-muscles not being frozen enabled him to press the hand-heels tightly against the matches. Then he scratched the bunch along his leg. It flared into flame, seventy sulphur matches at once! There was no wind to blow them out. He kept his head to one side to escape the strangling① fumes② , and held the blazing bunch to the birch-bark. As he so held it, he became aware of sensation in his hand. His flesh was burning. He could smell it. Deep down below the surface he could feel it. The sensation developed into pain that grew acute. And still he endured it, holding the flame of the matches clumsily to the bark that would not light readily because his own burning hands were in the way, absorbing most of the flame.

At last, when he could endure no more, he jerked his hands apart. The blazing matches fell sizzling③ into the snow, but the birch-bark was alight. He began laying dry grasses and the tiniest twigs on the flame. He could not pick and choose, for he had to lift the fuel between the heels of his hands. Small pieces of rotten wood and green moss clung to the twigs, and he bit them off as well as he could with his teeth. He cherished the flame carefully and awkwardly. It meant life, and it must not perish. The withdrawal of blood from the surface of his body now made him begin

① strangling: killing someone by pressing their throat so that they cannot breathe

② fume: strong and thick smoke

③ sizzling: making a sound like food cooking in hot fat

to shiver, and he grew more awkward. A large piece of green moss fell squarely on the little fire. He tried to poke it out with his fingers, but his shivering frame made him poke too far, and he disrupted the nucleus of the little fire, the burning grasses and tiny twigs separating and scattering. He tried to poke them together again, but in spite of the tenseness of the effort, his shivering got away with him, and the twigs were hopelessly scattered. Each twig gushed a puff of smoke and went out. The fire-provider had failed. As he looked apathetically about him, his eyes chanced on the dog, sitting across the ruins of the fire from him, in the snow, making restless, hunching movements, slightly lifting one forefoot and then the other, shifting its weight back and forth on them with wistful eagerness.

The sight of the dog put a wild idea into his head. He remembered the tale of the man, caught in a blizzard[①], who killed a steer and crawled inside the carcass, and so was saved. He would kill the dog and bury his hands in the warm body until the numbness went out of them. Then he could build another fire. He spoke to the dog, calling it to him; but in his voice was a strange note of fear that frightened the animal, who had never known the man to speak in such way before. Something was the matter, and its suspicious nature sensed danger — it knew not what danger, but somewhere, somehow, in its brain arose an apprehension of the man. It flattened its ears down at the sound of the man's voice, and its restless, hunching movements and the liftings and shiftings of its forefeet became more pronounced; but it would not come to the man. He got on his hands and knees and crawled toward the dog. This unusual posture again excited suspicion, and the animal sidled mincingly away.

The man sat up in the snow for a moment and struggled for calmness. Then he pulled on his mittens, by means of his teeth, and got upon his feet. He glanced down at first in order to assure himself that he was really standing up, for the absence of sensation in his feet left him unrelated to the earth. His erect position in itself started

① blizzard: a severe snow storm with strong winds

to drive the webs of suspicion from the dog's mind; and when he spoke peremptorily, with the sound of whip-lashes in his voice, the dog rendered its customary allegiance and came to him. As it came within reaching distance, the man lost his control. His arms flashed out to the dog, and he experienced genuine surprise when he discovered that his hands could not clutch, that there was neither bend nor feeling in the fingers. He had forgotten for the moment that they were frozen and that they were freezing more and more. All this happened quickly, and before the animal could get away, he encircled its body with his arms. He sat down in the snow, and in this fashion held the dog, while it snarled and whined and struggled.

But it was all he could do, hold its body encircled in his arms and sit there. He realized that he could not kill the dog. There was no way to do it. With his helpless hands he could neither draw nor hold his sheath-knife nor throttle the animal. He released it, and it plunged wildly away, with tail between its legs, and still snarling. It halted forty feet away and surveyed him curiously, with ears sharply pricked forward. The man looked down at his hands in order to locate them, and found them hanging on the ends of his arms. It struck him as curious that one should have to use his eyes in order to find out where his hands were. He began threshing his arms back and forth, beating the mittened hands against his sides. He did this for five minutes, violently, and his heart pumped enough blood up to the surface to put a stop to his shivering. But no sensation was aroused in the hands. He had an impression that they hung like weights on the ends of his arms, but when he tried to run the impression down, he could not find it.

A certain fear of death, dull and oppressive, came to him. This fear quickly became poignant① as he realized that it was no longer a mere matter of freezing his fingers and toes, or of losing his hands and feet, but that it was a matter of life and death with the chances against him. This threw him into a panic, and he turned and

① poignant: saddening, shocking and upsetting

ran up the creek-bed along the old, dim trail. The dog joined in behind and kept up with him. He ran blindly, without intention, in fear such as he had never known in his life. Slowly, as he ploughed and floundered through the snow, he began to see things again, — the banks of the creek, the old timber-jams, the leafless aspens, and the sky. The running made him feel better. He did not shiver. Maybe, if he ran on, his feet would thaw out; and, anyway, if he ran far enough, he would reach camp and the boys. Without doubt he would lose some fingers and toes and some of his face; but the boys would take care of him, and save the rest of him when he got there. And at the same time there was another thought in his mind that said he would never get to the camp and the boys; that it was too many miles away, that the freezing had too great a start on him, and that he would soon be stiff and dead. This thought he kept in the background and refused to consider. Sometimes it pushed itself forward and demanded to be heard, but he thrust it back and strove to think of other things.

It struck him as curious that he could run at all on feet so frozen that he could not feel them when they struck the earth and took the weight of his body. He seemed to himself to skim along above the surface, and to have no connection with the earth. Somewhere he had once seen a winged Mercury① , and he wondered if Mercury felt as he felt when skimming over the earth.

His theory of running until he reached camp and the boys had one flaw in it; he lacked the endurance. Several times he stumbled, and finally he tottered, crumpled up, and fell. When he tried to rise, he failed. He must sit and rest, he decided, and next time he would merely walk and keep on going. As he sat and regained his breath, he noted that he was feeling quite warm and comfortable. He was not shivering, and it even seemed that a warm glow had come to his chest and trunk. And yet, when he

---

① Mercury : refer to Mercurius, a major Roman god, the patron god of financial gain, commerce, eloquence (and thus poetry), messages/communication (including divination), travelers, boundaries, luck, trickery and thieves; guide of souls to the underworld; the son of Maia and Jupiter in Roman mythology touched his nose or cheeks, there was no sensation. Running would not thaw them out. Nor would it thaw out his hands and feet. Then the thought came to him that the frozen portions of his body must be extending. He tried to keep this thought down, to forget it, to think of something else; he was aware of the panicky feeling that it caused, and he was afraid of the panic. But the thought asserted itself, and persisted, until it produced a vision of his body totally frozen. This was too much, and he made another wild run along the trail. Once he slowed down to a walk, but the thought of the freezing extending itself made him run again.

And all the time the dog ran with him, at his heels. When he fell down a second time, it curled its tail over its forefeet and sat in front of him, facing him, curiously eager and intent. The warmth and security of the animal angered him, and he cursed it till it flattened down its ears appeasingly. This time the shivering came more quickly upon the man. He was losing in his battle with the frost. It was creeping into his body from all sides. The thought of it drove him on, but he ran no more than a hundred feet, when he staggered and pitched headlong. It was his last panic. When he had recovered his breath and control, he sat up and entertained in his mind the conception of meeting death with dignity. However, the conception did not come to him in such terms. His idea of it was that he had been making a fool of himself, running around like a chicken with its head cut off — such was the simile that occurred to him. Well, he was bound to freeze anyway, and he might as well take it decently. With this new-found peace of mind came the first glimmerings of drowsiness. A good idea, he thought, to sleep off to death. It was like taking an anaesthetic① . Freezing was not so bad as people thought. There were lots worse ways to die.

He pictured the boys finding his body next day. Suddenly he found himself with them, coming along the trail and looking for himself. And, still with them, he came around a turn in the trail and found himself lying in the snow. He did not belong with

---

① anaesthetic: a substance that makes you unconscious

himself any more, for even then he was out of himself, standing with the boys and looking at himself in the snow. It certainly was cold, was his thought. When he got back to the States he could tell the folks what real cold was. He drifted on from this to a vision of the old-timer on Sulphur Creek. He could see him quite clearly, warm and comfortable, and smoking a pipe.

" You were right, old hoss; you were right," the man mumbled to the old-timer of Sulphur Creek.

Then the man drowsed off into what seemed to him the most comfortable and satisfying sleep he had ever known. The dog sat facing him and waiting. The brief day drew to a close in a long, slow twilight. There were no signs of a fire to be made, and, besides, never in the dog's experience had it known a man to sit like that in the snow and make no fire. As the twilight drew on, its eager yearning for the fire mastered it, and with a great lifting and shifting of forefeet, it whined① softly, then flattened its ears down in anticipation of being chidden by the man. But the man remained silent. Later, the dog whined loudly. And still later it crept close to the man and caught the scent of death. This made the animal bristle and back away. A little longer it delayed, howling under the stars that leaped and danced and shone brightly in the cold sky. Then it turned and trotted up the trail in the direction of the camp it knew, where were the other food-providers and fire-providers.

Topics for discussion

1. How does London use the repetition's writing style in " To Build a Fire"?

2. What do you think the comment that " To Build a Fire" is London's most mature expression of his pessimism?

3. " To Build a Fire" is regarded by many American as a classic, and what do

① whine: complain or express disappointment or unhappiness repeatedly you think of the comment?

4. Dogs often become heroes of London's works such as Buck in *The Call of the Wild*, White Fang in *White Fang*, and a big native husky in " To Build a Fire". Why does London use dogs in his works? Discuss the different character of these dogs.

References for further reading

[1] Hedin, Robert, and Gary Holthaus. *Alaska: Reflections on the Land and Spirit*. Tucson: The University of Arizona Press, 1898.

[2] Perry, John. *Jack London: An American Myth*. Nelson Hall, 1981.

[3] Pizer, Donald. *Jack London: Novels and Stories*. New York: The Library of American, 1982.

[4] Sinclair, Andrew. *A Biography of Jack London*. New York: Harper and Row, 1977.

[5] Walcutt, Charles Child. *Jack London*, Minneapolis: University of Minnesota Press, 1966.

Sherwood Anderson (1876 — 1941)

Death in the Woods

Introduction to the author

Sherwood Anderson (September 13, 1876 — March 8, 1941) was an American novelist and short story writer. Sherwood Berton Anderson was born in Camden, Ohio, a farming town. He was the third of seven children of Irwin McLain, a former Union soldier and harness-maker, and Emma Jane Anderson. After Erwin's business failed, the family was forced to move frequently, finally settling down at Clyde, Ohio, in 1884. Young Sherwood found various odd jobs to help his family. He left school at the age of 14. His works are based on his own experience in the American Midwest at the end of the nineteenth century. His hometown, Camden, Ohio, is the setting of his most notable work. He once took a job as a laborer, an advertising salesman in Chicago, served in the army, started a business, finally devoted himself to be a writer at the age of 37. Anderson's marriage is not happy, he divorced twice and married Copenhaver finally, who traveled, often studied together, and participated in the trade union movement. Anderson died of peritonitis at the age of 64 during a cruise to South America. Anderson was buried at Round Hill Cemetery in Marion, Virginia. His epitaph reads, " Life, Not Death, is the Great Adventure"

He influenced many young writers including Hart Crane, William Faulkner, Ernest Hemingway, John Steinbeck, and Thomas Wolfe. Anderson's first two novels, *Windy McPherson's Son and Marching Men* are usually considered his " apprentice novels", which are successful men who abandoned their selfish aims to become populist heroes. His masterpiece, *Winesburg, Ohio* is a collection of tales of the " grotesque" inhabitants of a small town in Ohio. Anderson's *Many Marriages* and *Dark Laughter*, exploring the new sexual freedom of the 1920s, were not successful as before. In the 1930s, Anderson published *Death in the Woods* (short stories), *Puzzled America* (essays), and *Kit Brandon: A Portrait* (novel). His novel *Beyond Desire*, dedicated to Copenhaver, was set during the 1929 Loray Mill Strike in Gastonia, North Carolina.

Anderson reveals the frustration, loneliness, and longing in the lives of his characters. Anderson was one of the first American novelists to introduce new insights from psychology, including Freudian analysis.

Major works by Sherwood Anderson

Novels

Windy McPhersons' Son 1916

Marching Men 1917

Poor White 1920

Many Marriages 1923

Dark Laughter 1925

Tar: A Midwest Childhood 1926

Alice and The Lost Novel 1929

Beyond Desire 1932

Kit Brandon: A Portrait 1936

Short Story collections

Winesburg, Ohio 1919

The Triumph of the Egg, 1921

Horses and Men 1923

Death in the Woods and Other Stories

1933

Poetry

Mid-American Chants 1918

A New Testament 1927

Drama

Plays, Winesburg and Others 1937

Nonfiction

A Story Teller's Story (1924, memoir)

The Modern Writer (1925, essays)

Sherwood Anderson's Notebook (1926, memoir)

Hello Towns! (1929, newspaper articles)

Nearer the Grass Roots (1929, essays)

The American County Fair (1930, essays)

Perhaps Women (1931, essays)

No Swank (1934, essays)

Puzzled America (1935, essays)

A Writer's Conception of Realism (1939, essays)

Home Town (1940, photographs and commentary)

Appreciation

" Death in the Woods", written in 1926 is typical of Anderson's abiding interest in everyday, unimportant people. It is presented as a first-person narrative by an unreal narrator, who tells the story of an old woman, Mrs, Grimes. She lives on the edge of society and survives by selling egos and using the proceeds to buy food for herself, her small family and the animals in her care. Mrs. Grimes' husband and son treat her badly. She does not know life could be changed. Her main concern in life is taking care of, and feeding the animals and people in her care. On her way home, she leaves the road and walks through the woods, probably a short cut. On this shortcut she reaches a clearing where she sits down to rest. While sitting down, she dies. The dogs, that had been following her, run around her in circles, then rip the pack away from her and devour the food inside. The body is discovered by a hunter, who goes into town and tells everyone about the body in the woods. A group of men and some boys, including the narrator, walk into the woods to examine the body and bring it back. The narrator, looking back, tries to organize his memories and create meaning and beauty from them. Rather than remembering an aged woman, he remembers a beautiful, " statueque" and almost marble figure. She became an image rather an aged woman.

" Death in the Woods" describes a simple story of the life and death of a poor farm woman. The narrator observes her dead body as a man and an artist. When he puts together the pieces of her story, the story takes on mystery and mythic meaning as he reflects back on it years later. The story reflects Anderson's death consciousness — birth-death-rebirth.

Selected Reading

Death in the Woods

I

She was an old woman and lived a farm near town in which I lived. All country and small-town people have seen such old women, but no one knows much about them. Such an old woman comes into town driving an old worn-out horse or she comes afoot carrying a basket. She may own a few hens and have eggs to sell. She brings then in a basket and takes them to a grocer. There she trades them in. She gets some salt pork and some beans. Then she gets a pound or two of sugar and some flour.

Afterwards she goes to the butcher's and asks for some dog-meat. She may spend ten of fifteen cents, but when she does she asks for something. Formerly the butchers gave liver to any one who wanted to carry it away. In our family we were always having it. Once one of my brothers got a whole cow's liver at the slaughter-house near the fairgrounds in our town. We had it until we were sick of it. It never cost a cent. I have hated the thought of it ever since.

The old farm woman got some liver and a soup-bone. She never visited with any one, and as soon as she got what she wanted she lit out for home. It made quite a load for such an old body. No one gave her a lift. People drive right down a road and never notice an old woman like that.

There was such an old woman who used to come into town past our house one Summer and Fall when I was a young boy and was sick with what was called inflammatory① rheumatism.② She went home later carrying a heavy pack on her back. Two or three large gaunt-looking dogs followed at her heels.

The old woman was nothing special. She was one of the nameless ones that hardly any one knows, but she got into my thoughts. I have just suddenly now, after all these years, remembered her and what happened. It is a story. Her name was Grimes, and she lived with her husband and son in a small unpainted house on the bank small creek four miles from town.

The husband and son were a tough lot. Although the son was but twenty-one he had already served a term in jail. It was whispered about that the woman's husband stole horses and ran them off to some other county. Now and then, when a horse turned up missing, the man had also disappeared. No one ever caught him. Once, when I was loafing at Tom Whitehead's livery-barn, the man came there and sat on the bench in front. Two or three other men were there, but no one spoke to him. He sat for a few minutes and then got up and went away. When he was leaving he turned around and stared at the men. There was a look of defiance in his eyes. "Well, I have tried to be friendly. You don't want to talk to me. It has been so wherever I have gone

---

① inflammatory: intended or likely to cause anger or hate; annoying

② rheumatism: a medical condition that causes stiffness and pain in the joints in this town. If, some day, one of your fine horses turns up missing, well, then what?" He did not say anything actually. " I'd like to bust one of you on the jaw," was about what his eyes said. I remember how the look in his eyes made me shiver.

The old man belonged to a family that had had money once. His name was Jake Grimes. It all comes back clearly now. His father, John Grimes, had owned a sawmill when the country was new, and had made money. Then he got to drinking and running after women. When he died there wasn't much left.

Jake blew in the rest. Pretty soon there wasn't anymore lumber to cut and his land was nearly all gone.

He got his wife off a German farmer, for whom he went to work one June day in the wheat harvest. She was a young thing then and scared to death. You see, the farmer was up to something with the girl — she was, I think, a bound girl and his wife had her suspicions. She took it out on the girl when the man wasn't around. Then, when the wife had to go off to town for supplies, the farmer got after her. He told young Jake that nothing really ever happened, but he didn't know whether to believe it or not.

He got her pretty easy himself, the first time he was out with her. He wouldn't have married her if the German farmer hadn't tried to tell him where to get off. He got her to go riding with him in his buggy① one night when he was threshing on the place, and then he came for her the next Sunday night.

She managed to get out of the house without her employer's seeing, but when she was getting into buggy he showed up. It was almost dark, and he just popped up② suddenly at the horse's head. He grabbed the horse by the bridle and Jake got out his buggy-whip.

They had it out all right! The German was a tough one. Maybe he didn't care whether his wife knew or not. Jake hit him over the face and shoulders with buggy-

① buggy : carriage

② pop up: to appear or happen, especially suddenly or unexpectedly whip, but the horse got to acting up and he had to get out.

Then the two men went for it. The girl didn't see it. The horse started to run away and went nearly a mile down the road before the girl got him stopped. Then she managed to tie him to a tree beside the road. (I wonder how I know all this. It must have stuck in my mind from small-town tales when I was a boy) Jake found her there after he got through with the German. She was huddled up in the buggy seat, crying, scared to death. She told Jake a lot of stuff. How the German had tried to get her, how another time, when they happened to be alone in the house together, he tore her dress open clear down the front. The German, she said, might have got her that time if he hadn't heard his old woman drive in at the gate. She had been off to town for supplies. Well, she would be putting the horse in the barn. The German managed to sneak off to the fields without his wife seeing. He told the girl he would kill her if she told. What could she do? She told a lie about ripping her dress in the barn when she was feeding the stock. I remember now that she was a bound girl and did not know where her father and mother were. Maybe she did not have any father. You know what I mean.

Such bound children were often enough cruelly treated. They were children who had no parents, slaves really. There were very few orphan homes then. They were legally bound into some home. It was a matter of pure luck how is came out.

II

She married Jake and had a son and daughter, but the daughter died.

Then she settled down to feed stock. That was her job. At the German's place she had cooked the food for the German and his wife. The wife was a strong woman with big hips and worked most of the time in the fields with her husband. She fed them and fed the cows in the barn, as a young girl, her life was spent feeding something.

Then she married Jake Grimes and he had to be fed. She was a slight thing, and when she had been married for three or four years, and after the two children were born, her slender shoulders became stooped.

Jake always had a lot of big dogs around the house, that stood near the unused sawmill near the creek. He was always trading horses when he wasn't stealing something and a cow. They were all pastured in the few acres left of the Grimes place and Jake did hide enough work.

He went into debt for a threshing outfit and ran it for several years, but it did not pay. People did not trust him. They were afraid he would steal the grain at night. He had to go a long way off to get work and it cost too much to get there. In the winter he hunted and cut a little firewood, to be sold in some nearby town. When the son grew up he was just like the father. They got drunk together. If there wasn't anything to eat in the house when they came home the old man gave his old woman a cut over the head. She had a few chickens of her own and had to kill one of them in a hurry. When they were all killed she wouldn't have any eggs to sell when she went to town. And then what would she do?

She had to scheme all her life about getting things fed, getting the pigs fed so they would grow fat and could be butchered in the Fall. When they were butchered her husband took most of the meat off to town and sold it. If he did not do it first, the boy did. They fought sometimes and when they fought, the old woman stood aside trembling.

She had got the habit of silence anyway — that was fixed. Sometimes when she began to look old — when the husband and son were both off, trading horses or drinking or hunting or stealing, she went around the house and the barnyard muttering to herself.

How was she going to get everything fed — that was her problem. The dogs had to be fed. There wasn't enough hay in the barn for the horses and the cow. If she didn't feed the chickens how could they lay eggs? Without eggs to sell how could she get things in town, things she had to have to keep the life of the farm going? Thank heaven, she did not have to feed her husband — in a certain way. That hadn't lasted long after their marriage and after the babies came. Where he went on his long trips she did not know. Sometimes he was gone from home for weeks, and after the boy grew up they went off together.

They left everything at home for her to manage and she had no money. She knew no one. No one ever talked to her in town. When it was winter she had to gather sticks of wood for her fire, had to try to keep the stock fed with very little grain. The stock in the barn cried to her hungrily, the dogs followed her about. In the winter the hens laid few enough eggs. They huddled in the corners of the barn and she kept watching them. If a hen lays an egg in the barn in the winter and you do not find it, it freezes and breaks.

One day in winter the old woman went off to town with a few eggs and the dogs followed her. She did not get started until nearly three o'clock and the snow was heavy. She hadn't been feeling very well for several days and so she went muttering along, scantily clad,① her shoulders stooped. She had an old grain bag in which she carried her eggs, tucked away down in the bottom. There weren't many of them, but in winter the price of eggs is up. She would get a little meat in exchange for the eggs, some salt pork, a little sugar, and some coffee perhaps. It might be the butcher would give her a piece of liver. When she had got to town and was trading in her eggs the dogs lay by the door outside. She did pretty well, got the things she needed, more than she had hoped. Then she went to the butcher and he gave her some liver and some dog-meat.

It was the first time any one had spoken to her in a friendly way for a long time. The butcher was alone in his shop when she came in and was annoyed by the thought of such a sick-looking old woman out on such a day. It was bitter cold and the snow, that had let up during the afternoon, was falling again. The butcher said something about her husband and her son, swore at them, and the old woman stared at him, a

① scantily clad: wearing very little clothing

look of mild surprise in her eyes as he talked. He said that if either the husband or the son were going to get any of the liver or the heavy hones with scraps of meat hanging to them that he had put into the grain bag, he'd see him starve first.

Starve, eh? Well, things had to be fed. Men had to be fed, and the horse that weren't any good but maybe could be traded off,[①] and the poor thin cow that hadn't given any milk for three months.

Horses, cows, pigs, dogs, men.

III

The old woman had to get back before darkness came if she could. The dogs followed at her heels, sniffing at the heavy grain bag she had fastened on her back. When she got to the edge of town she stopped by a fence and tied the bag on her back with a piece of rope she had carried in her dress-pocket for just that purpose. That was an easier way to carry it. Her arms ached. It was hard when she had to crawl over fences and once she fell over and landed in the snow. The dogs went frisking about. She had to struggle to get to her feet again, but she made it. The point of climbing over the fences was that there was a short cut over a hill and through a woods. She might have gone around by the road, but it was a mile farther that way. She was afraid she couldn't make it. And then, besides, the stock had to be fed. There was a little hay left and a little corn. Perhaps her husband and son would bring some when they came. They had driven off in the only buggy the Grimes family had, a rickety thing, a rickety horse hitched to the buggy, two other rickety horses led by halters. They were going to trade horses, get a little money if they could. They might come home drunk. It would be well to have something in the house when they came back.

The son had affair on with a woman at the county seat, fifteen miles away. She was a rough enough woman, a tough one. Once, in the Summer, the son had brought

① trade off: to accept a disadvantage or bad feature in order to have something good her to the house. Both she and the son had been drinking. Jake Grimes was away and the son and his woman ordered the old woman about like a servant. She didn't mind much; she was used to it. Whatever happened she never said anything. That was her way of getting along. She had managed that way when she was a young girl at the German's and ever since she had married Jake. That time her son brought his woman to the house they stayed all night sleeping together just as though they were married. It hadn't shocked the old woman, not much. She had got past being shocked early in life.

With the pack on her back she went painfully along across and open field, wading in the deep snow, and got into the woods.

There was a path, but it was hard to follow. Just beyond the top of the hill, where the woods was thickest, there was a small clearing. Had some one once thought of building a house there? The clearing was as large as a building lot in town, large enough for a house and a garden. The path ran along the side of the clearing, and when she got there the old woman sat down to rest at the foot of a tree.

It was a foolery to do. When she got herself placed, the pack against the tree's trunk, it was nice, but what about getting up again? She worried about that for a moment and then quietly closed eyes.

She must have slept for a time. When you are about so cold you can't get any colder. The afternoon grew a little warmer and the snow came thicker than ever. Then after a time the weather cleared. The moon even came out.

There were four Grimes dogs that had followed Mrs. Grimes into town, all tall gaunt① fellows. Such men as Jake Grimes and his son always keep just such dogs. They kick and abuse them, but they stay. The Grimes dogs, in order to keep from starving, had to do a lot of foraging② for themselves, and they had been at it while the old woman slept with her back to the tree at the side of the clearing. They had

① gaunt: very thin, especially because of sickness or hunger

② foraging: to go from place to place searching, especially for food been chasing rabbits in the woods and in adjoining fields and in their ranging had picked up three other farm dogs.

After a time all the dogs came back to the clearing. They were excited about something. Such nights, cold and clear and with a moon, do things to dogs. It may be that some old instinct come down from the time when they were wolves and ranged the woods in packs on Winter nights, comes back into them.

The dogs in the clearing, before the old woman, had caught two or three rabbits and their immediate hunger had been satisfied. They began to play, running in circles in the clearing. Round and round they ran, each dog's nose at the tail of the next dog. In the clearing, under the snow-laden trees and under the wintry moon they made a strange picture, running thus silently, in a circle their running had beaten in the soft snow. The dogs made no sound. They ran around and around in the circle.

It may have been that the old woman saw them doing that before she died. She may have awakened once or twice and looked at the strange sight with dim old eyes.

She wouldn't be very cold now, just drowsy.① Life hangs on a long time. Perhaps the old woman was out of her head. She may have dreamed of her girlhood at the German's and before that when she was a child and before her mother lit out and left her.

Her dreams couldn't have been very pleasant. Not many pleasant things had happened to her. Now and then one of the Grimes, dogs left the running circle and came to stand before her. The dog thrust his face close to her face. His red tongue was hanging out.

The running of the dogs may have been a kind of death ceremony. It may have been that the primitive instinct of the wolf, having been aroused in the dogs by the night and the running, made them somehow afraid.

" Now we are no longer wolves. We are dogs, the servants of men. Keep alive,

---

① drowsy: feeling sleepy

man! When man dies we become wolves again."

When one of the dogs came to where the old woman sat with her back against the tree and thrust his nose close to her face he seemed satisfied and went back to run with the pack. All the Grimes, dogs did it at some time during evening, before she died. I knew all about it afterward, when I grew to be a man, because once in a woods in Illinois, on another winter night, I saw a pack of dogs act just like that. The dogs were waiting for me to die as they had waited for the old woman that night when I was a child, but when it happened to me I was a young man and had no intention whatever of dying.

The old woman died softly and quietly. When she was dead and when one of the Grimes, dogs had come to her and had found her dead all the dogs stopped running.

They gathered about her.

Well, she was dead now. She had fed the Grimes, dogs when she was alive, what about now?

There was the pack on her back, the grain bag containing the piece of salt pork, the liver the butcher had given her, the dog-meat, the soup bones. The butcher in town, having been suddenly overcome with a feeling of pity, had loaded her grain bag heavily. It had been a big haul for the old woman.

It was a big haul for the dogs now.

IV

One of the Grimes dogs sprang suddenly out from among the others and began worrying the pack on the old woman's back. Had the dogs really been wolves that one would have been the leader of the pack. What he did, all the others did.

All of them sank their teeth into the grain bag the old woman had fastened with ropes to her back.

They dragged the old woman's body out into the open clearing. The worn-out dress was quickly torn from her shoulders. When she was found, a day or two later, the dress had been torn from her body clear to the hips, but the dogs had not touched her body. They had got the meat out of the grain bag, that was all. Her body was frozen stiff when it was found, and the shoulders were so narrow and the body so slight that in death it looked like the body of some charming young girl.

Such things happened in towns of the Middle West, on farms near town, when I was a boy. A hunter out after rabbits found the old woman's body and did not touch it. Something, the beaten round path in the little snow-covered clearing, the silence of the place, the place where the dogs had worried the body trying to pull the grain bag away or tear it open — something startled the man and he hurried off to town.

I was in Main street with one of my brothers who was town newsboy and who was taking the afternoon papers to the stores. It was almost night.

The hunter came into a grocery and told his story. Then he went to a hardware-shop and into a drugstore. Men began to gather on the sidewalks. Then they started out along the road to the place in the woods.

My brother should have gone on about his business of distributing papers but he didn't. Every one was going to the woods. The undertaker went and the town marshal. Several men got on a dray and rode out to where the path left the road and went into the woods, but the horses weren't very sharply shod and slid about on the slippery roads. They made no better time than those of us who walked.

The town marshal was a large man whose leg had been injured in the Civil War. He carried a heavy cane and limped rapidly along the road. My brother and I followed at his heels, and as we went other men and boys joined the crowd.

It had grown dark by the time we got to where the old woman had left the road but the moon had come out. The marshal was thinking there might have been a murder. He kept asking the hunter questions. The hunter went along with his gun across his shoulders, a dog following at his heels. It isn't often a rabbit hunter has a chance to be so conspicuous. He was taking full advantage of it, leading the procession with the town marshal. " I didn't see any wounds. She was a beautiful young girl. Her face was buried in the snow. No, I didn't know her". As a matter of fact, the hunter had not looked closely at the body. He had been frightened. She might have been murdered and some one might spring out from behind a tree and murder him. In a woods, in the late afternoon, when the trees are all bare and there is white snow on the ground, when all is silent, something creepy steals over the mind and body. If something strange or uncanny has happened in the neighborhood all you think about is getting away from there as fast as you can.

The crowd of men and boys had got to where the old woman had crossed the field and went, following the marshal and the hunter, up the slight incline and into the woods.

My brother and I were silent. He had his bundle of papers in a bag slung across his shoulder. When he got back to town he would have to go on distributing his papers before he went home to supper. If I went along, as he had no doubt already determined I should, we would both be late. Either mother or our older sister would have to warm our supper.

Well, we would have something to tell. A boy did not get such a chance very often. It was lucky we just happened to go into the grocery when the hunter came in. The hunter was a country fellow. Neither of us had ever seen him before.

Now the crowd of men and boys had got to the clearing. Darkness comes quickly on such winter nights, but the full moon made everything clear. My brother and I stood near the tree, beneath which the old woman had died.

She did not look old, lying there in that light, frozen and still. One of the men turned her over in the snow and I saw everything. My body trembled with some strange mystical feeling and so did my brother's. It might have been the cold.

Neither of us had even seen a woman's body before. It may have been the snow, clinging to the frozen flesh, that made it look so white and lovely, so like marble. No woman had come with the party from town; but one of the men, he was the town blacksmith, took off his overcoat and spread it over her. Then he gathered her into his arms and started off to town, all the others following silently. At that time on one knew who she was.

V

I had seen everything, had seen the oval in the snow, like a miniature race-track, where the dogs had run, had seen how the men were mystified, had see the white bare young-looking shoulders, had heard the whispered comments of the men.

The men were simply mystified. They took the body to the undertaker's, and when the blacksmith, the hunter, the marshal and several others had got inside they closed the door. If father had been there perhaps he could have got in, but we boys couldn't.

I went with my brother distribute the rest of his papers and when we got home it was my brother who told the story.

I kept silent and went to bed early. It may have been I was not satisfied with the way he told it.

Later, in the town, I must have heard other fragments of the old woman's story. She was recognized the next day and there was an investigation.

The husband and son were found somewhere and brought to town and there was an attempt to connect them with the woman's death, but it did not work. They had perfect enough alibis.①

However, the town was against them. They had to get out. Where they went I never heard.

I remember only the picture there in the forest, the men standing about. The naked girlish-looking figure, face down in the snow, the tracks made by the running dogs and the clear cold winter sky above. White fragments of clouds were drifting across the sky. They went racing across the little open space among the trees.

The scene in the forest had become for me, without my knowing it, the

① alibis: proof that someone who is thought to have committed a crime could not have done it, especially the fact or statement that they were in another place at the time it happened foundation for the real story I am now trying to tell. The fragments, you see, had to be picked up slowly, long afterwards.

Things happened. When I was a young man I worked on the farm of a German. The hired-girl was afraid of her employer. The farmer's wife hated her.

I saw things at that place. Once later, I had a half-uncanny,① mystical adventure with dogs in an Illinois forest on a clear, moon-lit winter night. When I was a schoolboy, and in a summer day, I went with a boy friend out along a creed some miles from town and came to the house where the old woman had lived. No one had lived in the house since her death. The doors were broken from the hinges;② the window lights were all broken. As the boy and I stood in the road outside, two dogs, just roving farm dogs no doubt, came running around the comer of the house. The dogs were tall. Gaunt fellows and came down to the fence and glared through at us, standing in the road.

The whole thing, the story of the old woman's death, was to me as I grew older like music heard from far off. The notes had to be picked up slowly one at a time. Something had to be understood.

The woman who died was one destined to feed animal life. Anyway, that is all she ever did. She was feeding animal life before she was born, as a child, as a young woman working in the farm of the German, after she married, when she grew old and when she died. She fed animal life in cows, in chickens, in pigs, in horses, in dogs, in men. Her daughter had died in childhood and with her one son she had no articulate relations. On the night when she died she was hurrying homeward, bearing on her body food for animal life.

She died in the clearing in the woods and even after her death continued feeding animal life.

You see it is likely that, when my brother told the story, that night when we got

---

① half-uncanny: near to strange or mysterious ; almost difficult or impossible to explain

② hinge: a piece of metal that fastens the edge of a door, window, lid, etc home and my mother and sister sat listening, I did not think he got the point. He was too young and so was I. A thing so complete has its own beauty.

I shall not try to emphasize the point. I am only explaining why I was dissatisfied then and have been ever since. I speak of that only that you may understand why I have been impelled to try to tell the simple story over again.

Topics for discussion

1. Do you find Mrs. Grimes a sympathetic character? Why or why not?

2. The narrator states that it was the woman's destiny to " feed animal life." What do you think of his statement?

3. In his preface to *Winesburg, Ohio*, Anderson describes his characters as " grotesques." How do you understand the idea of " grotesques" in Mrs. Grimes of " Death in the Woods"?

4. What do you think of the role of narrator in " Death in the Woods"?

References for further reading

[1] Burbank, Rex. Sherwood Anderson, New York: Twayne, 1964.

[2] Dunne, Robert. *A new book of the grotesques: contemporary approaches to Sherwood Anderson's early fiction*, Kent : Kent State University Press, 2005.

[3] Rideout, Walter B. *Sherwood Anderson: a writer in America*, Madison: University of Wisconsin Press, 2007.

[4] Small, Judy Jo. *A Reader's Guide to the Short Stories of Sherwood Anderson*, New York:G. K. Hall, 1964.

[5] Townsend, Kim. *Sherwood Anderson*, Boston: Houghton Mifflin, 1987.

[6] White, Ray Lewis. ed. *The Achievement of Sherwood Anderson*, Chapel Hill: University of North Carolina Press, 1966.

Mary Flannery O'Connor (1925 — 1964)

A Good Man Is Hard To Find

Introduction to the author

Mary Flannery O'Connor (March 25, 1925 — August 3, 1964) was one of the most important American short story writers of the twentieth century, a Southern Roman Catholic writer. She wrote two novels and 32 short stories, and a number of reviews and commentaries. In her works, she adopted a Southern Gothic style, regional settings, violent plot elements and grotesque characters, and frequently explored problems of morality and ethics.

Mary Flannery O'Connor was born on March 25, 1925, in Savannah, Georgia, the only child of Roman Catholic parents, Edward F. O'Connor and Regina Cline. When she was sixteen, her father died from degenerative lupus, and the same disease later took her life. O'Connor graduated from Georgia State College for Women (now Georgia College & State University) in June 1945 with a Social sciences degree. She later received a master's degree in writing from Iowa State University in 1947. Then O'Connor attended the prestigious Yaddo writers' colony, working on her first novel Wise Blood. In 1951, she was diagnosed with systemic lupus erythematosus. Then O'Connor moved back to Milledgeville, where she lived the remainder of her life with her mother. On August 3, 1964, she died at the age of 39 at Baldwin County Hospital and was buried in Milledgeville, Georgia, at Memory Hill Cemetery. In her life, O'Connor delivered many lectures on faith and literature and kept correspondence with friends, family, and famous writers including Robert Lowell and Elizabeth Bishop. She remained single all her life.

In O'Connor's fiction, southern characters are fundamentalist Protestants and they experienced pain, and violence. O'Connor also explored contemporary issues including the Holocaust, race and holy pursuit. From 1956 through 1964, O'Connor wrote over 100 book reviews which consistently confront theological and ethical themes. The Flannery O'Connor Award for Short Fiction was established for an outstanding collection of short stories in 1982. O'Connor won three O. Henry Memorial Awards for her short stories, *a Ford Foundation grant*, a National Institute of Arts and Letters grant in literature and two honorary doctor's degrees during her lifetime. After her death, her fiction won a National Book Award, and her collection of letters *The Habit of Being* won an award from the Library Journal.

Major works by Flannery O'Connor

Novels

Wise Blood, 1952

The Violent Bear It Away, 1960

Short story collections

A Good Man Is Hard to Find, 1955

Everything That Rises Must Converge, 1965

The Complete Stories, 1971

Other works

Mystery and Manners: Occasional Prose, 1969

The Habit of Being: Letters of Flannery O'Connor, 1979

The Presence of Grace: and Other Book Reviews, 1983

Flannery O'Connor: Collected Works, 1988

A Prayer Journal, edited by W. A. Sessions, Farrar, Straus and Giroux, 2013

Appreciation

" A Good Man Is Hard to Find" was published in 1955. The disturbing and humorous story exhibits a violent action and underscores her devout Roman Catholic faith. Through an escaped murderer, O'Connor explores the Christian concept of " grace", that is, so long as a person asks frequently, God will give him a divine pardon. At the moment of her death, Grandmother reaches out to the Misfit and recognizes him as one of her own children, thus attaining grace.

The story portrays a family's vacation. The story's primary action involves a family car trip on which they encounter an escaped criminal and his gang. The story is told from the Grandmother's perspective. She packs herself in the car with her son Bailey, his wife, and their children — June Star, John Wesley, and the baby, especially including secretly her cat, Pitty Sing. At Red Sammy Butts' barbecue place, Grandmother discusses the escaped murderer known as the Misfit. Red Sammy tells the Grandmother that a good man is hard to find these days. Back on the road, the Grandmother convinces her son to visit an old plantation. Later, she suddenly realizes that the plantation is not in Georgia but in Tennessee. Her unexpected reaction upsets Pitty Sing, and the cat leaps out onto Bailey's shoulder, and Bailey loses control of the car and rolls it into a ditch. The children view the accident as an adventure. Unfortunately, they ran across the infamous and his fellows, carrying guns. Her family members are shot in nearby woods, and Grandmother tries to flatter

The Misfit and save her life, but without any effect on him. In her final moment, the Grandmother reaches out and touches the Misfit, whispering " You're one of my own children!" Her religious idea at the story's end provides the philosophical thrust behind the narrative.

The Grandmother is selfish and pushy in some sense and she strongly believes in the salvation of religion. The Misfit unburdens his soul to the Grandmother about his father's death, his own mistreatment, and his feelings about the world's injustices. The story demonstrates racial and class prejudice through the Grandmother's words and actions, and shows O'Connor's idea of grace that God's love and forgiveness are available to people in everyday life. Meanwhile, the story contains violence, and the family members including the grandmother are shot to death one by one. Grace is realized in territory held largely by the devil. In " A Good Man Is Hard to Find", O'Connor shows characters' state of mind by skies, weather and old house. Foreshadowing, an indication of future events, occurs several times in the story. Irony also appears in dramatic situations and dialogues. " A Good Man Is Hard to Find" combines humor, detachment, irony, and seriousness in tone. O'Connor presents a situation in which average people confront a force of pure evil. The story is structured to fall into two sections, each written in a distinctive tone — a humorous and light one and a dark and serious one. The story portrays an unremarkable family and then moves into themes of death, grace, forgiveness and injustice.

Selected Reading

A Good Man Is Hard To Find

The grandmother didn't want to go to Florida. She wanted to visit some of her connections in east Tennessee and she was seizing at every chance to change Bailey's mind. Bailey was the son she lived with, her only boy. He was sitting on the edge of his chair at the table, bent over the orange sports section of the Journal. " Now look here, Bailey," she said, " see here, read this," and she stood with one hand on her thin hip and the other rattling the newspaper at his bald head. " Here this fellow that calls himself The Misfit is aloose from the Federal Pen① and headed toward Florida and you read here what it says he did to these people. Just you read it. I wouldn't take my children in any direction with a criminal like that aloose in it. I couldn't answer to my conscience if I did."

Bailey didn't look up from his reading so she wheeled around then and faced the children's mother, a young woman in slacks,② whose face was as broad and innocent as a cabbage and was tied around with a green head-kerchief that had two points on the top like rabbit's ears. She was sitting on the sofa, feeding the baby his apricots out of a jar. " The children have been to Florida before," the old lady said. " You all ought to take them somewhere else for a change so they would see different parts of the world and be broad. They never have been to east Tennessee."

The children's mother didn't seem to hear her but the eight-year-old boy, John Wesley, a stocky child with glasses, said, " If you don't want to go to Florida, why dontcha③ stay at home?" He and the little girl, June Star, were reading the funny papers on the floor.

" She wouldn't stay at home to be queen for a day," June Star said without raising her yellow head.

" Yes and what would you do if this fellow, The Misfit, caught you?" the grandmother asked.

" I'd smack his face," John Wesley said.

" She wouldn't stay at home for a million bucks," June Star said. " Afraid she'd miss something. She has to go everywhere we go."

---

① the Federal Pen: the Federal Penitentiary

② slacks: loose trousers, pants

③ dontcha: don't you.

" All right, Miss," the grandmother said. " Just remember that the next time you want me to curl your hair."

June Star said her hair was naturally curly.

The next morning the grandmother was the first one in the car, ready to go. She had her big black valise that looked like the head of a hippopotamus① in one corner, and underneath it she was hiding a basket with Pitty Sing② , the cat, in it. She didn't intend for the cat to be left alone in the house for three days because he would miss her too much and she was afraid he might brush against one of her gas burners and accidentally asphyxiate③ himself. Her son, Bailey, didn't like to arrive at a motel with a cat.

She sat in the middle of the back seat with John Wesley and June Star on either side of her. Bailey and the children's mother and the baby sat in front and they left Atlanta④ at eight forty-five with the mileage on the car at 55890. The grandmother wrote this down because she thought it would be interesting to say how many miles they had been when they got back. It took them twenty minutes to reach the outskirts of the city.

The old lady settled herself comfortably, removing her white cotton gloves and putting them up with her purse on the shelf in front of the back window. The children's mother still had on slacks and still had her head tied up in a green kerchief, but the grandmother had on a navy blue straw sailor hat with a bunch of white violets on the brim and a navy blue dress with a small white dot in the print. Her collars and cuffs were white organdy trimmed with lace and at her neckline she had pinned a purple spray of cloth violets containing a sachet. In case of an accident, anyone

---

① Hippopotamu: (also hippo) large African river animal with short legs and thick dark skin

② Pitty Sing: a character in The Mikada (1885) by Sir Arthur Sulliven (1842–1900) and Sir William Gilbert(1836–1911)

③ asphyxiate: cause (sb) to become ill or to die by preventing enough air from reaching the lungs; suffocate.

④ Atlanta: capital of Georgia in U.S.A.

seeing her dead on the highway would know at once that she was a lady.

She said she thought it was going to be a good day for driving, neither too hot nor too cold, and she cautioned Bailey that the speed limit was fifty-five miles an hour and that the patrolmen hid themselves behind billboards① and small clumps of trees and sped out after you before you had a chance to slow down. She pointed out interesting details of the scenery: Stone Mountain;② the blue granite that in some places came up to both sides of the highway; the brilliant red clay banks slightly streaked with purple; and the various crops that made rows of green lace-work on the ground. The trees were full of silver-white sunlight and the meanest of them sparkled. The children were reading comic magazines and their mother and gone back to sleep.

" Let's go through Georgia fast so we won't have to look at it much," John Wesley said.

" If I were a little boy," said the grandmother, " I wouldn't talk about my native state that way. Tennessee has the mountains and Georgia has the hills."

" Tennessee is just a hillbilly③ dumping ground," John Wesley said, " and Georgia is a lousy state too."

" You said it,④ " June Star said.

" In my time," said the grandmother, folding her thin veined fingers, " children were more respectful of their native states and their parents and everything else. People did right then. Oh look at the cute little pickaninny⑤ !" she said and pointed to a Negro child standing in the door of a shack. " Wouldn't that make a picture, now?" she asked and they all turned and looked at the little Negro out of the back window.

---

① billboards: (US) large outdoor board for advertisements; hoarding

② Stone Mountain: a famous sight near Atlanta of Georgia, some distinguished characters including Jefferson Davis, Robert E. Lee and Stonewall Jackson are carved in the mountain stone

③ hillbilly: (US infml usu derog) unsophisticated person from a remote rural area, esp the mountains in the south–eastern US

④ You said it: you are right totally

⑤ pickaninny: (also piccaninny) young Negro or Aboriginal child

He waved

" He didn't have any britches[①] on," June Star said.

" He probably didn't have any," the grandmother explained. " Little riggers in the country don't have things like we do. If I could paint, I'd paint that picture," she said.

The children exchanged comic books.

The grandmother offered to hold the baby and the children's mother passed hım over the front seat to her. She set him on her knee and bounced him and told him about the things they were passing. She rolled her eyes and screwed up her mouth and stuck her leathery thin face into his smooth bland one. Occasionally he gave her a faraway smile. They passed a large cotton field with five or fix graves fenced in the middle of it, like a small island. " Look at the graveyard!" the grandmother said, pointing it out. " That was the old family burying ground. That belonged to the plantation."

" Where's the plantation?" John Wesley asked.

" Gone With the Wind,[②] " said the grandmother. " Ha. Ha."

When the children finished all the comic books they had brought, they opened the lunch and ate it. The grandmother ate a peanut butter sandwich and an olive and would not let the children throw the box and the paper napkins out the window. When there was nothing else to do they played a game by choosing a cloud and making the other two guess what shape it suggested. John Wesley took one the shape of a cow and June Star guessed a cow and John Wesley said, no, an automobile, and June Star said he didn't play fair, and they began to slap each other over the grandmother.

The grandmother said she would tell them a story if they would keep quiet.

---

① britches: beeches

② Gone With the Wind: It is a novel written by Margaret Mitchell, first published in 1936. The story is set in Clayton County, Georgia, and Atlanta during the American Civil War and Reconstruction. It depicts the experiences of Scarlett O'Hara, the spoiled daughter of a well-to-do plantation owner, who must use every means at her disposal to come out of the poverty.

When she told a story, she rolled her eyes and waved her head and was very dramatic. She said once when she was a maiden lady she had been courted by a Mr. Edgar Atkins Teagarden from Jasper, Georgia. She said he was a very good-looking man and a gentleman and that he brought her a watermelon every Saturday afternoon with his initials cut in it, E. A. T. Well, one Saturday, she said, Mr. Teagarden brought the watermelon and there was nobody at home and he left it on the front porch and returned in his buggy to Jasper, but she never got the watermelon, she said, because a nigger boy ate it when he saw the initials, E. A. T. ! This story tickled John Wesley's funny bone and he giggled and giggled but June Star didn't think it was any good. She said she wouldn't marry a man that just brought her a watermelon on Saturday. The grandmother said she would have done well to marry Mr. Teagarden because he was a gentle man and had bought Coca-Cola stock when it first came out and that he had died only a few years ago, a very wealthy man.

They stopped at The Tower for barbecued sandwiches. The Tower was a part stucco and part wood filling station and dance hall set in a clearing outside of Timothy.① A fat man named Red Sammy Butts ran it and there were signs stuck here and there on the building and for miles up and down the highway saying, TRY RED SAMMY'S FAMOUS BARBECUE. NONE LIKE FAMOUS RED SAMMY'S! RED SAM! THE FAT BOY WITH THE HAPPY LAUGH. A VETERAN! RED SAMMY'S YOUR MAN!

Red Sammy was lying on the bare ground outside The Tower with his head under a truck while a gray monkey about a foot high, chained to a small chinaberry tree, chattered nearby. The monkey sprang back into the tree and got on the highest limb as soon as he saw the children jump out of the car and run toward him.

Inside, The Tower was a long dark room with a counter at one end and tables at the other and dancing space in the middle. They all sat down at a board table next to

① Timothy：a small town in Georgia

the nickelodeon[1] and Red Sam's wife, a tall burnt-brown woman with hair and eyes lighter than her skin, came and took their order. The children's mother put a dime in the machine and played " The Tennessee Waltz," and the grandmother said that tune always made her want to dance. She asked Bailey if he would like to dance but he only glared at her. He didn't have a naturally sunny disposition like she did and trips made him nervous. The grandmother's brown eyes were very bright. She swayed her head from side to side and pretended she was dancing in her chair. June Star said play something she could tap to so the children's mother put in another dime and played a fast number[2] and June Star stepped out onto the dance floor and did her tap routine.

" Ain't she cute?" Red Sam's wife said, leaning over the counter. " Would you like to come be my little girl?"

" No I certainly wouldn't," June Star said. " I wouldn't live in a broken-down place like this for a million bucks!" and she ran back to the table.

" Ain't she cute?" the woman repeated, stretching her mouth politely.

" Arn't you ashamed?" hissed the grandmother.

Red Sam came in and told his wife to quit lounging on the counter and hurry up with these people's order. His khaki trousers reached just to his hip bones and his stomach hung over them like a sack of meal swaying under his shirt. He came over and sat down at a table nearby and let out a combination sigh and yodel.[3] " You can't win," he said. " You can't win," and he wiped his sweating red face off with a gray handkerchief. " These days you don't know who to trust," he said. " Ain't that the truth?"

" People are certainly not nice like they used to be," said the grandmother.

" Two fellers come in here last week," Red Sammy said, " driving a Chrysler.

---

① nickelodeon = jukebox

② number: (music) song, dance, etc, esp. in a theatrical performance

③ yodel: sing or utter a musical call with frequent changes from the normal voice to high falsetto notes, in the traditional Swiss manner. Here mean sigh

It was a old beat-up car but it was a good one and these boys looked all right to me. Said they worked at the mill and you know I let them fellers charge the gas they bought? Now why did I do that?"

" Because you're a good man!" the grandmother said at once.

" Yes'm,① I suppose so," Red Sam said as if he were struck with this answer.

His wife brought the orders, carrying the five plates all at once without a tray, two in each hand and one balanced on her arm. " It isn't a soul in this green world of God's that you can trust," she said. " And I don't count nobody out of that, not nobody," she repeated, looking at Red Sammy.

" Did you read about that criminal, The Misfit, that's escaped?" asked the grandmother.

" I wouldn't be a bit surprised if he didn't attact② this place right here," said the woman. " If he hears about it being here, I wouldn't be none surprised to see him. If he hears it's two cent in the cash register, I wouldn't be a tall surprised if he..."

" That'll do," Red Sam said. " Go bring these people their Co'-Colas," and the woman went off to get the rest of the order.

" A good man is hard to find," Red Sammy said. " Everything is getting terrible. I remember the day you could go off and leave your screen door unlatched. Not no more."

He and the grandmother discussed better times. The old lady said that in her opinion Europe was entirely to blame for the way things were now. She said the way Europe acted you would think we were made of money and Red Sam said it was no use talking about it, she was exactly right. The children ran outside into the white sunlight and looked at the monkey in the lacy chinaberry tree. He was busy catching fleas on himself and biting each one carefully between his teeth as if it were a delicacy.

---

① Yes'm = Yes, madam.

② attact = attack.

They drove off again into the hot afternoon. The grandmother took cat naps and woke up every few minutes with her own snoring. Outside of Toombsboro① she woke up and recalled an old plantation that she had visited in this neighborhood once when she was a young lady. She said the house had six white columns across the front and that there was an avenue of oaks leading up to it and two little wooden trellis arbors on either side in front where you sat down with your suitor after a stroll in the garden. She recalled exactly which road to turn off to get to it. She knew that Bailey would not be willing to lose any time looking at an old house, but the more she talked about it, the more she wanted to see it once again and find out if the little twin arbors were still standing. " There was a secret panel in this house," she said craftily, not telling the truth but wishing that she were, " and the story went that all the family silver was hidden in it when Sherman② came through but it was never found..."

" Hey!" John Wesley said. " Let's go see it! We'll find it! We'll poke all the woodwork and find it! Who lives there? Where do you turn off at? Hey Pop, can't we turn off there?"

" We never have seen a house with a secret panel!" June Star shrieked. " Let's go to the house with the secret panel! Hey Pop, can't we go see the house with the secret panel!"

" It's not far from here, I know," the grandmother said. " It wouldn't take over twenty minutes."

Bailey was looking straight ahead. His jaw was as rigid as a horseshoe. " No," he said.

The children began to yell and scream that they wanted to see the house with the

① Toombsbora: a city in Georgia

② Sherman: (William T. Sherman, 1820–1891) , was a General in the Union Army during the American Civil War (1861–65), for which he received recognition for his outstanding command of military strategy as well as criticism for the harshness of the "scorched earth" policies that he implemented in conducting total war against the Confederate States.

secret panel. John Wesley kicked the back of the front seat and June Star hung over her mother's shoulder and whined desperately into her ear that they never had any fun even on their vacation, that they could never do what THEY wanted to do. The baby began to scream and John Wesley kicked the back of the seat so hard that his father could feel the blows in his kidney.

" All right!" he shouted and drew the car to a stop at the side of the road. " Will you all shut up? Will you all just shut up for one second? If you don't shut up, we won't go anywhere."

" It would be very educational for them," the grandmother murmured.

" All right," Bailey said, " but get this: this is the only time we're going to stop for anything like this. This is the one and only time."

" The dirt road that you have to turn down is about a mile back," the grandmother directed. " I marked it when we passed."

" A dirt road," Bailey groaned.

After they had turned around and were headed toward the dirt road, the grandmother recalled other points about the house, the beautiful glass over the front doorway and the candle-lamp in the hall. John Wesley said that the secret panel was probably in the fireplace.

" You can't go inside this house," Bailey said. " You don't know who lives there."

" While you all talk to the people in front, I'll run around behind and get in a window," John Wesley suggested.

" We'll all stay in the car," his mother said.

They turned onto the dirt road and the car raced roughly along in a swirl of pink dust. The grandmother recalled the times when there were no paved roads and thirty miles was a day's journey. The dirt road was hilly and there were sudden washes in it and sharp curves on dangerous embankments. All at once they would be on a hill, looking down over the blue tops of trees for miles around, then the next minute, they would be in a red depression with the dust-coated trees looking down on them.

" This place had better turn up in a minute," Bailey said, " or I'm going to turn around."

The road looked as if no one had traveled on it in months.

" It's not much farther," the grandmother said and just as she said it, a horrible thought came to her. The thought was so embarrassing that she turned red in the face and her eyes dilated and her feet jumped up, upsetting her valise in the corner. The instant the valise moved, the newspaper top she had over the basket under it rose with a snarl and Pitty Sing, the cat, sprang onto Bailey's shoulder.

The children were thrown to the floor and their mother, clutching the baby, was thrown out the door onto the ground; the old lady was thrown into the front seat. The car turned over once and landed right-side-up in a gulch off the side of the road. Bailey remained in the driver's seat with the cat gray-striped with a broad white face and an orange nose clinging to his neck like a caterpillar.

As soon as the children saw they could move their arms and legs, they scrambled out of the car, shouting, " We've had an ACCIDENT!" The grandmother was curled up under the dashboard, hoping she was injured so that Bailey's wrath would not come down on her all at once. The horrible thought she had had before the accident was that the house she had remembered so vividly was not in Georgia but in Tennessee.

Bailey removed the cat from his neck with both hands and flung it out the window against the side of a pine tree. Then he got out of the car and started looking for the children's mother. She was sitting against the side of the red gutted ditch, holding the screaming baby, but she only had a cut down her face and a broken shoulder. " We've had an ACCIDENT!" the children screamed in a frenzy of delight.

" But nobody's killed," June Star said with disappointment as the grandmother limped out of the car, her hat still pinned to her head but the broken front brim standing up at a jaunty angle and the violet spray hanging off the side. They all sat down in the ditch, except the children, to recover from the shock. They were all shaking.

" Maybe a car will come along," said the children's mother hoarsely.

" I believe I have injured an organ," said the grandmother, pressing her side, but no one answered her. Bailey's teeth were clattering. He had on a yellow sport shirt with bright blue parrots designed in it and his face was as yellow as the shirt. The grandmother decided that she would not mention that the house was in Tennessee.

The road was about ten feet above and they could see only the tops of the trees on the other side of it. Behind the ditch they were sitting in there were more woods, tall and dark and deep. In a few minutes they saw a car some distance away on top of a hill, coming slowly as if the occupants were watching them. The grandmother stood up and waved both arms dramatically to attract their attention. The car continued to come on slowly, disappeared around a bend and appeared again, moving even slower, on top of the hill they had gone over. It was a big black battered hearse-like automobile. There were three men in it.

It came to a stop just over them and for some minutes, the driver looked down with a steady expressionless gaze to where they were sitting, and didn't speak. Then he turned his head and muttered something to the other two and they got out. One was a fat boy in black trousers and a red sweat shirt with a silver stallion embossed on the front of it. He moved around on the right side of them and stood staring, his mouth partly open in a kind of loose grin. The other had on khaki pants and a blue striped coat and a gray hat pulled down very low, hiding most of his face. He came around slowly on the left side. Neither spoke.

The driver got out of the car and stood by the side of it, looking down at them. He was an older man than the other two. His hair was just beginning to gray and he wore silver-rimmed spectacles that gave him a scholarly look. He had a long creased face and didn't have on any shirt or undershirt. He had on blue jeans that were too tight for him and was holding a black hat and a gun. The two boys also had guns.

" We've had an ACCIDENT!" the children screamed.

The grandmother had the peculiar feeling that the bespectacled man was someone she knew. His face was as familiar to her as if she had known him all her life but she could not recall who he was. He moved away from the car and began to come down the embankment, placing his feet carefully so that he wouldn't slip. He had on tan and white shoes and no socks, and his ankles were red and thin. " Good afternoon," he said. " I see you all had you a little spill."

" We turned over twice!" said the grandmother.

" Once", he corrected. " We seen it happen. Try their car and see will it run, Hiram," he said quietly to the boy with the gray hat.

" What you got that gun for?" John Wesley asked. " Whatcha gonna[①] do with that gun?"

" Lady," the man said to the children's mother, " would you mind calling them children to sit down by you? Children make me nervous. I want all you all to sit down right together there where you're at."

" What are you telling US what to do for?" June Star asked.

Behind them the line of woods gaped like a dark open mouth. " Come here," said their mother.

" Look here now," Bailey began suddenly, " we're in a predicament! We're in..."

The grandmother shrieked. She scrambled to her feet and stood staring. " You're The Misfit!" she said. " I recognized you at once!"

" Yes'm," the man said, smiling slightly as if he were pleased in spite of himself to be known, " but it would have been better for all of you, lady, if you hadn't of reckernized me."

Bailey turned his head sharply and said something to his mother that shocked even the children. The old lady began to cry and The Misfit reddened.

---

① Whatcha gona = What you got to.

"Lady," he said, "don't you get upset. Sometimes a man says things he don't mean. I don't reckon he meant to talk to you thataway."

"You wouldn't shoot a lady, would you?" the grandmother said and removed a clean handkerchief from her cuff and began to slap at her eyes with it.

The Misfit pointed the toe of his shoe into the ground and made a little hole and then covered it up again. "I would hate to have to," he said.

"Listen," the grandmother almost screamed, "I know you're a good man. You don't look a bit like you have common blood. I know you must come from nice people!"

"Yes mam①," he said, "finest people in the world." When he smiled he showed a row of strong white teeth. "God never made a finer woman than my mother and my daddy's heart was pure gold," he said. The boy with the red sweat shirt had come around behind them and was standing with his gun at his hip. The Misfit squatted down on the ground. "Watch them children, Bobby Lee," he said. "You know they make me nervous." He looked at the six of them huddled together in front of him and he seemed to be embarrassed as if he couldn't think of anything to say. "Ain't a cloud in the sky," he remarked, looking up at it. "Don't see no sun but don't see no cloud neither."

"Yes, it's a beautiful day," said the grandmother. "Listen," she said, "you shouldn't call yourself The Misfit because I know you're a good man at heart. I can just look at you and tell."

"Hush!" Bailey yelled. "Hush! Everybody shut up and let me handle this!" He was squatting in the position of a runner about to sprint forward but he didn't move.

"I pre-chate② that, lady," The Misfit said and drew a little circle in the ground with the butt of his gun.

"It'll take a half a hour to fix this here car," Hiram called, looking over the

① mam = madam.

② pre-chate = appreciate.

raised hood of it.

" Well, first you and Bobby Lee get him and that little boy to step over yonder with you," The Misfit said, pointing to Bailey and John Wesley. " The boys want to ast you something," he said to Bailey. " Would you mind stepping back in them woods there with them?"

" Listen," Bailey began, " we're in a terrible predicament! Nobody realizes what this is," and his voice cracked. His eyes were as blue and intense as the parrots in his shirt and he remained perfectly still.

The grandmother reached up to adjust her hat brim as if she were going to the woods with him but it came off in her hand. She stood staring at it and after a second she let it fall on the ground. Hiram pulled Bailey up by the arm as if he were assisting an old man. John Wesley caught hold of his father's hand and Bobby Lee followed. They went off toward the woods and just as they reached the dark edge, Bailey turned and supporting himself against a gray naked pine trunk, he shouted, " I'll be back in a minute, Mamma, wait on me!"

" Come back this instant!" his mother shrilled but they all disappeared into the woods.

" Bailey Boy!" the grandmother called in a tragic voice but she found she was looking at The Misfit squatting on the ground in front of her. " I just know you're a good man," she said desperately. " You're not a bit common!"

" Nome, I ain't a good man," The Misfit said after a second ah if he had considered her statement carefully, " but I ain't the worst in the world neither. My daddy said I was a different breed of dog from my brothers and sisters. 'You know,' Daddy said, 'it's some that can live their whole life out without asking about it and it's others has to know why it is, and this boy is one of the latters. He's going to be into everything!" He put on his black hat and looked up suddenly and then away deep into the woods as if he were embarrassed again. " I'm sorry I don't have on a shirt before you ladies," he said, hunching his shoulders slightly. " We buried our clothes that we had on when we escaped and we're just making do until we can get better. We borrowed these from some folks we met," he explained.

" That's perfectly all right," the grandmother said. " Maybe Bailey has an extra shirt in his suitcase."

" I'll look and see terrectly①," The Misfit said.

" Where are they taking him?" the children's mother screamed.

" Daddy was a card himself," The Misfit said. " You couldn't put anything over on him. He never got in trouble with the Authorities though. Just had the knack of handling them."

" You could be honest too if you'd only try," said the grandmother. " Think how wonderful it would be to settle down and live a comfortable life and not have to think about somebody chasing you all the time."

The Misfit kept scratching in the ground with the butt of his gun as if he were thinking about it. " Yes'm, somebody is always after you," he murmured.

The grandmother noticed how thin his shoulder blades were just behind his hat because she was standing up looking down on him. " Do you every pray?" she asked.

He shook his head. All she saw was the black hat wiggle between his shoulder blades. " Nome," he said.

There was a pistol shot from the woods, followed closely by another. Then silence. The old lady's head jerked around. She could hear the wind move through the tree tops like a long satisfied insuck of breath. " Bailey Boy!" she called.

" I was a gospel singer for a while," The Misfit said. " I been most everything. Been in the arm service both land and sea, at home and abroad, been twict② married, been an undertaker, been with the railroads, plowed Mother Earth, been in a tornado, seen a man burnt alive oncet③," and he looked up at the children's mother and the

① terrectly = directly.

② twict = twice.

③ oncet = once.

little girl who were sitting close together, their faces white and their eyes glassy; " I even seen a woman flogged," he said.

" Pray, pray," the grandmother began, " pray, pray..."

" I never was a bad boy that I remember of," The Misfit said in an almost dreamy voice, " but somewheres along the line I done① something wrong and got sent to the penitentiary. I was buried alive," and he looked up and held her attention to him by a steady stare.

" That's when you should have started to pray," she said. " What did you do to get sent to the penitentiary that first time?"

" Turn to the right, it was a wall," The Misfit said, looking up again at the cloudless sky. " Turn to the left, it was a wall. Look up it was a ceiling, look down it was a floor. I forget what I done, lady. I set② there and set there, trying to remember what it was I done and I ain't recalled it to this day. Oncet in a while, I would think it was coming to me, but it never come."

" Maybe they put you in by mistake," the old lady said vaguely.

" Nome," he said. " It wasn't no mistake. They had the papers on me."

" You must have stolen something," she said.

The Misfit sneered slightly. " Nobody had nothing I wanted," he said. " It was a head-doctor at the penitentiary said what I had done was kill my daddy but I known that for a lie. My daddy died in nineteen ought nineteen of the epidemic flu and I never had a thing to do with it. He was buried in the Mount Hopewell Baptist churchyard and you can go there and see for yourself."

" If you would pray," the old lady said, " Jesus would help you."

" That's right," The Misfit said.

" Well then, why don't you pray?" she asked trembling with delight suddenly.

---

① done = did.

② set = sat.

" I don't want no hep[①] ," he said. " I'm doing all right by myself."

Bobby Lee and Hiram came ambling back from the woods. Bobby Lee was dragging a yellow shirt with bright blue parrots in it.

" Thow me that shirt, Bobby Lee," The Misfit said. The shirt came flying at him and landed on his shoulder and he put it on. The grandmother couldn't name what the shirt reminded her of. " No, lady," The Misfit said while he was buttoning it up, " I found out the crime don't matter. You can do one thing or you can do another, kill a man or take a tire off his car, because sooner or later you're going to forget what it was you done and just be punished for it."

The children's mother had begun to make heaving noises as if she couldn't get her breath. " Lady," he asked, " would you and that little girl like to step off yonder with Bobby Lee and Hiram and join your husband?"

" Yes, thank you," the mother said faintly. Her left arm dangled helplessly and she was holding the baby, who had gone to sleep, in the other. " Hep that lady up, Hiram," The Misfit said as she struggled to climb out of the ditch, " and Bobby Lee, you hold onto that little girl's hand."

" I don't want to hold hands with him," June Star said. " He reminds me of a pig."

The fat boy blushed and laughed and caught her by the arm and pulled her off into the woods after Hiram and her mother.

Alone with The Misfit, the grandmother found that she had lost her voice. There was not a cloud in the sky nor any sun. There was nothing around her but woods. She wanted to tell him that he must pray. She opened and closed her mouth several times before anything came out. Finally she found herself saying, " Jesus. Jesus," meaning, Jesus will help you, but the way she was saying it, it sounded as if she might be cursing.

---

① hep = help.

" Yes'm," The Misfit said as if he agreed. " Jesus shown everything off balance. It was the same case with Him as with me except He hadn't committed any crime and they could prove I had committed one because they had the papers on me. Of course," he said, " they never shown me my papers. That's why I sign myself now. I said long ago, you get you a signature and sign everything you do and keep a copy of it. Then you'll know what you done and you can hold up the crime to the punishment and see do they match and in the end you'll have something to prove you ain't been treated right. I call myself The Misfit," he said, " because I can't make what all I done wrong fit what all I gone through in punishment."

There was a piercing scream from the woods, followed closely by a pistol report. " Does it seem right to you, lady, that one is punished a heap① and another ain't punished at all?"

" Jesus!" the old lady cried. " You've got good blood! I know you wouldn't shoot a lady! I know you come from nice people! Pray! Jesus, you ought not to shoot a lady. I'll give you all the money I've got!"

" Lady," The Misfit said, looking beyond her far into the woods, " there never was a body that give the undertaker a tip."

There were two more pistol reports and the grandmother raised her head like a parched old turkey hen crying for water and called, " Bailey Boy, Bailey Boy!" as if her heart would break.

" Jesus was the only One that ever raised the dead," The Misfit continued, " and He shouldn't have done it. He shown everything off balance. If He did what He said, then it's nothing for you to do but thow② away everything and follow Him, and if He didn't, then it's nothing for you to do but enjoy the few minutes you got left the best way you can by killing somebody or burning down his house or doing some other meanness to him. No pleasure but meanness," he said and his voice had become almost a snarl.

---

① a heap of = a lot.

② thow = throw.

" Maybe He didn't raise the dead," the old lady mumbled, not knowing what she was saying and feeling so dizzy that she sank down in the ditch with her legs twisted under her.

" I wasn't there so I can't say He didn't," The Misfit said. " I wisht[①] I had of been there," he said, hitting the ground with his fist. " It ain't right I wasn't there because if I had of been there I would of known. Listen lady," he said in a high voice, " if I had of been there I would of known and I wouldn't be like I am now." His voice seemed about to crack and the grandmother's head cleared for an instant. She saw the man's face twisted close to her own as if he were going to cry and she murmured, " Why you're one of my babies. You're one of my own children!" She reached out and touched him on the shoulder. The Misfit sprang back as if a snake had bitten him and shot her three times through the chest. Then he put his gun down on the ground and took off his glasses and began to clean them.

Hiram and Bobby Lee returned from the woods and stood over the ditch, looking down at the grandmother who half sat and half lay in a puddle of blood with her legs crossed under her like a child's and her face smiling up at the cloudless sky.

Without his glasses, The Misfit's eyes were red-rimmed and pale and defenseless-looking. Take her off and thow her where you thown[②] the others," he said, picking up the cat that was rubbing itself against his leg.

" She was a talker, wasn't she?" Bobby Lee said, sliding down the ditch with a yodel.

" She would of been a good woman," The Misfit said, " if it had been somebody there to shoot her every minute of her life."

" Some fun!" Bobby Lee said.

" Shut up, Bobby Lee," The Misfit said. " It's no real pleasure in life."

---

① wisht = wished.

② thown = threw.

Topics for discussion

1. At Red Sammy Butts' barbecue place, Grandmother discusses the escaped murderer known as the Misfit. Red Sammy tells the Grandmother that a good man is hard to find these days. Why?

2. At the end of the story, The Misfit said that Grandmother would be a good woman if it had been somebody there to shoot her every minute of her life. What does he mean?

3. The Misfit said. " It's no real pleasure in life." Does the statement remind you of some philosophy?

4. Some critic says, " O'Connor tells us quite directly that the inescapable threat of death shatters the Grandmother's complaisance and makes her look at the essential." Do you agree? How do you look at the function of death in the story?

5. O'Connor is a Catholic writer. Do you think Grandmother is an agent of grace?

References for further reading

[1] King, Richard H. *A Southern Renaissance: the Cultural Awakening of the American South, 1930-1955*. New York: Oxford University Press, 1980.

[2] Smith, David L. *A Handbook of Contemporary Theology: Tracing Trends and Discerning Directions in Today's Theological Landscape. Grand Rapids*, Mich.: Baker Books, 2000.

[3] Spivey, Ted Ray. *Flannery O'Connor: the Woman, the Thinker, the Visionary.* Macon, GA: Mercer University Press, 1995.

[4] Whitt, Margaret Earley. *Understanding Flannery O'Connor*. Columbia, SC: University of South Carolina Press, 1995.

[5] Wood, Ralph C. *Flannery O'Connor and the Christ-Haunted South*. Mich.: William B Eerdmans, 2004.

References

1. Ashton, Rosemary. *George Eliot: A Life*, New York: Penguin Press, 1996.
2. Batchelor, John. *H. G. Wells*. Cambridge: Cambridge University Press, 1985.
3. Bauer, Helen Pike. *Rudyard Kipling: A Study of the Short Fiction*. New York: Twayne,1994.
4. Beer, Janet ed. *The Cambridge companion to Kate Chopin*, New York: Cambridge University Press, 2008.
5. Beer, Janet. *Kate Chopin, Edith Wharton, and Charlotte Perkins Gilman: studies in short fiction*, New York: St. Martin's Press, 1997.
6. Briggs, Julia. *Virginia Woolf: An Inner Life*. New York: Mariner Books, 2006.
7. Bulson, Eric. *The Cambridge Introduction to James Joyce*. Cambridge and New York: Cambridge University Press, 2006
8. Burbank, Rex. *Sherwood Anderson*, New York: Twayne, 1964.
9. Cloy, John D. *Pensive jester: the literary career of W.W. Jacobs*. Lanham, Md. : University Press of America, 1996.
10. Coulombe, Joseph L. *Mark Twain and the American West*, Columbia: University of Missouri Press, 2003.
11. Curle, Richard. *Joseph Conrad: A Study*, New York, Doubleday: Page & Company, 1914.
12. Dalgarno, Emily. *Virginia Woolf and the Visible World*. Cambridge University Press, 2007.
13. Fernihough, Anne. ed. *The Cambridge Companion to D H Lawrence*, Cambridge,

Cambridge University Press, 2001.

14. Ginden, James. *John Galsworthy's Life and Art*. University of Michigan Press, 1979.
15. Gordon, Lyndall. *Virginia Woolf: A Writer's Life*. New York: Norton, 1984.
16. Hayes, Kevin J. ed. *The Cambridge companion to Edgar Allan Poe*. Shanghai : Shanghai Foreign Language Education Press, 2004.
17. Hughes, Kathryn. *George Eliot: The Last Victorian*, New York: Farrar Straus Giroux, 1998.
18. Hutchisson, James M. ed. *Edgar Allan Poe: beyond gothicis*. Newark: University of Delaware Press, 2011.
19. Jones, Kathleen. *Katherine Mansfield: the story teller*, Edinburgh: Edinburgh University Press,
20. Keith Brown, ed. *Rethinking Lawrence*, Milton Keynes: Open University Press, 1990.
21. McCourt, John, ed. *James Joyce in Context*. Cambridge and New York: Cambridge University Press, 2009.
22. McDowell, Margaret B. *Edith Wharton*. Boston: Twayne Publishers, 1991.
23. Messent, Peter ed. *A companion to Mark Twain*, Malden, MA: Blackwell Pub, 2005.
24. Meyers, Jeffrey. *Joseph Conrad: A Biography*, New York: Charles Scribner's Sons, 1991.
25. Nevius, Black. *Edith Wharton, A Study of Her Fiction*. Berkeley: University of Californian Press, 1953.
26. Patricia Lengermann, G. ed. *Charlotte Perkins Gilman*, Farnham, Surrey: Ashgate Publishing Limited, 2013.
27. Pizer, Donald. *Jack London: Novels and Stories*. New York: The Library of American, 1982.
28. Ricketts, Harry. *Rudyard Kipling: A Life*. New York: Da Capo Press,2001.

29. Semrau, Janusz. *New essays on the short stories of Nathaniel Hawthorne*, Frankfurt am Main ; Berlin : Peter Lang, 2012.

30. Small, Judy Jo. *A Reader's Guide to the Short Stories of Sherwood Anderson*, New York:G. K. Hall, 1964.

31. Smit, J. Henry. *The Short Stories of John Galsworthy*, Haskell House, 1996.

32. Smith, Harriet Elinor ed. *Autobiography of Mark Twain*, Berkeley: University of California Press, 2010-2013.

33. Spivey, Ted Ray. *Flannery O'Connor: the Woman, the Thinker, the Visionary*. Macon, GA: Mercer University Press, 1995.

34. Stape, J. H. ed. *The Cambridge Companion to Joseph Conrad*, Cambridge: Cambridge University Press, 2006.

35. Townsend, Kim. *Sherwood Anderson*, Boston: Houghton Mifflin, 1987.

36. Turner, Arlin. *Nathaniel Hawthorne: A Biography*, Oxford: Oxford University Press. 1980

37. Walcutt, Charles Child. *Jack London*, Minneapolis: University of Minnesota Press, 1966.

38. Warner, Charles Dudley. *Washington Irving, Boston : Houghton Mifflin Co.*, 1909.

39. Wells, Geoffrey H. *The Works of H. G. Wells*. London: Routledge, 1925.

40. Whitt, Margaret Earley. *Understanding Flannery O'Connor*. Columbia, SC: University of South Carolina Press, 1995.

41. Williams, Stanley Thomas. *The life of Washington Irving*, Oxford: Oxford University Press, 1935

42. Wilson, James D. *A reader's guide to the short stories of Mark Twain*, Boston, Mass: G.K. Hall, 1987.